365 Life Shifts

Pivotal Moments That Changed Everything

Jodi Chapman, Dan Teck

& Over 250 Soulful Contributors

DandiLove Unlimited

This book comes from our hearts and is here to support you in connecting with pivotal shifts in your life. Please know, though, that it is not a replacement for therapy or medical advice. If you are feeling like you could use some extra support, please seek out a professional in your area.

The views represented in this book are not necessarily a reflection of the publisher. Each author wrote their story in a way that they remembered the events happening. Please note that the publisher accepts no responsibility for any inaccurate information portrayed.

The authors who contributed to this book are from all corners of the world, and we have kept their native English spelling for each of their pieces. For this reason, you will see words like "color" and "colour" or "realized" and "realised" throughout the book – just depending on what part of the world the author is from. We also wanted to find a balance of maintaining consistency throughout the book while still honoring each author's belief system. For this reason, you will see that some words are capitalized in some pieces and not in others. For the most part, we capitalize words relating to God, Source, the Universe, and a Higher Power.

Ordering information available at:
www.365lifeshifts.com.
For wholesale inquiries, please write to: info@365bookseries.com.

Printed in the United States of America
ISBN: 13-978-0998125107
Library of Congress Control Number: 2016917154

www.365bookseries.com

DEDICATION

We would like to dedicate this book to each of the contributing authors who bravely shared their truth and, in doing so, gave each of us permission to do the same.

We would also like to dedicate this book to those of us who view the world through such a lens that every single moment contains the possibility for wisdom and growth. It's not always the easiest to walk through life in this way, but we've found that when we do, we're rewarded with beauty and magic, which make it all worthwhile.

Table of Contents

Chapter 2 – Believing in Myself 49

Chapter 3 – Shifts in Perception.. 99

Chapter 5 – Animals & Nature 193

Introduction

E very so often, we have an experience – a shift – that alters the course of our lives and changes who we are forever. Sometimes these moments fill us with rapture and flood us with insight. Other times, they are blessings in disguise that don't reveal their treasure until years later. However they show up, these moments can inspire us to live richer, deeper, and more authentically soulful lives.

Throughout this book, you'll find 365 true stories of such life-changing moments – experiences that inspired, uplifted, shook each author to their core, got them back on track (or onto a new track altogether), and led them toward their true selves. While the experiences themselves vary greatly, each of these moments transformed the authors and helped them shift in a positive way.

It's our hope that while reading this book, you can flip to any page and find a story that will provide insight, inspiration, and encouragement for your own life journey – offering a reawakened sense of awe and a renewed reverence for life itself.

One of the things that we most love about this book is the variety of life shifts that are shared. Over 250 co-authors came together to create this book – each of whom is unique. We are spread out all over the world, speak different languages, have different professions, follow different religions, are different races, have unique experiences and points of view...our list of differences goes on and on. Yet, no matter how different we are, we each go through similar life experiences here on Earth. What we continue to find throughout this book is how similar we truly are. We all want to feel loved and to offer love, to express our deepest truth, to be seen and understood, and to feel peace and happiness. We all want to embrace our time here on Earth. And we all know that shifts occur in our lives to help us learn, grow, and discover a deeper part of ourselves or another that we hadn't seen before.

The shifts cover many different life experiences, and because of that, we could never have written this book on our own. Each of the true stories was needed to create the depth and richness that you'll find throughout this book, and we're truly grateful to everyone who is part of it. The pieces were written with love and infused with the intention that you'll be able to discover the beauty in your own life shifts, too.

Throughout this book, each of the authors has shared about their personal shift openly and honestly. It takes bravery to share in such a heartfelt way, and we are inspired by each of them for doing so.

Examples of Life Shifts

Here are just a few examples of the types of life shifts that the authors share throughout this book:

- discovering their purpose
- experiencing a spiritual awakening
- leaving their job to follow their dream
- leaving a relationship that no longer felt right
- bravely choosing to open their heart to love
- having a child and seeing the world through their eyes
- hitting rock bottom, finding themselves completely transformed, and lifting themselves back up
- learning about themselves and their loved ones through death and grief
- leaving a religion or finding a new religion
- going through a physical trauma or near-death experience and transforming because of it
- receiving messages from beyond and opening to their wisdom
- communing deeply with animals and nature
- believing in themselves and feeling strong enough to speak their truth

How to Read This Book

One of our intentions when creating this book was to show that life shifts can happen at any time. They can appear huge and "in your face," and they can also be subtle and take time to reveal the depth they hold. As we do with all of our books, we gave each of the co-authors free rein with their pieces and trusted that the book would come together in a cohesive way once we received them all. And that's exactly what happened. The pieces fell into 10 categories, which became our chapter titles:

1. Divine Guidance
2. Believing in Myself
3. Shifts in Perception
4. Relationships
5. Animals & Nature
6. Divine Unfolding
7. Everyday Shifts
8. Physical Healing & Self-Care
9. Transitions
10. Living My Purpose

As is true with all the books in this series, there are many ways to enjoy this book: you can read each entry in order on the day it appears, or you can flip through at random and let your soul guide you. Perhaps you have a favorite day of the year (such as your birthday or an anniversary) and want to see which piece appears on that day. Or maybe a certain chapter's theme is calling for you to turn to it and flip through and choose a piece that way. For example, if you've recently left your job to pursue your purpose, you may want to start by reading pieces in Chapter 10. Or if you're wanting to connect with the divine in some way, you could start with the Divine Guidance chapter.

There is no right or wrong way to read this book. You can read one piece each morning or night as part of your spiritual practice. Or you can read it in the carpool lane while picking up your kids from school.

Another suggestion for reading this book is to keep a journal nearby to jot down any thoughts and inspirations that enter your heart as you read the pieces – even if they don't make sense. Chances are, they will when you most need them to. By reading this book, you're consciously opening your heart to finding the gifts in your own life shifts, and we believe that the clarity around them will begin to flow in.

You can also read this book with your friends as a way to deepen your relationships and share about your own shifts together! You can meet (either in person or online) and go through the days, or you can pick and choose them at random and share what you learned about yourself after reading them and taking them into your heart.

However and wherever you choose to read it, know that it's a powerful book – one that we believe will help you feel inspired, uplifted, and more attuned to the blessings from the shifts in your own life. Just by having it around, you will be opening your heart and raising your own vibration toward embracing shifts that are happening all around you.

Giving Back

Because we've both experienced beautiful life shifts in nature and with animals, we'll be donating 5% of all profits from sales of this book to the Jane Goodall Institute. (You can learn more about this charity by going to www.janegoodall.org.)

Thank You

Thank you for being part of this journey with us. We hope you enjoy each of the pieces in this special book. We felt our own hearts expand while compiling them, and we hope that you'll experience that while reading them. We'll all go through many shifts throughout our lives, and it's our hope that after reading this book, you'll see how powerful, magical, and transformative each shift can truly be.

Hugs, love, and gratitude,
Jodi and Dan

Chapter 1
Divine Guidance

We believe that there is far more to this magical universe than we'll ever know – far more than what we can see, feel, hear, and touch. While we tend to be on the skeptical side, we have had firsthand experiences that can only be described as miracles and encounters with the other side that defy rational thought and explanation.

We have been touched by angels and communicated with by our loved ones who have passed on, and have received a deep inner knowing time and time again from our soul that simply couldn't be ignored. Because of these experiences, we now listen closely when we receive messages and guidance from the divine. We love knowing that we all have an entire team that constantly surrounds us – wanting nothing more than to support us in living our best life.

Each piece in this chapter shares a moment when someone received a loving message from the divine and shifted their life because of it. Many of the stories defy logical explanation. Many will give you goosebumps. And many will fill your heart with reverence for what is possible in our amazing universe.

We never know when divine guidance will appear, and it's up to us to be ready when it does. As you'll see on the pages that follow, our lives can change in such beautiful ways when we stay open to this magical world. Ours certainly have.

The Angel of Highway 35

By Lucy V. Nefstead

I've always loved to travel, and I especially loved to visit my grandma and great-aunt several states away. The distance never bothered me, but a certain large city did. It terrified me! Nothing was ever easy going through it, no matter how many prayers I said. That city was always draped in problems for me.

During one trip, panicky with fear, I pulled into a country gas station only minutes from "the city." The station was empty except for an inside attendant who watched me unsuccessfully attempt to pump gas.

Frustrated after several unsuccessful attempts, I noticed a smiling, light-haired, husky, middle-aged man clad in a plaid shirt, jeans, and boots walking toward me. Talking in a pleasant, gentle, and confident manner, he got the pump going and filled my tank.

Thanking him profusely, I told him how I feared the city ahead. Smiling, he assured me there was nothing to fear. His blue eyes sparkled as he took a map of the state from his back pocket and outlined a detour around the city. I repeated the directions as he gave me the map, clasped his hands lovingly over mine, looked into my eyes, and told me calmly to never fear anything – God was with me always, as were the angels.

He smiled, then he turned away and was gone...*gone*...vanished! He wasn't in the parking lot, the field, the side road, or inside the station. He had no car. No one had picked him up. Vanished. Chills went through my body as I stared into space. The realization hit me: He was an angel! He had to be! I had spoken to and touched an angel!

Time stood still. I was dazed...numb. I knew my life had changed forever – it would never, *could* never be the same. The magnitude of the message was overwhelming: God and His angels are with me always – anywhere, any time, any place...even on Highway 35.

Let Go. Let Us Drive.

By Michelle Radomski

When I first heard about self-driving cars, I was horrified.

"No way," I told my husband. "I could never give up control and let a car drive itself!"

For as long as I can remember, I have been controlled by an unrelenting need to control. So imagine my reaction when, in the midst of a desperate struggle to control the uncontrollable, I heard these words whispered into my soul: "Let go of the wheel. Let us drive."

"No!" I shouted back. "I am the only one who can control this car called 'my life.' No one else is driving! Ever!"

"Look around," the voice encouraged. "You have lost your way. Your journey has stalled. You are running dangerously low on fuel. *Let us drive.*"

In that very moment something shifted, and I found myself entertaining these thoughts: *What if the Universe does know a better way to travel this road? Maybe I don't have to do this all alone. Maybe I can let go just a little.*

So slowly – one reluctant, resistant finger at a time – I loosened my grip on the metaphorical wheel of my life. I was terrified, but I had to try. I had to see what would happen and where the Universe could take me if I let go of the need to control *every…single…thing.*

What happened was a miracle.

For the first time in ages, I took a deep, full breath. I felt a surge of energy run through my body. I started to create things. I made connections. Opportunities appeared. Money flowed to me. Worry (which had previously ruled my life) drifted away.

As an active participant, but no longer the driver, I felt no need to control. My hands (and my heart) were unclenched and open. I looked around and saw that I was moving steadily forward in the direction of my dream.

I was no longer alone. I was happy. I felt free.

Maui Healing

By Angie Carter

After the sudden loss of my 19-month-old daughter, Bella, I instinctively knew I needed to be away from home to start the healing process. When an opportunity presented itself to attend a Hay House Writer's Workshop in Maui, I couldn't pass it up. At the workshop, I met Doreen Virtue and Wayne Dyer and shared my story with them. I spent time with many like-minded souls who willingly spoke about my loss without judgement. I openly shared about my ongoing connection with my daughter. It was enlightening to see how many people share my beliefs about life after death.

I spent the majority of the week physically alone, but Bella's presence was strong. The time I spent on the beach was sacred; I was able to communicate with Bella, process my grief, and finally let go. As I stepped into the ocean, I felt Bella's love surround me and allowed the pain of grief to take over. The waves swallowed me, then spit me out aggressively onto the shore, then swallowed me again. During this process, I explored every thought and feeling that had been burning inside me. With every wave, I felt the pain subside as I released it. Healing finally began!

Another pivotal moment occurred when a group of us from the workshop went to the Haleakala summit to watch the sun rise, which was breathtaking. On the summit, we stood in a circle while one of the women led a group meditation. She went around the circle and said something personal to each of us. When it was my turn, she spoke about Bella. My eyes were closed as she spoke, yet I saw a gigantic ball of light hover above me. This light was energy and emanated pure love: it was Bella! The light came toward me and entered my body. It filled all the cracks in my broken soul with love! I felt her with me, inside me, and I knew instantly that she would never leave.

Two weeks after I returned home, I discovered I was pregnant!

The Question That Changed Everything

By Aliza Bloom Robinson

"Are you willing to serve creation?" In my heart sounded a clear and resounding *YES!*

"Then you will be asked to surrender everything."

What??? my mind thought, but out of my mouth came simply, "Okay."

Those were the words I heard during a mystical experience in 2010. Those words changed my life.

I had been going along, minding my own business, when I came into an experience that blew the circuits of my mind and turned my life upside down. I had, however, been asking for more – more connection, more purpose, more passion, more meaning. This life-shift moment was like a boomerang that totally undid what I was and catapulted me into an entirely new dimension of my being-ness.

I was asked in the depths of my soul to give up everything…and I did: I left my job, I left my relationship, I left my career, and I went on the road for what I thought would be three months. It turned out to be closer to 18 months living in my car, completely untethered to what the world believes is stability.

I was also led into a purging of emotions I didn't even know I had: anger, rage, and fear, to name a few. I surrendered all aspects of being a victim in my life and in the world. Each surrender was excruciating in the moment and yet led to a creation of spaciousness and quiet within my soul.

I was then led to dismantle my beliefs – nothing was left out. I was left for a time with complete emptiness. There was nothing in me except space and quiet. No emotion, no thought, no belief. It was the dismantling of the egoic personality that led me to a deeper realization of my Essence.

This experience ultimately changed everything. I now live as the light and love of the Universe; the work that I offer is pure in Spirit. I see with new eyes from a greater and deeper perspective, and I know in my bones that all is well. And so it is.

One Way to Slow Down

By Hue Anh Nguyen

Who would have thought that an afternoon out shopping for our Boy Scout celebration would change my life forever?

It was a very clear day outside; inside my mind, however, was anything but clear! As I stopped at a light before making a right turn, 1,000 distracting thoughts raced through my head: my business, my relationships, kids in daycare, a ringing phone, setting up the Boy Scout to sing the opening for the ceremonies...

Suddenly, I saw a car making a turn right in front of me. I stomped on the brakes and...*BOOM!*

The airbag popped out. My face felt like it was on fire. I heard a siren in the distance. People gathered around, helping me out of the car. I was dazed, and my car was totaled, but THANK GOD the kids were okay!!! They had been securely strapped in and didn't move an inch. Scared but safe.

The Divine has a way of speaking to us; this time it was really loud and clear: *Slow down!* Like my car, my life came to an abrupt halt.

I spent months going from one therapy to another, searching for a way to relieve the pain. During this time, I had many long hours to contemplate what my life was about and to rediscover the magic to heal from within.

Looking deeper within myself at who I was and how I wanted live, I was able to sort out my priorities. The crash and the subsequent healing process made me realize what I truly valued the most: When you have children, the most important job is being a parent. Money, business, and everything else can wait. It doesn't really matter how much money you have in bank; it's meaningless if you don't have health, peace, and love in your life.

Angel Nurse

By Charlene Williams

My four children were upset that I might not be home with them for Christmas since my due date for their little sister was December 26. After talking to my obstetrician, we decided that I would be induced on December 20. Being that this was my fifth baby, we figured that it would be a piece of cake!

After 17 hours of non-productive labor, my doctor determined that I was too exhausted and we would resume the next morning, so I was fed and given a sleeping pill, and I drifted off.

I awoke suddenly in transition and in so much pain. The contractions were strong at first but then weakened – so, again, an IV was started to induce labor. The intermittent contractions went on for another 12 hours, after which I was completely exhausted, dehydrated, and scared since things were not going as expected.

The next thing I knew, I woke up on my hands and knees, supported by two nurses who were massaging my belly rigorously. The room was filled with people, one of whom told me that I had stopped breathing and they had lost my baby's heartbeat! My doctor said that I needed a C-section. At that point I didn't care, though I'd never had one before.

In the operating room, they started to prep me when the double doors opened and a woman walked in and stated, "You are not cutting this woman!" All else faded for me as her beautiful face leaned down, nose to nose with mine. She told me her name was Jaime and to listen only to her and that she would help me deliver my daughter. With her help and firm coaching, I delivered my healthy baby girl.

In recovery for the next two days, I kept asking for Nurse Jaime, and I was told there wasn't anyone on staff by that name or resembling the woman I described to them! I know in my heart that Jaime was an angel sent to me and my daughter, and I will always remember and be forever grateful that we were both home for Christmas!

Visitor from the Ocean

By Lori Kilgour Martin

Life's events have brought me to the floor, to the edge, many times. When thoughts of giving up washed over, the light arrived, bringing the return of magic, mystery, joy, and love.

During one of the lowest points on this journey, I experienced great personal and career losses. I was deeply grieving while, at the same time, overwhelmed with debts and gasping for air. It had reached the point where I was paying for food, health treatments, and rent with credit-card cheques.

I soon found myself caught in a flood of collection calls and letters. With no let-up, the waters were dark; I was swimming in fear and regret. Being hit from all sides, each waking moment was filled with dread, worrying about which bank was going to call next. My heart and soul were crumbling; there was no one to turn to except for God and Jesus.

A visit to my sister's cottage one weekend allowed for a short break from the intense energies. While there, he appeared. The dream was unlike any I have ever experienced, and it is still as clear as if the encounter had taken place last night.

An orca was waiting at the dock. I approached him slowly, then placed my hand on his forehead. Looking into those deep, rich navy-blue eyes, his mighty energy felt warm and comforting. This was a completely new and unexpected occurrence. When I awoke, it took a while to return to this earthly plane. I was in a state of awe. An adjustment had occurred. I had been lifted into a state of peace and acceptance of this life.

I felt understood; the silent call for help was heard. His appearance created the spark of self-forgiveness – acknowledgement that I was doing the best I could, given the lessons that had brought me to that point. I knew that my life would one day turn around. Today, slowly and steadily, it is doing just that.

Even now, I feel the orca's presence. This gentle surprise encounter, for which I am incredibly grateful, remains a wondrous moment in a place beyond time.

Guidance from My Earth Angel

By Michelle Anne Gould

I had reached a point in my life where I was over just being "Mum." With three children under five years of age, I had not taken time out for myself in years. My smile was fading each day, and my usual optimism had gone missing. A quiet voice inside had been attempting to get my attention, urging me to stop living this way, but I did my best to ignore it for as long as I could. Now, I was burned out and on the verge of a meltdown.

One day, I found myself alone in a local park, crying, screaming, and pleading to God. My shouts echoed against the sky, and I became engulfed in a tidal wave of emotion. Deep inside, I knew that there was more to life, more to me. I deeply wanted to be happy, but I knew that I was not truly living; I was just existing. This was not life.

I kept breathing until I calmed down. Through the silence, I heard a gentle, loving voice ask me, "What would you like to do?"

"I don't know," I said. "I want to become a coach!"

At that moment, I felt a loving presence and eyes following me. I turned around, and time stopped. I found myself in a surreal time warp. A flash of light enveloped me as I locked eyes with an angel in human form. My surroundings whirled in a rainbow of colours as the whole world fell away. All around me, I heard invisible angels laughing.

The only way I can explain it is to say that, in a divinely arranged meeting, God sent me an angel, a mentor. I had never experienced such a deep soul connection. Just hearing my Earth Angel's voice captivated me. On a whole different level, my soul knew this soul even before meeting.

With guidance from my Earth Angel, I started to find myself again, piece by piece. I peeled back layers that were not serving me and rediscovered joys I had abandoned, including angels and crystals. I deepened my awareness of the unseen beauty that always surrounds us. My Earth Angel reminded me of my divine spark and reconnected me to love.

A Life's Work, One Step at a Time

By Andrée Joubert

Once upon a time, there was a mother who had two wonderful little boys...

Oh, wait!! This isn't a fairy tale; it's reality...MY reality! The year is 1997. I am 33 years old, the mother of two wonderful sons, and I have just received my diploma. I'm also divorced and unemployed. I've left my church and am living without electricity or running water. Everything I knew about life – all of my values and beliefs – is shattered...*I* am shattered!

How do I get out of this mess? This is bigger than me. I cannot pray to God because I have broken too many rules...and I don't even go to church anymore! Yet I could talk to the Angels because aren't they God's intermediaries?

Here, my spiritual journey began. In my despair, the Angels whispered, "You will walk this life's journey one step at a time. Your steps may be little, but what you build will be solid."

I began to live and make decisions. I am not proud of all of them and am sorry for some, but I have tried! I got a job...I moved...I left a job...I got another one. I was scared, I got discouraged, I learned, I built, I let go, and I moved...forward.

Eventually, I was led to Dr. Joe Dispenza's book *Breaking the Habit of Being Yourself*, which brought me to a new understanding about life, creation, and equilibrium. In a life-changing moment, I realized that life is about *balance* – balance between pain and joy; heart, brain and soul; humanity and spirituality. The sum of my experiences came together, and my life finally made sense. I understood that what I had learned from church made perfect sense. I saw that letting go is possible, not only with our heart, but also by engaging our brain. And I understood that we, as human beings, are the Creators of our lives.

The experience was big; the steps it led me to take were often small, but they were significant. Today, I work for the government of Canada, I am about to start my own business, and I am continuing to consciously create a more solid life, one step at a time.

A Message of Hope Received

By Jerri Eddington

It was a beautiful Mother's Day, and I was just getting ready to head out for dinner when my phone rang. It was my brother, Ed (who is eight years older than me but has always been close), calling to tell me he was in trouble with his work. The night before, while under the influence of alcohol, he had gone to work to see a college play he was directing and had acted inappropriately with a female student. Little did he know how dramatically his life would shift. When the college learned about the incident, he was placed on administrative leave. I became his lifeline of support.

The following Wednesday morning, I was doing my morning meditation in my spa and sobbing, thinking about Ed. Within minutes, I had a visitation from my mother's spirit (which startled me, since we weren't that close when she was alive). She said, "Tell Ed it is no accident that things came to a head on Mother's Day. It is time for him to get help." Then she vanished. I quickly got out of the spa to call Ed.

I went into my bedroom to sit in my recliner. Suddenly, my bedroom became a raging ocean, and I was standing up a small wooden boat, trying to navigate through the storm while Ed was crouched down in the boat with his hands covering his head. I then realized that I would be a navigator for my brother's healing process. I began crying again. Ed called me before I could call him. I delivered the message from our mother and shared my ocean vision.

Ed retired from his teaching position, which had been a positive career until this incident. He went into treatment to deal with his alcoholism and received support from our extended family. Seven months later, the legal issues were resolved on our mother's birthday.

It has now been over four years since the incident, and Ed is still working an active recovery program with a sponsor and me as his spiritual advisor and energy healer.

A Gift from Source

By Faye Rogers

Although it was almost 14 years ago, it seems like only yesterday that I was attending my first healing workshop. I came home from the workshop so excited because an entire new world had opened up for me, a world of helping others. I was so inspired that I started attending other workshops, and in time, I started teaching healing to others.

Almost a decade later, in January 2013, I was recovering from the aftereffects of whooping cough. During this time, I was pacing myself and only accepting the odd request for Animal Communication and Healing sessions that I considered ultra-urgent. I had just connected to a beautiful horse named Evie who told me that the Universe had been trying to get my attention, to stop what I was doing and listen. I was then given a gift from Source: "The Sacred Christed Energies" for healing, for humanity, for the ascension of the planet, and to teach to others that the planet was now ready for this Ray of Healing due to the Crystalline Energy, which could now anchor the frequency.

The Sacred Christed Energies are the healing codes of Christ Consciousness, the universe of beauty that exists in us and exists in the Greater Universe, reaching the core of the Divinity.

Within a week of being gifted these Sacred Energies, I unexpectedly had six people turn up on my doorstep asking for healing. I live in a rural area, and these people had never visited me before. I'd never even had contact with five of them before they knocked on my door – yet they somehow found their way to me, which is quite a mission in itself as I don't advertise my home address! And they all came bearing the same message: the Universe had sent them.

I knew then that it was time to share my gift from Source.

A Soul-Level Healing

By Sara Martin

Years ago, I met a man who activated part of my soul story that had previously been dormant – a story of love, loss, and guilt. We had shared a life together in a previous incarnation. In that life, he died and I was left alone. Consequently, I sequestered myself in my parents' home, mourning my loss and feeling guilty for living off of their wealth.

This person made a profound impression on me in my current life. However, he left the picture. This action triggered my past-life memory, and I experienced a dark night of the soul, which led to an obsessive search for answers. In the process of seeking healing for my loss, I also uncovered the root cause of my migraines – two issues that might seem unrelated but, as I learned, were closely intertwined.

I had been seeking relief from migraines since childhood. My mother and I spent years trying many approaches, from alternative to conventional, but nothing helped. When I began exploring this past-life story, however, I realized that my soul had created these headaches as a way to remember the story in order to heal it. Simply gaining a conscious understanding of *why* was enough to clear them!

I rarely have migraines anymore, and I have a new perspective around the old soul story. I also experienced another epiphany as I contemplated how I, at the soul level, could create such a condition to remind myself of a story I needed to revisit and heal. I wondered, *Who would consciously choose to experience pain like that?* The migraines certainly didn't seem to be in my highest good, but I finally realized that sometimes we create negative experiences for our soul's growth and healing.

Through my experiences with this past-life story (and the spiritual and healing work it led me to, including learning to read the Akashic Records), I have gained the understanding that we really are Divine Beings, creating in each moment – the good and the bad. This was quite a lot to take in; ultimately, though, it was very freeing and empowering for me.

The Words That Changed My Life

By Noemi Grace

On September 11, 2001, I was stuck in a train station near Boston after the terrorist attack. The fear within me and around me was palpable. It was then that I uttered a pivotal prayer from deep within my heart.

Because I had grown up in a family that prayed daily, I had a fundamental understanding of prayer. But at the time, I felt spiritually adrift; the days blended together without purpose.

Yet on that day, I knew I had to pray, even if my prayer was never answered. It was then that I spoke words I had never said before: "Use me for the healing of the world." I really meant those words and felt compelled to speak them for hours to keep the fear at bay.

I never told anyone about this experience and rarely considered it. But I occasionally wondered if my prayer would be answered and why I chose to meet fear with hope and willingness on that day.

Over a decade passed. Then, on March 3, 2012, I heard these marvelous words: "Love is the fabric of freedom. Forgiveness paves the way to freedom." Those words stopped me in my tracks! As someone who had secretly harbored judgment and guilt, I knew that those words were not mine. Yet I heard them as deeply and felt them as strongly as I had felt fear on 9/11.

Since that first message, I have become a channel for spiritual wisdom, and I have received hundreds of messages as powerful as that first one, which shook me to my core. I have also learned that these messages are the answer to the prayer I uttered in desperation on 9/11.

On that day, I had no idea of the power of the words I prayed. But they helped me rise above the collective fear around me and embrace hope. They even opened the door for me to become a spiritual channel. Now the words I receive every day are blessing me and those around me.

The Miracle of Reiki

By Farah Joy Rupani

I stood beside her hospital bed where she lay terminally ill. I held her hands gently and lovingly, my eyes glued to hers as the tears rolled down my face. "May you be free from suffering; may you be at peace," were the only words I offered to my great-aunt. Just then, a subtle yet powerful energy started pulsating through my hands. A bright glow of light surrounded our hands, as if this light was meant to help her in some way. As the light became more prominent, my cries became louder and my heart pounded faster.

Suddenly, my daughter awakened me. I was sobbing heavily. Curiously, I questioned myself, *Was that a dream?* The experience of being with my great-aunt was so vivid that I couldn't imagine it to be anything but real. My soul kept guiding me to learn about the energy I witnessed in that dream.

That afternoon, my mother called to share that my great-aunt had departed. I stood in utter disbelief, as I had planned to visit her that day at the hospital. I somehow felt responsible for her death. With guilt washing over me, I sensed that the prayers I offered in the dream had caused her to pass. I carried that guilt for months.

A year after her death, I stumbled upon the energy-healing modality of Reiki. I became intrigued that others could be healed naturally with the channeling of universal life-force energy through one's hands. I realized that what I offered to my great-aunt in the dream was, in fact, Reiki. I had finally discovered my calling.

As I began my healing journey with Reiki, I realized that I didn't harm my great-aunt in any way. I only helped end her suffering in this world. It is said that Reiki flows wherever it is meant to for one's highest good. Reiki found me when I needed it the most to heal my grief and guilt. That was the gift that my great-aunt had left me with: a true healing miracle of Reiki.

A Beautiful New World

By Mathew Hart

On December 31, 2011, I awoke from a deep sleep remembering a fascinating dream in which I was given a positive vision for the future of humanity, and words in support of that vision – words that I was told during my sleep would be part of an event that was going to happen within one month's time. I was also shown a video that I was to make by holding up the words of the vision on a series of white cards.

That morning, I wrote down those words and then contemplated what to do with them. Back then, I belonged to only one Facebook group, and it suddenly occurred to me that I should share it there since the members of that group were open-minded about messages received from spirit. So I composed a post and fully intended to share it, but when the time came, I found myself overcome with fear – fear of judgment, fear of ridicule, fear of not being understood. I pushed the fear aside and posted anyway.

A few minutes later, the first person to respond was a women from Jerusalem, who I didn't know, who said, "Your vision is my vision." She then went on to ask if she could use the words of my vision as the basis for a worldwide online meditation event she was planning to have in three weeks' time.

I answered, "Yes!" as I immediately knew that her meditation event was the event foretold in my dream.

The next day, the same woman sent me a second message: "Do you think you could make a video in support of the meditation event? It would help to promote the event."

"Yes," I said again, as I knew exactly what to do and went ahead and made the video.

The video, entitled "A Vision of a Beautiful New World," was released on January 3, 2012, and within a matter of days received thousands of views and more than a hundred comments – all very positive and supportive.

All in all, it was an exciting experience and a real turning point, something I will never forget.

More to Life Than Science

By Anita D. Marshall

In 2010 my focus was on my new business, not finding a relationship. As for motherhood, I had set the idea aside after receiving the devastating news three years earlier that my chances of having children naturally were extremely low. But I still had hope because three different palm readings from teenage years onwards said "two children," plus the amazing insights from being a Soul Plan Practitioner/Coach suggested that fertility was not meant to be an issue.

In September of that year, my car broke down and I did something I would never have considered doing before: I boldly asked the lovely repairman who came to my rescue for a date! We ended up falling in love. He had two children, so I started thinking that maybe this is what the palm readers meant; but still, inside, there was a seed of belief.

Then, after a couple of years, he suggested trying for a baby. The doctors' tests resonated in my ears, and I was now 38, but we both had fertility as positive soul-plan energies. *Was it possible? Could science be wrong?*

I became pregnant but lost the baby at nine and a half weeks. Because I had learned to count my blessings, I thanked the little soul for giving me the chance to learn about the transience of life and experience pregnancy, however briefly.

Three months later, a palm reader told me that I had one child...with a second as an option! She said that my partner had three...with maybe another possible! Ten days later, I found out I was expecting.

Giving birth to our gorgeous son was life changing and confirmed that shifts happen when you are willing to let go of what science knows and trust in more.

And the second child? I continued to believe and count my blessings through two more miscarriages. Then, as I trained in Soul Transformation Therapy, I was on the receiving end of this powerful healing practice and experienced a cathartic energy shift. I was pregnant again within the month, and at nearly 43, as I write for this book, we welcomed our second son into the world.

Polywogs

By Charlene Williams

I was a shy, frightened child who desperately wanted to believe that there was a God who saw me and heard my prayers. I often played on the far side of the house in a dirt pile with my brother's Matchbox cars. I created roads that became shopping centers with parking lots, expressways, and the road to my house.

My brother would bring home buckets of polywogs from the nearby creek. I watched in fascination as their tails shortened, their legs grew, and they would jump from the bucket! There were also some who simply died, and it made me so sad to witness their short lives. One day, when I was about eight or nine, I buried a few in the dirt and asked God to please take them to Heaven. I waited maybe five minutes and dug through the dirt but couldn't find the polywogs! I knew that things decomposed, so the next time I wrapped the little bodies in tissues so I would find them. Once again I prayed, waited five minutes or so, and began to dig. Once again…no polywogs! Perhaps things decomposed quickly? I wanted to make sure, so the next time I wrapped them in tissue and then put them in the tiny matchboxes that my parents used for the fireplace. I buried the little amphibians in their tiny coffins, mounded the dirt, put little twigs at the top of their graves (so there would be no mistaking where they were buried), and waited another five minutes or so. I dug everywhere, deeper than they were buried, in the exact spot where I placed them, but could never find any trace of the polywogs, tissues, or matchbox coffins!

Ever since that time, whenever I've had doubts about the existence of a Higher Power or God, I've thought about the beautiful gift of God hearing an innocent little girl's heartfelt prayer for confirmation of his presence. I will never forget the polywogs!

My Past-Life Awakening

By Jane Francis

I enjoyed smoking, and for 25 years I smoked two packs a day and believed that cigarettes were getting a bad rap. I often said, "I will smoke until I die...and it will NOT be from cigarettes!"

It was suggested that I have a past-life regression as part of my spiritual-healing journey. The concept was new to me, so I had no idea what to expect. I simply asked my angels to reveal what would help me now.

During the session, the regressionist had my body resting in a peaceful garden while my spirit was to travel back to the past, yet I could not relax into it. After 45 minutes, we finally went back to "get my body." (As an experiential learner, I believed I needed it!)

Once I "had my body," I immediately zoomed to a life as a man wrestling with someone. I dispassionately observed my head being slowly pushed under mud. I felt mud fill my mouth, I died, and I went to the afterlife...all in less than two minutes!

I went to another lifetime right away. In this life, I was awakening to consciousness knowing that dirt was being shoveled over me. I calmly witnessed my struggle to breathe and quickly went Home once more. A third experience once again had me suffocate and die immediately.

After experiencing three lives (and three suffocations) in five minutes, we asked my higher self about the significance and were told that I was to experience dying and going Home.

Despite the experiences and the message, I personally thought of myself as a regression failure. The following week, however, someone pointed out to me that the cigarette I had prior to my regression was the last one I smoked. WOW! I had made no conscious decision to quit!

The regressionist later told me, as I trained under her tutelage, that I was the most challenging client she ever regressed with the most bizarre experience she ever witnessed! (Thankfully, I have never regressed anyone as difficult as myself either!) Odd as it was, I am grateful to be 20 years smoke-free! I truly smoked until I died...and it was NOT from cigarettes!

A Class-5 Angel

By Maureen Hollmeyer

It was 11 o'clock on a Friday night at the University of Cincinnati when my friend asked if I wanted to go on a whitewater rafting trip. The bus to West Virginia was leaving in an hour. I said, "Yes!"

The following morning, we woke up on the bus to pouring rain. All I could think was how horrible my hair would look wet! We put on our wetsuits and piled into the rafts.

Halfway through our journey, the raft guide reluctantly told us that we were going to go through a Class-5 rapid. "Hold on tight!" he shouted. The last thing I remember was watching helplessly as the six people sitting in front of me flew out of the raft.

Then everything went black.

I had no idea where I was or what was happening. Suddenly, I was shown an image of a newspaper swirling around and around. When it stopped, I read the headline: "UC Student Dies Whitewater Rafting." I realized that the headline was referring to me and I was going to drown!

I struggled to push myself toward the surface, but I had no concept of which way was up. Then, it was as if someone yanked me by my lifejacket and pulled me to the surface. My head popped up, and I could breathe!

I floated the rest of the way on my back, with my feet facing the aggressive currents. It's a miracle I made it to dry land.

The entire incident was captured on video. Watching it later, I couldn't believe my eyes. I had flown out of the raft about 50 feet! I wasn't even wearing a helmet. How did I survive?

At that moment, I realized I was saved by my guardian angel. I was given the chance to live my life's purpose. I became a social worker, and through my career, I have been a lifeline for other people over the past 15 years.

This experience left no doubt in my mind that we all have guardian angels!

Your Soul Always Knows Your Destiny

By Christine King

By the mid-1980s, having already established a successful holistic practice in the U.K., I had an experience during a deep meditation that made me feel ready to expand spiritually by taking further training.

A short time later, somebody handed me a leaflet about a New Thought Science of Mind teacher from America who was offering metaphysical training in the U.K. I attended the lecture and was excited about the training. The course was full, however; so, concluding that I had misread my guidance, I continued with a previously planned trip to the U.S.

There I met a lady who was studying metaphysics with Science of Mind in Los Angeles. She invited me to a meeting, and I felt the same sense of excitement that I'd experienced at the lecture in London.

Days later, at a different event, a woman approached me, saying that she had a spiritual message for me: I should go to the Bodhi Tree metaphysical bookshop because there was an important book there for me. She had no title but said I would be intuitively led to it.

Arriving at the bookshop, I was overwhelmed by the thousands of books on display. How would I ever find the "special" one?

A large, impressive, leather-bound title enticed me. My ego spoke: "That must be it!" As I reached up to coax it down, a small, insignificant-looking paperback came hurtling into my hands.

Casting it aside, I noticed the title: *You Can Heal Your Life*. (This was years before Oprah promoted it on her show; so, like most people, I had never heard of it at that time.) Something prompted me to look inside. I couldn't believe it. The author, Louise Hay, was trained in the Science of Mind teachings. Just what was going on? Those teachings were following me around.

I returned to the U.K., intrigued by all of these coincidences. Upon opening my front door, I saw a letter from the course teacher. Somebody had dropped out. Would I like the space?

I then trained with the Science of Mind organisation for three years, which was a life-changing chapter in my journey.

The Message of the Tattoo

By Mauri Barnes

I was spending time far from home, in my mother's condo, after her sudden and unexpected death. My heartbreaking task was to empty her home and finalize the sale of her condo at the end of the month.

I'd brought my dogs with me for companionship and love, and to help ease the pain of this overwhelmingly sad time. As the days of June grew warmer, the poodles needed haircuts. I dropped them off with a groomer and looked around for something to do while waiting. With time to explore, I headed across the street to satisfy my curiosity. Enchanted by the variety of exquisite tattoo designs and amazed at the skilled artistry displayed in this boutique, I spent hours browsing.

The owner had been tattooing since she was 12, having learned from her father. She would replicate any picture for me. I just didn't know which design to choose. I was excited to be tattooed at the age of 55 and scheduled an appointment for the next day. This was my gift to myself. It was symbolic of a shift into becoming the family elder that began with Mom's passing.

That night, I dreamed of Pegasus, my animal spirit guide. This mythological winged horse had been a familiar figure to me ever since childhood, when my father wore a red Pegasus on his uniform while working at our family's gas station and garage.

The next day, I told the tattooist that I wanted a tattoo of Pegasus...with a twist: instead of soaring above the clouds, my Pegasus would rise out of the sea.

"That doesn't make sense," the woman said. "Why would a flying horse be coming out of the water?"

"It's what I want," I told her.

In less than two hours, she easily created the design. My beautiful Pegasus, rising from the waves, is now forever a part of me.

A few weeks later, while packing to leave for the last time, I reached for my mother's bookbag, noticed the logo, and just stood there smiling with wonder. Pegasus was rising from the waves! The *Reader's Digest* gift to Mom became her message to me: She likes my tattoo!

The Day My Angels Reached Me

By Patricia LeBlanc

During a period of several weeks in early 2016, I would play with my angels and ask them the exact same question over and over: "In which direction should I take my business?" Each and every time I asked this question and pulled a card, I would get the Spiritual Teacher card, as well as the Healer card and/or the Support card.

One day, I think they got fed up with me asking the exact same question, getting the same answer, and yet doing nothing about it. I pulled out the first card: the Spiritual Teacher. My angels started yelling at me: "Spiritual Teacher!"

I asked for confirmation: "So you are telling me that I need to be a spiritual teacher?"

They yelled back, "Yes! Yes! Yes!"

"Okay," I answered back. "I hear you. I need to become a spiritual teacher again."

The next card I pulled was the Healer card, and once again, my angels yelled at me, "Healer!"

"Okay," I replied. "I hear you!"

Once again, the third card I pulled was the Support card. I asked my angels, "Are you letting me know that you support me and I will be able to make a living by being a spiritual teacher?"

Again, they answered, "Yes."

From that day forward, I have been paying close attention to any guidance I receive from my angels – whether it's through the cards, through a feeling, or through a nudge in a certain direction. Since I began paying closer attention to – and *following* – the angels' guidance, my life has been flowing with ease and grace.

Letting Go of Judgment, Embracing Goodness

By Teresa Velardi

Are you kidding? A cardinal? That woman is out of her mind!

As I listened to the woman speak about how she knew that God was watching over her anytime she saw a red cardinal, I made a judgment that she was crazy. Her view of God certainly didn't fit with my religious upbringing, which taught me about a vengeful, punishing God – a God I had long before decided didn't love me anymore.

Long ago, I had made a decision against that still, small voice inside, which I have since come to know as my inner guidance or the voice of God. Because I didn't listen, I was being punished. That's why my life was such a mess, and I wasn't going to God with any of the hurt and pain plaguing my life. I believed it was all punishment from Him. I was miserable! I wanted to die!

One morning while I was out for a walk, trying to shake off the effects of being abused the night before, I finally cried out to God. I was desperate and had nothing to lose. With tears streaming down my face, I asked for a sign that God was with me and that I could still turn to Him. Just then, I heard a little peep of a bird, one I was familiar with. Sure enough, sitting in the majestic red maple in our front yard, there it was: a red cardinal! Seriously? I remember saying out loud, "Very funny, God!" I even heard a little giggle inside.

In that moment, I renewed my relationship with God and began to trust again. With gratitude, I let go of the judgment of the woman's cardinal story, and cardinals have been with me ever since. They nested in that maple tree for years, and when I moved, they showed up in the apple tree outside my bedroom window.

There are many opinions and meanings connected to these beautiful birds. I choose to believe they are a little bit of Heaven, a whisper from God, and a wink from my parents.

God is good!

Open to Learning

By Stacey Hall

I was looking forward to a gathering of silent meditation followed by socializing. As the facilitator helped us focus our thoughts and energies into a quiet, meditative state, I gently relaxed into the deliciously luxurious space to receive Divinely connected inspirations. Almost immediately, other attendees began chatting in loud whispers. I lost my Divine connection as even more conversations could be heard.

My feelings of frustration and anger rose into a white-hot flame as I felt powerless. I was agitated that the facilitator was not requesting that the room return to silence, irritated that I did not have the courage to request quiet, and disappointed that I was unable to tune out the noise.

I chose to leave. On my way out of the room, some of the other attendees smiled warmly at me and a few encouraged me to stay – not knowing why I was leaving. I was so angry, all I could do was throw daggers at them with my eyes.

At home, I decided to return to my meditative state. I was still so angry, I began yelling at God for not helping me so I could have remained at the gathering in a peaceful state. My outburst was interrupted as the lights around me dimmed, all sound went quiet, and I was transported to somewhere between Heaven and Earth. And then, a deep masculine voice boomed, "If what they were doing was so wrong, then why are they still there enjoying each other's company while you are here yelling at me?"

Shaking and trembling, I replied, "I am open to learning."

The voice (which I'm sure was Divine) responded, "Trust that you will be receiving guidance in how to be happy and loving."

The next day, I began receiving unsolicited invitations to transformational workshops and suggestions of books to read. New people came into my life as I explored each of these suggestions and invitations. The anger I'd felt, which had been simmering within me on a low flame for many years undetected, began to cool. It was replaced by more loving, generous, compassionate feelings for others.

Every day since then, I wake up and remember that experience, and I have the most glorious day with others, living fully!

Angels by My Side

By Rose Kaplan

On July 15, 2005, life as we knew it was forever changed. Scott – our beloved son, our only child – was gone. A car accident had taken his life.

It was 10:30 a.m., and Scott was late arriving home from swim-team practice. I thought perhaps he'd gone straight to his job to pick up his schedule and paycheck. It was unlike Scott not to call.

I was meeting friends for lunch in the same strip mall where Scott worked. Looking out the restaurant windows, I checked as SUVs passed by, hoping to see Scott's. Just as we ordered, my husband called and said to come home, RIGHT AWAY! I knew it had to be serious and feared it was about Scott. Heart racing, I sped home to find police cars in front of my house.

Even in my anxious state, as I walked up the driveway, I couldn't help but notice the thin line of small grey feathers, not askew but placed almost symmetrically along the entire length of the lawn leading up to the house. I knew they weren't there when I had left less than an hour before to meet my friends.

Although I couldn't absorb it at the time, those feathers were a sign from my angels letting me know that we were not alone.

Looking back, my angels had made their presence known months prior to the accident. A unique pattern had emerged. No matter where I went or how crowded the lot, a parking spot near the door would become available. Although I had never asked for one, it was obvious that I now had a parking angel. What a blessing!

At the time, I didn't understand why I was receiving angelic signs, but I now know that the angels were showing me that in good times as well as bad, they are always by my side.

I Got Carried Away

By Marla David

Imagine that you are in a super comfortable bed with a down comforter, feeling more like you were surrounded and supported by clouds, floating in the cosmos. You want to relish that feeling for as long as you can, not wanting to leave the warmth, the comfort, and the safe haven. You pull the comforter right up over your head and cocoon yourself. This is what I experienced during a dream that shifted my very existence and what I know of life.

My body lifted up and began floating. Sometimes in my dreams I fly, but this was different. Arms of light held me and circled around and around. As if in a cocoon, I was comfortable and secure, feeling extreme happiness and joy. I was overcome with pure love, more love than I had ever conceived. It was like seeing the sun and feeling its warmth, but so much stronger than anything I'd ever experienced or even imagined. Although the light was bright, it did not bother me. It was radiating, like heat does. I was aglow with arm-like bands that kept me encapsulated inside a vortex of love.

I am unsure if I was moving or being rocked, like in a cradle, but it felt peaceful. I'm not even sure whether I stayed in that place or traveled somewhere else, but it didn't matter. I didn't want this experience of beautiful and loving acceptance to stop. I just let it be.

When I jerked awake, I felt a bit disoriented for a few moments. Sitting on the end of the bed, I tried to make sense of what had just transpired. Surely it was just a dream, yet it seemed so real...and also surreal. I knew I had just had a life-shifting encounter...with Source. Tears flowed freely as I smiled, knowing that I was loved, *really* loved, just as I am, with all my imperfections and with all the mistakes I have made. I was loved as me!

The Voice

By Missy Conley

I finally got the nerve to go to Mom and Dad's grave two weeks after my mom passed away. I was glad that it had snowed enough that day to cover the fresh dirt of her grave. My heart had been broken before, but I'd never experienced anything worse than the heartbreak of losing my parents. I was too young to be left here without them.

My knees hit the snow, and I began to sob. Tears poured down my cheeks as I screamed to them aloud: "Why did you leave me? Why did you come here, have me, and then leave me alone? I have no brothers and sisters or anything! How could you do this to me? I am so mad at you! What am I supposed to do now?"

I shifted my anger toward God. I didn't even know if there was a God. If there was, why would he take my mom and dad from me? I roared these words into the air around me: "Why, God? Why would you take them from me? I don't understand! Why?!" I lay there in the snow, crying until I exhausted myself. After I stopped struggling, eventually I reached a moment of silence.

I stood up in shock when I heard a voice come into my mind – seemingly from out of nowhere – and make a very clear statement. It was so clear, in fact, that I thought someone had spoken the words: "If I had not done things this way, you would have never come back to me."

I knew who it was. It was God, and it was real. I knew that I had a purpose for staying here without them. I was instantly filled with peace and comfort. I left the cemetery that day feeling that something had definitely shifted in me. If I was important enough to receive a real message from God, then I must have an important purpose for being here.

Never again have I felt alone.

My Journey to Oneness

By Valerie Cameron

I was brought up in a Christian home. My grandfather was a reverend and a scholar who spoke seven languages fluently. Because I loved him so much and didn't want to go against my upbringing, it took me many years before I branched out into spiritual realms of self-discovery beyond the church.

Eventually, I made a personal choice to leave the dogmatic religious system I was raised in and search for my own spiritual identity. But it seemed that no matter how much I looked outside myself for something, I could not find it. I felt such an emptiness within, like part of me was missing – although, for a long time, I wasn't even sure what it was.

During these years of my spiritual journey, I experienced many great dreams and visions, yet I never understood what they meant. It was not until I went through a very deep depression, even to the point where I had planned to commit suicide, that the Voice within me spoke to me: *It is time.*

When I heard these words, I immediately understood their message: What I had been looking for on the outside was already within. I knew that it was okay for me to grow and experience in my own way. I was on the path I needed to be on for my own personal evolution.

As I expanded my awareness of the Universe, I became more balanced and discerning. I saw the world and people from a different perspective. I saw things as a whole rather than from their individual parts. I gained greater empathy because I came to understand what was going on in many people, even if they didn't see it themselves. I realized that, although the details of our stories may vary, my journey is no different from anyone else's. And I realized that my love for life and the compassion I feel for others is how I can be of service to humanity.

Visions of Fire and Feelings of Dread

By Gretchen Oehler Hogg

Have you ever wondered what it would be like to glimpse into your future? If you had a prophetic vision, would you make different decisions that would change your future's trajectory? I had just such a vision merely one week after I was married. I found myself desperately trying to ignore my intuition, as visions of fire began dancing in my head, and feelings of dread permeated my body.

February 21, 1982, one week after our wedding, my husband and I prepared for our first day back at our respective jobs: I as a nurse at a General Intensive Care Unit, and he as a pilot. As we got dressed for work, I couldn't shake a horrible sense of foreboding. I kissed him goodbye with promises to lovingly embrace one another after work.

At the start of my shift, my routine continued as I received my patient assignments for the evening. Yet again, visions of fire danced across my eyes, and an unyielding sense of dread took hold. I intended to call our landlord as soon as I got out of report and ask her to go check our apartment. Did I leave the stove on? Did I leave the laundry basket too close to the wall heater?

There was a call at the nurses' station for me. I heard my husband's best friend and fellow pilot on the other end of the phone. "There's been a crash," he started. I could tell he was crying.

I started uncontrollably sobbing, knowing that I had to ask him the most dreaded question imaginable: "Is he alive?"

From that moment onward, everything became surreal, as I began to float above my body, gazing at it from the ceiling. Curiously, I began feeling a sense of divine love, protection, and a knowing that everything would be okay. Next, I observed people dragging me, hysterically sobbing, back into the nurses' report room; then I suddenly found myself back in my body.

Those prophetic visions, along with the divine reassurance I felt during that time of crisis, shifted my life in profound and mysterious ways. My intuition became my compass rose, like a trusted navigation system that would guide me through stormy seas into safe harbors along the journey of my husband's turbulent, yet complete, recovery.

Hugged by an Angel

By Andrea Detchon

My life from the outside looked great, but inside my head and home I was stressed, depressed, self-medicating, trying to escape, and putting myself at risk by drinking most nights and every weekend. I didn't care whether I was alive or dead. I knew that if I died, people would be sad, but they would get over it.

After one night of particularly heavy drinking, I dropped into a deep sleep and dreamed about being dead, about floating away and leaving my body. I hoped my family would be okay, but I felt so free, comfortable, safe, protected, accepted, and peaceful. Above all, I felt loved – *truly* loved – the kind of love that overwhelms your emotions and makes every cell in your body vibrate.

When I started to wake up, I realized that I wasn't actually dead, but that feeling of unconditional love stayed with me. I felt like I was inside a giant hug from a giant, soft bird – an angel holding me, bringing me back. I dared not open my eyes, wanting to hold on to this feeling. The sun felt bright around me. I knew that things would change.

When I finally opened my eyes, the day was cloudy and I was alone. But every cell in my body knew that something had changed. Everything was different. I was *aware*.

It took time for some of the changes to show up in my life, and some of them were uncomfortable and painful. But after that moment, I found alternative ways of living, alternative ways of healing. I couldn't go back. My eyes were open.

I have never forgotten – and I never will forget – that feeling, that sensation of being hugged by an angel, of being safe, of the total, overwhelming, unconditional love and the desire for me to be alive and well and truly living life.

In the years since then, I've seen other angels, felt their energy, and listened to their messages. I now help other people to transform their lives, do what they really want to, and live with more happiness and joy. This amazing journey all began with that one profound dream – my awakening – and I am grateful beyond words for this blessing.

January 31

A Shift into Knowing

By Nancy Merrill Justice

Suddenly, out of the corner of my right eye, I saw two headlights racing toward the passenger side of my car. In that brief, slow-motion moment just before impact, I had a life-shifting experience – one that left an indelible imprint on my soul.

I was driving home after a long walk, hoping to ease my heavy heart filled with grief over the recent death of my younger sister, Carol. While she gracefully battled recurring breast cancer, I was in awe of the strength and comfort she derived from her unwavering faith in Jesus Christ and the Christian teachings. Yet, as I observed in admiration, my own internal conflicts over the teachings of organized religion swelled.

I have always felt God's presence everywhere as unconditional love. But when I would go to services in official places of worship, I not only heard uplifting messages of hope, salvation through Christ, and eternal life, I also heard undertones of individual unworthiness (labeling us as "sinners"), God-fearing rhetoric, and conflicting messages about wealth and abundance. These messages caused me such internal unease and angst that I stopped participating in organized religious worship. Instead, I found my strength and celebrated a spiritual connection with God in nature. Even so, my rational mind kept me a disbelieving skeptic about a spiritual afterlife.

Then, in that suspended moment just before impact, with no time for rational thought, I saw my sister's image and three angels of light surround and protect the right side of my vehicle. And instead of instinctively stiffening to brace for the impact, I felt a wave of peaceful energy sweep through my entire body, and I relaxed into the force of the crash. My beliefs that spiritual connections to God end with physical death shifted into the certainty of knowing that our essence lives on.

This experience forever changed my core beliefs and awakened my soul – empowering and inspiring me to create and live my life's true purpose through transformational teaching, writing, and healing.

Journey to Source

By Jeanette St. Germain

Her soft voice rolled over the meditation group, lulling my senses into a deep relaxation. Following her suggestions of steady breathing and letting go, I slowly entered a more floaty state where I was able to notice everything without attachment. Her voice grew deeper, inviting us to take a soul journey removed from time, and I felt myself shift higher.

The healer brought us to a sacred garden, a place filled with bright light, colorful plants, and sparkling waters. There was an expectant curiosity here, and even though I seemed alone, I somehow knew there were thousands of "others" joining me, filling the space with welcoming. Together, we explored magenta roses, climbing ivy, and violet fountains.

After allowing my consciousness to enjoy the wonders in the garden, I finally settled at the edge of a crystalline pool. Peering over, I gazed at my reflection. Startled, I blinked rapidly, confused by the many faces of "me" looking back. The healer's voice was barely perceptible at this point, but she encouraged me to sink further into the eyes shining up at me. She asked them to take me to the beginning, to the first spark of life I could remember.

There was a quick rush of warm electricity, and I was suddenly transported to another place. Stretched out before me was an infinite cloud of spiraling light. There was every color imaginable and a swelling in and out, like breathing. I could feel a pulsing vibration in the air, a kind of silent song that my spirit knew and embraced, a great cosmic heartbeat infusing ALL. I felt safe, as if I were being cradled in the arms of a mother. Tears streamed down my face, pure adoration pouring from every atom of my being.

We shared all-encompassing, thick, true love. I started to panic, feeling not worthy, wanting to flee the magnificence laid before me as my own. The energy seemed to understand and, with a jolt, filled me with certainty, a life-shifting moment of perception far greater than any fear or doubt...the only truth is love.

Beads of Hope

By Susan Elizabeth Schoemmell

The rosary beads in my mother's hands were tangled and gnarled into a ball of despair. It was as if her emotions of frustration from being left in the nursing home without my daily visits were all tangled into those beads.

It was a difficult decision for me to leave and attend a workshop in Kauai, Hawaii, but it was an invitation that I could not resist. The author of the book *Are You Really Too Sensitive?* had unlocked several issues of my life, and I desperately needed to understand more of who I was and how to take care of myself. However, as I sat there and saw the level of frustration this had brought on, I felt a rush of guilt come over me. I was overwhelmed with the need to untangle both the rosary beads and my mother's emotions. Since my father's death, I had become my mother's caretaker, and although she was in a nursing home, it wasn't an easy compromise.

As I took the rosaries from her hands and said, "God listens if you pray softly," a miracle transpired. At that moment, the beads miraculously became untangled as if someone had touched them with a magic wand. Suddenly, they lay in my hands, totally free of any knots.

I was shocked, but at the same time, I sensed that God was watching and listening. My guilt dissolved as a shift in my thinking became clearer. What had just transpired could not be explained except that my mother's beads of despair had been turned into beads of hope. Even if my mother was not aware of what had just transpired, I was. I had been shrouded in guilt, but as I placed the untangled rosaries back into her hands, I felt at peace. Through all of this emotional pain, I truly felt that I had been touched by the Hand of God.

Ready to Listen

By Cathy Duesterhoeft

God gave me a sign! During devotions, I read 1 Peter 3:3 about not adorning myself or focusing on beauty because that should start on the inside. I thought it was interesting, as my husband and I had recently talked about this. In addition, just a couple of hours later, the radio DJ talked about her disappointment when looking in the mirror, and she read 1 Peter 3:3 – *Don't be concerned about the outward beauty that depends on jewelry, or beautiful clothes, or hair arrangement.* The same verse from two different sources within hours of each other couldn't be a coincidence. I was being sent a message, and I was ready to listen.

Now I needed to figure out why I had been sent the message. Was I being called to the pulpit, or was there a different reason? The first thing I did was to shed my vanity by shaving my head. Being bald was my way to focus on determining why I had received my sign from God and what plans he had for me.

After much praying and studying, I decided that I did not need a pulpit to stand behind in order to empower others. My baldness shows that I am comfortable with myself and I can be a positive influence on others dealing with depression, low self-esteem, and many other social stigmas. My sign from God was a prompt to aid others.

I found it ironic when I was at the refrigerator one day and there, staring me in the face, was an inspirational verse I had hung: 1 Peter 3:3. The date on the verse was exactly one month prior to my sign. God had tried to get my attention, but I was not ready to listen. When God deemed that I was ready, he sent the same message *twice* because he wanted to make sure I was listening – and this time I was!

Seven Angelic Keys

By Ted Brooks

From the age of seven, I could cross the veil of time and space and see beyond the illusory world of form. I can see auras, a gift that I find helpful in doing energy work, allowing me to facilitate the reversal of negative body events such as health issues (which the world labels as "healing"). Hundreds of times in my life, Spirit has told me to let pure consciousness move through me to the soul in front of me, and they have been changed and restored.

Then, four months ago, angels came to me and said that it was time to begin fulfilling my agreements made before time, space, and form. They showed me the reasons for all events in my life thus far, as well as what my path was to be in this time experience, and I was given "Seven Angelic Keys," three of which I will share here:

1. Judge nothing (as best you can in each moment); judgment is not our role.
2. Love unconditionally in all situations.
3. Upon waking each morning, seek with gratitude that which you believe to be the Kingdom of Heaven.

Practicing these Keys has already created major shifts in my life. Since receiving them, I have released five out of my six health concerns, including releasing 12 medications. I have also cut my debt by more than a quarter million dollars! And, most of all, I'm happier to be alive than I've ever been. I feel connected to all of life. My spiritual connection and gifts have increased exponentially, and I know that life is good!

My goal in writing this is to share a way for everyone who reads this and follows these three steps to experience their own specific shift. I know that you, too, can be lifted to joy, peace, and the biggest shift of all: love.

Inspired Direction

By Sharon Rothstein

Once upon a time, I was alone, asleep, and frightened. Then I, the princess of my reality, woke up and realized that there is a greater power than me watching over me and working on my behalf.

Call it God, Spirit, Source, or my Inner Being. Call it what you may, I am not alone. I have been awakened. There is a guide protecting me and showing me the way through this human journey. I simply had not noticed or did not recall.

Once introduced to the glorious world of Spirit, I searched for a deeper connection and belief. There revealed a far greater peace in me than I had ever known – a lightness of being, a knowing so profound, a special trust that I might now live in a consistent state of inspired direction.

Inspired direction connects me to my inner knowing, providing much more to me than this physical Earth being named Sharon. It is my quiet zone, void of self-imposed challenge, where I am able to find more solutions than problems.

The incessant chatter of my mind slows down. I no longer give power to my ego voice. It may be the voice of protection, yet it is also the voice of negativity that tells me lies. I can choose not to believe this fabricated nonsense.

When falling into unnecessary fear, worry, or doubt, I stop, breathe, and ask, *Is this true?* I immediately recognize, *All is well, and I am safe.* The torture ceases. In my life review, everything has always worked out for me; therefore, I assume that this shall continue.

It has become my norm to listen to my guide within. Inner calm confirms that my choices are appropriate; if not, I respond with a new inspired decision. With inspired direction, my needs are met and timing is perfection. I reside happily in my now, knowing that my future will take care of itself.

I've evolved into a fully unlimited being, assisted in this joyous dance of life, asleep no more.

Dancing with Synchronicity

By Farah Joy Rupani

The phenomenon of recurring numbers has always fascinated me. In 2011, I began noticing certain numerical patterns in various places. I told a dear friend at the time that I was seeing my birthday (413) everywhere: the clock, license plates, street addresses, numbers on receipts, even the number of Facebook post likes. My friend laughed and abruptly dismissed my experience, but I was convinced that these numbers were appearing in my life to convey messages.

As I grew increasingly curious about the ways that numbers were materializing, I started seeing 444, 777, 111, and my very favorite one, 143, which signifies "I love you." Every time that I saw 143 appear, I would dance in joyful excitement because I instinctively knew how much God loved me.

Right after recovering from a distressful accident in 2014, I started receiving even more intuitive messages through the recurring numbers. I began to notice alpha-numeric combinations on license plates that carried their very own meanings for me. While driving, I would come across cars with the word "CRY" on the license plate. Interestingly, this would happen when I was very well aware of grief and sadness that needed to be released from my heart. I would see the word "FLY" on the license plates just when I needed to trust myself more and spread my wings. As I focused more on this phenomenon, I started hearing songs with synchronistic messages at opportune times, exactly when I needed to hear those words the most.

At one point in my life, I thought these were mere coincidences. Later, I learned that these messages carried an intuitive meaning that is deeply connected with God. Now, I revel in the fact that I have found my path illuminated through the constantly repeating words, numbers, and songs. My heart knows there are no coincidences in life, only divine synchronicity. And I sure love it when the synchronicity shows up and I can dance with it.

Ancestral Grace

By Aprile Alexander

For 10 years, I'd felt impelled to make a Camino de Santiago pilgrimage, although I didn't know why. Last year, through circumstances I had never anticipated, I was able to journey to Spain with enough time to walk the final 112 kilometers from Sarria to Santiago de Compostela.

In order to live by trust day by day, I chose not to pre-plan or pre-book. I walked mostly alone, my constant companions for the next seven days of pilgrimage being my backpack and the mantra "God is the ground of my being."

When I finally climbed the steps of Santiago de Compostela's ancient cathedral, I felt myself joyously surrounded and welcomed by invisible multitudes of pilgrims from the last 1,000 years!

While waiting for the pilgrims' service to begin, a surge of energy came towards me from the side of the altar, and I recognised a stream of my ancestors, almost tumbling over each other, so jubilant were they at my presence. Their warmth and their love enveloped me; tears came to my eyes as I felt healing, not just within myself but also in the ancestral line.

This experience was affirmed several weeks later when I learned that the land I'd walked through was once settled by my ancestors, the Portuguese.

Receiving such profound love, approval, and healing from these ancestors was one of the most grace-filled times of my life. I give thanks to my ancestors for the paths they forged for me.

The Seer

By Katrina Elkins

In between the space of wakefulness and sleep, I was visited by the Divine Feminine with a vision of a female Pope. The Pope was in her vestment robe. Her long brown hair draped over the off-white fabric, and her eyes perfectly matched her hair. She seemed at peace but preoccupied with something not yet apparent.

"I see you," I said.

The Pope's eyes looked into mine. "Oh, you are one who can see," she said.

Her entire demeanor changed. She was no longer the embodiment of the masculine as we know it in the Pope. She was a woman, a young woman, who held a secret. She raised her left hand as her shoulders hunched forward and her gaze turned to the ground.

It was a vision for my eyes only. The robe slid down her arm and showed me her pale, fragile forearm and wrist bone. I could see that she carried within her the ache of the incarnation of the feminine. The life force of love was almost non-evident, and her bones and skin longed for the nourishment that had been blocked for eons. The deprivation had left her pale, papery skin scarred with deep shadows in the folds of her fragile form.

I was shocked that a woman of such privilege had revealed something so personal. She was the Pope and yet harbored unbearable pain – an ache that mirrored my own.

"We have much to do. I have seen such pervasive heartache. And now it is time to lend a hand to all of humanity," she stated.

In that vision, the Pope showed me my own sorrow. For most of my life, I had neglected the Divine Feminine within my own body. I became aware of the gift of receiving all that she is and the abundance of joy that grows from unconditional self-love. I became aware that the Divine Feminine is a powerful force within us all – a force that can change your life, as it did for me.

Listen When Angels Talk

By Trish Mckinnley

When I was asked to give a talk on angels at a local retirement community, I couldn't wait! I had so much juicy, inspiring information to share. I planned and prepared an impressive PowerPoint presentation, created handouts, and even put together swag bags. Upon hearing that the residents were grumbling over my topic, I became even more dead set that I would show them. I was in complete control, and this would be the best presentation ever. Everyone would love it!

The day before my talk, my computer file corrupted. A sign? Well, I wasn't going to let that stop me! I completely re-created the PowerPoint presentation from scratch. Then, my printer broke when attempting to print the handouts, the retirement community had a glitch with the Wi-Fi connection, and the cord to my computer was the wrong compatibility and their computer couldn't read my flash drive. Ultimately, my computer crashed at the site. I had no choice! I finally got the message.

As I vulnerably opened my talk with my story of thinking I was in control, everyone warmed. Still smiling, I apologized, saying I was going to trust and wing it. After sharing my own stories about angel encounters from my heart, I intuitively felt I should ask if anyone had their own angel story. The response was overwhelming! This was what was supposed to happen! By the end, each person (all 110 of them) had shared an angel encounter. The lines of communication in this world and the next had been opened up in profound, unimaginable ways. Thanks to releasing control and allowing the event to go the way it was supposed to, we all left that day blessed.

I still plan my workshops, but without the anxiety and stress. I remember the loving lesson from my angels and simply allow the material that's meant to be shared to flow, while consciously releasing the outcome. It is empowering to realize that by giving up control, I truly gain control.

Write My Story

By Janet G. Nestor

In May 2014, I received an unexpected gift. Just after my morning self-care routine, I heard a voice say, "Write my story." I was stunned into silence. My head went wild with thoughts too numerous to mention. Because of my delay in answering, the voice spoke a second time: "Write my story." His words sounded like a question, but I knew there was only one answer I could give.

I heard myself say, "Yes, I'll write your story." Then I panicked because the question was asked by Yeshua, the Christ.

I knew that there would be 100 stories to write. Every day, I wrestled with the task at hand, until I finally realized I'd have all the answers I needed if I asked Yeshua for his help. I did, and the instructions began to flow: I was told to make a computer file and wait at the computer. I waited for three days, but nothing happened. On the fourth day, I sat at the computer wondering what to do next, when suddenly Yeshua began to speak a message to me. His voice was slow, steady, and all business, yet I could literally feel his presence around me and hear his words in my mind as clearly as if he had spoken them out loud. I typed every word he said as he spoke it.

Each day I'd sit at my computer, prepared to write. Some days we'd write one or two stories, but after I became used to the process, we'd sometimes write as many as five. On August 8, 2014, message 100 was completed, and I knew it was time to prepare for publication.

If anyone asked me about the book or why I'd been asked to write it, I'd burst into tears. I'd lived within Yeshua's energy 24 hours a day for 45 days, and I was still vibrating with the essence of his determination and his love of humanity.

Tears seldom come now, but his passion about protecting our planet and our need to unify with love still burns inside me. My perspective is forever broadened, and believing in the love of creation is no longer just a philosophy but a reality. I am, as all living beings are, spirit first. And spirit is 100% pure love filled with the sparkles of life, wisdom, and light.

Shattered

By Jane Francis

I had developed the habit of locking my painful feelings in a sturdy chest in my mind. But in 1996, at 42 years old, I saw a psychologist who counseled me to "feel my feelings." I mentioned several times that if I actually felt them, I would shatter into a million pieces and die. Still, she kept urging me to "feel – deal – heal" them.

Spirit works in mysterious ways…I was asked to change my regular Tuesday appointment to the next day – the date my birth-son was born, a secret I never shared. That chest held 24 years of agony, shame, and recriminations about placing him for adoption…yet I decided to open it and *feel* while in the waiting room.

A bolt of intense pain shot through me; I gasped and frantically tried to slam the chest closed. No luck – like Pandora's box, once open, it was too late. I paced, focusing on breathing deeply until I went in for my session.

"What happened?" my therapist asked wide-eyed in alarm.

I choked out, "I placed my baby for adoption."

CRACK! Pieces of me flew everywhere.

Although not dead, I was out-of-body. From far above, as a spirit, I watched my psychologist murmuring gently as she led Jane's earthly body to the couch. All I heard was white noise and a gentle "Shhh."

The therapist was silently holding Jane like a mother comforts a child, while I was in soothing dimness. Serene, totally at peace, cocooned in Love, I was in Oneness. I had no pain, no breathing body, just "essential Me" unconditionally loved in the heart of God.

When the hour was up, I was back within Jane's body, yet NEW. I knew peace, I knew worthiness, and I knew I was loved without judgment. I knew that the power and intensity of pure Divine Love is beyond words.

Did I still have to "feel – deal – heal" my feelings?

YES! I did two more years of psychotherapy and energy work to heal my deeply stuffed feelings. But I have always remained grateful for the out-of-body experience that shattered me wide open and started my healing journey.

Listening to the Quiet Voice

By Lori Thiessen

Life had fallen apart. My marriage had ended, and my ex had moved out with his half of the belongings. I had kept the house, which was now a total mess. Physically, mentally, and emotionally, my life was in shambles.

In the midst of all this, I received an email from Jodi Chapman inviting me to her *Coming Back to Life* ecourse, a six-week interactive program to get my life back on track. *That's what I need*, I thought, but I did nothing.

The following week, I saw another email reminding me of the ecourse's start date. The sign-up button was right there. I thought again, *That's what I need*, but again, I did nothing.

A third time the email reminder came. The course was starting the next day, and there was still time to sign up. I didn't. Instead, I turned my computer off, turned the light out, and went to bed.

As I lay there in the dark, I heard that quiet Voice tell me, "Sign up now." I rolled over.

The Voice said, "Do it."

I thought, *Now? Really? My computer's turned off, and I'm in bed with the lights out.*

The Voice said, "Yes, now. Do it."

But the light's going to be bright and hurt my eyes, I inwardly grumbled. I lay there longer but couldn't shake the feeling.

The Voice said, "This is important."

I finally gave in and got up. Shielding my eyes, I turned on the light and turned on the computer. I clattered around, dug out my credit card, and signed up for the course. It took all of three minutes.

It was life changing. It's led to amazing growth, new friendships, and wonderful opportunities. Partway through the ecourse, Jodi asked us to tell why we signed up. I didn't have an answer because I didn't know why; I just knew I was supposed to do it. And I knew that my life had shifted in that moment when I listened to that quiet Voice and took a tiny step forward.

Forever Love

By Charlene Williams

My friend's aunt, Jean, was in town. They hadn't seen each other in many years, so we brought Jean back to the house for a visit. I left the two of them alone so they could talk privately. I tried to go about my business but was very aware that a male energy was speaking to me about the love he felt for Jean. I kept experiencing this sweet, gentle, all-encompassing, unconditional love that he felt for his wife! It felt like a warm blanket enveloping me. I realized that this was her late husband, whom she missed very much.

I shared my psychic experience with Jean, telling her how much her husband loves her and is always around her. This information was met with a raised eyebrow and a slightly suspicious look. I don't think she was quite ready to believe what I was sharing with her.

As we were driving back to the hotel where Jean was staying, I received a vision in the back seat of the car: I saw a darkened room with a tall dresser in the corner; on top of the dresser was a wooden tray with shiny brass trim around all four sides. The tray held a comb, hairbrush, shaving brush, and cuff links. I asked Jean if this had meaning for her. She let out a gasp, and tears came to her eyes. She said that she had bought the set for her husband on his birthday, and it still sat on his dresser at home!

This was such a wonderful confirmation for all of us that love doesn't end – it simply changes form.

Hallelujah! – How I Met the Angels

By Melody R. Green

I'd never really thought about having angels in my life until they arrived. I believed they existed but felt sure they weren't part of my daily life…until I first heard an angel's voice! It wasn't accompanied by lights, harps, and a feeling of well-being. Instead, my very first encounter was a loud, booming voice near my ear saying "Hello! I'm one of the angels, and we want to remind you, it's time!"

After that, I became aware of angels all around me for the next several days. At first I attempted to ignore them, but I eventually blurted out, "I have one question: Who are you, and why are you here?"

"We're glad we don't need your math skills, because technically that's two questions! We are the angels, and we're here to remind you that it's time for you to begin your work with us."

"Why can't I see you?"

"Well, you do wear glasses!" they said laughing at their own joke. "You can't see us because you don't believe you can, but you can feel our presence and hear us, and that's enough."

"How will I know you're here?"

"We're with you all the time, but over the next two days, we'll give you proof so you won't be in doubt."

The next day I was in my local mall when I heard Handel's *Hallelujah Chorus* blasting from the sound system…*and it wasn't even Christmastime!* As suddenly as the music started, it stopped. Later, at the dress shop, I couldn't decide between two blouses. As I lifted the turquoise blouse, suddenly the *Hallelujah Chorus* played loudly. When I lifted the green blouse, there was only silence.

Suddenly I heard, "Yes, we like that one. By the way, we quite like shopping. Can we come again?"

This was more than 20 years ago, and since then the angels have continued to be part of my daily life. They have been companions through all the ups and downs of life and are my go-to business partners in my work as an Angel Communicator. They are why I came here, and they help me complete my soul's mission for this lifetime.

Awakened by the Light

By Angie Carter

The day I lost my daughter, my entire universe came crashing down around me. Initially, I was numb – in shock and disbelief. Babies don't die! The thought of living without my child was utterly unbearable.

The following day, while surrounded by my family, I felt anxiety begin to surface. It was the first thing I had felt since leaving my daughter's side, and instead of trying to push it aside, I let it take me over. I began screaming at the top of my lungs and didn't think I would ever be able to stop. I screamed until I passed out and stopped breathing.

The bright white light I've read about appeared, and I instantly felt my daughter's presence. I wanted to stay with her; she told me it wasn't my time but that she would always be with me. When I woke up in the hospital, everything had changed. I knew that Bella was with me because I could physically feel her!

For the next two weeks, I felt Bella's arms around me, as though she were hugging me. Feeling her presence gave me the strength to get through the worst days of my life. She began sending me signs of her presence, which included rainbows, rocks (that I would find in strange places), and electronics and battery-operated toys that would work on their own (even when the batteries were dead).

I would feel her energy, which felt like tingles, and occasionally I would see her energy, which looked like static. I would also hear her; she would speak to me often in the months following her transition to the spirit world. The most beautiful messages from Bella were about the power of love. She said that "love heals all" and "love is all you need."

My near-death experience changed my perception of death and has opened me up to another dimension, the one where my daughter now resides. Death is an illusion, and although my daughter is not here in physical form, she will always remain very present in my life.

Embraced by the Angels

By Courtney Long

"Do you know Archangel Michael?" my naturopathic doctor asked, staring at me through her big brown eyes.

"No," I responded shyly.

For months, I had seen Dr. Kim for various health concerns. She had never mentioned angels before. All I knew of angels were statues and Christmas ornaments at my aunt's house.

"Archangel Michael can protect you and help you feel confident," she said. "Plus, Archangel Raphael helps with healing. Are you open to asking them for help during acupuncture today?"

Curious and intrigued, I nodded in agreement, hopped on the acupuncture table, and lay down. As usual, Dr. Kim inserted tiny needles into my body's acupuncture points. Despite the temporary discomfort, I always loved the warm, tingling sensations that flowed through my body once the needles were in place. Dr. Kim then placed her hand on my arm and started to sing, "Mi-cha-el. Mi-cha-el. Ra-pha-el. Ra-pha-el." She asked the angels to help with my healing.

I'll never forget what happened next: The table beneath me seemed to transform into a soft blanket that surrounded me like a cocoon of light. I could feel Archangel Michael and Archangel Raphael lifting me up and holding me in a loving embrace. My body relaxed and melted into the warmth and comfort. I had never felt such sensations of love, comfort, and peace. I thanked the angels for being with me. *Well*, I thought, smiling through my tears, *I guess angels are real!*

This sweet introduction was the start of a major life shift and meaningful relationship with the angels. Little did I know that my spiritual gifts include communicating with angels. I later traveled to Hawaii to become an Angel Therapy Practitioner®, certified by Doreen Virtue. My life purpose has involved sharing the angels' loving messages with others through intuitive readings, classes, retreats, books, and healing guided meditations. The angels have filled my life with love, abundance, magical blessings, and opportunities to help others. Apparently, they were patiently waiting for me to wake up to their presence. Thankfully, Dr. Kim heard and honored their call!

Chapter 2
Believing in Myself

S ometimes our true selves can get lost, buried underneath all the demands from life, our family and friends, our job, and our circumstances. At times like this, it can feel disheartening and overwhelming to realize that we had given away our power without even realizing it. Just trying to remember who we once were before our inner spark dimmed can be exhausting.

We've both definitely experienced this. Thankfully, we know with complete certainty that our spark never goes out – no matter how much gets piled on top of it. Each of us can always find a way to uncover the layers that are keeping us from shining bright; we can always find a way to soar, to believe in ourselves again, and to live a conscious and empowered life. We can always find a way to speak our truth and to shift toward living a life again that feels good to us. Always.

Throughout this chapter, you'll read empowering stories from authors who found themselves in these moments – feeling stuck or disempowered – and discovered an inner strength that they'd forgotten (or never even knew they had), a strength that helped them find their way toward loving and believing in themselves. While the external circumstances vary greatly, what each piece has in common is the author's shift toward remembering that they are powerful beyond measure and that they are here for a beautiful reason. After reading these inspiring stories, we hope you'll feel empowered and believe in yourself more than ever.

Never Too Old to Dance

By Candy Motzek

I'm sitting in my parked car. It's pouring rain, and the wipers are madly flapping back and forth. It's chilly, but my palms are sweating and my stomach is in knots. *Why am I doing this? People are going to think I'm crazy,* my inner voice chatters. Finally, I draw on my courage and walk into the class.

It's my first ballet class, something I've dreamed of for years. But I'm 42 and my dance mates are barely 13. They are beautiful, graceful young ladies; I am short, round, and "mature."

Class starts, and we each step forward, place our left hand on the barre and prepare. The first exercises in every class are always *pliés* – deep bending of the knees while moving in time to the music. I forget my embarrassment and concentrate. Everything in ballet is hard work with lots of sweat. My teacher says, "There is the *easy* way and the *right* way. If it's easy, it's not ballet."

I struggle to coordinate my posture and to get my hands, arms, legs, feet, and head to synchronize. But then the music speaks to me, dredges up emotions; and in that instant, I am spirit. This timeless, connected feeling is why I am here.

Weeks pass and somehow I commit to taking an exam. I practice relentlessly at home, in the office elevator, and with my ever-patient teacher. Finally, exam day arrives. As I walk in for my 30-minute solo, the examiner politely stifles a laugh. Surprisingly, I'm confident because I know I've earned this time. This is *my* performance, the only chance I will ever have for this unique expression. Later, I hear that she is motivated to begin dancing again with her friends.

It's many years later, and I still dance. I dance because I'm alive. This creative expression feeds my soul. Every class, every performance is different. I've danced to heal from grief, illness, and burnout. Most of all, I dance for creative joy. And somewhere along the way, I've transformed from a woman who takes dance classes into a *dancer.*

The Day I Chose to Live

By Martina E. Faulkner

I sat on the living-room floor with a 10-month-old puppy in my lap as I watched my husband and his mother passively discussing whether he could reasonably taper himself off the narcotics again.

As their words ran in circles, it suddenly occurred to me: *This is never going to change.*

In that moment, something rose up from deep within me, like a plea from beyond anything I knew, but somehow remembered; I heard a voice in my head: *I'm dying.*

I *was* dying. In fact, in many ways, I had *already* died and was lucky to be alive at all. Over the years, I had lost count of the number of times I had wished for death instead of the endless drain on everything in my life that went along with being married to an addict. The half-hearted attempts I made at making death a reality weren't lost on me.

The voice came louder now: *I'm dying!*

I listened. Shock, followed by acceptance, and then survival kicked in. I had been dying all along, and now, after supporting him through two rehabs and three relapses, my soul – my spirit – was on its last. I had lost myself. My core had methodically been buried six feet under without my realizing it. I had to choose myself or I'd be gone forever.

As they continued their empty words of accountability, I stood up, walked down to the basement, and dumped two weeks' worth of laundry into a suitcase. Climbing back up the stairs, I grabbed a leash and my handbag and headed out the door with the dog.

From behind me, as he peered into the refrigerator searching for anything to fill his internal void, I heard him: "Where are YOU going?"

"I love you, but I'm done." And I was.

He paused and then, with the most venomous sarcasm he could muster, replied, "Good luck."

I walked out of the house, got in my car, and drove a block away before breaking down sobbing. "Good luck" – the angry last words of a 13-year relationship. And yet, I *was* lucky. I survived. Somehow, I hadn't died. And now, in a single moment, I listened to myself and chose freedom. I chose to live again.

Losing to Win

By Nicole Black

225 pounds. This surely cannot be right. Perhaps the scale needs new batteries? Batteries replaced – sure enough, that was what I weighed. Self-reflection about how I let myself get to this weight revealed that years of sadness and depression and ice cream had all led me down a dangerous road. The problem was that I was too sad to even think about doing something about it.

Fast-forward to a family vacation: I went to a store where I sat in a hammock, and all of a sudden, I realized I was sitting on the floor. The hammock had collapsed under my weight. I laughed hysterically because it was funny – that is, until I looked up and saw people laughing and videotaping my mishap. I needed to make a drastic change. Immediately.

Having been the ultimate yo-yo dieter since I was 15, I knew that surgery was my only viable option. I opted for gastric sleeve surgery. In Mexico. So many people thought I was making a huge mistake. I knew in my heart that it was my only hope and that I would do everything in my power to lose the weight. The doctors told me that, at best, I could hope to reach 160 pounds. "It's been too many years with too much weight on your frame," they said.

One of the things that kept me going was thinking about how my daughter felt when she came home from school one day and told me that her friend had said I was fat. I told her that I was fat but that I was doing something about it. Determination is something I have never shied away from, and I was determined to get it off and keep it off.

Now, over three years later, I weigh 125 pounds and have managed to keep the weight off. Learning to love myself again was one of the hardest things I have ever had to conquer. I know how much I had to lose to win my own self-respect back. If I had to do it over again, I wouldn't change a thing.

Net-Worth Loss, Self-Worth Gain

By Nicole Levac

Looking around with my eyes full of tears, I made the decision. Joe wanted to keep trying, but I couldn't go on any longer. We'd spent years losing sleep, struggling to make ends meet, and worrying about our dire financial situation. Exhausted, I finally gave in to this dreaded outcome: foreclosure.

Even in my lowest moment, however, I knew that I was giving up on the house, not on myself. I knew that this was the beginning of a new life, a fresh start. And I knew that I was not going to let my self-worth be defined by my credit rating.

Taking in this lesson, I asked the Universe to guide us to our next step. We knew we had to leave our house, and we had nowhere to go. We set out in a new area, trusting that this was the right thing for us.

After seeing a few places in town, we decided to look at a rural area where we found a farmhouse for rent. While sitting in the driveway, calling the rental agent, Joe's cell went off. He was being offered a job that he had been wishing to get in the same area as this house. With this new beginning, we signed the lease.

Once we had everything lined up for our new beginning, we received the notice from the bank to evacuate in two months. Within one month, we were moved and had a fresh start. Everything was working out.

I knew that the Universe had given us the biggest lesson about self-worth and personal value. We could have chosen to walk with our heads bowed down in shame, yet we chose to look at it as a time to empower ourselves – *we* defined how we were dealing with this and how we would see ourselves.

No matter what, we had everything we needed, and it did not come from what we owned. We could get through this foreclosure with our heads held high because we owned something much more valuable than any THING would ever be worth.

Choosing to Follow My Heart

By Cynthia Starborn

The spring of my second year in a graduate program for French, I started to feel like I was living a double life. On the surface, everything looked *magnifique*: I had a full fellowship at my university, excelled in all my classes, and was on track to earn a Ph.D. in a couple more years. Everyone around me expected me to become a college professor. On the inside, though, I was feeling increasingly disenchanted. While I loved French, writing 15-page papers analyzing the existentialism of Jean-Paul Sartre's *No Exit* just wasn't satisfying my creative spirit anymore.

One night, I found myself unable to push through another page of left-brained literary criticism, and I burst into tears. "I don't want to keep living like this!" I exclaimed. Hearing this shocking statement out loud gave me the courage to finally get out of my head, out of a seeming prison of rational expectations, and into an emerging new space in my heart. Realizing that – unlike the characters in Sartre's famous play – I wasn't stuck in one place for eternity, I decided that night to exit the Ph.D. program and to graduate that spring with a master's degree instead.

Announcing this choice to my professors – particularly those who had recommended me for doctoral studies – was not easy. Yet I felt a huge sense of relief, and the universe quickly showered me with support for my new path. Before graduating, I easily landed a full-time job teaching foreign language to middle- and high-school students.

In retrospect, I am immensely grateful that I made the choice to switch tracks. I can't imagine suffering for a couple more years to get a Ph.D. and then teaching college-level literary analysis for the rest of my life. However, since graduating with my master's degree, I have experienced great joy teaching children and youth in a wide variety of creative roles.

Sometimes, the smartest choice we can make is the choice to exit the narrow confines of the rational mind…and to explore instead the happy, open playground of the heart.

The Big Chop

By Tanya Destang-Beaubrun

A few months ago, I did what's known as "The Big Chop" – I cut off my previously chemically straightened, shoulder-length hair.

For years I'd thought of doing it, but coming from a culture where long, straight hair is sought after, I just never followed through. A few months into what I call my "year of living deeply," however, I felt that it was time. I announced to my family and friends that I was tired of chemically treating my hair and that my life as a physician, coach, student, homemaker, and budding author/artist no longer suited the time and energy it took to manage my hair.

As I entered the salon, I showed the stylist a photo and excitedly stated that I was here for a similar cut. As several inches of hair fell to the ground, I felt something bubbling up, invading every cell of my body: pure, unadulterated JOY.

I gingerly touched my hair, reconnecting with its naturally soft, curly texture. It had been many years since we had last connected. Years since I had truly connected with myself – my dreams and desires, my purpose.

As the weeks passed, I realized how much of myself I had hidden behind my hair. Now there was no hair to hide a bad-skin day or when going makeup-free.

Along with my hair, it seemed that some layers of the old me had also been cut away, revealing my long-lost friend: the ME who used to be playful and vivacious, who had big dreams of changing the world. I was eager to play with her again, to find out what made her tick.

Together, we plunged into new experiences, feeling braver than we had in the past. Seeking new ways to find joy. Dreaming again. We smiled and laughed more, falling more and more in love with our *self*, falling in love with life.

I became infinitely more grateful – for my family, for my career, for life, and for the world in all its beauty. Grateful that I had finally found myself again – this time a more confident, carefree, purposeful, and powerful version.

From Fear to Courage Overnight

By Lupe Ramirez Peterkin

By the time most people are 18, they are off to college or the military. At that age, I was unhappily married and feeling trapped in a life of domestic violence.

One day, when my beautiful daughter, Veronica, was five months old, I decided to go to the gym despite my hesitancy toward leaving her with my then-husband. When I came back, I could tell that Veronica had been crying. My husband disregarded my questions.

Coincidentally, my baby already had a check-up appointment scheduled. When the doctor examined her, she found bruising on her torso. She immediately reported it to Child Protective Services, who came out to investigate. After a brief interview, Veronica and I were taken to a women's shelter. We slept in a closet on the floor that night.

After months of separation and counseling, my husband and I reconciled. Against the advice of my mentor, I moved back in. A brief honeymoon stage resulted in a second pregnancy with my son, Victor. But, shortly thereafter, the physical abuse resumed and actually worsened.

One day, I had bruising on my body, yet I was terrified to call the police because of what might happen if my husband found out. My nonexistent self-esteem kept me imprisoned in this relationship. The bruises faded along with my hopes for a happy life.

One night, months later, we argued violently and I got struck. The babies came out of their room terrified. The looks on their faces wiped the fear right out of my soul. In that moment, I told myself that no one would ever treat us like that again. I made a plan to escape. Resources fell into my lap very quickly, allowing me to leave that relationship.

There were several attempts made on my life after that, but my children had given me the courage to look past the terror and not give up on our happiness. I made it out alive! In October 2016, I celebrated my 50th birthday. My kids are now 31 and 30, living happy, healthy lives.

Accepting My Gift

By Trish Mckinnley

I know we all have intuition, that sixth sense; I just was born with an extra dose. My mom always said it was a gift, but it didn't always feel like one. Often, my intuitiveness felt like a curse, an embarrassment, or both. So I shut down. But after years of ignoring my intuitive gifts, connecting with angels, and anything remotely metaphysical, I had a wake-up call that forced me to never disregard it again.

I was a "normal" young mom with a three-year-old and a 19-month-old, and I was seven months pregnant. Like most young moms, I was exhausted. One crisp fall afternoon while the kids were napping with the windows open, it seemed like the perfect opportunity to sink into my waterbed cocoon and get a quick snooze. But I just could NOT get comfortable – not because of my pregnancy but because my intuition was blaring, telling me that something wasn't right.

A cute little child's voice drifted through the window, interrupting my thoughts. I assumed a toddler was playing outside. "SOMETHING IS OFF!" my intuition screamed. Then, I heard an invisible, powerful voice: "Get up! Get up, now!" Struggling to get out of the waterbed, I was suddenly hoisted as if a crew of people had lifted me and pushed me out of my room. "Go! Now!"

As I entered his room, I saw my three-year-old son teetering from his window. The screen was missing, and his diaper waistband seemed to be holding him from falling the two stories to the concrete below. I barely made it. He was slipping as I grabbed his ankles. Yanking him into my arms, I cried. I knew what my stubbornness and disregard of my intuitive gifts had almost cost.

"It's okay, Mommy," he soothed. "He told me you were coming."

"Who?"

"Michael."

"Who's Michael?"

"My angel. He was holding me while we waited for you."

I shifted to recognizing that my mom was right – my intuition IS a gift, and I haven't stopped listening since. I am forever grateful to Archangel Michael, my son, and my profound intuition.

Partnership with God

By Manpreet Komal

In December 2015, a person I trusted gave me a Sikh mantra to bring myself back to health. I recited this mantra morning and night. Along with this, I was reading a book that was guided by Jesus Christ.

On December 2, 2015, after an ISIS terrorist attack, a Sikh temple was vandalized. All of the pain from the 9/11 attacks began to resurface within me, including memories of how many Americans confused Sikhs for Muslims because they were brown and wore turbans. So many people were full of hatred and anger, wanting to beat someone up for their pain, and either didn't know or didn't care that the Sikh religion was formed to protect others and celebrate oneness with God.

I was afraid because my dad wears a turban, and I felt a burning desire to educate the world about who a Sikh truly is: a savior, not a murderer. I reached out to several friends who were popular and in the field of films to make a documentary or a video, but no one did anything.

Then one day I woke up and felt a strong urge to make and post this video before even getting out of bed. The video described how Guru Nanak, the founder of Sikhism, went into a lake for three days before being resurrected, the same as Jesus Christ. Both of these ascended masters were selflessly on a mission to help the world find oneness with God.

My video went viral, and Sikhs and many others around the world blessed me. I also received threats of hate crimes against me, but I stood my ground and found strength in God to protect me. A week later, the mayor of Fresno made a video opposing crimes against Sikhs and respecting the turban. The message was spreading, and I felt that God was behind it all!

I feel I was destined to get the mantra and pray for the world. As I look back now, I also see that God was clearly guiding me to not only believe in my message but also in the power of my own ability to make a difference.

The Healing Power of Love

By Isabella Rose

Right around Christmas 2014, I asked my late aunt and the Universe to give me the courage and strength I needed to learn to love myself and take my power back from those whom I had allowed to control or hurt me. A few weeks later, I set that as my full-moon intention, and so began my healing journey of body, mind, and spirit to break the cycle of trauma and abuse that ran throughout my ancestral lines for generations.

Over the next 22 months, I would change the way I viewed myself and the world around me and take the biggest risk I have ever made: to allow love into my heart.

I slowly learned to love, accept, and approve of ALL of me – both the light and dark aspects of myself and my past. As I did, I began shedding the layers of masks I wore, and the fortress of protection I had spent a lifetime building around my heart began to crumble away. I had worn these as shields to prevent myself from feeling the continual hurt, judgment, repeated abandonment, disappointment, and betrayal by loved ones from happening again and again.

With the love, support, encouragement, wisdom, and guidance of my sisterhoods and the man who would break open my heart to allow love in, I replaced the outdated, false belief systems – that I am not lovable, good enough, worthy, or deserving of good things – with the knowing that *I AM*.

I saw that I had the same beauty inside and outside of myself that I saw in others and nature. I was no longer afraid to share my rawness, vulnerabilities, and Truth (my divine and authentic Truth rather than the "truth" of the false belief systems I once perceived to be true). As I began trusting more in myself, intuition, and divine guidance, I gained confidence and began feeling more comfortable sharing my spiritual gifts and talents, which I had kept locked inside since early childhood. With the healing power of love, I began to make my childhood dreams a reality.

Prayer for Change

By Katie Kieffer

As if the conception itself woke me, I opened my eyes in the dark, knowing I was pregnant. At 22, in an abusive relationship and feeling stuck there, the idea of pregnancy terrified me. For me to remain was one thing, but to bring a child into such an environment? No. I absolutely couldn't do that, so I prayed for change. Little did I know that this spark of life was the catalyst for the change I prayed for.

At four months pregnant, I found myself against the wall by my throat. After months of him tearing up the house but not hitting me, the moment I knew would come did. Every feeling that had kept me in that relationship vanished, like a light switching off. No love, hatred, sympathy, or ill will. Just nothing. My only fear was of the unknown. Even though I had been the only income provider, I was afraid of not having transportation to work. I never was okay with relying on others, asking for help repeatedly due to my bad decisions.

As I look back over the last 16 years, my son has been my greatest hero. He helped me leave the abuse and exercise personal responsibility. He then helped call in my husband and soulmate, the only dad he knows. My quest to help this boy who tics and had meltdowns almost daily sent me down the rabbit hole of alternative health, wellness, and education information, and eventually onto my spiritual path. Intuitively, I have always known there is a way; I just had to find it.

As I continue to learn and grow, my family also shifts and changes. My son is nearly grown, doing very well, and continuing to amaze me. Our family certainly doesn't fit the norm, and I am perfectly happy with that. In many ways, my son helped us all come together. What I have learned most from him is to follow my intuition and know that it's okay to be unique. I am excited about the adventure ahead. Sometimes it's maddening, sometimes it's easy, but it's always interesting.

Will I Ever Be Good Enough?

By Lynn Paterson

For as long as I could remember, I'd always felt that I wasn't good enough, that somehow I was lacking in some important way. When I awakened to my spiritual path, this was the overriding theme that kept on returning time after time, despite my many years of inner work, therapy sessions, and holistic training. Somehow they were never enough either. Despite doing well in my field and having a great relationship, it was never enough to dispel the deep depression and suicidal thoughts that plagued me from time to time.

Then, one evening as I was lying in bed reading, I felt the energy of a presence that immediately made me pay attention. It was incredibly loving, so gentle that I could offer no resistance to it. I felt loved in totality by this presence, which I will call Source or God. In that moment, I knew that there was nothing I had done or could do that would ever change that Love for me. This Love undid me; it unravelled me.

In that single moment, I saw that everything I had ever done – including those things I had believed were done without thought of reward or compensation – was, in fact, done because I believed I wasn't good enough! Furthermore, I realised that I believed, on a previously unconscious level, that by doing all of these things, I could somehow make up for my unworthiness and could then be accepted by God! In my head, the accompanying words to this "seeing" were, *Surely I've done enough by now. Have I done enough to come back into the Garden now? Please?*

I found this revelation so hilarious that I burst into a fit of laughter! As that subsided, I was left with an enduring sense of utter delight, peace, and knowing that I was completely and eternally loved. Indeed, anything less was not even a possibility. It is this knowing that helps keep me sane when life brings up challenges, as it always will.

Living Outside the Comfort Zone

By Emma Porter

I logged in to social media, and there she was! A friend had allowed her body to become a canvas for a local artist of body paintings. She was stunning. The level of detail and creativity had me mesmerized. I admired my friend's vulnerability and the courage it took to present herself to the world through this medium.

Looking through the artist's website, I was blown away by his creations – so much so that I decided to get a body painting to celebrate turning 40 the following year, which would give me time to lose some weight.

I began to read the comments posted by strangers online who were interested in being painted yet, due to insecurities about their weight and other physical features, didn't feel ready. It saddened my heart and prompted me to reflect on how often people delay things or never say yes to experiences because of their insecurities and fears.

Physically at my heaviest, I had recently become my lightest and healthiest in terms of self-worth. Filled with a sense that society needs examples that *all* shapes and sizes can be celebrated, I questioned myself – *Why wait?!* – and enthusiastically booked my appointment!

At first, I felt self-conscious and timid about my body; however, I soon relaxed and enjoyed the experience – enough to want to return for another painting! It was a key shift for me to appreciate my body, which had survived a past of disordered eating, and to ultimately transcend society's judgments and my own fears.

When I looked in the mirror at my transformation, I remembered that I wanted to live life fully and joyfully – without conditions and not confined to a comfort zone. This painting was a turning point for me, something for me to embrace at this point and a reminder, moving forward, to do even more of what my heart desired.

Falling Down Is Getting Up

By Michele Silva-Neto

I had just finished stretching, and I felt so refreshed. As I walked to the kitchen to get some water, I congratulated myself on trying to be healthy.

The next thing I knew, I was on my butt at the bottom of a step. Alarm bells were ringing in my head, and the adrenaline was surging. Then the feeling came back into my body. I felt tremendous pain in my lower back. My husband carefully helped me up and into bed.

We were on vacation in Brazil.

Five months earlier, my husband had told me that while he loved me, he wasn't in love with me. I had no idea what that meant; I only knew that my life was ending. All my plans for the future were in question; everything I had planned for my life was in doubt.

We had been married 17 years. We had three children together. We even owned a business together. In consideration of these facts, we decided to work on the marriage. This trip was one of the things we tried. We spent time together as a family, we went riding every day, and things had been going well. And then I fell.

I was stuck in bed, no way I could leave the house.

Nonetheless, my husband woke up every morning at 5:00, made his plans for the day, and was gone by 6:00. I didn't see him again until his return in the evening. He made no effort to accommodate my changed needs.

By the end of the holiday, I decided to move out.

I was so upset. If only I hadn't fallen, it would have been a wonderful vacation and our marriage would have remained intact.

Then again, if I hadn't fallen, I would have stayed with a man who ignored my needs, was incapable of being loving and supportive, and who didn't encourage me to follow my dreams. If I hadn't fallen, I wouldn't be writing now. I wouldn't be living an authentic, creative life.

I'm so glad I fell!

Cruising Outside the Box

By Kristy Carr McAdams

"Fear is the cheapest room in the house.
I'd like to see you living in better conditions." - Hafiz

"This is a blessing," I kept repeating to myself as I packed my suitcase at the last minute for my first cruise. I was scared, which isn't the typical reaction to going on a cruise! For my 15th anniversary, we were hopping on a boat to Bermuda.

The only thing was, I had been living afraid for years and didn't know it until I booked the trip. Now I realized that I was afraid to be confined to a boat, away from my children and all the known elements of my everyday life. It dawned on me that I had built my life into a small, predictable zone: I only drove locally and shopped the same stores all the time. I had securely planted myself within the four walls of my house, living in a beautiful box.

I challenged myself to step outside the box by planning this trip, determined to find my inner "Indiana Jones" explorer. I decided to tap back into that part of me that saw new things not as sources of fear but as adventures, the way I did when I was a child. It was time to bring out my "Indiana Joanie"!

As I entered the cruise ship and saw the tiny room and the vast ocean beyond, I felt overwhelmed. Taking a deep breath, I sought out the schedule of events. I decided to book excursions based on this question: *What would I do if I weren't afraid?*

With this newfound perspective, we went cave exploring and walked undersea with "astronaut-suit helmets." I was scared at the beginning of each adventure (especially when I was alone in a dark cave with just my flashlight for 10 minutes, whispering "Indiana Joanie" over and over!), but I did it anyway! My true spirit of adventure had been tucked away for too long, and a whole new world opened up to me!

I had booked the cruise to celebrate love of marriage, and I ended up also finding an ocean of love and growth for myself when I lived outside my fears.

My Rolling Stones Epiphany

By Annalene Hart

In the summer of 1972, just days before my 18th birthday, I read an article in the *Toronto Star* about the upcoming Rolling Stones concert at Maple Leaf Gardens. I decided to go just to soak up the ambience but without any intention of purchasing a ticket.

Lingering with the crowds outside the Gardens, I was happy just to hang out there, feel the electricity in the air, and be part of this cosmic hub. When the doors flung open, a young man wearing a black motorcycle jacket approached me. "Would you like a ticket?" he asked in a thick French-Canadian accent. I told him no, thank you, but he persisted. "You could be my guest," he pleaded. By this point, a row of his friends had appeared, all wearing motorcycle jackets. Once I agreed to join them, he swung his arm victoriously over my shoulder, pronouncing, "You're my girlfriend for the evening!"

After we were inside the Gardens, he shared with me that he was married but that he and his wife had an open marriage. He also confessed that he and his buddies had done a "Brinks." I had no idea what that meant, so he explained how they had robbed a Brinks truck, and one of their buddies was the fall guy in jail.

Once the concert began, I got caught up in watching Mick strutting and singing on stage with the group. Miniature bottles of liquor were being passed around, along with joints. I graciously declined. Meanwhile, my companion's hand roamed up and down the side of my body. At one point, he decided to dangle me above the railing so I could get a better view of the crowd below. Someone a few rows away from us threw up.

As the concert was coming to a close, he invited me back to their hotel room. I started to get anxious about my plan of escape. How would I do this without inciting them? I figured my best window of opportunity would be to leave before the end of the show.

When the mini liquor bottle was passed to me yet again, I handed it back, got up, and started flying down the cement stairs. As I ran, I felt a sense of relief, liberation, and inner strength I'd never been aware of before. I suddenly knew I could take care of myself and hold my own in the world. It was a defining moment for me.

Breaking Through the Illusion

By Debbie Carcuffe

It became apparent to me that the role I had been playing in most of my intimate relationships was that of the inferior, insignificant, and unimportant person. In order for me to excel at this role, I had to downplay my own wants, needs, and desires. I was utilizing my strengths, talents, and abilities, but not to advance my own life. Instead, I used these attributes to enrich the lives of those I considered most dear to me.

I was completely unconscious of the fact that I allowed myself to be manipulated based on a self-created illusion. As a young child, I adopted the belief that to feel safe, worthy, loved, and approved of, I had to compromise my own desires. I agreed to the illusion that others' needs were more important than my own, and my responsibility was to devote myself to enriching their lives.

Each one of my relationships and the part it played for me became the perfect match to achieve this self-realization and turn my life around. These relationships magnified my smallness and the position I was playing as the "lesser" one by not allowing myself to shine. Each relationship dynamic magnified my unconscious illusion and became a stepping stone toward my evolution.

Like a script, the scenes played out so I could identify behaviors that were not in alignment with my soul's purpose. I saw all the times I was playing supporter, rescuer, and savior. I saw how I played the enabler so beautifully, feeding into the other's role of being "weak" or "the victim" so I could be "the strong one" who would "save the day." Until I could objectively see my shadow and my pattern as the weaker partner (disguised as the hero), I couldn't claim my true identity and take charge of my life.

My pivotal moment – identifying this pattern so that I could *change* it – set me free to give love and support to others without compromising my own goals and dreams. Once I abandoned my old role, I could embrace my authentic nature as a confident, independent leader with the self-love required to move forward, fulfilling my soul's true purpose in this lifetime.

Reawakening During a Life Shift

By Nancy Ferrari

As I celebrated my 60th birthday last year, I was reminded of Dr. Christiane Northrup's quote, "Getting old is inevitable; aging is optional." Despite the comments that it was time to retire, I logically knew that age is just a number. Nonetheless, I was feeling the vibe, especially as I was hearing and reading more about life shifts after 40 or 50 – and here I was at 60!

I decided I was not going to allow the start of a new decade to define me and affect my ability to stay the course with my career as a life coach, multimedia producer, and host of my radio show. Unfortunately, a persistent bout of back-to-back sinus infections during the summer months of 2016 sidelined me and led me to a difficult decision to take an indefinite break from my work so that I could practice self-care.

My decision brought forth a myriad of opinions, including my mother's comment, which paralyzed me: "It's no wonder you quit, because you didn't make much money from your radio show." I immediately felt like a child again as I heard all those negative words of not being smart enough, pretty enough, and all those other beliefs that kept me playing small and lacking in self-worth.

Seven years earlier, in 2008, I had experienced my awakening and proclaimed, "I AM ENOUGH!" This was my time of transformation, connecting with my soul truth, and living life as it was intended to be. Yet here I was, sliding quickly toward old mental habits after one negative comment.

I knew I had to snap out of this while allowing myself to feel the feelings and incorporate forgiveness so I could let go and be free once again. I reminded myself that if I allowed others to direct my life path, I would spiral back into the dysfunction that was once "normal" for me.

With the power of meditation, journaling, and prayer, I embraced myself and my accomplishments, and I decided that where I go from here would be on my terms. Trust and self-love came back to me, and I now know that wherever my life path leads me, I am living my soul's destiny. No one can take that away from me!

Trading In the Script for Authentic Living

By Teresa Velardi

"Who are you, and why are you here?"

That was the question I asked myself when I looked in the mirror on a morning when I wanted to be anywhere else but in my own life. I didn't know who I was. I had let go of all my friends, my talents, and most everything I had previously held dear, including my relationship with God.

Years before, I had married a man, knowing he was the wrong choice. I didn't have the courage to say "No" at the altar, even though I heard God say to me, "Teresa, don't do this; I have something so much better for you." When I said those two magic words, "I do," I felt like I had turned my back on God. My life was no longer my own from that day until the morning in the mirror when I came face to face with that big two-part question.

Although it has taken time for me to answer that question about who I am authentically, that moment in the mirror changed everything for me. I was taking 100% responsibility for my life, I was no longer going to enable, and I would most certainly no longer be living what I now call a "scripted life." That's a life you seem to watch from the outside in, kind of like watching yourself play a part in a movie.

Contrarily, we are meant to live life from the inside out, using the gifts and talents God gave us and enjoying every moment. I believe that each of us is here to make a difference in the world somehow. Only you know what that is for you, but you will never find it if you sacrifice yourself for a scripted life.

I vowed "till death do us part." On that morning, when I realized I was dead inside, I began the process of parting. I've never looked back. Now I write, make pottery, and help others unlock the story inside themselves.

Total Bankruptcy

By Donna Davis

As I stumbled through my doorway and fell to the floor, I realized that complete and utter exhaustion had taken over. The angels must have driven me home because I couldn't remember much of the hour-plus ride.

A series of events in my life had left me feeling empty, bankrupt. All the years of traumas, disappointments, and abuse had me wondering if I could possibly survive and get back on my feet again. I felt like I had nothing left to give – to myself or anyone else.

When you hit bottom you have two choices: *Give up or get up.*

There's nothing easy about getting up. The decision alone is weighty. Adding in the fact that you are emotionally, physically, and financially spent makes it feel almost impossible.

I was so used to being independent and self-sufficient. I was so strong for so long. I prided myself on sharing smiles and encouragement with others and didn't even notice the effects of all the challenges that had come my way. My body was shutting down, and I felt myself sinking into an abyss of sadness and apathy.

After surviving numerous painful obstacles, I was now faced with rebuilding my life, but I didn't even know where to start. *How do I do this? Which way is up?*

Thank God for answered prayers! I learned that friends, family, and professional guides can help you get back on your feet…if you allow them to. It needs to be a two-way street.

Letting people help me was not easy. I didn't know how to receive. The process of receiving was a journey that led me to know myself, get back on my feet (literally and figuratively), and thrive! Through patience and allowing, I learned how to reap all the love that I had sown.

Bankruptcy showed me just how empty I was. The process through it to the other side showed me just how full and free I could really be.

Shift Happens: The Power of Self-Love

By Jody Vehr

In 2006, I experienced devastation beyond anything I could have imagined. For the past six years, I had been studying Shamanism with a teacher who I trusted with my life. When we first met, I was coming off a seven-year run of hard partying in the rave scene and was very vulnerable. In this state, my teacher lured me into a romantic relationship, convincing me of how important it was to keep it a secret. With a foggy mind and no self-esteem or self-love, I agreed. I saw him as the saving grace from my dark life.

After his death, I discovered that I was one of at least 30 women he had secret relations with, including a secret wife of 20 years. This experience knocked me so far off my path that I didn't even recognize myself. My world was shattered.

The beauty is that I was unknowingly receiving an answer to my prayers, even though it looked quite different than I might have expected. At that time, I was praying to be shown the path of truth, to know God more deeply, and to know myself and love myself the way God loved me. I eventually came to see that this experience wasn't some grave misfortune that had happened to me; it was a tremendous blessing – a gift and a shift that was happening *for me*. All of it! Every moment of friction was shining the gem of my true self.

Through the crack of my broken heart, enough light shone so that the miracle of healing could transpire. With my willingness to forgive myself, I opened my heart to love. I learned the absolute truth in the saying, *If you do not love yourself, you cannot love another.* By learning to love myself, I created the space to share a profound love with my husband.

Even though the path was painful at times, in hindsight, I clearly see the miraculous gift of it all. Without those heartbroken, rock-bottom moments, I never would have been able to create the beautiful life I now live. I am eternally grateful for the lessons and wisdom I gained in those hard years that taught me the power of self-love.

Pushing Through Fear

By Sheila Callaham

Having recently relocated to San Antonio, Texas, I've been on the hunt for dancing venues. Sadly for me, ballroom isn't as popular here as it was in my former digs, but I've made inroads. Since my husband doesn't dance, I've been going solo to these new places, hoping to enjoy a few dances.

At one venue, I walked in to find most of the tables reserved, but I found an open table in the back. I saw a water bottle and hankie at one chair and assumed it was a lady who had stepped away. A few moments later a gentleman returned. I smiled and said hello, but his reaction was far from inviting. Concerned that this was another reserved table, I asked if I could stay. He told me he didn't know how many friends would be joining. I asked again if I needed to move, but he ignored me.

I scanned the room for free tables. Reserved. Reserved. Reserved. I looked back at Mr. Rude and was hit with the fight-or-flight dilemma. Should I fight the discomfort and see how it goes, or should I get the heck away? My inner wisdom said stay, so I practiced deep breathing, put a smile on my face, and watched the couples on the floor.

When Mr. Rude's friends arrived, the lady who sat next to him was quick to make introductions. Her name was Judy, and she was sitting with Alfred, who managed a stiff nod. I was introduced to the two other couples, and conversation ensued. When I mentioned to Judy that I was new in town, she took it upon herself to introduce me to everyone she knew.

Finally, I was asked to dance a rumba. With the first dance out of the way, it wasn't much longer before another invitation followed. Then another. I even danced with Alfred.

As I drove home, I considered how events unfolded. I thought about my initial trepidation and how I wanted to run away from Alfred. I was so glad I listened to the inner guidance that told me to stay. It was a reminder that the real reward lay on the other side of fear. All I had to do was move through the moment to reap the reward.

One Tall Latte, Hold the Tears

By Jacynthe (Jaz) Villemaire

"Have a great day," said the cheerful barista as she handed me my favourite flavoured coffee. Tears filled my eyes. I rushed to the bathroom and wept.

For 14 years, I lived under a constant cloud of darkness. I felt sad and disillusioned. I would cry myself to sleep wondering, *What is wrong with me? Why can't I enjoy what I have created?* I have everything I could ask for. Yet the dream I thought I should have for my life wasn't fulfilling at all.

For 14 years, I thought I should stay in my stable job with the pension and great salary. I was even gaining influence with the decision makers. I thought I should continue to do what was expected of me. I should be the good girl. I should quiet my heart's longings, which cried out for freedom, magic, and fresh air.

I felt stuck and miserable. My health was in decline. I couldn't even order a coffee without crying. It was time to do something about my depression.

Although I was taking Reiki training and reading many New Age books, I was ignoring my soul's whispers. I had chosen to shape my life around other people's expectations instead of shaping it with the love and guidance of my soul.

I took a long walk along the river. I opened my senses to Nature and her beauty. The dark cloud lifted. I found a new mantra for making my life decisions: "Because I love myself, I choose to…" And in that moment, I chose me. I chose life. I chose happiness. I chose to quit my job.

In my spiritual work, I've learned that depression often happens when the soul's calling is ignored. When I chose to ignore it no longer, my spiritual coaching business was born. That was three years ago, and I've not regretted that choice for a single day. Today, my life is magic.

Just Around the Corner

By Kathy Kane

For ages, the only person I told was my husband. I was that heartbroken to be suddenly tossed out of my writing group.

A writing group is a place where our vulnerability is a second skin. I had placed my trust in our group leader, let myself be emotionally naked; I had been all in. Then she made a ridiculous accusation that knocked the wind out of my sails. In spite of the untruths, I tried to satisfy her demands. When that didn't work, she threw me out of the group. She took me off her email list and disconnected from me in every way possible. I was bereft.

Why do I do this? The tape in my head was set on "repeat." *Why do I lay myself in the shadow of someone I trust and admire?* This was not the first time I had allowed myself to feel knocked down, but I'd always managed to pull myself up and keep going. Not this time, though. My Irish stoicism no longer worked.

It seemed that I needed to get ejected from the cocoon of a writing group to finally reach out for help, share myself with others, examine the narratives of my life more closely, discover and polish the parts of myself that were beautiful, and send loving kindness to those parts that hurt.

When we choose a life of personal growth, the path is labyrinthine. We are seeking the center in which we will find self-actualization. As we wend our way, we may pass familiar places, learning lessons over and over, but never on the exact same path and never as the same person.

And then there are the moments when we turn a corner, the view changes, and everything shifts.

Camino Frances: Journey to the Core

By Leslie Moe-Kaiser

What is the life I'm meant to live? The answer lay on the 500-mile Camino de Santiago in Spain, a pilgrimage I undertook in the spring of 2016. Some say if you return the same person, you need to walk again. In 2013, I walked 197 miles of the Camino, fulfilled, yet sensed there was more to discover. In 2016, I undertook the entire pilgrimage, all 500 miles. I came to know that the Camino unfolds on its own, and its message would be revealed as I opened to what it chose to show me.

After my 2013 Camino journey, living the rhythm and pace of a new retirement life, a pivotal moment emerged as a question that would not be stilled: *Is this all there is?* After months of training, a plane ride to Madrid, on to Pamploma, a shuttle ride over the Pyrenees to St. Jean Pied de Port, I began living the question until the answer found me.

I discovered: The Inner Camino is earned with every blister, pain, and day of utter exhaustion; finding an available bed without bed bugs, hot water, minimal snoring in mixed-gender dorm-like hostels, and toilet tissue in the middle of the night equals success; and boot-sucking mud, wind, rain, heat, rock trails, a 15-pound backpack (considered light), and occasional starvation can be overcome!

For 35 days, during 12- to 18-mile hikes up and down mountains, through villages and the flat desolate meseta, I came to accept my limitations while believing in my ability to just do it. Choosing to cross the Pyrenees, via the steeper Route Napoleon, taught me courage and perseverance despite injury. Leaving my burdens, represented by a small stone, to God at the foot of Cruz de Ferro brought lightness within and tears without. Lighting a candle in Iglesia de Santa Maria Real in O'Cebreiro brought peace and energy. These insights followed painful climbs. Coincidence?!

Ultimately, the Camino showed me that acceptance comes with surrender, and expectations are best when realistic. It fostered a deep appreciation of simple things – clean clothes and the goodness of strangers – inspiring a deep faith that the universe provides whatever you need.

We All Have an Aunt Della

By Kimberly A. Elliott

My Aunt Della is sassy. She's stern. She's been married for over 40 years...to the same man. And, without a doubt, she has my best interest at heart. "You have to work through challenges," she tells me. "Nothing is easy all the time. I just want to see you happy, Baby."

In retrospect, however, I see that focusing too much on what others determine as "my happy" has turned seemingly temporary detours into extended stays in disaster. Now, don't get me wrong, I'm not ascribing any of my previous bad choices to well-intentioned advice from my Aunt Della. Surely, I navigated those all on my own. For example, my first two marriages were to men Aunt Della never even knew. It was my recent decision *not* to continue an engagement with someone Aunt Della approved of that resulted in a life shift for me.

You see, Aunt Della is often that inner voice that chides me to seek approval and to shrink at the thought of disapproval – or the misguided thought process that overrides my sense of nurturing what makes me thrive, and instead continues to plant seedlings in already neglected space. Caring for others has never truly been the problem. The problem has often been *not* ascribing enough value to *myself*.

Breaking off my engagement was a sincere moment of truth. At that time in my life, marriage wasn't what I wanted; it was what I believed *others* wanted for me. I was actively wrestling with uncertainty, which would certainly jeopardize a sustainable relationship. Realizing that I was uncomfortable even acknowledging my reservations (especially about a decision that would so dramatically impact my own life) confirmed that I had not embraced the trust needed for a foundation of future growth.

I don't accept any pressure to label my current relationship. Yes, Aunt Della still offers her wonderful advice, and I love her! But I now collaborate with my own inner voice and determine what's valuable for me as I make plans to move forward. All advice is filtered by my unmistakable aim to recognize and possess "my own happy"!

Embracing Who I Am

By Ginger Gauldin

Several years ago, I had a friendship that meant the world to me. Then one day it completely blew up in my face, leaving me feeling bewildered, abandoned, and betrayed. I bumped into a mutual acquaintance I hadn't seen for quite a while, she gave me some startling news, and my reaction of surprise was totally twisted into a tall tale of drama and lies.

I'd never experienced anything like it before in my life and had no reference for how to manage all of the feelings that flooded my mind, body, and soul. I was so devastated I wanted to die, realizing my dear friend believed these lies rather than who she knew me to be.

I would have done anything to change the situation because I couldn't bear thinking that my friend would believe that I could be so unkind. At this point, I was willing to betray myself to save the relationship. I asked myself how it could have happened and wondered how I managed to attract this horrible situation.

After deep soul-searching in the days that followed, I found comfort when I realized that God knew my heart and I was in integrity with myself; I hadn't done or said what I was being accused of.

As I worked through my grief and practiced forgiveness, compassion, and honoring myself, I began to see that my inner design is a spirit of kindness and love. Even if others don't get me – if they misinterpret my intentions or I'm just too much for them – I have to stay true to who I am. The best thing I can do for myself and others is to not take things personally. Others' perceptions of me, no matter how awkward it makes either of us feel, have nothing to do with me. They are seeing life through their own filters.

Rather than choosing to dim my light in the world, I'm choosing to embrace who I am: a spark of the Divine, a sparkling light of love and grace.

Becoming Enough

By Mindi Burke

I was very young, perhaps five at the time, hiding behind the crib in the nursery of my aunt's house, crying. No one was calling my name. No one was looking for me. I was left alone with my thoughts telling me that no one loved me. No one cared about me. I was unimportant.

Recently, 35 years later, I sat amidst 250 seminar participants in a hotel conference room. Deep in guided meditation, we were encouraged to think of a current situation where we felt stuck in our results. That was easy – I'd started a new business and wasn't having as much success as I would have liked.

Next, we were to scan our bodies, searching for tension or discomfort. I found it in my neck at the base of my skull.

"Think back to the first time you ever remember feeling this way," came the next instruction. BANG – hiding behind the crib!

One seemingly had nothing to do with the other, but for some reason, my subconscious mind made the connection.

I'd been in and out of depression multiple times throughout my life – once even attempting to end it all. I'd carried this feeling that I wasn't enough – smart enough, pretty enough, lovable enough, important enough – and suddenly I understood how my lack of success and happiness was all interwoven!

The crazy part? I'd always projected this lack of confidence onto my relationship with my parents...and they weren't even aware of my childhood experience!

When I arrived home, I told them about my discovery and how I felt it had affected my feelings about myself and my relationship with them. I already knew the answer, but I asked them if they loved me unconditionally.

My father looked at me with tears in his eyes and responded with more love and appreciation than I ever thought possible, and in that moment I knew – that little girl who felt alone, afraid, and unimportant was gone. In her place sat a woman, full of confidence, full of love, full of appreciation and gratitude, for I know that I am enough.

Shifts Come from Within

By Mimi Quick

As lovely as life is, there are moments that can be a bit dark – like when you're in pain or when you're really struggling to achieve the success, relationship, or good health you once took for granted. All of these amazing experiences come up now and then to help us create the necessary skills to move into the next level of our lives. Many people don't see it that way, though.

For me, back in 1994, it was all of these: my marriage was over, my health was getting worse, and success had decided to slow down. So what changed? Nothing…

…until I stepped into my power.

…until I made a decision.

…until I very clearly and powerfully claimed my good health, a loving marriage, and a prosperous business.

…until I said "I love you" to myself – and truly felt and accepted it.

This was the shift that made all the difference. And you know what? It came from within. Nothing outside of me was needed for this new way of living and being. Yes, I had help from a caring, loving, and extremely wise mentor who reminded me of my power and guided me to use it; but, again, the magic all started happening not because someone told me about my power but when I started to *use* it in ways that would be of great service, joy, and love for all.

Through my shift, I learned that you can bring light to every dark situation and heal it. We all have the power, and I invite you to use your power today. It can be as simple as saying "I love you" to yourself. Feel it, accept it. This simple saying can shift your life quickly, as it did with mine. Good health, relationships, and success are there for you, and love is the power to fuel you to get there.

Wounds Liberated by Compassion

By Star Staubach

"No matter how nice you are, you'll never be enough."

I lived *decades* with this critic screaming at me, both from external sources and in my mind. This message was continually reinforced throughout my childhood. I could feel the toxicity of these words – the toxic feeling of black tar smeared on my insides consumed and overwhelmed me.

There were moments of clarity, though – a voice from within, calling me to my truth: "Your pain does not define who you are. You are an evolving, playful, multi-faceted, uncontainable free spirit, a human sparkler of love." But, time and again, this clarity would be followed by a breakdown, accompanied by an inner voice luring me to a false reality: "You are none of these; you are a phony."

Confused and unsure of who I was, I spent decades in counseling, dealing with this painful inner dialogue.

One time, while I was still in the grip of this inner tug-of-war, my mother visited me in Australia. One week into her eight-week scheduled visit, I knew that we wouldn't survive one another unless we saw a counselor together.

When asked what were we there for, Mom answered, "I grew up in a family of 12. I witnessed abuse..." She elaborated.

After several minutes, the counselor said, "Mary Jo, these are your own stories of childhood and pain. Why is Star here?"

It was in that moment that I felt the years of self-blame wash away. Another decade would pass before I could understand that Mom's pain was not her fault. A generation of wounds had been passed down unconsciously. In one raw moment, a breakthrough.

I asked my mother, "What messages did *you* grow up with that *your* mother never intended you to receive? What messages did your mother want you to hear?" Mom and I spoke of what we unconsciously received and what we missed hearing as children. We asked the same questions and discovered the same wounds, slightly altered. The healing through compassion was (and still is) profound: *You are enough. You are loved. The pain you experienced was never your fault.*

Thriving After 18 Years with a Narcissist

By Maryann Candito

The narcissist at first is disguised by his/her charm. Over time, however, you see the charm fade. You notice the manipulation, the lack of empathy, the control, the anger, the extreme self-centeredness, and the unrealistic demands they place upon you. Little by little, they chip away at your confidence, your self-esteem, and your authenticity, with the aim of molding you into the image that they hold for you. But you can never live up to a narcissist's vision of who they need you to become, because no one is as perfect as the image they hold of themselves.

After 18 years of mental and emotional abuse, I knew I was at the end of my rope and I'd had enough. It was time to end our marriage, move on, and heal from the devastating effects of years of abuse and crazy-making. I remember that day as clearly as if it were yesterday: the feelings of despair, self-loathing, unworthiness, fear, and intimidation. I didn't know how I was going to make it out of that situation. Lying alone on my bedroom floor on that rainy Saturday morning, thinking about how he had taken everything from me – my heart, my self-confidence, and my fun and lively spirit – I suddenly sat up and declared that he would not take my soul! It was at that moment that I decided that – regardless of how difficult he would make this divorce, no matter the threats, the scare tactics, the vicious and vindictive words he could spew at me – I would not cower any longer. I had to rise up to face the bully.

I'm not sure how, on that Saturday morning, I found the strength to stand up for myself, but I did. I knew that no one could save me except myself.

That was 10 years ago. I not only survived it, but I'm now thriving! I'm in a healthy and happy relationship, engaged to be married to the sweetest, kindest man. I'm living my dream. I'm empowered, and I speak my truth without fear! And most importantly, I will never again let anyone dim my light.

Have Confidence, Dear Friend

By Ellouise Heather

I sit at my desk preparing resources on how to improve self-confidence, and I am suddenly very aware of what I'm doing. If you had told me 15 years ago that I'd be helping women with their self-esteem, I probably would have just stood there waiting for the punchline. Yet here I am!

It was 15 years ago when, as a teenager still in school, all I wanted was to fit in with everyone else. It was apparent to me that I did anything but, and I was often reminded of this by some of the other kids. Looking back, I can see that what was said about me was completely untrue. But since I was often told that I was fat and ugly, I started to believe that this was really how the world saw me. While I wasn't overweight, the almost daily name-calling affirmed the belief that I was. On a subconscious level, I took this unofficial lesson with me after leaving school. In my early 20s, I did gain weight, as I'd developed an unhealthy relationship with food resulting from low self-esteem.

Through personal growth, my confidence gradually improved. Interestingly, the real transformation began in my late 20s when I realised this: I had so much love and compassion for other people, but when it came to myself, I could be quite unkind and critical. This is when I began to treat myself in the way that I would a dear friend. I discovered a sense of self-worth that I'd never known before by making this simple shift.

Since then, I've done my best to be mindful of my internal self-talk. I've also slipped up and forgotten to use this approach at times, but now when this happens, I remember to be kind rather than critical of myself. From learning to know my worth as a human being, my self-esteem has improved to the point where I've discovered that a deeper, more authentic confidence lies within.

Finding Freedom Just as I Am

By Cynthia L. Ryals

Years ago, I left a successful career in media and ministry to return to college. I loved the freedom of those days. After years of struggling with my sexual identity, I was finally able to explore without fear or judgment. I immersed myself in the LGBT (lesbian, gay, bisexual, and transgender) community. I was out, proud, and fully me.

After graduation, I settled into a new career and joined a local church that taught that being gay was condemned by God. In anguish, I begged God to change me, to no avail. So I found ways to twist myself into a mold that made other people comfortable and hoped that God would accept me.

Later, I moved to a large city and decided to avoid all things gay. Working in mental health, one of my first new clients was a suicidal gay teenager. As many more LGBT youth crossed my path seeking acceptance and support, the façade that I so carefully crafted began to crumble. I was no longer able to hide.

I fell into an emotional and spiritual tailspin. Looking for a place to belong, I became deeply enmeshed in a tight circle of friends who formed a small Bible study group. We began a liberating study series on homosexuality. Afterward, needing acceptance, I met a friend for dinner with the intent of coming out.

As we sat in the crowded restaurant, it seemed that we were encased in a bubble; all the sound disappeared, as though we were alone in the world. I nervously shared my history and came out to him as bisexual. There was silence, as if the universe were holding its breath. He exhaled, and spoke his truth: "Let me put your mind at ease; I'm gay."

Air and sound flooded the room again, and I felt immediate relief! A tremendous weight was lifted, and my entire life shifted. I learned the power of speaking our truth to not only set us free but to liberate those around us. Most importantly, I learned that I was loved and accepted by God, just as I am.

My Path to Self-Acceptance

By Linda Graziano

I live with bipolar disorder, and I've been through many deep depressive episodes in my life.

In 2010, I was in a job that was not suited for me. The environment was all wrong for me. It didn't support who I was as a person. But I didn't know that then, and it took a toll on me. Or I should say, I took a toll on myself *because* of it.

I was pressuring myself to stay at the job. I thought there was something wrong with me because I couldn't handle the job or the people I worked with. I was being so critical of myself, doubting myself, and feeling queasy in the stomach even at the *thought* of going to work.

I could feel that I was about to go into a spiral of depression. And this was scary because when I've been at the bottom of the pit in the past, there was just about no getting back out.

Then I began to search online for some help and came across a life coach who worked with people who were highly sensitive. As I read about this, I realized that I was a highly sensitive person. And it brought a sense of relief. I could now look at my qualities of being quiet, introverted, and sensitive to others' feelings and thoughts as a gift and not as if there were something wrong with me.

This started the beginning of my true self-acceptance.

I enrolled in a course that this life coach offered. This was the catalyst I so needed in my life. It allowed me to get to know who I was and to value exactly how I was as a person. It helped connect me to my soul.

As I began to embrace who I was on the inside, the bouts of depression disappeared! I found what worked, and I've been sustaining my wellness ever since.

This experience has guided me toward my passion to become a life coach. I'm now helping others with bipolar disorder or depression to embrace who *they* are!

From Fear to Flow

By Simone Wiedenhöft

For more than 30 years, I had been what I now call an active depressive. I seemed to function quite well in everyday life – I even finished university with best degrees – but at the same time, ugly monsters fought their brutal wars inside me, making me feel like a fraud, a loser, a *nothing* most of the time.

This changed on a day in March 2012 in the snowy woods of Switzerland. I was part of a coaching training, and for this day my personal task was to overcome a course made out of trees and bushes with my eyes blindfolded and no further guidance except one question I was allowed to ask: *Am I able to overcome this obstacle?*

At first I was full of fears and doubts, super self-conscious about what I was doing and asking tons of questions. Surprisingly, after a while, something changed. I stopped questioning, fearing, and doubting, and I just walked my path.

When my coaches told me to stop and take off my blindfold, they were laughing and nearly dancing. I felt calm and peaceful at this point. What were they so excited about? "See what you have done at the last obstacle," they said. "If you had asked whether you'd be able to overcome it, we would have said no, but you didn't even ask – you just made it, and you were incredibly fast!" When they showed me the place, I started crying.

It took me weeks to realize what this experience had taught me about myself. I, the fraud-loser-nothing depressive, was obviously able to make the biggest switch of all: from panic to performance, from fear to flow. I had never believed that I could live my life from full capacity – too many fears inside. Now I knew I could.

In that moment, I made the most important decision in my life: to bring this shift into my everyday life – to live a life of bliss, flow, and wonder. On a day in September 2015 when I discovered my intuitive energy work, I reached my goal.

Silenced No More

By Lynn Spiro

In 2015, I attended a spiritual business retreat in the peaceful Berkshire Mountains of Massachusetts. I had been waiting for this conference for over six months and was ripe with anticipation. However, I did not expect, nor was I prepared for, the profound change I would experience there.

On the first day, the leader broke the attendees into smaller groups. I chose a meditation workshop, as I had woken up that day feeling terribly under the weather. Although I was excited to be there, I was just too tired to be interested in a lot of activity.

My group was led into a small, quiet room and asked to settle onto the floor. The topic was Changing a Limiting Belief. I wiggled around, found a comfortable position, breathed in several times, and followed the directions of the meditation.

I found myself at a place in my very early childhood and heard the words, "Shhh…don't bring attention to yourself. He might hurt you." It was a reminder designed to protect me from the irrational behavior of my unstable father. I was 53 years old, and I never remembered it until that day. Afterwards, each of us spoke about what we experienced.

My discovery brought forth that my long struggle with public speaking stemmed from my early childhood experience of squashing my words for fear of being harmed or unloved. As an adult, that belief was no longer valid; it was now safe to speak out. Here I was thinking I'd experience a relaxing meditation, and instead I found an epiphany!

Ironically, shortly after the meditation, I became completely bedridden from a raging throat infection and couldn't attend the rest of the conference. But I had already experienced a huge shift.

My epiphany led to the decision to share my childhood struggles through writing and speaking so others would not feel alone. Whenever I lose sight of that purpose, all I have to do is say, "Shhh." That one word reminds me that I never have to be quiet again. Finally, I could be silenced no more.

A Gift of Freedom

By Viknesvari Piche Muthu

I love singing! This is the time when I'm fully connected to who I really am. It is my soulful expression to the world. When I'm singing, I know that I'm happy. I know that everything is alright. When I don't sing for months, I know that something is wrong and that I haven't been completely honest with myself.

As a child, my shelves carried notebooks with carefully written lyrics. The door to my room was always closed when I sang my heart out. The freedom of my voice rushed through my entire body. Though I felt extremely shy singing publicly, I found joy in singing the songs requested by my friends.

One day, I decided to step out of my bubble. Although I didn't have any experience or training, I decided to sign up for a singing competition. Standing in front of a panel of judges, I sang a song that I had been practicing for weeks.

Sadly, I didn't qualify.

My head hung low with failure, and I found myself standing at a crossroads: Do I give up singing because I didn't get through, because I'm not good enough? Or do I keep singing anyway?

I had a choice to make.

I've heard that the Universe conspires to bring to you that which you desire. All you've got to do is ask.

I signed up for vocal lessons, which began as a journey of self-improvement and evolved into an opportunity for me to become a vocal coach. My self-confidence and self-belief soared. I stepped out of my comfort zone, into what I like to call "the magic zone," and shared my gift of song.

For over four years now, I've watched my students transform by embracing their inner voices and expressing their whole hearts through song. Together, we embodied bigger, bolder, braver versions of ourselves.

I chose to keep singing because it makes me feel free! I chose what I love. I chose to make it work. And it is my hope that you will give this gift to yourself, too. What are you waiting for?

Choosing Me

By Pam McKinney

I was pacing the floor, talking on the phone to the man I believed I loved. He had once again done something heartbreaking, and I was in tears. This wasn't a *new* event, just a *different* event. I always rationalized much of my heartbreak away. I must be doing something wrong – if I could just be enough, give more, and love deeper, everything would work out and we'd have a wonderful life. I didn't feel the strength, courage, and self-love to step away – much less *run* away as fast as I could!

This wasn't the first relationship I'd been challenged with – most were similar stories. I would try to adapt myself to whatever my significant other wanted me to be. My boundaries were weak or non-existent in this area of my life. I had been taught to be compliant, quiet, a peacemaker, and to always think of others' needs before my own. But this simply wasn't working, and I knew I had to change my beliefs.

When I hung up the phone, I felt totally defeated. I had bent over backward to make this work, and it was still a mess. I broke down and cried my heart out.

Finally, I had enough of believing I wasn't enough! I vowed that I would no longer measure my worth using someone else's ruler. I was inherently worthy, and I needed to start recognizing and accepting this as my truth. I had the strength, courage, and grace to live my life a completely different way. I took responsibility for my life.

Each and every moment, I have the opportunity to choose what's in my highest good. And I've learned that taking care of myself, making *me* my priority, is an empowering way to live. I'm now better able to help others as I choose to take care of myself first.

I ended the relationship. While I won't say I've never been challenged again, I will say that I more easily come into alignment with the choice that's in my highest good. And when that happens, all are blessed.

Finding My Voice

By Carrie Kondor

I was elated about my pregnancy and the upcoming birth of my baby! I was working on my master's degree in Education and was learning so much about early learning and child development. When my baby boy, Dakota, was born, I held my bundle of joy and felt the Divine speaking into and though me.

One and a half years later, Dakota was not speaking in a way that others could understand. Other signs also pointed to a need for him to receive testing. We still did not yet understand the scope of what he was challenged with. The tests revealed high-functioning autism, Asperger's, ADHD, and sensory-integration issues.

Intuitively, I began taking him to various therapies and children's play groups. I also spoke to insurance companies and counselors to support Dakota's development. Some people, including his dad, strongly disagreed, yet I continued to speak what I knew in my heart. I had almost never spoken up for myself in the past, yet for the most precious gift I was given by the Divine, I found my voice. I climbed any mountain to ensure that my child would receive the love and the best support he could, so he could blossom into the best he could.

Since then, my life has shifted in such a miraculous way with my son. Dakota, now 17 years old, reads, writes his own comic books, draws, reads facial expressions, and continues to amaze me with his quick-witted humor – all the things he wasn't supposed to be capable of. And in successfully speaking up on his behalf, I found the bravery in my own voice, too. Ahh, the hidden gifts from the Divine.

Intuition, Sensitivity, and Being an Empath

By Sharon Hickinbotham

I've always been sensitive to energies, but not until recently, in my adult life – having gone through many of life's experiences, both good and bad – have I really understood what it is that I'm feeling or sensing around or within me.

Being very sensitive has taught me how to use the gifts of seeing, hearing, touching, tasting, and smelling in my everyday life. But my sensitivity goes beyond our five senses, as I realized when I discovered that I was an empath.

Being an empath means that you have the ability to pick up on people's emotions or to be aware of the mental state of others around you. Being an empath has helped me understand why so many times I've felt certain ways, never fully knowing why I felt this or that until now. But it also means that I've had to learn to find balance and grounding to protect my own health and well-being. I've learned to realize that not everything I feel is actually my own feelings. Sometimes, I'm picking up on someone else's emotions, which can drain my life force and leave me struggling for energy.

When I began awakening to my intuition, I had to learn to tell the difference between my own feelings and the energy of other people – or even places or objects – which could make me feel anxious, unbalanced, or uneasy. As I ventured into this unknown life, I decided to trust my heart, to have faith, and to let love lead the way.

As I've become more aligned and in tune with my higher self and the universe's love and guidance, my relationship with God, my spirit guides, and nature has become more intimate. I've found that with love, prayer, faith, an open heart, and raised vibrations, you can receive signs from your higher self (God, angels, or Mother Nature), and the answers you seek will flow through you endlessly.

Soaring in the Andes

By Lore Raymond

"Little by little, one walks far." - Peruvian proverb

If someone asked, "Do you know who you are?" what would you say? Would you list your driver's-license information, job title, graduation degree, or favorite hobbies? The answers are as unlimited as the blue skies over the Andes Mountains. As children of the *Pachamama* (Mother Earth), we are always changing, responding to the windswept questions and the circumstances around us.

It was freeing to give my ego a rest that crisp, sunlit morning many years ago. I shared a rock bench with Don Jorge Luis Delgado, a new shaman friend and my co-leader of our Peruvian church tour. He had just completed a cleansing ceremony. In his tradition, he burned Palo Santo wood and stoked it with his impressive feather fan with a silver and gemstone hilt.

We silently watched group members complete their releasing rituals at the sacred portal, the Doorway of Aramu Muru. Unexpectedly, he turned to me. Then, from his shamanic fan, he pulled out and handed me a shiny, black condor feather – the sacred bird of the Incas, the great messenger who holds the "big vision" for our world.

"Do you know who you are?" he softly asked.

I paused and whispered, "No."

Louder, he said, "You are a *chacaruna* – a bridgekeeper – and it's your job to connect people here on Earth to their Heaven."

Gratefully, I detached from any previous ideas about myself. I no longer carried the load of wondering about my true identity, which was now soaring on condor wings! I had walked many miles in my 55 years.

Now, every morning, standing at my Writers' & Angels' Altar, I see my condor feather wrapped in a brightly colored, handwoven Andean altar cloth. Don Jorge later told me that the feather was a gift from the Doorway.

His precious gift serves to inspire my dreams of soaring like a condor. I am taking more steps toward my big vision! Thanks to Don Jorge, I know who I am.

Trust Your Instincts

By Randi Goodman

My first son was born, forced out, six days late. He was quick to learn, quick to walk, and quick to talk. When my second son was born, it was a beautiful delivery and he came out perfectly, like a cherub. At a young age, however, he developed health problems. He would choke approximately 100 times per day and, therefore, could not be left alone. When we needed to get out of the house, we took him wherever we went – even to the movies.

At one year old, the choking subsided, but he still wasn't talking, walking, or crawling. I questioned this but wasn't horribly concerned yet. At 18 months, he was just starting to crawl, but we still had to carry him almost everywhere we went. At two years old, he still wasn't speaking, although he did make sounds.

At his two-year appointment, I asked the doctor what I should do to figure out what was happening with my son and how I could help him. The doctor said not to worry, he's fine. After some back and forth, I said, "We'll have to agree to disagree; just tell me where to begin."

He suggested a lovely speech therapist who immediately told me to get him into the nursery school I had planned on putting him in when he was two and a half. They were wonderful there and wanted to do their own assessment, which led to many helpful therapies outside of school. We were lucky enough to be able to afford private help each week and got him every type of assistance we could.

Today, he is flourishing. He has graduated high school, entered massage-therapy college, and earned certificates in the health sciences. I am so grateful that I've gotten to share his journey and see him thrive. I'm also glad I trusted my instincts that day at his two-year appointment, questioning the doctor's initial response and reaching out for further help. This decision created a major shift for me and my son, paving the way for a vibrant, healthy life. It also reinforced one of the best lessons I could ever learn or share: *Trust your instincts, as a parent and in other areas of your life. You will always know best.*

My Declaration of Independence

By Mallory Riley

I don't own many things. To be honest, I barely "own" anything. Sure, I have the basic necessities, as well as a few luxuries – Sperry boots; groovy thrift-store clothes that, when paired with accessories, look avant garde; department-store makeup that gives me that "glow" – but as for "grown-up" possessions…not much. At age 26, a newlywed still figuring out my life, I am not an Owner.

This realization may have knocked me right out of my boots if it weren't for also seeing this: I own ME. My medical messes, exhausting emotions, reckless radiance, awesome awkwardness, chatty mouth operated by a poorly patched heart…all mine. I can sing any child to sleep. I love till I'm exhausted. These intangible things, I own. I claim, flaunt, frolic, and rejoice in *me*.

But there was a time – 72 hours ago, actually – when I wanted nothing to do with owning something so flawed and messy. I had put my value in the hands of someone who once sang me Billy Joel lullabies, who wore Cosby sweaters, who made me feel like Princess Buttercup when I was in middle school and my braces were the wrong color. Someone who literally made half of my heart and then continued to thoughtlessly break it over and over again. Songs, smells, the lace gloves I wore as we walked down the aisle toward my future – all these very real memories seemed forever tainted.

And then that song, "You Don't Own Me," finding me everywhere, telling me I had permission to declare ownership of my Self. Of my new husband and our future family. To claim the beautiful truth of that little girl who loved the stars and chocolate kisses.

My own Declaration of Independence. I looked straight into our same-blue eyes and spoke my truth. Because if I didn't, I'd risk losing myself to those lullabies he stopped singing long ago. No, my childhood is not lost. And now, neither is my womanhood. For now, my DaddyMan, I let you go. You don't own me.

I Can Be Your Hero, Baby

By Manpreet Komal

I was at a stoplight, sitting in my car, when I saw a woman in a cute white dress walking alone on Highway 1 in Half Moon Bay. She approached me and said, in an accent, "We can't figure out why our rental car isn't moving."

I thought, *What the heck? I'm no mechanic, but you never know — maybe I'm supposed to help them. After all, random strangers have pulled my car uphill to a gas station.*

Cars were pulling up behind me, so I parked around the corner to avoid danger. I walked to their car to take a look, climbed into the passenger's seat, and sat next to a man who also had an accent and seemed very frustrated.

I love accents, so I had to ask where they were from. He said they were from Germany. "Oh cool," I replied. "I have never been there."

The car's gear was in drive, but it wasn't moving. I pulled up the handbrake and tried to shift the gear into park, but it didn't work. Then I pressed a small button labeled *Shift Lock Release* and once again tried to put the car into park. This time it worked! He turned on the engine switch successfully.

"How did you do that?" he asked. I pointed to the shift lock release button, feeling quite proud of myself and rather amazed by my own hidden talent. I had never used that button before. I felt like quite the hero!

The woman asked how I did it. I smiled and pointed to the button, happy to see them happy.

While I was walking back to my car, a man on the street who had been looking on in amazement asked me, "You fixed it?!"

"Yes," I said, laughing. "Who would have known that a woman could fix a car?"

If we allow ourselves to trust the difficult circumstances that are placed in front of us, even if we have no experience dealing with them, we can do almost anything!

Reconnecting to Oneness

By Isabella Rose

As a young child, I always knew I had a special connection to God and the Spiritual realm. I was raised in the Protestant faith, believing that God is loving. Whenever I felt scared or alone (which was quite frequently, growing up in a "perfect" dysfunctional, alcoholic family), I found solace and nurturing in my Grammie, nature, and the night sky (the feminine/motherly aspect of deity), as well as through visions and connection with the Divine. When I spoke of these experiences to my parents, however, I was repeatedly told, "You are just a child; no one will believe you." Slowly, I began to hide my gifts.

In seventh grade, I began to question if everything I had learned in Sunday school was true and started to shift my perspective to believe that God was judging. In youth group, we were asked to draw a picture of how we saw our family in the future. I drew three children, one of whom was handicapped. My teacher reacted with shock, questioning how I could possibly draw one of my children as handicapped. Her disapproval contradicted my firm belief that we are all perfect in the eyes of God. After that, I stopped spreading the word of Love.

A year later, at the age of 14, I was raped by an upperclassman. My father had me talk to his priest, who placed all fault and blame on me.

With each traumatic experience, I became closer to the feminine/motherly archetype of deity and more disconnected from the male archetype of deity. I could no longer relate to God as I had known him and began exploring my Pagan roots.

As an adult, I eventually hid those beliefs because I got tired of defending them after being ridiculed or called a Satan worshipper. In my 30s, I began reconnecting to my soul, the Angelic realm, and magick. After communication with my late aunt, four months after she was murdered in 2013, I committed to healing my body, mind, and spirit. In late 2015, I reconnected to the loving God and replanted my roots into Oneness.

Acknowledging How I Feel

By Janet Dhaenens

"Aza, I need some information from you." No response. He was busy at the computer.

"Aza, I need to get this paperwork for recertification of food stamps in the mail today. I need to know about your income in the last six months."

I had interrupted his focus, and he responded with frustration: "I don't care about your damn paperwork!"

I felt hurt. What I was doing was part of how I kept food on the table and took care of our needs. When Aza got to a stopping place in what he was doing, I told him I felt hurt by his response and suggested how he could have responded instead. He apologized; together, we finished the paperwork.

I realized that the most important part of what happened was that I told Aza how I really felt at the time I felt it. I spoke simply, without anger or criticism, just sharing my experience. I knew that my habitual way of responding, by keeping my pain inside and not sharing it, caused irritation and resentment. I wanted to make new choices and change my pattern!

I saw that it was not his apology that helped me feel better. Although that was nice to receive, it was my acknowledgement of how I felt that freed me to feel differently. Suddenly, I realized that it was my old choice to *not* acknowledge the truth of how I felt that had kept me feeling the same way for so long.

Although this interaction with my son occurred years ago, it stands out in my memory as a turning point in my understanding about emotions and how to work with them. It felt to me like I lived in a storm of emotions most of the time, and I really wanted to change that! This experience with Aza gave me a key piece of how to do so.

The simple act of acknowledging how I feel leaves me free to feel differently almost immediately. I use this awareness daily now, whether I am telling someone else how I feel or simply being honest and real with myself.

Loving the Skin We're In

By Elizabeth R. Kipp

Feeling comfortable in my own skin and understanding my true beauty has taken a good portion of my life, and it took a major shift for me to truly see it.

I was born into a family where beauty abounded. My grandmother, also named Elizabeth, was a fashion model. She died before I was born, but I saw stunning pictures of her as I grew up. She positively beamed when she looked into a camera lens. In some of her pictures, she has an expression like she is privy to some secret that the rest of us have yet to discover. No one in the family spoke much about her, so I was left to my imaginings.

I never imagined I could ever match Elizabeth's beauty – either inside or out – until I realized that I had some interior housekeeping to do. I had to shift my perspective. To achieve this, I had to find a way to stop the war going on inside me – the one between me and myself where I told myself that I didn't measure up to other people's expectations of me or to my own expectations for myself. I felt full of shame about how I looked.

The shift in my perspective on true beauty lay in me accepting my body as an expression of the Divine, with all my seeming imperfections: my nose is a funny shape, my legs are too short, my thighs are too fat, etc. I finally realized that these "imperfections" are part of who I am. I thought, *Who am I to question the Divine? The Divine made me just the way I am.* I found such peace and relief in deeply understanding that my external beauty truly is a reflection of my perception of myself on the inside.

Maybe I discovered Elizabeth's secret after all! I learned how to channel my own inner goddess and live in the true beauty that I am. And I learned the truth that we are *all* beautiful as creations of the Divine, whatever skin we are in.

The Moment I Realised That I Belong

By Lisa Hawkins

I've never quite fit in or belonged. Or, at least, I never *felt* like I did. I always thought I was a good person, but I never felt supported or understood, so I never built up any confidence. I just never seemed to connect with those around me. I always felt like an outsider.

So I started to tweak and edit myself to suit those around me. But no matter what I did, it just never seemed to be enough. Eventually, I felt completely lost and didn't even know who I was anymore.

When I started looking at myself, I actually liked the person I was on the inside and on the outside. I loved the fact that I was compassionate and helpful, caring and kind. Yes, that was still me, but I wasn't honouring myself the way I should have. I was depleted and exhausted from the years I'd spent trying to fit in – trying to be accepted on someone else's terms, more focused on what others thought than on what was right for me.

Then, while walking the dog on the beach one day, I had an a-ha moment: I realised that I didn't need to fit in to be accepted and to belong. I just needed to be *me* and live my life purpose. It's not about what I do, where I live, or whom I associate with that allows me to belong. No. I'm here to live my purpose. To be true to myself for the greater good. To remember and honour what I came here to be. I'm here in this city with these people doing what I'm doing because that's what I came here to do. It's about my connection with myself and being the best expression of that person that I can be. That's my purpose, and that's where I belong.

It was just a moment in time, but that moment changed my life.

Freedom to Become Me

By Elaine Lockard

You never know when a shift will happen – that a-ha moment or epiphany when you know that your life has changed forever. This happened to me on my wedding night, but not in a way you might expect.

You see, I had a very domineering and controlling father who kept me close to home and did not allow me to experience a lot of the activities that children normally participate in. I couldn't belong to clubs or stay after school for activities, and he never took the family a lot of places either. In addition, I had many responsibilities placed on me from an early age due to my mother being confined to a wheelchair.

So, day after day, my routine was to go to school and come home; always to go and do what had to be done and then come straight home.

When I started dating my future husband (and this was only because my mother allowed me to date while my dad worked second shift), I started to get a taste of freedom. There was so much to experience and learn about in the world around me!

Four years later, on our wedding night, my new husband and I were quietly watching the sunset from the balcony of our hotel room when, out of the blue, he said, "I don't have to take you home tonight."

That one statement turned my world on end. Everything became so surreal. He was right! I never had to go home again unless it was MY choice! I now got to choose what I did, where I did it, and when I did it. My dad had no say in the matter any longer.

An unfamiliar feeling of freedom rushed over me. Yes, I knew that things would change when I got married, but I did not fully comprehend what that could mean until that moment. I could experience and live the life I chose! It was my first chance to explore, find out who I was, and become ME!

Chapter 3
Shifts in Perception

Have you ever looked at a Magic Eye stereogram and gradually watched a 3-D picture emerge from what had initially looked like a random collection of dots? Or perhaps you've looked at some classic examples of Gestalt-shift images (such as the duck/rabbit or the old lady/young lady) and seen them shift appearance right before your eyes – not because the picture itself changed but because the way you looked at it changed. Your perception shifted.

This doesn't only happen with special pictures. When your perception changes, the way you see yourself, others, and the entire world changes. You can shift from pessimism to optimism, from guilt to gratitude, from fear to freedom.

In our own lives, we've often experienced shifts from spiritual tools and teachings, such as the Law of Attraction. Seeing the world through this new lens, our lives shifted into clearer focus. We were able to make connections between our thoughts, vibrations, and external realities. Like a Magic Eye picture, we saw clear patterns emerging out of a world that had previously looked like random chaos.

In this chapter, you'll read stories about life shifts caused by perceptual shifts. You'll find stories of shifts toward gratitude, forgiveness, and seeing goodness in others. You'll read about people shifting their perception about parenting. You'll read about how a short quote or even a single word helped people see the world differently. And you'll read stories about using vision boards and other tools to turn new ways of looking at the world into glorious new realities!

As you read these pieces, we hope you'll gain insight and inspiration from the authors' experiences...and possibly even experience a perceptual shift of your own!

A Picture Is Worth a Thousand Words

By Sylvie A. Savoie

Someone once told me that turning 29 is often a time of transitions. I was 27 when my seven-year relationship ended. I was devastated. I went from thinking I had it all to finding myself alone and living on less than minimum wage. Life…was…hard.

Then one night, in a moment of clarity, I became painfully aware of the role I had played in creating my reality. Thinking he was "The One," I had built my entire life around a man who did not feel the same about me. I had chosen poorly and lost myself in the process.

Now, as I suffered the consequences, I knew something had to change. It was time for me to decide I was worthy of more – time to get clear about what that meant. So I made a list of my dream life, dream job, and dream partner. After a while, I realized that words were not enough. That's when it came to me that if a picture is worth a thousand words, I would use images to complement my list.

For the first time in months, I began to feel optimistic about my future as I flipped through magazines, looking for pictures to reflect the essence of my list. I chose a couple smiling at each other while painting the walls of their home. Another, slow dancing in their living room, their reflection in a window overlooking water. I added an image of a lake house. I cut out phrases such as "business is booming" and "freedom 55."

With my list complete, I spent the next year focusing on getting on track. I followed any lead that seemed in line with my new goals and let go of anything that wasn't.

Slowly, like pieces of a puzzle, my life began to shift. I started putting more energy into my small business. I met and married the most amazing man. I retired at 42. Together, we built our dream home.

To this day, life continues to be amazing. Now and then we even slow dance in our living room, overlooking the lake.

Power of Words

By Trish Mckinnley

"Sticks and stones may break my bones, but words will never harm me" may have been a popular phrase, but one I had never found to be true. Words *had* hurt me. Every time someone had called me ugly or stupid, it had hurt. For the first four decades of my life, those nasty comments piled up. On the other hand, anytime some kind person tried complimenting me, I retorted with explanations of why I wasn't worthy of accepting their gracious offering, probably insulting them in the process. Not a way to live! Then a divine moment happened.

One of my kids had left the TV on. I could hear a man's voice preaching. He was saying how some people are mean, having a bad day, or just making an off comment. "Doesn't mean you deserve their nastiness. It's not about you. It's about them," I heard him say as I snuggled in the chair, all else forgotten. He shared why words have no hold, no connection, and no power until given power. I felt like he was speaking directly to me! "They're just words," he said, "You choose what you want to do with them."

What a message! Just because someone points out a flaw, which may even have strands of truth, doesn't mean I have to wear it on my heart as a negative label. They're just speaking words. Take it or leave it. From that moment on, I have chosen to leave it!

Sometimes if harsh words still linger, I ask myself why. *Is an old label or insecurity being tested? Why does my spirit feel aligned with this insult? What do I need to do to release that belief?* That open conversation with myself enables me to delete the harsh words and do my best to save the kind, loving ones.

I actively speak kindly to myself, consciously celebrating my flaws as well as my strengths. I fill my soul with love and self-respect. I finally feel and believe I am worth it. The declaration *is* true. Words will never harm me. That's the power of love.

A Different Perspective on "Up-Hill" Battles

By Connie M. Warden

I cannot believe I am now "one of them"! For 30 years, as I watched people jogging and biking up the big hill on the street where I live, I thought, *Don't they know that's hard and painful?* Now I've joined them, and I've learned many important lessons about training for "up-hill battles" with grace and resilience – on the hill and in life!

I practice mindfulness. As soon as I begin the ascent, I focus more on the sensations of my body. As my body becomes more stressed and I feel more pain, I become present to my breathing and my legs. I *have* to focus on the effort I am exerting on the climb. I've also found that when dealing with any uphill situation in life, bringing mindfulness allows me to be more grounded and present, to release the monkey-mind chatter about what-ifs, to connect to the things I *can* control, and to let go of those things that I can't.

I back off on the tension. While biking up a hill, I lower the tension of the chain and downshift. If I'm jogging, I have to back off on my stride and ease up on the amount of road I cover. I've also found this to be a great analogy to what happens when we're in an uphill life situation – and the importance of easing up on ourselves and the amount of productivity we feel may be necessary during these times.

I move slower. Because I'm easing off of tension, I *have* to move slower. I used to try to go faster so I could get done with the hill faster, but someone wiser than me suggested that it wasn't necessary to keep the same pace as when we're moving on level ground.

I smile more. This was a trick I learned from a young lady who was a competitive runner in college. She played with the idea of smiling when running, especially during sprints when it was the most painful for her body. It really helps the attitude!

I increase my capacities. Running and biking up hills increases my lung and muscle capacity, and I become physically stronger than if I only ran and biked on level ground. Just like in life, we expand our capacities by working through our challenges.

I hope life is smooth sailing for you right now; if not, maybe you could try one of these tips and see if it helps your own uphill climb!

Finding the Roses

By Jen Flick

"I can complain because rose bushes have thorns, or I can rejoice because thorn bushes have roses." - Junius (Edgar Allan Moss)

I was 14 years old when I first read this quote, and it was like experiencing an individualized Big Bang. The words exploded my consciousness and began to establish a whole new world within me. A life-shifting awareness came crashing through: I have the power to choose my viewpoint...about everything! A-HA!

Ten years prior to this, my mother's untimely death affirmed that life flirted dangerously with devastation, and sometimes the consequences were shattering. My belief system was that life couldn't be trusted, happiness would always be stolen away, and heartache was a constant companion. Simply put, life was one giant, prickly thorn bush.

But this quote blew open a brand-new door of perception and began to dramatically transform my mindset. Like a rush of refreshing wind, it cleared the sour air and clingy cobwebs that had oppressed my consciousness for too long. Yes, life has its thorns, but what if I tried focusing on the roses?

Miraculous shifts began to occur. Instead of being gridlocked in grief over losing my mother to cancer, I began to connect with her more deeply in prayer. Soon, my mind opened to a whole new appreciation for my father. I realized how strong he was, carrying our family through her illness and death, and I honored him for holding us together when we easily could have crumbled apart. In my prayers, I thanked my mother for choosing to marry *him*. Looking for the roses lightened my mourning and rerouted me to gratitude.

As my mindset shifted, I was able to recognize the silver lining in many of my challenges, which resulted in an appreciative perspective of every bumpy road. Although these roads aren't necessarily enjoyable while I'm *on* them, I have learned to see the gift inside the struggles. Life is quite remarkable when I'm able to find the glorious, triumphant rose among the thorns.

Choose Love

By Monica Laws

Many months ago, I happened upon a YouTube video of Jim Carrey giving an inspiring commencement speech. He talked about the fact that our decisions are based out of love or out of fear.

I listened to that speech many times, pondering the central idea: *We make decisions all day long; do they really come down to these two options?* It made sense. Becoming aware of this changed everything for me.

Before hearing this speech, I had been trying to understand why I would sometimes be in such a happy mood and then suddenly feel sad, even though my circumstances were the same. I was (and still am) on a journey where I am endeavoring to be more present. To live a conscious life of awareness. That speech helped me understand my moods and my life, and it led me to ask myself: *How I am choosing? Why I am choosing? What am I choosing?*

I decided to choose love. All day. Every day.

Now, when I am in the elevator, I say hello and smile to people. I choose love. Not fear (of rejection or anything else). Yes, it is practical to not speak, to not be vulnerable, to not open up. (And, as Jim Carrey mentions in his speech, choosing fear is often disguised as practicality.) But I do not grow or live by choosing fear.

I also encourage others to choose love. Support those at work. Stand up for others. Risk speaking up. Risk being heard. Risk making a joke without people laughing. Risk getting on that dance floor. Risk loving yourself. Risk loving others.

All day. Every day. Walk and say thank you to yourself with each step. Be conscious of every move you make. Let each action you take be out of choosing love. For yourself. For that stranger you open the door for, or smile at, or wish a good day.

Jim Carrey ends his speech by saying, "You will only ever have two choices: love or fear. Choose love. Don't ever let fear turn you against your playful heart."

Only those two choices! And yes, I have a playful heart. A loving heart. I am inspired. I am inspiring. I am caring. I am engaging. I choose love.

The World Was My Oyster

By Tara Leduc

I was at the top of my class, top of my school, top of my small world. So I tried what made sense in my young mind: go to a huge university, study, become a doctor, save lives, make a difference. As a big fish in a small town, I didn't realise that, in a large university, I'd be the tiniest of minnows.

Rather than flourishing in this unfamiliar environment, I failed. Just like that, I fell from the top of my class to the bottom of a pit of low self-esteem. What I didn't know at the time, however, was that failing out of university would lead to the greatest education possible. The world was my oyster, but even an oyster needs grit to create a pearl.

Ten months later, I left to travel across Asia, solo. As I landed in Hong Kong, I could smell adventure, newness, and difference, along with the scent of spice in the air. I experienced chaos and struggle on that trip. I witnessed the best and the worst of humanity's conditions, from the poorest begging for scraps, to the opulence of Raj palaces. I saw cruelty. I saw diversity. And I saw kindness.

When I found myself stranded in Burma – wallet lost, needing to ride a train to get to help and safety – I saw the best that humanity has to offer. I begged to ride that train. I'd sleep on the floor. I didn't need a seat. I just needed a break. Risking his livelihood, the conductor let me stay.

The sun rose the next morning to reveal the lessons. The train staff invited me to join them. They shared their meager breakfast with me. Then the passengers began to pass food along the aisle to me: tea, bread, jam, eggs. I never could have known that this chaos would show me the generosity in people. Most poignantly, an older gentleman approached me as he alighted. He looked in my eyes and pressed cash into my hand. "For tomorrow, Miss. Thank you for visiting our country."

As a girl of 19, I failed out of university but gained the best education possible. I learned that while you may "fail," you can never *Fail*. And, time and time again, I learned that while we are all different, we are also the same. People are kind. People are generous. People are good.

The Drive That Taught Me How to See

By Helen Ferrara

I'm driving early one cold winter morning, on my way to hold a dance workshop at a bookshop café. The memory of the warmth, light, and aroma that envelops me there is like a blanket around me, keeping out the chill.

It's still a little dark, and I come across banks of thick fog. Slowing down at these, I wonder at how solid they look, and how grey and dismal it feels to be inside them.

Then, just as my eyes begin to adapt to this darkness, the pre-dawn light starts to shine through the fog and amazingly reveal it to be just mist. As I drive on, it looks more and more wispy and insubstantial, scattered here and there. I watch it dissipate as the glorious pinks and gold of the dawn take over until I feel I'm part of this, and I imagine blowing it away myself or, better still, *thinking* it away.

At that moment, the remnants of the fog transform before me, and in my mind's eye they become the things that I've felt as being solidly oppressive in my life. I can see scenes of conflicts that have seemed irreconcilable, from those among my friends and family to those that are still causing wars. All manner of other things present themselves before me – things that I've feared in the past and others that I'd still rather not look at, as I feel unable to face them.

When seen in this magnificent dawn light, they look so flimsy, as though there's nothing to them – shadowy tatters of thoughts. The light shining through them is much more real and strong!

I realise then what a gift I'm being given through this remarkable spectacle. There before me, all that causes me any kind of pain – and stops me from being fully myself – is being shown for what it is: dark thoughts and feelings that can only maintain their solidity in the absence of light. As I drive on, I whisper my gratefulness, knowing I'm being shown the way forward.

Feeling and the Shift from "Or" to "And"

By Elizabeth R. Kipp

For a long time, I believed that I could only hold one feeling state at a time. I felt grief in one moment. I felt longing in another moment. I felt love in yet another moment. I felt one way or the other. I believed that I *had* to be one way or another. It was a choice, really, because of the belief that I held about how feelings worked.

I lived in the "or."

Then one day, I noticed how much tension I had around my feeling state in general. I felt fragmented, as if I had lost touch with pieces of myself. I became curious and asked, *Is my belief true, or is something else possible? Why am I feeling so much tension? Could it be that being human can be different from the way I think it should be?* My curiosity opened me to the potential for new experiences.

I awoke one morning and was graced with such an experience. I suddenly felt three things at once: I found myself able to hold the deep grief of loss of my parents; the intense longing to embrace my son, who was half a world away from me; and the great joy of being part of a community of people who truly love me. I held these all together at the same time.

I learned to embrace the "and."

Yes, I felt filled to the brim, but the tension I had been experiencing utterly dissolved. I felt such a sweet expansion within myself. I thanked the Divine for showing me a way to shift from living splintered in the "or" to embracing the expansive "and" of the human experience.

What a gift!

Replacing Anxiety with a "Loveburst"

By Elyse Jarard

Everyone said that raising teenage girls was hard, but I wasn't prepared for the lack of sleep. I found myself waking up with a jolt in the middle of the night in a full-blown anxiety attack, worrying about my daughter. Usually, it came to me in some form of a dream where something horrible had happened to her.

These episodes caused me to worry about her all the time. *Is she going to be okay? Will she get into college? If not, is she going to get a job, or will she live with us forever?* My mind buzzed out of control with fear for her safety, her future, and our financial security. I was letting the fear consume me.

My attacks revealed my weaknesses. By giving in to these fears, I was forgetting that God had a plan for her – I had a hole in my faith. I knew that my negative energy was transmitting to her, invisibly. I knew she felt my lack of faith in her. Most of all, my fears and insecurities reflected my lack of faith in myself and in the greatness that God has planned for both of us.

I could feel how this was compounding the conflict already in our relationship. I don't know what did it, but I finally realized that I had the power to change this. Whenever I started to feel anxious, I transformed that energy and imagined giving her a big hug, feeling the love for her that was deep in my heart. I acknowledged that God's plan for her was different from mine, and that it was glorious. Even though it was all in my head, I knew that my "loveburst" was penetrating the walls of our house, just as my fear and anxiety once had.

After that, our relationship changed. I knew that she would be okay, and I could tell that she sensed a change in me. Her own natural fears about her future lessened, and things were different for both of us after that.

Am I Creative?

By Michele Silva-Neto

I am not creative.

I am very left-brained. I love numbers. I love accounting. I hated English class – all that symbolism. Why not just say exactly what you are thinking? I don't have time to figure out what you're saying. Get to the point!

I think logically, therefore I can't be creative. How do artists create? I have no clue. I can't begin to imagine how that process works. It is utterly foreign to me.

I couldn't be creative if my life depended on it.

It was so difficult to do creative writing in school. It was painful. I had nothing to say. My mind was blank. I felt that I had nothing in common with others who were creative.

But…

When I do share my creative writing, I am praised for the work. Looking at home-design books gives me such peace. I love looking at fashion magazines. Taking a design from a magazine and interpreting it into my style is so enjoyable. Expressing my heart through the fashion I choose gives me such freedom. Whatever mood I'm in today is reflected in the clothes I wear.

Wait…

Doesn't that mean I'm creative? Can I be creative *and* logical?

I am creative.

That feels weird, yet…I feel something shaking loose, a piece falling away.

I am creative.

Something is happening in my chest. Something is becoming unclenched. Oh, that's scary. I need a pen and paper. The ink is flowing, my heart is exploding, and I can breathe. It feels like I've never truly taken a breath before.

I am creative.

I can breathe, I can love, and life flows easily.

Because I am creative.

Shifting Consciousness

By Lindsay S. Godfree

Looking back, the depression that felt like it would swallow me whole turned out to be a blessing, motivating me to do everything I could to feel better. First, I followed the steps in *Infinite Possibilities: The Art of Living Your Dreams* by Mike Dooley. I decided that the only thing that mattered to me was my connection to Source and believed that I would find the peace – and even the *happiness* – I sought.

What happened within a few months' time was totally unexpected. I was just walking down my lane, turning the corner by my house, when everything shifted. I suddenly saw life from a completely different dimension. I had no idea what was happening to me or why, but I could see/sense Divinity everywhere. I felt connected to the trees and all of nature, alive with consciousness. I saw everyone as part of the Divine.

I was wandering around in awe of life, laughing and crying for a week or two. I would shake people's hands, pass out money to the poor, and send love and blessings to everyone. I was so overflowing with love and had absolutely no fear. I knew that my life had been perfect and that no matter what happened next, including death, it would also be perfect.

That experience faded, however, and so I continued my journey integrating the presence of the Divine into daily life. I can testify that we are bathed in continual light and love – that we are forever a part of Divine Oneness. I have experienced it in a way that shifted my very being in a sensual, experiential way that can never be denied.

I believe that we are living in a time of the evolution of humanity, a time of major shifts in life as we know it. I think that everyone will shift to greater consciousness as the vibrational frequency of the planet is raised. I am speaking out so that as each of us is touched by Spirit, we will share our experiences and rise together. As Ram Dass said, "We are all just walking each other home."

The Missing Piece of the Puzzle

By B. J. Garcia

It didn't matter how far I had come or how deep I had grown through my years of striving to attain higher levels of integration in my spiritual/psychological journey, there was still this pressing question: *Why do I keep falling back into my patterns of suffering?* A friend suggested I might want to explore shame. Shame? Shame was not anything I had examined before, but if it meant getting to the bottom of my suffering, I was game!

In my willingness to invite shame in, I described it as dark, hidden, and painful. Picking up a black, blue, and purple pencil, I began to draw shame. Opening up more to experiencing shame, an intensity and vulnerability was growing within me. My drawing began to take form. I added red, representing the anger I was feeling as I examined shame. The finished drawing took the shape of a bruise.

As I gave voice to my drawing, it began to shapeshift, growing bigger and bigger. I experienced shame as consuming my whole being. It had me completely!

I *was* this bruise!

Shame was crying out to be found deep within every crevice of my being. My heart broke open and tears rolled down my face. With intensely painful feelings of devastation, I was brought to the core of my suffering.

The process continued into the night. I dreamed of a soccer ball being kicked around by a girl. When I awoke, I asked myself, *When have I felt kicked around?* The answer was, *My whole life!*

I realized that the shame went even beyond the scope of my own lifetime. It had been passed down through generations, and it veiled the tender innocence within.

Closing my eyes and holding myself in love, I breathed into this painful truth. As I relaxed deeper into gratitude and forgiveness, a puzzle appeared in my mind's eye. It was a puzzle of my journey through life. All the pieces were put together except for one missing piece. I placed the piece of shame into the puzzle, and it began to melt and dissolve. What remains is Light and Love.

The Gift of Free Will

By Lori Evans

Sometimes I feel like an alien on Earth, observing humans' choices as they balance the good with the bad, the joy with the sadness, the peace with the pain – it's the ultimate teeter-totter act! In amazement, I see the resilience that humans have, not just to survive but to thrive.

Like many others, I am called "Survivor" – survivor of child and adult abuse, of emotional neglect, of numerous hardships. Surviving, though, feels heavy, complicated, dark, and depressing. I've lived my life in survival mode, and it's led me to choices based on flight, fight, or freeze. The choices weren't thought out, researched, or even intuitively guided. They were strictly ways to feel safe and get my needs met.

During a recent move, I found myself in flight mode. I hadn't asked others for help, nor did I have a well-thought-out plan; I just fled. Moving in this state of emergency created three months of self-inflicted hell.

I was grieving my father's death while dealing with the abuse and betrayal of family members; letting go of past choices that were bringing up resentment and regret; and, for the first time in my life, experiencing daily depression.

This move was supposed to liberate me! Yet, thousands of miles away from the threats, I felt hopeless. I was so scared that I'd never be happy again. The deeper I dug into the darkness, the more trauma bubbled to the surface. I was suffering like I'd never suffered before, and it *hurt*!

Then one day, I made the decision: *I've done enough suffering in this lifetime; I want to spend more of my human time in peacefulness.*

I asked my angels to assist me, and they showed me how to release and clear my negative emotions – keys to abolishing the suffering that blocks healing.

Through my decision, I found that we have the power to change anything in our lives, in an instant.

Free will is our gift. What are you choosing today? I choose peace.

Not Your Hollywood Psychic

By Jacynthe (Jaz) Villemaire

If you would have asked me years ago whether I was a psychic clairvoyant, I would have answered, "No! Of course not!" And yet…

I was a strong healer. I was able to guide clients through past-life issues that I would see unfolding in my imagination during Reiki sessions. I had vivid dreams, many of which were visitations and premonitions. But I would still stubbornly declare that I was not a psychic.

My inner whisperings were becoming louder, demanding that I start teaching psychic development. I felt really stumped because of my beliefs about psychic powers – and my beliefs that I didn't have them. My beliefs were based on Hollywood versions of witches, gypsies, and charlatans. I was expecting clouds to part and to hear a thundering voice. I was expecting to see misty figures as clear as day with my naked eyes. I was expecting to see auras in Technicolour around everyone. None of that was happening, therefore surely I wasn't psychic; yet my inner whisperings were relentless!

Then one day, I started to research the psychic senses. One concept gave me a shock of awakening, as if I had been hit on the side of the head by Spirit, saying, "I told you so!"

I read in a medical article that not everyone can see images in their mind's eye. Not everyone can see like a movie unfolding when they read a book nor decipher images and get visual impressions when talking to others. I was floored! I thought everyone could see in their imagination, and that surely the visions I had were not a special gift.

Once I shifted this belief, I became more confident in affirming that I do have psychic abilities. My mind opened up to new possibilities. My heart opened up to more magic. My fear of psychic powers in the likes of dark Hollywood witches vanished, and I was able to embrace my own gentle powers.

My inner whisperings are now happy that I have stepped up to the task, teaching others how to develop their own psychic senses!

Ripples Through Time

By Karen Hicks

A gratitude practice isn't something I automatically do each day. This doesn't mean that I am not thankful; I often say thank you to the Universe throughout the day. As a dedicated practice, though, apparently I need more discipline. From time to time, however, I reserve space in my day to express gratitude in a conscious way. This is the story of one of those times.

Not so long ago, as I lay in bed, giving thanks for the blessings in my life – my capable body, my amazing partner, my kids, my work – I had an epiphany. As I was expressing thanks to all the generations of women who came before me, whose decisions and beliefs helped to shape my life, my thoughts began to wander, and wonder, about the impact of my decisions and beliefs on my children. This wasn't a new thought; from time to time, through my children's actions, I can see my influence.

On this night, though, a new thought surfaced: The impact of my decisions and beliefs do not stop with my children. The impact will be felt by *their* children, grandchildren, great-grandchildren, and so on. In essence, the impact has no ending...wow! This realization took my breath away.

With this new awareness, I began to think about how I spend my time and invest my energy. Were the things I focused on worthy of my investment? Were they worthy of future generations? I considered the legacy of my fears and insecurities. Interestingly, this new awareness caused me to feel excitement.

Like many others, when I am standing on the threshold of a big decision, I can allow limiting beliefs to overwhelm and distract me from taking action. In this case, though, understanding the responsibility I have for those yet to come caused my limiting beliefs to lose some of their hold, and I felt myself becoming braver, knowing that this understanding and bravery would produce positive ripples through time for generations to come.

Sure! Why Not?

By Anne Bradley

I've always been positive and enthusiastic, seeing the good in everyone. So for a long time it didn't make sense to me how I could have been divorced six times.

Looking back, I could see varying reasons why those marriages ended disastrously. Yet somehow, in spite of my good intentions, I was always surprised and stunned as each marriage crashed spectacularly.

My sixth marriage could actually have ruined the rest of my life. Luckily, I came to my senses and was able to get out in time. After that close call, I slammed on the relationship brakes and took a serious look at my life.

As I reflected on my marriages, I had a moment of clarity when I spotted one common thread. No matter how different each husband was, no matter how differently each marriage ended, they all began in exactly the same way. Whatever the situation, no matter who the prospective husband was, when someone proposed, my answer was always, "Sure! Why not?" That realization was my "a-ha moment" – things suddenly made sense.

Who would have guessed that one simple phrase could have caused one disaster after another through 50 years of my life? It was more than three simple words. It represented my happy-go-lucky approach to everything, actually, including marriage. Right then and there, I vowed to never, ever say "Sure! Why not?" again. After that one simple decision, things completely turned around for me.

Just like that, the "curse" was lifted. I finally spent some time alone, focused on my personal growth, and really got to know myself and who I wanted to be. And, in an amazing twist brought about by one of my divorces, I met my soulmate and am living the life I always dreamed of.

Now, at the urging of my amazing husband and family, I am writing my memoirs, sharing the most ridiculously funny and embarrassing episodes of marital disaster that all began with me saying "Sure! Why not?" I never dreamed that this wonderful marriage, happy life, and becoming an author could have come about after so many wrong turns.

Awakening to Peace

By Regina J. Dekker

While I have taken many leaps of faith throughout my life, this time around I realized that what I really did was jump right into my Soul Purpose. It began at a point when I reached a level of burnout that brought me virtually to my knees. I can still hear myself pleading out loud, "God, please help me; all I want is some peace in my life!"

So, what was going on in my life that was causing me so much stress, anxiety, and emotional and physical pain? I was living in a chaotic bubble filled with the stress of being a single mother dealing with the ups and downs of raising my then-teenage son, a career in the corporate world that no longer made sense to me, and an unfulfilling 16-year relationship. I was living in a state of absolute overwhelm and was physically ill much of the time.

During this time, a dear friend invited me to attend self-help classes at a local church. I believed they were the answer to my plea for help. Shortly after embarking on this journey of my awakening, I took yet another leap of faith and began to accept that my son was on his own journey and I needed only to support him with unconditional love and let go of my need to fix everything. I resigned from my job without having any other work lined up, and I ended that 16-year relationship. And I did all of this within a few days! Through all the tears, I understood clearly that having peace in my life was not possible while holding on to these very things that were keeping me from it.

No words can truly articulate how my life has changed for the better through this major shift. I now live on purpose – my Authentic Soul Purpose. I believe that life is a process of unfolding, and I can now say that I am at peace most of the time. And I am grateful.

Life Through Rainbow-Colored Glasses

By Karen A. Foli

Throughout my life, there have been little flashes of color to guide me in discovering that big changes were in the works. I wore a red dress when Mr. Right appeared, and soon after taking on the title of *Mrs.*, I became *Mom*. Sunshine and green spaces helped me balance those roles by honoring my intuition and gave me blazing courage to stand when I needed to speak my truth.

Numerous volunteer roles in my community and family activities colored my daily schedule. Those leadership positions taught me life and business skills and also satisfied my desire to serve. Family vacations to the calming blue ocean balanced my busy life with much-needed respite to contemplate spiritual questions that flashed guiding signals to search deeper into myself for answers.

A few years after moving from a big city to a country home in a small town, I experienced the "empty nest," which gave me time to delve into spiritualism via books and the internet. Guided by my passion, I widened my spiritual searchlight and found teachers online, in my town, and at a big-city expo. I took a frequency-healing program and explored a variety of other modalities, including energy medicine, Reiki, crystal therapy, and color therapy.

During one online healing meditation, I realized I was playing small in my volunteer choices. I gained the courage to act on my soul's urge to step out and expand – inspiring me to share the tools I'd learned with my community and with anyone else willing to open their eyes, minds, and hearts.

Every colorful experience on my spiritual journey has led me to tools of knowledge, allowing me to help others live a richer spiritual life guided by love. I'm exploding with excitement and dancing with my soul's desire to serve as a catalyst for positive growth and change.

My own transformation from volunteer to entrepreneur has materialized at a stage in my life where many individuals choose to retire. I finally discovered my true self at the perfect time.

The Locket That Opened Doors

By Holly Berkley

As I handed over the antique gold locket, I thought, *This is crazy, but let's see what she comes up with.*

I was standing in the living room of my college roommate's home, and her genteel Southern mother was offering to "read" my jewelry. Sarah had described her mom's ability to tune in to personal objects and recount their history, but I had my doubts.

After all, I was the daughter of an engineer, an ex-Marine no less, who had instilled in me the importance of thinking things through, relying on brainpower and verifiable facts. I was graduating with a chemistry degree. None of this airy-fairy stuff for me!

Mrs. Martin cradled the locket in the palm of her hand, went quiet for a minute or two, and then began to describe the strong woman who had worn it as she made the arduous journey from Illinois to California via horse-drawn wagon in the 1840s.

I was flabbergasted! She was describing my great-great-grandmother, and everything she said was accurate, down to the route.

I peppered her with questions: What was she feeling, exactly? How had she learned how to do this? I wasn't even sure what to ask, but I knew I wanted to know more!

Many years and many certifications later, I look back on this brief interaction as the door that opened the world of subtle energy to me, showing me that frequency and vibration are the underlying signature of all matter. And that all matter, including our body, holds the imprint of significant events.

Now I, too, am able to read energy as easily as Mrs. Martin could, and I use it, along with leading-edge neuroscience, in my leadership-development work with aspiring businesswomen. Together, we clear the "inner glass ceiling" of Imposter Syndrome and other limiting beliefs so they can have the impact and success they were meant to have.

One of the first things I teach them is to pay attention to those gentle inner nudges that may reveal their greatest joy and life purpose – and to keep those intuitive antennae turned on!

You Are What You Think

By Fiona Louise

Somewhere along the way, I lost my self-worth. Experiences with bullies made me question my own value. I grew up not believing in myself, constantly judging and comparing myself to others, and always coming off second best. I mentally beat myself up and valued others' opinions over my own. I even went into a career that undervalued my actual talents and wasn't aligned with my true self.

When my brother committed suicide, I built up walls and held on to a lot of blame, guilt, and anger. I was closed off from any joyful experience and consumed by grief. I met a lot of people who took advantage of my low self-belief and zapped what little energy I had left. I developed autoimmune disorders where the immune system attacks healthy cells, mistaking them for foreign invaders. My body was literally trying to kill itself!

This illness was not surprising, considering how little I thought of myself. My body was just reacting to the toxic thoughts and feelings. Every action, every moment required so much effort. Still requiring energy to work, I did the exact wrong thing – chain-drank caffeine, which further depleted my reserves until I could no longer work. Under constant threat, exhausted, and in perpetual pain, my body gave up. I was bedridden for six months. My body just had nothing left.

Or so I thought.

It turned out that the enforced rest was exactly what I needed. Little by little, my energy started returning. Listening to and respecting my body, I stopped drinking caffeine and began eating healthily. Noticing the negative thoughts, I held up a STOP sign. Every day, I recited positive affirmations until they became truth. I meditated. I began to value my inner voice and gain self-respect.

My newfound self-worth stopped attracting bullies and freed up space for genuinely loving and trustworthy people. I learned to grieve, move on, and heal.

Finally, I believe in myself. What a blessing the illness was; it brought me worthiness and inner peace, and it put me back onto the right life path.

Ripple Effect of Change

By Sophie Maya

My daughter was nine when I noticed she was struggling socially and academically. Our doctor diagnosed her with ADHD and suggested that she take medication. I chose to find a holistic cure instead and reached out to an acupuncturist, asking if he could heal her. I was shocked when I heard him say, "Chinese medicine believes that if you want to heal a child, fix the parent." I translated his words to mean that I was a terrible parent, causing my daughter's pain. I put him on my enemy list and prayed for another solution.

A week later, a neighbor-teacher told me that she believed ADHD was a reflection of problems in the home. What?! Again, I felt offended and wanted to put her on my enemy list, too, but since I was in an unhappy marriage at that time, I wondered if maybe she and the acupuncturist were right. So I chose to listen and put my attention on healing myself.

I sought out healers and therapists who helped me see my inner critic – the voice that told me I wasn't good enough. I also saw how I'd projected this unconscious aspect of my psyche onto my daughter, believing that she needed to change to be good enough. I was doing to her what my mom had done to me: focusing on what was wrong instead of what was right. I decided to stop this pattern of mental and emotional abuse, to be kinder to my daughter – and myself – giving us both what we needed.

I began celebrating my daughter's unique creative spirit and way of being in the world, allowing her to choose her clothes, friends, beliefs, and activities, without judging her choices. As I changed my ways, my daughter became more confident and peaceful. I let her know that there were no mistakes, only opportunities to learn, and that I loved her unconditionally. The more I celebrated my daughter's unique way of being in the world, the more her body and mind relaxed, and her academic and social life flourished naturally!

Finding the Hidden Treasure

By Joy T. Barican

As my name was called to receive the valedictorian award, tears of elation and relief flooded my mum's face as she proudly beamed at me. Being granted a full university scholarship lifted a huge financial pressure that had been weighing heavily on our minds.

Since Mum's divorce when I was three, she had worked hard to provide for me materially, but the lasting gifts she strived to give me were education, spirituality, and character. The seeds Mum had sown while I was growing up bore fruit that day and well into my future.

A sense of entitlement initially caused me to feel resentment towards my father, knowing that financial assistance from him would have eased our burden. Looking back, though, I see that his failure to assist us was a blessing in disguise. It taught me important life lessons of self-reliance and dependence on God. With Mum's gentle coaching, I accepted that his absence in my life meant that I had to double my efforts and triple my frequency of praying. From then on, I knew that if I did my best, God would take care of the rest.

I've also come to see the wisdom in the Shannon L. Alder quote, "Forget what hurt you...but never forget what it taught you." These words remind me to look for opportunity in every difficulty I encounter in any aspect of my life. It has taken discipline, fortitude, and Mum's unconditional love for me to continually search for the hidden treasure behind each trying situation, issue, or person. I am grateful for the times when I recognise the blessings quickly, because they help me become the best I can be. And I am humbled by the times when I fail, for they remind me that I am far from what I once was but not yet what I am going to become.

Unanswered Prayer

By Ioana Adriana Terec

As a child growing up in Romania, my favorite time of the year was summer when my brother and I spent time with my grandparents in their small village. Everything there was amazing…except the water.

My grandparents had a water fountain in the back yard, but that water was not safe for people to drink. Instead, like the rest of the village, they had to get water from a spring that was about three miles away from their house. Every day, my grandmother went to the spring – walking up and down the big hill, which seemed even bigger if you were carrying water!

I sometimes went with my grandmother, just to keep her company, and we often had to stop to catch our breath. One day, while we were stopped on the hill, she told me that her prayer had not been answered. Her prayer was that somehow the hill would disappear, which would make it easier to get water. She had also talked to the leaders of the village to do something about it, but her request remained unanswered.

I often thought that God didn't listen to her prayer, or perhaps it was just too hard a request. I found out later that she was asking for the wrong thing. She asked for the hill to change, instead of asking for an easier way to get water. Her need was water.

A few years ago, my grandparents passed away and my parents decided to sell the home. It was hard to sell because of the water problem. When the house finally sold, the buyer did some research about the water. To everyone's surprise, he found fresh, drinkable water just across the street from the house!

All that time, the water had been so close, but my grandma never asked for it; she asked for a totally different thing. What a life lesson this was for me: Be careful what you ask for…and how you ask for it!

Co-Creation

By Linda Voogd

I have had many shifts in my life – some big, some small. Each took me deeper into the river of life. Some opportunities were grasped; others went untouched. All moved me further on my journey. Yet no shift felt as strong as finally seeing the infinite possibilities life offered me.

Being a therapist, I've long known that our thoughts create our feelings and, ultimately, our behaviors. But I didn't understand how they send out rockets of desire that result in creation. As I practiced changing my concept of self and re-examining my beliefs, a higher self emerged. This self saw my unlimited potential. It drew strength not only from *my* energy but from all existing energy. The universe itself supported my quest to fulfill my life's purpose.

I can't say how or when this happened, only that it did. The more I read and learned, the more I felt my power grow stronger. I forever left victimhood and became a co-creator of my world.

As a co-creator, I use my imagination to bring my dreams to fruition. I set daily intentions for what I want to manifest in my life. Now I visualize and think from the end, as if what I want to happen already exists. And so it comes into being. I changed my language to reflect this new self – *I can't* turned into *I can* – and everything was possible. This shift in perception led to increased confidence in my abilities and resulted in creating successful workshops, public speaking, and eventually co-authoring a book.

With this new awareness, I wake up each morning feeling joy and gratitude for life's endless opportunities. We are all connected to a universe that gives us the ability to manifest our desires. How exhilarating to know that we all get to choose our experiences! This realization was my greatest gift and my biggest shift – to know that I am a co-creator and that I use my dreams to shape my reality.

The Biggest Lie

By Suzanne Zupancic

What was I waiting for? A raise? A new car? The perfect job? The perfect weight? Why did I wait to be happy? Why did I base my happiness on getting something or somewhere? Why couldn't I be happy *now*, as is, without changing anything: in this job, in this body, with this house? My life is happening right now, in the present moment, yet how many days have I lost dreaming or worrying about the future and regretting or reliving the past?

I knew that I wasn't alone in my search for happiness. There are over 75 million Google search results for the term *happiness*. Clearly, we are all looking for happiness in one form or another. But, ultimately, I found happiness when I *stopped* searching, when I stopped wanting, when I stopped chasing the imaginary thing that I thought would make me happy, when I remembered that my happiness does not depend on something else.

I finally realized that happiness is a choice: *we* get to decide whether we are happy, even if things are not perfect. And it's a choice I have to make each and every day. Some days it's a breeze, and some days it's harder than others. On the hardest days, the days when nothing is going my way, I have to make a conscious choice to start and end each day with happiness.

My life shifted when I realized that the biggest lie we tell ourselves is that "I'll be happy when…*xyz*." The truth is, my happiness does not depend on something else. If I am always chasing something – if I am willing to sacrifice my *now* for some imagined future – then what happens to my life, to the present moment, the only place that life exists?

Sure, I can wish for things to be different. I can wait to be happy until I fit into those jeans or until I have a bigger house, but where does that get me? It gets me straight to unhappiness! It supports the illusion that things can be different from the way they are. In truth, I cannot control what happens in my life; my control lies in how I react to what happens. That is *my* choice. And I, for one, choose happiness.

From *Not Losing* to *Winning*

By Mary Meston

Standing poolside amongst 50 of my fellow bestselling authors, I admired each for their resolve and eagerness for upcoming possibilities. All of us were receiving a distinguished award for our contributions to a well-known author's book on success.

I was part of, and overheard, story after story of each contributor's personal path to success and how they set their sights on being a bestselling author. Little did I know that those stories would provide me with a new clarity, a new perspective, and a life shift.

You see, ever since I can remember, I have been striving to win. As a very small child, I was the first to ride my bike. As a high school senior, I was at the top of my class. I was first in anything I endeavored to do, and if I couldn't be perfect and be first or the winner, I wouldn't try it.

While I always believed I approached everything from a "winning" frame of mind, it took 50 of my newly minted bestselling authors, a historic hotel, and that a-ha I didn't know I needed. At that moment, I realized that I had never truly played to win; I had only played to NOT LOSE.

"What's the difference?" you might ask. It is a very subtle and ever-so-powerful shift. It is the mindset and energy with which you approach a goal, mission, vision, or path. Playing to win is an expansive, encompassing, and anything-is-possible approach, whereas playing *not to lose* is a state of contraction – in the sense of *not* making a mistake, *not* reaching too far or stretching beyond what is known, and *not* seeing the possibilities and opportunities.

By playing *not to lose*, I hadn't lost, but I also hadn't experienced the vastness the world offered. My fellow authors spoke of incredible opportunities and reaching afar. I found my self-imposed limitations stunted, stilted, and stale in comparison to their stories of possibility. In hindsight, I had never really won; I just hadn't lost.

From that moment on, my new approach has been to expand to the possible. *That* is truly winning in life!

Falling In and Through

By Marta Mrotek

I remember my daughter shrieking in the most disturbing way, yelling nearly unintelligible threats about leaving, or worse. That's what I remember most. My husband was yelling too, but I knew exactly what he was saying. He was asking her why, both hands on her shoulders – tight, angry and afraid – begging her to stop. I was sitting on the bed just a few feet away, perfectly still. I could hear and see everything that was happening, but it was as if someone had turned down the volume and dimmed the lights. I was somehow distanced, and there was a feeling of falling – falling in, and then falling through all the noise and fear to a place inside where it was quiet enough to take a breath.

Being born into a home with a slowly dying parent and growing up to have two children in active addiction taught me to retreat from upsetting circumstances with some amount of dexterity. But this was something different. This wasn't something I had conjured. It was a reprieve that came without warning and left almost as quickly, granting fleeting protection from the intensity of the experience and a shift in my perception. My daughter's journey into recovery and the purpose of my own life would be marked in so many ways with this specific memory where pain and chaos met an indescribable instant of peace.

There is no way I could have known that the events of that evening would pave the road for so much healing – not just healing for my children, not just for me or our family, but healing that would spread through us and out into the world in unexpected ways. Since that night, I have witnessed similar moments of transformation. I have come to recognize these painful experiences and the miracles that happen in their midst as teachers that hold invaluable information for falling with intention. I still fall sometimes, but now I rise even stronger, with a sacred calling to share what I have learned about how to land in a peaceful place.

Spiritual Power

By Melissa Feick

As an introspective person, I've come to have a different perspective on power. To be true to the loving power within you, you have to be aware that there is a spiritual power and be aware of how the ego can sabotage that power.

For example, once I was teaching a class, and a fellow teacher was not happy with the way the class went. On my way home, my ego started to drone on about how those who attended had been *my* students and how *her* students didn't like me. An insecure energy came over me, and I felt powerless – a feeling that often ensues when the ego gets involved.

My ego whined on: *Of course I'm not liked by her group. I don't fit in; I'm the odd one out again.* I started to feel like I was in high school again. I felt insecure and fearful, which made me want to hide.

At last, my higher consciousness chimed in and I heard, "What would you do differently in order for them to like you or for them to accept you as part of their group?" This question stopped me dead in my tracks.

My honest answer was, "Nothing!" I wouldn't have done *anything* differently. At that moment, the insecure, powerless feeling left me, and I felt something else: a sense of spiritual power.

There is a difference between spiritual power and ego power. This insight helped me realize the ability of the ego to take over in a stealthy way, to demolish joy, spiritual power, and inner peace. Needing to be liked is the ego's desire, but we don't have to give our power to the ego or to others.

As a result of this realization, I came to see that being in your spiritual power happens when you take responsibility for your actions while not changing who you are in order for someone to like you. If you allow your spiritual power to wane, just to be liked, then you aren't in your integrity. So the next time you find yourself wanting to be liked, ask yourself if you really need to change or if it's just your ego talking. That's what I continue to do, and my entire life has changed for the better!

Peace Is the Way

By Karen Bomm

"There is no way to peace; peace is the way." - A. J. Muste

I had had enough; the pain was too great! So I dug into those real memories that brought up all those horrific layers of ugly feelings. I allowed all the hurt, manipulation, disrespect, frustration, sickness, hatred, and anger to surface.

I reflected on what Granddad did, the disrespectful treatment by Dad, how my older brother had taken advantage of me, my sister's abusive coercion, and all the disappointing relationships with people who seemed to be attracted to me for all the wrong reasons.

I discovered how raw my emotions were. My anger was real. My body hurt! I believed in a world of peace, but *how could I make this pain go away?*

I felt alone, disconnected, and alien to people with holier-than-thou attitudes who put others down to make themselves feel better, who slighted others in order to satisfy their own love of money and power over others.

I knew I did not belong here, but I needed to be careful not to get stuck in "rebellious" or "victim" behavior. I chose to deal with my feelings of pain, anger, and distrust head on. I moved through my "radical" and "why me" behavior toward forgiveness.

I recalled telling my mother before she passed what her father did to me when I was five years old and how I forgave him. I called my dad to apologize for expecting him to be the kind of dad I *wanted* rather than honoring who he *really was*, and I told him I loved him unconditionally. Also, out of respect for different views of life, I reaffirmed my need to maintain my healthy space of self-respect.

I forgave them all, including myself! I stopped the pain, stepped into my power, embraced self-love, and celebrated my authentic contributions and place in the world. I felt the goodness of life! My life shifted to smiles, creativity, love, and respect as my heart filled with peace.

Finding Freedom

By Brenda M. Wiener

When I was seven years old, I saw a dog attack a cat and felt helpless to stop the cat from dying. I didn't know what to do or how to stop it from happening. The worst part is that my aunt and I were blamed for letting it happen.

As a small child, I accepted that I was at fault and that I had let an animal die, no matter what the reality. I wasn't equipped to understand all the variables at play that day.

This experience continued to impact every one of my decisions, even into adulthood. In the spring of 2016, I was attending a retreat and staying with someone who had some food allergies/sensitivities. When I realized I had incorporated a restricted food item into a meal we shared the night before, it shut me down! I didn't know what to do or what would happen to my friend's health.

Fortunately, my mix-up did not create a life-or-death situation, and my friend was fine. I was relieved and also saw this experience as a blessing because it helped me grow and heal from my childhood experience. What I came to realize that day was that I had been responding to basically all of life as if my decisions were a matter of life or death. It did not matter if I was just buying toilet paper or deciding what to make for dinner; I was always on edge, anticipating that my next decision would result in death – NOT an enjoyable way to live!

At age 50, I found freedom – freedom to enjoy life and respond from a place of life and love rather than death.

The Power of Yes

By Cathie Bliss

Yes! What a difference one word can make! Yes opens doors and expands our lives. It gives us the power of choice. Yes is the gateway to all opportunity.

Now imagine you had no Yes. Imagine not being able to express yourself. Your every thought, feeling, and desire is trapped inside you. No way to mention you really want enchiladas for dinner, or remind Mom that it's purple-shirt Friday and she's picked blue. Imagine having severe pain and not being able to say where it hurts.

Our first child and only daughter, Cailey, is a beautiful, funny, sweet, and brave soul. She was injured shortly after birth by kernicterus (severe, mismanaged newborn jaundice). Kernicterus doesn't affect cognitive ability, but it can cause cerebral palsy, hearing loss, visual impairment, and digestive disorders. Cailey had them all.

Cailey was incredibly social, and her motivation to connect was strong. She had so much to say, yet Cailey was non-verbal. She couldn't speak or effectively use her body.

Over time, she learned several ways to communicate. Diagnosed with profound hearing loss, she learned American Sign Language, but the cerebral palsy was so severe that Cailey couldn't sign back. She tried to express herself with body language and eye gaze, but these were frequently misinterpreted. Wonderful specialists developed low- and high-tech communication solutions, but accessing technology was an exhausting physical effort.

By the age of 10, Cailey was sticking out her tongue. No, she wasn't trying to offend; it was a breakthrough! She'd created a reliable, wonderful way to say Yes! She now had direct input into her own life, a gift of empowerment in a world of dependence on others.

As her Yes became more sophisticated and refined, Cailey enthusiastically shared her love of movies, restaurants, music, and dance, smiling with her whole body at the results. By combining Yes with a three-choice method, her self-expression grew quickly. She loved being with friends and family and was wholeheartedly engaged in all that this life offers! Oh, the doors that opened when Cailey discovered the power of Yes!

It's Up to Me!

By Shelley Lundquist

As I look back on my life, I find myself utterly amazed at how easily I used to surrender my power and cling to the notion that "more" was not meant for me. I would throw in the towel before ever stepping into the ring to face my fears. Plagued by the "poor me" syndrome, I would sit back in a defensive position, waiting and hoping that someday things might get better.

Alas, life doesn't work that way. Life gets better when we learn to value ourselves and we find the courage to step into the power to which we were born.

A pivotal moment came for me while celebrating a success at work. I was struck by the mind-blowing epiphany that if I had the power to direct and create one outcome, then certainly I possessed the power to create the results I desired in other areas too. Holy moly!

In accepting responsibility, I could see that doing nothing was still making a choice. Life was not just happening to me; I was an active and powerful participant!

Excited and focused on possibility, I made room in my life for my hopes and dreams. Things began to fall into place as I honoured my desires in action.

My path was no longer determined by my emotions, fears, or excuses; I simply followed my heart. I became attuned to the awareness that my choices, perception, mindset, and ability to work with whatever the present moment brings would allow me to create the life of my choosing.

Success rippled through all areas of my life because I envisioned what I wanted and moved toward it.

Relationships were mended because I let go of judgment and focused on caring instead of being right. My career flourished because I believed in myself and honoured my choices. I had more energy, and my overall health even improved because I made better dietary choices and added exercise to my routine. Choices = results!

How wonderful it is to finally see that how I live my life is always up to me!

The Lesson of the Zipper

By Pami Woodruff

"I can't! I can't!" The frustration was written all over my five-year-old son's face, and he was near tears as he kept trying to get the bottom parts of his coat zipper aligned. "I can't!"

"Keep trying," I encouraged. "You've almost got it."

He glanced up at me, dubious, then concentrated on his zipper once more. "I can't, I can't…," he muttered. Then, a pause, and a surprised "I DID IT!" accompanied by a triumphant grin.

I smiled, remembering the same transformation when he finally "got it" when learning to tie his shoes. "Yes, you did!" I told him. "I knew you could."

It had been a momentous day of firsts. He'd read his first independent words – "hot dog" on the menu – and mastered a coat zipper. I pondered how quickly his defeated "I can't" had changed to a triumphant "I DID IT!"

I wondered, *Do I do that as well?*

Does success seem furthest from our grasp when it is only one more attempt away? I wondered how many times I had given up, just one try shy of success. Could I have finally mastered the hula hoop or gotten the hang of roller skates? Was a successful cartwheel just one more attempt away?

A can-do attitude is important in life, and it is one of the things I teach through the medium of old-fashioned home skills that most have never had the opportunity to learn. But is this a lesson I need to remind myself of, even today? Do I only need to write one more email, one more Facebook post, or one more blog entry to gain the momentum I desire in my business?

When tempted to say "I can't," I've learned to ask "How can I?" instead. But today, I wonder if looking back from my future – when I can say "I DID IT!" – might not be even more helpful. Maybe I can ask my future self, "How did you do it?" and listen for the reply.

It might be just that simple – just like the zipper.

The Lecture That Shifted My Perspective

By Lori Thiessen

It was a typical summer weekend afternoon. The air had the warm, humid scent of July. A light breeze tickled my bare arms as I walked across the parking lot to my office. I punched in the security code and knew I was the only one in the building, again. I was once again stuck inside my cold, claustrophobic office facing stacks of work and looming deadlines. My hoodie wasn't enough to ward off the chill of the air conditioner. My hands were freezing cold. So was my heart. Cold and angry. I did NOT want to be here again, day after day, missing out on the fun of another all-too-short weekend.

Work had been like this for a few years now. My thoughts lashed out at the unfairness of it all: *Is this really how the months and years ahead are going to continue? Work, work, work, with no end in sight? I don't know if I can keep doing this.*

A quiet but distinct Voice replied, "Stop saying that."

The Voice continued with a full-on lecture: "Remember what happened last time you said those words and gave up? Remember all those dark years of depression because you thought your situation was permanent and gave up? Don't do that again. You know now that no situation is permanent, that life is so much bigger and broader than what you can see right now. This WILL NOT be what the rest of your life looks like. This WILL CHANGE. It ALL will change. That's how life works. Think about that before you give up again."

I did stop and think.

The Voice was right. What is in my face right now is not the totality of my life. One day, I will no longer walk into this building and sit at this desk.

As I realized the truth in all this, my life shifted. My struggles are not permanent. I went back to my computer with a peaceful attitude and more balanced perspective, determined to be present, stay patient with the challenges, and cherish the good.

Do You Hear the Wind?

By Laura Young

I was sitting outside on our deck with my husband the day after he got his hearing aids. It was early summer and a clear, quiet, beautiful night. Suddenly, I noticed him looking at me funny. I asked him what was wrong.

"Nothing," he said. Then he blurted out, "Is it normal to hear your own voice inside your head?" He had suffered with tinnitus and severe hearing loss for most of his life, and apparently that had drowned out his inner voice. I was shocked! Something that I'd taken for granted all my life – that crazy voice in my head – he hadn't been aware of for decades!

I was in deep thought about this when he hit me with another question. "Do you hear that?" he asked.

"No," I replied. "Hear what?"

Suddenly he was excited! "Do you hear the wind?"

No, I didn't. I did not hear the wind. Because, just like I had conditioned myself to hear my mostly mean inner voice, I had also pushed away the beautiful sounds of the outer world.

I was in tears as I sat there wondering what it must be like for him to hear the wind. When had I stopped hearing it? Could I ever hear it again? What else wasn't I hearing?

I remember a friend once saying that *silent* and *listen* had the same letters. Now it all made sense! To really listen, you must be silent. My husband finally had silence in his head. And that silence allowed him to hear!

I do hear the wind now. And the rain, and the birds, and even the *nice* voice in my head that had been long ignored. I realized that I can choose what I want to hear. Whether it is inside or outside of me, I have the choice!

And so does my husband. And I now know when he's done listening to me: when he takes his hearing aids out!

What's the Best That Could Happen?

By Sophia Ellen Falke

I sat there crying – something I tried not to do. But once I started talking, all the misery I was feeling poured out. "I don't know what to do," I confided to my friend. "I used to love going to work, but with the new bosses, I feel like I'm not valued – or wanted – anymore." It was the first time I expressed out loud what I'd been suppressing for months.

When I finished my story, my friend sat quietly for several minutes. Finally, with eyes filled with compassion, he said, "I don't usually give direct advice, but I think you should leave your job."

Ack! Leave my job? My mind went straight to all the reasons I couldn't or shouldn't: *I don't have another job lined up. I have a mortgage. You don't just give up.* All this and more sped through my mind. And then I remembered another friend who would always ask me, "What's the worst that could happen if…" and she would ask me to fill in the blank related to whatever was stressing me at the time.

So I asked myself, *What's the worst that could happen if I left my job?* I could lose my house. I could be jobless…I continued in this vein until I realized, *I can overcome even the worst.*

Then I asked myself, *What's the BEST that could happen if I left my job?* Ahh, *that* opened up a world of expansive, uplifting possibilities. The best? I would feel free – free from stress, free to fully express my creativity in the world, free to start new adventures, free to follow my dreams. I could again enjoy each day to the fullest. I could focus on promise rather than limitation.

I felt an immediate shift. "Yes, I can" became my mantra. Yes, I left my job. Yes, I had an adventure of a lifetime when I took my 75-year-old mother on a 2½-month, 11,000-mile camping trip to the Arctic Circle. Yes, I chose "the best" and created the life I would love.

Going Global

By Alison M. Stokes

Yad Vashem in Jerusalem is not for the faint of heart. As the National Holocaust Memorial, it contains the ashes of those who were exterminated in the 22 concentration camps during WWII. The Eternal Flame that burns here constantly reminds us of what can happen when we ignore dictatorship and genocide on our planet.

As the Irish Peace Delegate, I came to pay my respects to those who had died and to their surviving relatives, some of whom were with us. One of the museums is dedicated to the children (over one million) who died in these camps. It is an experience that I will never forget. On display were old photos of children, along with items that had been found or confiscated: the odd shoe, a tattered ribbon, a rag doll. A continuously playing tape listed the name and age of every child who had died.

Looking at these innocent faces who had been wiped out systematically was so REAL and so horrific. One of the men with me saw a photo of a little girl who looked remarkably like his daughter, and he broke down in violent sobs. I had to help carry him outside. Others emerged in a state of shock, and most were distraught.

I didn't cry. I don't know why. I remember sitting on the wall outside, trying to comfort those who were traumatized, and thinking, "How can I help prevent this kind of atrocity from happening again?" I realized I would need to shift the focus of my healing work in Dublin to a more global scale. It wasn't enough to concentrate on just my local community anymore; I would need to send healing energy to every single person in the world.

Now, that is exactly what I do every day. I sit and send loving, healing energy from my heart to the heart of every single being on this planet. It is only by being vigilant and aware and standing together that we can prevent history from repeating itself.

Living Fearlessly

By Lisa McDonald

Five years ago, when I embarked upon single-parenthood, I knew that a major "11th hour" would arrive in the summer of 2016 – when I would see whether I could hold on to my children's home by buying out their father's share.

I did not have a crystal ball five years ago; however, I did have (as I have always had when facing a personal tsunami) an indomitable mindset, fierce perseverance, and the ability to take massive action in my daily life for whatever I deem a do-or-die moment.

I remained steadfast in my conviction that I would in fact hold on to this house, and I entrusted the universe to carve out the roadmap to my non-negotiable outcome, all the while knowing I had the essential, intrinsic ingredients for this to come to fruition.

By choosing to put one foot in front of the other during this five-year marathon, I did finally secure my children's home. I did manage the buyout and prevented my children from seeing a "For Sale" sign on our front lawn – not by luck, loan, or lottery – I did this all by myself!

What I have learned in my many years of daily commitment to personal growth and personal development is that in order for one's life to shift, one's mindset must shift. One is the conduit to the other.

I am one of a growing many who believe, support, and understand this guiding principle to be essential to achieve fundamental change and success. A critical shift in thought and action must happen. It's called *living fearlessly*!

The shift is birthed out of clarity, desperation, pain, passion, gumption, and knowing how to turn even your darkest moments into the brightest blessings. Learning the principle of how to live fearlessly is the gift we give ourselves, the gift we share with the rest of the world.

Filters

By Karen Hicks

While coming home from vacation this past summer, I alternated my skygazing between the windshield and side mirror. (Clearly, skygazing is one of the benefits of being in the passenger's seat!) What was curious to me as I went back and forth was the apparent changing of the colour of the sky. Through the windshield, the colour was a very light blue, almost white; yet through the side mirror, it was darker. I could not figure this out! And then it hit me.

As I looked at the sky through the windshield, I had two obvious filters: my sunglasses and the glass of the windshield. In looking at the sky through the side mirror, I had three obvious filters: my sunglasses, the glass of the passenger window, and the side mirror. I glanced over to my partner. While he had the same number of filters, his sunglasses were different than mine. He saw a completely different sky colour than I did, regardless of where he looked. Same sky, different colour. Always.

The teaching was not lost on me. The realization was a gentle reminder that each of us has our own filters through which we look at the world. We use these filters to sort and process information; we use them to make sense of the world. And just as I was initially unaware of why the sky appeared to be different colours, many of the filters we use to make sense of the world sit below consciousness. Not one person shares my filters; they are uniquely my own. The filters of my partner, my children – they are uniquely their own. Some elements may overlap; however, they will never match completely.

Skygazing, sunglasses, windshields, and side mirrors: a simple demonstration of such an important awareness. I smiled and was thankful for the reminder.

Surrendering into the Unknown

By Jennifer Larkin

Recently, I found myself reaching a breaking point like none I'd ever experienced before. It required a severe, heart-wrenching shift. The experience unearthed an immense sea of bitterness and untethered rage. I had spent years challenging myself to grow beyond limitations and face deep pervasive demons – I had done "my work." Now, I wanted the "win" I was promised for keeping true to the path. I found that my resilience had reached its sell-by date.

Interestingly, during this period, the blows to my heart continued relentlessly. I rebelled against all the wisdom I'd ever learned, and the anger at my lot in life grew exponentially. I found myself thinking, *How is it possible that so many others who have done so little inner work have so much? Why is so much of what I choose so heavily peppered with tests and trials?*

I continued to do the only thing I knew how to do: persevere. Yet this was like trying to push numerous boulders up Everest in gale-force winds and hail without adequate tools or a support crew.

When I finally surrendered to the best of my ability and stopped my futile endeavors, I became aware of the internal residue of what felt like decades of too many traumas to count and burdens too heavy to bear. My nervous system was demanding me to press "Reset."

In the end, the only choice that offered any relief was surrendering repeatedly into the unknown and freefalling into possibility. This created many moments that were filled with deep, dark, uncomfortable feelings and a realization that the only thing I was willing to do in the moment was to accept that I could not accept the current situation. This permission to be real allowed me the time and space to get to a place where I could finally accept and allow for something different to emerge. Through this process, I discovered an immense capacity to create stillness, joy, and love for every moment, regardless of the circumstances.

My Concern Was Really Ingrained Terror

By Rozlyn Warren

The day I decided I would no longer entertain fear was the day everything shifted and my life began to expand into the amazingly beautiful place it is in today! This was not a decision that I took lightly. It meant that I had to disassemble all my beliefs, structures, and everything I held as truth.

In hindsight, I can really appreciate the change this allowed. Before this shift, I had often been concerned about the future, focusing on potential worst-case scenarios. Being a naturally happy and positive person, however, this kept me in inner turmoil, always feeling split in two.

What I finally came to recognize was that this "concern" was actually deeply imbedded terror – the result of my "fear training." Being raised by a fearful parent (whose word was law) and brought up in a religious setting that focused on what you mustn't do to keep yourself out of danger, most of my beliefs, ideas, and thoughts were fear based. This continued and worsened until the day I was so miserable that I was unable to cope with life any longer. This was the day I decided that if a thought, idea, or "truth" caused my heart to contract in fear, I had misunderstood it!

This Divine insight opened the door to my freedom. It allowed me to step away from the victimhood found in blame and take full responsibility for my misunderstandings. This also made it easier to let decades-old beliefs and paradigms just drift away to be replaced by new, love-based ones.

I often say, only half-jokingly, that the day I took Hell off the table as a possibility to be guarded against, my life completely changed! I no longer play it safe and focus on what has to be avoided. Paying attention to what brings me joy and satisfaction has "scared" this fear off for good!

Surviving the Shift

By Isla Selupucin

I believe our lives are made up of shifts that move us like tectonic plates; they can be gentle or can jolt us fiercely to move forward. Shifts ensure that we live the lives we have chosen, and while they can be beautiful, they can also be incredibly hard and deeply painful. Shifts are at the core of who we are; we adapt and we evolve. Sometimes they're anticipated, even welcomed, but sometimes they're like an earthquake in our lives.

I had one such shift several years ago – the kind that eventually sucks all the air from you, leaving your soul breathless. It started slowly with work troubles – bankruptcies and betrayals, which led to legal issues – but continued as cherished friendships ended abruptly. Life became disconnected. To cope, I disappeared. I'm not sure where I went, but it was a place of stress, strain, and loneliness. From the outside, I appeared to be a lioness moving forward with strength, but in truth, I was utterly lost. I often felt like I was holding on to a raft in the middle of an ocean of sadness; regardless, I fought, I kept swimming, and I kept listening to my soul.

I don't know why I didn't seek out new friends or share the burden I felt with those who remained in my life. What I do know is that I learned more about myself in the darkness than I had ever known in the light. I learned that true friends never disappear and that, regardless, we can never be truly alone when the universe is inside us. I also learned that our thoughts and feelings are symptoms of the process that we sometimes have to go through. And, most importantly, I learned that by focusing on the good, on the small things, light always comes after darkness.

Revising an Unrealistic Belief

By Connie M. Warden

It felt like I had tried to propel myself through a wall. I couldn't move my neck from side to side because of the pain. I felt physically and emotionally shattered. Something had to change.

A week earlier, during a parent-teacher conference with our son's fourth-grade teacher, we were interrupted by a school staff member who said that we needed to reschedule. The school had just been informed that my son's schoolmate, who had been missing for two days, was found dead (ironically, across the street from Columbine High School, just a year after the tragedy there). My husband, son, and I left the school, deep in thought and with much sadness in our hearts.

The next morning, as we were getting ready for school, I noticed my son lying on the floor, lethargic and listless. He said he was depressed and didn't want to go to school.

It was hard for me to see my son in any kind of depressive state, especially because the word "depression" had such a charge for me. When I was 11 years old, my mother had tried to kill herself. She was found and hospitalized before she could carry out the suicide attempt. Needless to say, this was a hard time for me and my family.

As a parent, I so badly wanted to protect my own children from any such pain, and I developed the belief that "If I'm a perfect parent, my children won't experience trauma, grief, or sadness." After the tragedy with the schoolmate, however, I realized that this belief simply wasn't realistic, and I had to revise it to "Teaching my children how to cope with trauma, grief, and sadness makes for a good parent."

My son stayed home for a day before going back to school, where he got wonderful help from teachers and the school counselor. The day he went back to school, however, my own pain started. But as soon as I revised my unrealistic belief, the pain began to dissipate. I feel fortunate to have transformed this belief, for my children's well-being and for my own.

The Shift from Doubt to Possibility

By Elizabeth R. Kipp

Where does self-doubt live?

Self-doubt lives squarely in the seat of fear, and fear lives anywhere but in the present. I fear the moment I am about to enter or an experience from my past. I am actually living in the future when I project what I believe might happen. I am not here, in this moment.

Yet it is here, in the present moment, where all the possibilities exist. The impossible becomes "I'm possible." I may feel excitement about the moment I am in, and that exists as a state of raised energy, but only my projections about what I believe might happen later lead me into a state of fear.

When I meet someone for the first time, I might feel fear about revealing myself. I try to predict the future by creating the story that they will not like who I am, so I fear allowing them to see the real me, based on past experiences of rejection when meeting someone new.

I create my own shift once I become aware that I have dropped out of the present and into the story that *this is how it was in the past, so it will be like this in the future.* With this new awareness, I can now tell myself a new story: *I am here in the present. All possibilities lie here. What can I create right now from what is here for me?*

When I break myself from the habit of projection, I find the sweet peace and flow that is found only in the present moment. I reconnect and reawaken to the eternal brilliance of the Infinite Light within me.

What a shift – from self-doubt to possibility and self-illumination!

My Daughter

By Janet Dhaenens

My relationship with my daughter, Amaryllis, has been challenging for me ever since she was a child. At times, I felt completely inadequate with her. My work in recent years has included looking for what caused me to feel uncomfortable and wrong in her company. I always wanted her to be different. I wanted *me* to be different, too!

One day last summer, I remembered a time when she was a few weeks old and I was at my sister's house. Amaryllis was in her little chair; I set her down somewhere and then I couldn't remember where. I was terrified that I had set her down on top of the car that had been driven away.

I found her a few minutes later – I don't even remember where – and she was fine. But *I* wasn't! I felt horrible! I thought I must be the worst mother in the world to be so irresponsible! My self-judgment was intense! What I suddenly realized last summer is that, at the time, I somehow managed to connect me feeling terribly wrong with *her*. All at once, I understood why I felt so uncomfortable. Her presence activated in me that feeling of being wrong.

This realization completely changed how I feel! I no longer feel inadequate in her company. I do not have any need for her to be different than she is or for me to be different than I am with her. I understand why she held herself separate from me and seemed guarded. She felt my self-judgment and feeling of being wrong. She interpreted this as either she was wrong or I was critical of her, or both.

This change in how I feel is a great gift for both of us! I enjoy giving her the support, encouragement, and love I always wanted to give her. I look forward to Amaryllis's trust in me growing as I continue to feel and express how much she means to me and how deeply I appreciate and value who she is, exactly as she is! I no longer need either of us to be different.

Finding Grace

By Fiona Louise

Although this may seem like a minor life shift, its effects are profound. Being gracious, experiencing moments of grace, and having gratitude for everything in life shifted my consciousness, allowing me to welcome unlimited abundance. I've found that the more gracious I am, the more I receive. The more thankful I am for opportunities, the more synchronistic miracles I experience and the more magical life becomes.

This shift occurred for me after years of feeling unworthy and full of self-doubt. It felt like everything was an uphill battle, with good things only happening to others. My self-defeating thoughts became self-fulfilling prophecies. The longer I lived with a cloud of misery above my head, the longer it took for my heart to open and my vision to clear.

Now I see opportunities to be grateful all the time: when hearing the birds sing, feeling the sun's warmth, enjoying a sunny day, or savoring a moment of silence. I am grateful when I complete my to-do list or find a parking space close to the supermarket. I'm gracious in interactions with friends and strangers, knowing that what we put out into the world, we receive back. I'm glad when I awaken feeling refreshed and when I bring dry washing in before it rains. I'm grateful for every breath I take and every moment as my body heals. I find grace in the blooming of a rose and in a vibrant sunset. I find grace in the garden and while singing in my car.

I even find grace in my illness, which has gifted me with time to heal my mind and body and to reconnect with my soul. Slowing down means I have time to appreciate small things. My choice to leave the corporate life enables me to align with my true self and follow a path that gives me a sense of peace and contentment.

This life shift makes the journey more enjoyable, and I live each day knowing that I am worthy. I am open to new experiences, and I know that all my needs are abundantly supplied beyond my wildest dreams – all thanks to grace!

Forgiveness Is Freedom!

By Laura Young

The earliest memory I recall from my childhood was in 1964, when I was three and a half years old. We were living at my grandparents' house temporarily as our family transitioned through a move from one city to another.

For some reason, everyone slept upstairs except for me and my grandfather. I slept on a cot in the living room, and my grandfather had his own room on the main floor as he was very ill and on oxygen for emphysema.

I remember lying on that cot on my back, looking up at the ceiling tiles, focusing in a meditative state, feeling my way through to the other side, and escaping from my physical body to a beautiful place above the clouds – full of angels and other nice people who watched over me – as my grandfather sexually molested me night after night. This was how a three-year-old coped as she was unknowingly developing PTSD.

Fast-forward to 2008. I'm at a workshop where we go back to a memory to do forgiveness work through guided meditation. Having thought I'd already worked through this trauma with various other processes, I did not expect my grandfather to be the one chosen for this practice. But my higher self proved me wrong!

I had never forgiven him. Why should I? He didn't deserve forgiveness! I relented to the process, however, and this is what I learned: *I* deserved to forgive him. I deserved it, not him. He was long dead, and the energy of the situation was affecting only me by preventing healthy relationships, a healthy body, and healthy self-esteem.

So I forgave him that day. I didn't condone his behavior, and I didn't let his actions not count for something, but I forgave him. And in doing so, I found freedom!

Do You Have *Yoyu?*

By Marci Kobayashi

When the cashier at my grocery store first started working, she was stiff and unfriendly. She never made small talk, and she never smiled. I worried about her and about the store. Customer service was clearly not her strength. Whenever I came through her line, I made eye contact and smiled. I wanted to make her sour face light up. Instead, she looked startled.

Months later, I noticed that the cashier was chatting with customers and she even smiled. The bitter, unapproachable mask she wore before was gone. I realized that I had misread her. The cashier was not a bitter, unfriendly person. When she first started working, it was all she could do to ring up the groceries. She had no extra mental or emotional wherewithal to interact with others because she was already running at full capacity. She had no *yoyu.*

Yoyu is a handy Japanese word to describe your capacity to afford something. If you want something but don't have *yoyu*, it means you don't have enough money and can't afford it. Likewise, if your spouse asks you to empty the garbage but you don't have *yoyu*, it means you don't have enough time or energy to do it. *Yoyu* also describes your personal capacity to handle or be in a situation.

Being mindful of someone's *yoyu* allows room for understanding and accepting what they are capable of in this moment. It's not about intelligence or ability. It's about how full their cup is right now.

Watching the cashier shift as she gained *yoyu* helped me learn to be kinder to myself. My Japanese father-in-law lives with us because he is struggling with Alzheimer's. Witnessing someone, especially a parent, navigate this disease is agonizing. I am the buffer between father and son. I hold the space. I have infinitely more patience until suddenly I don't. Now, thanks to the cashier, rather than give in to irrational outbursts and later beat myself up about it, I simply excuse myself. A few hours later, I happily return, drama-free and with my cup overflowing. I am full of *yoyu* once again.

Diving Deep

By Tonia Browne

I looked down into the sea. It seemed endless. I was standing on the edge of the boat with my full diving gear on. It felt heavy and restrictive. Was it too late to change my mind and not jump?

I hadn't dived like this for decades. The odd dive I'd done felt safer – shallower and closer to shore. This was different. It was a pivotal moment. Did I want a safe life or an adventure? If successful, it would be the shift I'd requested. Should I take the plunge or step back?

I jumped.

The world I knew disappeared, replaced by another, just like that. As I submerged, the surface of the water vanished from my sight. I looked around. In front of me was an expansive space of blue, and below was a coral bed alive with action and colour. I was instantly overcome by the beauty and magnificence of it all.

It was at these depths and in these beautiful waters where I realised there are two types of fear: the fear that protects you and the fear that prevents your life from being fun. Sometimes we need to go deep within ourselves and consciously make a decision to change. We need to push fear aside before that change can happen for us.

There is a beautiful world inside and outside all of us, full of opportunities and experiences. Our world is waiting for us to love it, to explore it, and to come to it in peace. It can all happen by saying the word "yes," and then jumping into action and diving deep.

Chapter 4
Relationships

Meeting, falling in love, getting married, and *being* married has certainly been the biggest – and the best! – life shift we've ever experienced (one which we both write about in our pieces for this book). We're so grateful that we get to share every day with our best friend, life partner, and soulmate. What a blessing!

We've found that a loving relationship allows you to express your true self, explore your spirituality, and share your soul. It's also a way to share everyday human experience, from the blissful (such as adventures and peak experiences) to the mundane (such as eating lunch or watching TV). A soulful relationship nurtures your deeper self and encourages you to become the fullest version of *you*.

But marriage is only one kind of relationship. There are also friends, lovers, and "it's complicated" relationships. There are relationships between students and teachers, mentors and mentees, and members of a group sharing a common vision. And there are relationships with family: parents, children, grandparents, ancestors, and "soul families" whose connections can run deeper than blood.

In this chapter, you'll find true stories that explore all types of relationships – covering the highs and lows of love, from the romantic sparks of love at first sight to the heartbreak (and, oftentimes, empowerment) of knowing when to walk away. You'll read stories of support, health, recovery, forgiveness, and many other life shifts that emerge from deep, soulful connections.

We hope you'll recognize some aspects of yourself in some of these stories, gain new insights, and perhaps even feel inspired to examine, explore, and celebrate the relationships that are most important in your own life.

The Prayer That Changed Everything

By Jodi Chapman

I hadn't even realized it, but somehow I had lost my way. Everything on the outside appeared fine. I had a husband I thought I wanted, a job I thought I wanted, a life I thought I wanted. I was comfortable, yet I found myself sleepwalking through my days.

And then 9/11 happened, and everything changed. I began to wake up, and I discovered that I no longer fit into my own life. It was a good life, but it wasn't mine. I didn't want to just go through the motions. I wanted to live fully and feel alive again. I didn't want to simply exist. So I did something that I hadn't done since I was a child: I dropped to my knees and prayed. I prayed for a best friend to come into my life – someone who would understand me, really know me, and help my heart expand.

Two weeks later, I was walking on a dirt road in the New Mexican mountains when I looked over and saw the most beautiful man. We started talking, and we both felt like we were just continuing a conversation. I knew him, and he knew me. For the first time in my life, I felt like I could fully exhale. I knew that he was what had been missing. I had been searching and searching, and finally we were back together – we were home.

We immediately became best friends, and within months I got divorced and we became a couple. Since that day, we have been inseparable. We knew how precious finding each other was, and we quickly rearranged our lives so that we could be together all of the time. Our lives have been filled with one heart-opening moment after the other ever since.

Asking for and then finding Dan completely opened up my soul and gave me such solid faith in our universe. My prayer was answered even more beautifully and perfectly than I could have ever imagined. I will forever be grateful for the greatest gift I have ever been or will ever be given. My love. My heart. My everything.

Home at Last

By Lori Santo

He was a wanderer, the Prodigal Son. He left after a difficult divorce and exile from his family, leaving six children and a lot of darkness in his wake. He was an abuser. My father. Oh, how I loved him. And despised him and his dark, brutal legacy.

Twenty years after his departure, I was immersed in meditation practices and Ageless Wisdom teachings when I began to receive his soul visitations. The more still I became, the more vivid his visits. He began communing with me on a nightly basis. I'd awaken from deep sleep in the middle of the night with images of him on the streets, homeless. He was hungry, frail, terrified, fiercely alone, and so very cold. Each dream delivered more vivid, explicit visions. I felt certain that he had moved closer, that he was local…sleeping under the stars on a bed of dirt, wrapped in an oversized blanket.

I felt an overwhelming urgency to find him, and I prayed for guidance. Like breadcrumbs, I followed my soul's urges, knowing that this rendezvous was imminent. I asked the heavens to part for me, for the courage to answer the call with formidable grace. And I surrendered completely.

Within days, on a poverty-stricken street littered with homeless tents and unimaginable filth, he heard my voice as I asked a stranger about him. He rose up from behind barrels and piles of flat tires, garbage, sewage, debris, and street grease. We embraced, and my heart cracked open like a rushing river, blasting love like diamonds and shooting stars straight from my soul to his. We had a profoundly loving hour of pure joy and connection, and I broke open for weeks afterward.

He died two months later in a junkyard car on that street. His body wasn't discovered for seven weeks. The most brutal ending imaginable…delivering the most profound lessons of my life: Don't question the Great Mysteries of your beautiful life. Listen. Trust. Learn the pulse of your soul's secret language. And be prepared for your life to take you to unimagined destinies.

You Can Always Stay with Us

By Karla Joy Huber

What most people call guardian angels, Buddhists call *shoten zenjin*. The protective forces of the Universe aren't always otherworldly; they can manifest in the love and generosity of living, flesh-and-blood people in our lives.

Long before I became Buddhist and understood this concept, my dearest friends, Cristina and Housein, became my *shoten zenjin*. This was in 2008 when, after being jobless for several months during the recession, I ran out of money and had to move out of my apartment within the month.

"I've started over again so many times I've lost count," Housein told me. Thinking about all of his and Cristina's ups and downs – including growing up in South America, traversing countries and continents as students and Bahá'í pioneers, and moving almost every year while in Michigan – how they handled these situations was always an inspiration to me. In contrast, I tended to get bent out of shape and complain when the unexpected or inconvenient happened.

I realize now that this tendency of mine is exactly why my karma attracted Cristina and Housein to help me overcome my fears about not being able to take care of myself. They reminded me that this was a great opportunity to get rid of unnecessary extras and realign my priorities. And then I realized that it wouldn't even have to be nearly as difficult as I'd thought when Cristina said to me, "You can always stay with us." A few days later, I took them up on their offer.

One night, after filling my car with a load of things to donate, I stood in the parking lot of my complex and gazed up at the cloudless, star-studded sky. I felt a calm wash over me as I stood there in the cold, pondering those points of light, and I had an epiphany: nothing earth-shaking, but it finally occurred to me that *I* wasn't a failure – my *circumstances* had failed me. And the Universe, through the help of my best friends and their demonstration of the virtues of our faith's teachings, had given me new circumstances. Simple as that, really.

Just Hit Send

By Jody Vehr

At the age of 33, after years of dysfunction and abusive relationships, I hit rock bottom. At that time, I was divinely guided to a master's program in Spiritual Psychology at the University of Santa Monica. While there, I was inexplicably drawn to a man named Steve Hardison, a world-renowned life coach. The draw was daunting, given that calling him a coach is like calling The Beatles a garage band. He is extraordinary, and I had little to no self-esteem at the time. Regardless, I chose to be bold and ask for what I wanted. With a courageous leap of faith, I just hit "Send" on an email, and my life was forever changed.

Although I didn't know it at the time, there was a deeper level to what was transpiring. My soul was being called to my future husband, John, who happened to be a client of Steve's. Their work together at the time had been to consciously create the ideal romantic partnership for John. In synchrony, I was creating the ideal relationship through my work at USM.

Steve and I had a 25-minute, life-changing conversation. After the first three minutes (during which he politely declined my request for mentorship), I surprisingly found myself pouring my heart out about a promise of my heart that I knew I shared with another – I simply hadn't met him yet. Steve, struck by the beauty of my words, thought I was quoting scripture.

From our conversation, a light sparked and I birthed the poetic words now called "A Promise of the Heart," which later became my wedding vows. Through a series of Spirit-led events, "A Promise of the Heart" landed in John's world, where he immediately fell in love with me without ever seeing or talking to me. We were married one year later on 12.12.12. Our love is the greatest gift and blessing God ever could have given me.

My intention in sharing this with you is to encourage you to follow the call of your heart, even if it is faint or doesn't seem possible. I encourage you to have the courage to "Just Hit Send" in your life and watch miracles transpire.

A Whirl of Emotion

By Edna Harris

It reminded me of a scene from *Father Knows Best*. My mother, sisters, and brothers flanked his bedside and hovered over him, seemingly ready and willing to meet his every need as he waited for open-heart surgery. He looked helpless, almost insignificant, as he lay silent on his hospital bed with tears in his eyes – a vast departure from the monster that had molested me throughout my childhood and ultimately raped me at the age of 16.

I continued to watch the goings on as I stood in the hall and stared through a window into his room, aghast at the way they rallied around him. In my opinion, his only claim to fatherhood was that he'd sired us. *Have you all taken leave of your senses?* I screamed inwardly. *Have you forgotten what he did to us?*

The memories bombarded me and spirited me away on a roller-coaster ride of emotions. I thought I'd forgiven him for his cruelty, but as my pain spilled out from behind the confines of its iron gates, it brought with it a raging river of emotions.

The memories continued to claw at me, suffocating me. I was transported back in time to a bottomless abyss, choked by the darkness of the trauma. I was reliving the pain of a little girl's wounded soul and spirit – the pain of betrayal by someone who should have been a trusted caregiver. Words could not express it, tears could not relieve it, and the salve of human kindness could not heal it. It was a pain that no human being could minister to, a pain that brought me to the brink of despair. Over the years, I'd learned to push it into the farthest corner of my mind, covering it with a sheet of denial and a thick blanket of numbness, but now it was back, stronger than before.

I took a deep breath, squared my shoulders, stuffed the emotions as far down as they would go, and walked into the room with the intention of forgiving my tormentor. When you forgive, you heal.

The Unexpected Journey

By Melisa Archer

My dad had never asked me for anything before, so receiving a phone call from him requesting that my husband and I move six hours north into his building was surprising. My life was already in limbo, as I was on an unpaid management leave, recovering from injuries. I prayed about it and asked my husband, expecting him to say no, but he said yes!

Not sure what this new life had in store for us, we relocated. Six weeks later, my dad had a stroke. I flew with him to a hospital four hours away. The doctor told me that he was brain dead and wanted me to sign for his heart donation. Because I see energy, I knew that my dad's journey was not over. I demanded for them to bring him out of the coma. As they started the process, I screamed, "DAD! DAD!" As his blue eyes locked on mine, I shouted, "Relax, so they can take the tube out of your throat."

My dad was released four days later; however, he soon suffered a second stroke. He became unaware of himself or his actions due to medications. I took him back to the hospital, begging for help. This went on for four weeks. I was being pressured to place my dad in a nursing home, but I refused. Thank God I was living here! I took it upon myself to care for him and research the medications, making a chart to slowly wean him off of them. Eight days later, my dad snapped out of it. He was back! Within three weeks, he had made a 100% recovery.

Many months later, my dad told me of how he heard me talking in another room, demanding to let me be there when they brought him out of the coma. He had seen himself in the hospital bed. This upset me to think that if I had not challenged the original decision, my dad would have died. I am blessed to continue having him in our lives, completely recovered. I love you, Dad!

Finding Family When Life Shifts

By Lisa Miles Brady and Cynthia L. Ryals

The first time I visited her website, I knew I liked her energy. I just didn't want to reach out.

We were part of a group-coaching program and were encouraged to seek an accountability partner. Although I was drawn to Cynthia's energy, I convinced myself that partnering with the only person who looked like me was not an exercise in "growth."

A few days later, she posted a vulnerable update in the Facebook group that broke me open. This woman was going through hell! Yet no one responded.

I didn't want her to feel alone. I've been there. A stranger from Beirut, Lebanon, held my hand through the worst period of my life. And now, just maybe, I could pass on that gift.

But the gift was mine to receive. Since we've been accountability partners, I have come to know and love myself more deeply. I am braver. I've embodied fierce presence. I *have* grown. More importantly, I have found my soul sister.

***

Who would have guessed that I would find family in a Facebook post? I had just buried my mother. The day she died, I lost my home and most of my belongings. I was back in my hometown, in my mother's home. It was the Christmas season, and the house had flooded. I was alone.

I signed up for a coaching program with the intent of throwing myself into my business. Never mind that I had so much healing to do.

When Lisa offered to be my accountability partner, little did I know that she would become my family. She held space for me through the darkest moments of my life. We have spent hundreds of hours on the phone but have never met face to face. Yet she couldn't be more of a sister to me than if we had shared a womb.

Lisa stepped into my world at a time when I didn't care much about my existence, and she loved me back to life. She was a rock that held me steady when my life shifted, and I'll be forever grateful.

Marching Forth from Second to First

By Scott Fjelsted

I have taken second place so many times in my life that I have lost count. From state and national Olympic Weightlifting competitions, to softball tournaments, to being the second-best player in any given position on youth sports teams, to almost winning my age group in a 5K race (yep, I took second there, too), winning has always been elusive to me. I was even born second!

To some, all of these seconds might not seem so bad. But for me, it was agonizing being so close to first so many times. It felt like I had a gift coming to me that got taken away right before I got to open it.

My life shift began in the year 2000 when a personal-training client of mine approached me about taking on a yearlong health project at a large corporation. Little did I know that this decision would affect my life way beyond my career.

It turns out that in the sea of thousands that this building employs would be the diamond in the rough that would change my life forever. On a random Tuesday afternoon, eight years after I first set foot in this building, across a crowded room filled with dozens of cubicles, my eyes met my soulmate. It felt as if time stood still and I was seeing the ocean for the first time.

A few months later, on *March 4th*, I got up the nerve to *march forth* and introduce myself. The rest is history.

She became my wife in October of the same year and is my number-one fan. For the first time in my life, I felt that I took first place. It was as if I finally got to open the big Christmas gift I had wished for, then I turned around to find that the tree had a thousand more waiting for me. I continue to feel that way eight years later. Since she is my second wife, maybe second isn't so bad after all.

Culture Shock

By Meredith Fjelsted

At almost 40 years old, I had made a life for myself…or so I thought. Back then, I had no idea what a big plan God had for me.

I still had never been married or had children, and my parents had given up asking me if any of the men in my life might be "the one." A couple of years earlier, I'd come to the conclusion that maybe marriage was not in the cards for me, so I decided to be the best single person I could be: I worked two jobs, owned my own home and a rental property, and had a dog and a lot of friends. My life had a rhythm to it, and when I prayed, "God, please give me a life," I thought this was it.

Then I saw a man walk by me at work. Our eyes met, and my heart leapt. I instantly knew he was "the one." It took him three months to introduce himself. It was so awkward! It was as if our mouths didn't need words as our hearts communicated in their own language. I knew nothing about him except that my spirit soared. I had thought I was happy. I thought I was making a life for myself by going on mission trips and traveling the world. In fact, I went on my second mission trip that year, right after I met my soulmate. Little did I know, it would be my last for many years. Three months later, he proclaimed his love for me and I for him. He moved in, and we were married by the end of that year.

We had never dated. I knew almost nothing about him except that he was divorced with two small children. Out of all the countries I'd been to, this one, *marriage*, was the biggest culture shock I'd ever known. I had lived in Mexico. I'd traveled to Europe, Central America, South America, and across North America. But I'd never experienced the life of marriage and an instant family. God had indeed given me a life – one bigger and better than I had ever imagined!

Friendships

By Lupe Ramirez Peterkin

In honor of "The Big Five-Oh," I decided to throw myself a big birthday party. A grand illusion grew in my head with specifics for my momentous day. My budget allowed for catered food, and a new friend offered to DJ for free. It was all coming together. So I created my invitation list and invited my chums.

As the days passed, I reflected on good memories I had with the friends I had invited. The excitement grew, along with my anxiety for a perfect outcome. I already felt fidgety about my upcoming milestone; adding to my nerves was the impending first anniversary of my mother's death, which would fall one day before my party. Sadness washed over me while thinking that my father would be next.

Despite my unrest, I felt pretty good on the day of my party. I worked hard to get my house ship shape, decorated for my happy experience, and was glad that the day was finally here!

My guests included a true friend who I'd known for 25 years, her spouse, my lovely neighbor, four of my children, my grandson, my youngest sister, my husband, and our DJ friend and his wife. Although my notions of a huge shindig had been scaled back somewhat, I appreciated the company of those who made the scene, and it was a wonderful night of dancing and eating.

The next day was my actual birthday, and I woke up feeling melancholy. But then I was struck with a jolt of enlightenment about the people in my life – they become either playmates, social acquaintances, intimate friendships, or simply precious memories. As life changes occur, so do our priorities, creating ongoing relationships or remembrances, and either way is perfectly fine. Memories make me smile, as do present moments. While I accept the present as the most meaningful state of mind, I understand the value of gratitude for those who show up in my life and for those who don't. I treasure every day and will continue to do so until I rest in peace.

My Divine Delivery from China

By Donna Cantone

My biggest life shift began with a shocking call from my infertility doctor in November 1995, three days before my birthday. Everything had been a "go" until he ran one last test. I was now told that I had only a 4% chance of becoming pregnant with IVF.

This news shook me to my core. I was ready for IVF, and I wanted a baby! I was too young to be in perimenopause! I had already tackled chronic health issues; this unexpected development simply wasn't fair – and it certainly did *not* fit in with the life my husband and I had planned: get married, buy a home in one year, pay off the furniture, then have a baby. Do you know the saying, "You make plans, and God laughs"? Well, when my husband arrived home that night, I was not laughing – I was in tears. My husband said maybe it wasn't meant to be, but I was determined.

We met with adoption agencies and attorneys and learned that, as "older" parents, we may not be chosen. Tearfully, I shouted, "God, why is this happening? Can you and the angels help me?" I loved angels but had never before asked for their help. As soon as I did, though, I got an idea: *Let's adopt from China!* Immediately, I knew that this was God's plan.

That night, I found a paper in our driveway – one that I had never seen before and haven't seen since. I sat down to read and saw that the main article was about adopting children from China! Due to overpopulation, boys were kept and girls abandoned – and we wanted a girl! Shortly thereafter, we heard an agency being interviewed about overseas adoptions. My husband called, and there was a seminar that weekend. I told him to bring our checkbook in case we applied. He thought I was crazy, but I knew that my daughter was in China and I had to bring her home!

We completed the many requirements and, after a few delays, flew to China in January 1997. Our divine delivery was seven months old. Today, Chelsea is a college junior, and she's still the light of our lives. And, in addition to my beautiful daughter, I now have stronger faith than ever in divine guidance!

We Were Not Alone

By Marla David

Prior to sunset, sitting on the beach, I watched with pride as my daughter and her fiancé stood under the wedding canopy, beautifully adorned with fabric and flowers. They exchanged vows as waves came and went gently on the shore behind them. It was a destination wedding, and we were in Eden.

I felt a presence and looked beyond the wedding area to see a group of locals admiring the nuptials from afar. On the tree above them sat a bird. I'd seen that kind of bird often throughout this trip. Because my late father and I had this thing with birds, I looked it up on the internet. It was a white-throated magpie-jay in all its glory with the crest of feathers on the head, common in the Guanacaste, Costa Rica region. It made its presence known with loud, intrusive calls.

The wind picked up, and I secured my flowers. Looking up, I saw my daughter smiling as her veil had blown off. I admired her beauty, her petite figure, and her confidence. My other two daughters stood to her left, completing the magical picture. It was a blessed moment of grace.

I smiled with contentment, then looked at the landscape beyond. The setting sun colored the sky in pink, yellow, and orange hues. My senses heightened – the sounds of the ceremony; the surrounding nature; the smell of the ocean; the taste of salty air; the feel of sand around my feet; the wind; the beautiful, serene setting; and the love tugging at my heart as my little girl, now a beautiful woman, was starting a new chapter in her life. I looked back to the bird on the branch. Then, the glass was shattered and they were officially married.

As pictures were taken, the waves rolled in and out, like the ebb and flow of life. The family was complete, including those who had passed. I could sense it so much it was palpable. I collected shells to place on my dad's grave back home, but I knew he was there…as he made his presence known. We were not alone.

Sacrificial Love

By Julie Jones

I grew up in a family of three girls and four boys. My oldest sister has always been my protector, my guardian, and my teacher. Because she was older, she was almost like a mother to me. My sisters and I shared a large room containing two beds and a cot. Since I was the youngest, I slept on the cot.

One of my favorite things in our room was my oldest sister's beautiful doll, which I admired so much. This doll was magnificent; standing up on her feet, she was about eight inches tall and had blond hair that was kept neatly under a Dutch bonnet. The cap was made of white cotton lace fabric, and the ends flapped up – it reminded me of a nurse's cap. Her shoes were wooden *klompen*, and her dress was a silky, blue material with a white undercoat and jacket. The dress stood out as if she were in a constant whirl. Her lips were painted red, and I thought she was the most beautiful doll that ever could exist.

One day, shortly after my birthday, I was sitting on my oldest sister's bed talking. I had wanted a doll for my birthday but did not receive one. Suddenly, my sister gave me her doll – for me to have, hold, and keep. It would be mine – just mine. She handed me the doll and said, "Here, it's yours."

I will never forget that moment and the appreciation I felt for my sister. I kept and cherished that doll for many years. As an adult, during a move from Chicago to North Carolina, the doll was taken out of a moving box and stored for transit – my heart was broken.

Thinking about this loving gift from my sister, I'm reminded of a quote from Pam Brown: "An older sister is a friend and defender – a listener, conspirator, a counsellor, and a sharer of delights. And sorrows too." My sister showed me deep love, generosity, and loving kindness. While I often think about my treasured doll, what I will always treasure even more is the knowledge and feeling that my sister cared deeply for me. So I write this in honor of my sister – you have impacted my life in more ways than you will ever imagine. Thank you.

All Things French

By L. A. Reeves

I remember it like yesterday. I had fallen truly and deeply in love with a Frenchman. With all my might I tried to win his heart, but alas, I could not. My heart took a real beating when we went our separate ways.

As fate would have it, a year later I found myself on a layover in the Charles de Gaulle Airport in Paris. As I sat there, my senses were assaulted by all things French (including a Champagne bar and *La Maison du Chocolat*), which brought back more memories than I could emotionally handle. I started to cry, and as hard as I tried to contain myself, the tears soon turned into sobs that rocked and cradled me right there in Terminal E34.

After 15 minutes in the throes of this heart-ripping hysteria, I found myself floating among the rafters of the airport, looking down on this pitiful, broken-hearted creature. In an instant, something mystical happened and I became a beautiful story. Then, an even more beautiful thought slowly drifted down from those fascinating French airport rafters and gently fell into my heart. It was as if the love I had hoped for whispered to me, "How many American women get to sit in Paris sobbing over a love affair gone wrong – and with a Frenchman no less?"

I raised my eyes to make sure someone had not noticed my breakdown and, in their compassion, begun to console me. But no one was there. It was just me and my most loyal companion from the last year: sadness.

As the last tears drizzled down my red and swollen cheeks, I heard my very own voice clearly say, "Oh my!" As those words wrapped around me, I actually felt *blessed*! Blessed for the short-lived love and even for the pain that lingered much longer. And on a much deeper level, I realized then that sometimes it only takes an instant and a bit of grace to shift your perspective and turn your heart around.

The Difference a Mentor Can Make

By Gabrielle Taylor

I remember sitting with my friend Natalia on the park bench in front of the little waterfall. We'd decided to paint our impressions of the water as it cascaded over the rocks below. The sound of the falls put me into a trance of sorts, and I painted: purples, blues, yellows, and pinks. It was a magical moment, followed by tea back at her house – a stark contrast to the deadlines, harsh neon lights, impersonal classrooms, and my frazzled life as a 20-year-old student.

We'd recently become good friends. Or rather, she had befriended me, an art student, adrift and searching for my place in the world. We met on a dark November evening at a lecture on the biblical prophets. Natalia, a 60-year-old Russian immigrant, struck up a conversation with me in her singsong voice. Within a few moments, I received a heartfelt invitation to her "Saturday evening dinner," a weekly get-together of lively and eccentric artists.

A few days later, I walked into her kitchen, where the smell of home cooking and the sound of laughter filled the air. Her imaginative spirit was visible everywhere: colourful sketches covering the living room walls, books and papers stacked up beside an old typewriter, surrounded by African violets.

Across the chasm of four decades between us, I felt a sense of authentic connection. Natalia seemed totally alive, and she helped light a flame within me that had been dimmed. On many an afternoon, she lent me an ear and shared from her wealth of experience. Under her influence, my floundering, anxious self found the courage to pursue my studies and passions and to reach for my highest potential.

Decades have passed, and Natalia is no longer with us, but she's no less an inspiration to me. Her warm demeanor, blue eyes, and slightly disheveled fair hair all spoke of someone who had lived, created, and loved. Today, when I get frazzled or discouraged, I remember her generous spirit, and it awakens my desire to carry and pass on the flame of that same generosity and presence.

A Match Made in Heaven

By Rose Kaplan

This is the story of the night I met my husband, Steve – a match that almost didn't happen were it not for some help from above.

I had a good job, a nice apartment, and dear friends. The only thing missing was that special someone.

On December 23, my girlfriend and I decided to go out and celebrate the holiday season. The night was fun and festive with everyone in the holiday spirit. After I was there a few hours, things were winding down and I was getting ready to leave.

Steve was there for a work-related holiday dinner and was also saying his goodbyes. Our angels must have been in a panic mode – they had gotten us both to come here, but we still hadn't noticed each other. The angels quickly went to work.

In the process of saying my goodbyes, I suddenly felt a tug on the strap of my shoulder bag. I turned my head to see what had happened. As Steve was passing by, the very thin strap of my shoulder bag had gotten caught on a button of his vest. We both laughed about it as we got untangled. We chatted briefly and he asked me to dance.

On the dance floor, I thought: *Handsome, great build, a good dancer (my favorite pastime), and a nice smile – he's got potential!*

Needless to say, neither of us left right away, as the sparks were flying. The angels must have been cheering: "It worked! Our job is done!"

Thirty-four years later, we still laugh about how we met and are in awe of the events and the life shift that transpired that night.

P.S. We still have the vest and shoulder bag!

Thank You, Abraham

By Janice Littler

We can find hope, inspiration, and gratitude in the most unlikely places.

In tracing my family history, spanning many decades, I have slowly uncovered details about an ancestor. Abraham Freidman, my great-great-uncle, began his working life in the 1840s as a poor farmer in the Ukraine, where he was unable to pay the levied taxes. Something stirred within his heart, soul, and mind that motivated him to leave his family and take a chance to start a new life somewhere else. He travelled to England and then to Australia, looking for opportunities and freedom.

Over the years, he built businesses, went bankrupt twice, and suffered great tragedy (his only children, two daughters, died in infancy). Abraham had the ability to become successful in business and bounce back after each defeat. Over a number of years, he paid for other family members' passages and financially supported them upon their arrival in Australia, including my great-grandfather Max and his family.

Abraham was a self-made man who had tremendous courage and guts when the going got tough. It would have been amazing to have the opportunity to sit with him and discuss his ideas on running businesses and what made him tick. Unfortunately, he died long before I was born.

Abraham has shown me by example what is possible when you have the dream, desire, and courage to seek something better. This has created a life shift in my mind, heart, and soul. With determination and grit, I realize that I can have whatever I want in life as long as I set my mind to it and, more importantly, act upon my thoughts. Just thinking about it is not good enough. When you have the desire, drive, and conviction, you can do anything. Using motivation and momentum, you can move towards achieving your goals.

Thank you, Abraham, for your example as a light to show me how taking a path and using determination can bring about internal behavioural changes. I am forever grateful for what I continue to learn from and about you through historical documents.

An Unexpected Saviour

By Marie Spencer-Rowland

I had been in a bad relationship for four years. It had gotten so bad that my health started to deteriorate. I was worn out and lost, and had no idea how to get *me* back.

I was constantly arguing with myself because I refused to believe that this was the life I had chosen for myself. I had watched my mum go through similar relationships, and I didn't want to relive her life.

I *knew* in the core of my being that I had to get out of this relationship. I believed that I deserved more and I could absolutely have better if I was prepared to jump and let the net catch me, but I was scared and honestly didn't know how I would survive on my own financially. I felt so trapped and worthless. I felt like I had nothing.

I sent out another prayer to the Universe, pleading for help. Two hours later, I was greeted by an advert for a credit card. I'm not sure why I applied, apart from a gut feeling to do so, but that one small advert gave me the courage to pack up my belongings, call a friend, and move out.

As soon as I left, everything started to fall into place. My health improved, literally overnight. I dropped two dress sizes over the space of a few weeks, simply because I was no longer stressed, and life became fun again. To top it all off, within three months, I met the man who I would eventually marry.

When I look back on it now, I realise that the Universe gave me a lot of chances to leave, but I was too afraid to let go...until I saw that credit-card advert. It seems like a strange thing to praise and give thanks for, I admit, but that's what finally made the difference for me.

In addition to all the external improvements, I learned a valuable lesson: Always trust your gut and your heart, because your life can turn around in an instant if you're brave enough to do what your heart is telling you.

Unveiling My Voice, Unleashing a Miracle

By Amy Gage

I am grateful that my mom and I are close these days, but we haven't always been that way. We had a lot of emotional walls built up over the years, and we didn't know how to be close to each other. Without going into the whole story of our relationship, I want to share the experience leading up to the part when we started getting close.

Singing was my constant growing up, and becoming a professional singer was my childhood dream. Along the way, I started doubting my abilities and my dreams. I continued singing privately to improve my voice, but mostly, singing was a sacred ritual for me. I desired to sing for others, but I was terrified to. I didn't think I was good enough and thought I may never be.

After about 15 years, I decided to share a recording of myself singing and playing piano for a Facebook challenge in a creative group. That recording was my musical diary, unedited, imperfect, and raw. Being heard and embraced in that vulnerability helped set me free, and it gave me more courage to share my singing with others.

My mom was the next person to hear me sing. One day while visiting her, I felt compelled to share the recording with her. I didn't expect her to say much about it. But to my shock, she started crying and hugged me afterward. Emotional walls came crumbling down, and I felt like that was when we truly connected for the first time. That was a miracle to me.

Since then, we've grown a lot closer. The shift I felt that day has continued to shape our relationship and the course of my life.

I always thought I needed to be great before I shared my voice. I discovered that wasn't true. When I unveiled my most honest and vulnerable self through singing, I opened the door to connecting more deeply with others and tearing down the toughest of walls. Ever since then, sharing my voice has been healing my life at a fundamental level.

A Momma Was Born

By Marla David

"Hello? The baby was born prematurely. It's a girl!" I put the phone down. I was thrilled, but after almost eight years, two failed adoptions, and one miscarriage, I didn't want to get my hopes up. It would be another two weeks until she gained weight. The day arrived, and at the hospital the nurse was given the things we brought for her to wear home, as we in turn were given a parcel the birth mother had left for us and the daughter she would not raise.

Entering the nursery, the first thing I remember seeing was the sun through the window, igniting the hair of a wee babe into the most incredible strawberry-blonde pile. In my arms for the first time, the tears flowed freely. It was hard to believe; it felt surreal.

She wouldn't be ours until the 21-day period was over. That meant we would hold her, care for her, and love her for an entire week while the birth mother could still change her mind. Talk about walking on eggshells! It was a hard week, but with hope and prayer, the victory call came. Oh, what a feeling! Weeks went by with feedings, appointments, and visits from family and friends to celebrate our daughter with us.

At this time, I developed a nervous stomach, which I at first attributed to the hormonal roller coaster I'd been through. However, an ultrasound revealed that I was pregnant, and it went full term. I believe that the love saturating my very being somehow made it possible. In just seven months after adopting, I held another baby girl, strong and healthy, with a full head of black, spiked hair. Ah, the tears…the miracle of life.

Time flew, as it always does. Two years later, I gave birth to another daughter – the biggest baby of all, at 7 lbs. 8 oz., also with black spiked hair. I was blessed with abundance and the fulfillment of my dream, which shifted my entire existence. A momma was born!

Love at First Sight

By Melisa Archer

I was 19 years old, moping around the house, when my dad announced, "I found the perfect guy for you." Dad jokingly said that this guy was just boring enough for me, as I did not smoke or party. Hours later, I was dragged out to my dad's pool league. At first sight of this mystery man, I had butterflies in my stomach and tingles up my arm. We shared a longer-than-normal stare. A part of me knew that my life would never be the same.

After pool league finished, this hunk of a man asked me if I would like to go to karaoke. I said, "Sure!" That night we sang "I Got You Babe." After sharing some laughs and a snuggly dance, he drove me home, where we shared our first kiss in the doorway of my childhood house.

The next day, he stopped by my house and brought back my gloves, which I had "forgotten" (wink, wink) in his car. He also surprised me with flowers.

We became inseparable. We would stay up talking till early hours and spend endless hours snuggling. It was amazing how drastically my life changed forever from just one prolonged glance.

I have always been very thankful that my dad insisted I go and meet his teammate. My dad was right in saying he had picked the perfect guy for me. Three years later, Dad walked me down the aisle to marry my best friend.

The days flew into weeks, then months into years. It's hard to believe we met 20 years ago.

I asked my husband if he knew that he loved me at first sight. He said that he was attracted to me and that there was a pull, and that he didn't want to let me go. And it's still true today – 20 years later, we're still like magnets, not to be separated.

A Little Help from My Friends

By Judith Clements

"What?" I whispered.

Patiently, my grandmother repeated, "The family wants to give you a two-week vacation in England. Your grandfather's sister, Inga, and her husband, Jehl, invited you to be their guest. All the travel arrangements are made."

"Oh, okay," I replied. I should have been thinking, *I am 19 years old, a mother, divorced, AND I should be questioning my family's authority.* Yet I felt that this trip, an unexpected surprise, was "right." At the deepest levels, I knew that my mother would continue to nurture my two very young children in my absence.

In June 1969, my life reflected the enormous changes occurring in America. The war in Vietnam, the women's movement, and The Beatles helped mold my personality. I possessed intellect without insight, empathy without empowerment. I was painfully conflicted and desperately seeking answers.

As I flew over the Atlantic, my great-aunt and -uncle were preparing to meet me. Informal therapy with Jehl, a retired psychologist, was certainly part of the family's unspoken agenda.

Venturing out from the cozy cottage in tiny Tunbridge Wells, Uncle Jehl and I experienced England's historic sites together. At night in the den, he introduced me to Carl Jung, Zen Buddhism, and the *I Ching*. I humbly absorbed the wisdom of the ancients. Gratefully, I relished his sharing and gifts, returning home with classic spiritual texts and a 15-inch antique wooden Buddha.

That precious summer, the *I Ching* counseled me, "Work on what has been spoiled," and affirmed, "It furthers one to cross the great water." Thereafter, my children and I thrived, adapting quickly to ever-changing conditions. In 1972, I embarked on a 39-year teaching career with underprivileged kindergarten students, which I found richly rewarding. This grandmother, writer, and seeker realizes that my great-uncle generated my mind-blowing, lifelong shift. Shifting from limiting personal perspectives to a multi-cultural perspective yielded abundant nutritious fruit for me.

Mixed Blessings

By Elyse Jarard

I sat in my car, crying – no, *screaming* – into the empty space. "Why did you give me children, God? I am not cut out for this!!!" I was at my wits' end with my oldest daughter. I don't even remember what caused me to feel such an intense level of frustration, but there I was, bawling like a two-year-old. I never knew that being a mother would be so hard on my ego. Parenthood is one of the most natural experiences in the world, so why was this totally out of my grasp?

My daughter and I had a tenuous relationship; someone was always vying for power. Why couldn't she just listen to me? She wasn't bad; she was just difficult. She just refused to do what others (namely me) wanted her to do. It amazed me when, at parent-teacher conferences, her teachers would say that she was so sweet. My husband and I looked at them, perplexed, and asked, "Are you sure you're talking about *our* daughter?"

Then, in an instant, everything changed for me. I found myself in Las Vegas for a mastermind meeting with a woman who specializes in helping female "soulpreneurs." During a roundtable discussion, a lightbulb went off in my mind that forever shifted my life, my soul, and my relationships.

I realized that for her entire life, my daughter has been teaching me the most important lesson of all: *unconditional love*. In her "difficult" moments, she was demanding that we love her as she is. She isn't here to fit our mold. She is who she is, and that is exactly perfect, whether we like it or not.

We learn at an early age that to be worthy of being loved, we need to please other people and be who they want us to be so they will like us. It took me 48 years and being a mom of "that kid" to find out that I am worthy just being me.

Saying Yes to Unconditional Love

By Emma Porter

After my 18-year marriage ended, I never intended to enter another relationship. I'd been living in Arizona for a little over five years, and family and friends imagined that my two sons and I might return to my birth country of England. Instead, I decided to relocate to Australia for a step outside my comfort zone and a fresh start. But my plans changed when, within 24 hours of setting an intention that I experience more laughter and playfulness, I met my loving, playful Earth Angel!

I noticed a man outside a café; he had been lost, needing directions, and now he was thirsty. We decided to have breakfast together. Our similarities flowed from us as we chatted. I was drawn to his happy, kind, funny, respectful, and uplifting energy. His eyes to me held a universe. The more we spoke or listened to one another, the more I appreciated what was extraordinary. Our magical connection deepened with our first kiss.

Having trained in cultivating my own inner peace and self-awareness, I recognized that this relationship would have a solid foundation of co-creation and respect. I observed him tenderly caring for wildlife and his dogs, and joyfully singing with my children. His soul gently yet brilliantly shone like the moon. He was present, thoughtful, and mindful of the moment, and we recognized that we both deserved this level of love.

I love inspirational signs from my experience of the Divine, and we had several: We had met on 3/3, he lived at house number 333, and I was joyously accepted by his sweet dog named Angel.

Without a doubt, the effortless connection of mind, body, and spirit I felt with this man shifted me into realizing that my calling was to say yes to unconditional love. I decided to stay in Arizona, where I'm now enjoying a healthy, loving relationship.

A Transformation from Grief to Peace

By Kim Marks

"This is Kim. How can I help you?" I cheerily answered the phone.

"It's Bessie."

Silence.

"Bessie?" I turned icy cold. My thinking and breathing stopped. Somehow, I managed to talk rationally. I had known this call would come, but no matter how I prepared, I wasn't ready.

I tend to adopt everything – cats, dogs, birds, you name it – and I planned to adopt Bessie as well. She would be my daughter. I would show her unconditional love. Love would heal everything.

But Bessie was unable to accept my love. In fact, love made her want to destroy. Destruction was what she did. The Destroyer in her wanted me gone. It took me years to get that message.

Bessie left our family, hoping to find the perfect family. After living in several institutions, she did find another family.

The separation took a tremendous toll on me. I fell apart. Grief racked me. I blamed everyone. I especially blamed myself. Slowly, I worked at healing my wounds and forgiving myself. I experienced a lot of personal growth. Eventually, I started to feel alive again.

Grief is not linear. It jumps, spirals, and appears when least expected. Bessie's call jolted me. I knew I had to do something before it happened again.

That's when I realized I was still playing the archetypal roles of Victim and Mother. Although I wanted a reciprocal relationship, I felt that, as a Mother, I was responsible for Bessie's emotional state. After the call, it occurred to me that while I had blamed everyone else, I had never blamed Bessie. As I realized this, I allowed myself to feel anger toward her for her lack of personal responsibility. By not allowing myself to express my feelings, I had given Bessie my personal power. By forgiving Bessie and myself, I immediately felt a new sense of strength and freedom. When the next call comes – and it will – I will use the archetypal energy of a Teacher and let go of the Mother. I have called back my power, released fear, and stepped into more joy and peace.

Love Awakening

By Jenny McKaig

"I want to be held."

My roommate patted the spot next to him on the couch, and I walked without hesitation from where I was slumped on the loveseat. I sat down next to him and leaned in.

I'd been doing a lot of crying then, but I'd also been feeling elated. I'd left a longtime partner, telling him I wanted to "fix myself" then come back to him. I quickly learned that I didn't need fixing; I was whole all along.

I don't think I cried that night when I leaned into my roommate's body. He had been respectful of my space. I had an interest in him, and he in me, but we had been clear in communicating: he was my roommate. He had a room for rent in his house and could drive me to work. The space I needed superseded interest, and besides, I was returning to my longtime partner.

That night though, with five words spoken and the way he patted the couch and the naturalness with which I walked to him and melted my head onto his shoulder – that was the night everything changed.

We fell asleep. The only way I can describe it is to say that everything tingled. I'm not talking sexually; we literally fell asleep, and we melted into one another.

My body tingled. It's what I know now as the telomeres of the body, a cellular activation, an awakening. It was the most beautiful feeling, as though everything dissipated. My fears, sorrow, doubts…gone, disappeared, vanished.

That cellular activation, that being held in the arms of a man who was radiating love, and the chance I took in listening to my heart and asking clearly for what I wanted are what brought me to the man who is now my husband and the father of our daughter.

When we woke up, we both knew. Everything was different.

I told my longtime partner that we wouldn't be getting back together. I couldn't. I spared him the why; in my heart, I knew. There was no going back; my heart had awakened. I knew a new love.

Sucks to Be You!

By Robin OK

I will never forget the chill of that semi-sunny January afternoon in the parking lot or the terrible truth of those words that fell out of my mouth. From my driver's seat, I waved at my gorgeous 14-year-old daughter. She gave me one of those "don't embarrass me by letting people know you're my mom" looks as she and her girlfriend approached. Before she got in, she was already telling me the latest drama at her dad's house: "…and can you believe he is going to take away my music and my makeup and – really, Mom – I didn't DO anything!"

"Sucks to be you," were the words I carelessly tossed back. At the time, I had no idea. There and then, I just knew that she was a spirited, rebellious teen and trusted that her father, with whom I was still figuring out "shared parenting," had her best interest at heart. I did not know that this afternoon's dialogue would be the beginning of a long and painful battle, a fight not only between father and daughter but also between father and mother. Nor did I know that it would mark the beginning of my own personal revolution.

Over her remaining high school years, I bore witness as he sent our highly sensitive Leo girl through one emotional hoop after another. I picked her up when he sent the police after her. I hired attorneys to defend her. I sent her to live with a friend in another state to shield her from our inability to share parenting.

My mama-heart broke again and again as I saw the shining soul of my strong, brave girl rally to be seen, known, and loved for who she was. Yet it was in this disgrace that I was finally able to comprehend the pattern in which I, too, had been ensnared. He treated her as he had treated me. I released myself from trenches of guilt, shame, and self-blame to a higher road of self-love and acceptance. Years later, I champion us both as, together, we declare our independence.

The Answer to My Prayers

By Netta de Beer

A few years ago, I was in a dark place where I could hardly muster up a smile. I felt I had no purpose, motivation, or joy. I prayed for a blessing to lift me up, but my prayers seemed to go unheard.

During that time, a friend of mine, a principal at an underprivileged nursery, asked me to help her. She wanted me to teach a group of mothers how to cook in order to provide for their families. I was shocked because I was not the best cook, but my friend believed I could make a difference. In a very loving but firm way, she let me know I needed to do this. So, with a heavy heart, I agreed to help, not seeing this as the blessing I'd been praying for.

I started the following week with a group of four mothers. As I expected, it did not go well. I went home crying my eyes out, determined never to go back. This thought was still in my mind when I heard my cell phone ring. My friend was on the line, telling me that we'd be able to bake at the church across the road, which had a better kitchen. I decided to give it one more chance.

The next week, I went back well prepared, organized, and determined to have a better experience. When I arrived at the church, I was greeted by a group of 12 mothers. Not expecting such a big turnout, I was in shock…but ready for my big challenge. *So*, I figured, *what's easier to make than coconut ice? Even I can make that!*

When the mothers saw the end result of their labour, they were thrilled! I also showed them how to package their food and create labels with their names on it. That day, a family was born. We laughed together, cried together, and prayed together. Regardless of our ages, backgrounds, or religions, we were one.

From there, I recruited as many ladies as I could find. We continue to bake, pack, and sell what we make. The women gain a skill and an income, and I gain the joy of seeing the light in their eyes and their tears of joy. I feel humbled, worthy, and needed once again. These women have given me back my spirit, my joy, and my love of life. They truly have been the answer to my prayers.

Unearthing Joy

By Shari Sorbo

I've heard it said that we are as sick as our secrets. I wasn't quite sure how that applied to me until recently when I experienced the death of a dear friend.

I experienced such deep grief about this person's death and couldn't seem to shake it. I allowed all the emotions to run through me, all the while thinking that there would be a lifting of the cloud of grief as time passed.

I made an appointment with my naturopath and spoke to him about this grief. It was there that, through his work of acupuncture and other techniques, I began to release my friend to the great unknown. Yet I still seemed to be holding on to something.

While speaking about this to my dearest friend, a secret came out about my relationship to my departed friend. What I found was that to be able to speak about this secret to my trusted confidant freed me from an enormous burden I had carried for several years. To top it off, I didn't know I had carried this secret and really didn't even know that it was a secret! A wave of grace came over me as I shared about my relationship with this person. From having a listening partner be present while I spoke my story, compassion and love began to change the direction of my life.

I had not known the shame and guilt I had been holding on to, thus developing an armor of mistrust that went before me in everything I had undertaken.

Since that day of discovery, there has been a lightening and enlightening of my soul. The armor of mistrust dropped away, replaced by compassion and forgiveness. Unearthing that secret buried deep in the shadows of my consciousness shed light and joy on the relationship I had with my friend, and from there I was able to send him on his way to the great beyond.

I've Got You

By Brenda Reiss

I didn't realize the depth to which I hadn't trusted anyone – not even God! I had experienced some pretty traumatic things in my life – abandonment, abuse, rejection from my father, failed relationships – and had built up a pretty good defense mechanism of operating from my head and not my heart. It was safer that way. I prided myself on all that I could do and how strong I thought I was.

Until I wasn't.

Eventually, I experienced something that overcame all of my defenses. It was bigger than me. It simply hurt too much. It was a divorce.

I had been divorced before, but it was nothing like this. I had become addicted to this person, which is co-dependence on steroids. I had given everything to him – all of me – and now I found myself in a run-down apartment with not a lot of anything, on the floor, holding my belly, sobbing deep, gut-wrenching sobs.

I didn't know where else to turn, so I cried out, "God, if you are truly there, take me now or hold my heart because I can't do this anymore!"

I was kind of hoping that he'd hear the "take me" part because I was so tired and part of me simply wanted to give up. Instead, what I felt were these arms wrap around me from behind, holding me in the most loving embrace I'd ever felt before, and I heard the words, "I've got you."

The experience of feeling that divine intervention still brings tears to my eyes each time I think about it, even as I write about it here. It was the first time in years that I felt my body relax and my broken heart open just enough to allow those words to enter the space I had been protecting since I was five years old. That night, I started my intentional spiritual journey, an amazing experience that has led me to my calling, a new love, and my *truest* love: me.

The Door Knocker

By Heather Wiest

Something seemed a bit strange. As my father and I walked up the dimly lit sidewalk, the brass door knocker was covered with white paper, a letter in my mother's handwriting stating that we did not live there anymore. Confusion flooded my 14-year-old body as my dad and I entered a neighbor's house to receive the full story. While I had been away on summer vacation, my mother and stepfather reached the pinnacle in their domestic-violence history. In an act that was later determined self-defense, my mother had stabbed my stepfather in the heart with a kitchen knife. He'd been air transported to the hospital, near death, and my mother was arrested and placed in jail for a week.

The next few months were a new season for my mom and me. We rented an apartment, I began high school, and she attempted sobriety and employment as a single parent. Within a year, my mom hit rock bottom in her addiction and found herself in another abusive relationship. At the age of 15, with the support of my father and dear friends, I left home and began life as an independent teen.

Tough love encouraged me to establish safer boundaries. I created a space free from substance abuse, instability, control, and violence – an environment where emotions were openly expressed and communication was clear, a setting of hope and opportunity. I began the long journey to healing and wholeness.

God supernaturally strengthened and comforted me during this time, speaking to me: "Keep on knocking, and the door will be opened to you." I chose to knock on a different door than in the past. The Divine gave me an undeniable purpose to help others as I pursued an education and career in social work. This path was confirmed by my life verse (2 Corinthians 1:4, NLT): "He comforts us in all our troubles so that we can comfort others. When they are troubled, we will be able to give them the same comfort God has given us."

Not all doors open upon knocking, but those destined to unlock are certainly divine life shifters.

Regaining Our Special Love

By Natasha Botkin

For years, I was haunted by a mistake that I made in my love relationship. Try as I might to alter the darkness of my "monstrous" past, my focus inevitably returned to my old sabotaging story, which inevitably led me to a misguided freak-out.

My thoughts about my past were so muddled that I was unaware that *I* was the one who sent *him* away. In spite of the break-up, we stayed close to one another. We were each given an opportunity to move away from the area, yet neither of us left. And we were each given an opportunity to begin another relationship, yet we both remained single. We each had the chance to pull away from the other, yet we both reached out to one another.

One day, he reached out to me during his time of need, and I helped him regain his strength and abilities. When a crisis erupted in my life, he texted with me until he knew I was asleep. And when I thought I would have to spend my first Christmas alone, we connected in a moment of unconditional love (an experience I wrote about in the story "When Love Knocks," which appears in *365 Moments of Grace*.)

After that connection, however, months of quietness passed. Still, my heart pleaded with me to not give up: *Be patient, dear one. Do not give up; many give up just before the miracle begins.*

Then, just as I was printing out the story "When Love Knocks," he sent me a text. With my happy heart leading the way, I quickly accepted his invitation to reconnect.

We reunited as two friends who still cared very much about one another. Very quickly, however, we resumed the dance of *us* – our special love that cannot be defined or explained; it just is. Following our admissions of undying love, we began writing the next chapter of our special love relationship.

The time we spend together zips by at an alarming speed. We explore each other's souls, darkness, light, and the differences between who we used to be and how we have grown. We know that we are each other's love, and yet we are able to fall in love all over again.

Connection

By Victoria McGee

I was nervous as I waited for the school principal. I wasn't in trouble; I was a new teacher anxiously awaiting the results of my first official classroom observation.

The principal came in, smiling warmly, and started off by saying she had a story for me. One of the freshmen in my Beginning Drama class had been ditching all her classes except mine. She came to school every day, but would hide, walk around, or go to a hangout off campus instead of going to class. I thought, *Well, of course, Drama is a fun class. She just wants to have fun.*

The principal went on to tell me she had called the student in to discipline her for the ditching. She asked her why she never ditched my class. The girl told her, "She's the only teacher who says she misses me when I'm absent."

I was floored. I tried to always tell my students I missed them when they were absent, but I didn't realize the impact it could have. The principal went on to share that this particular student had a terrible home life, bordering on neglect, with very few adults who cared about her comings and goings. "Welcome back. I missed you yesterday" meant more to her than I could imagine.

This taught me a valuable lesson as a young teacher and shifted my focus in education. It taught me that connections are so much more important than content. As I grew in my profession, I saw countless examples of this. Students need to feel that the teacher cares about them before they can care about learning. I saw this truth carried through from kindergarten through 12th grade.

I feel this truth in every aspect of life now. The little connections we make every day can make a huge difference to others. My heart connection to others is more important than the content of what I do or say. And my soul connection to God is more important than the content of my beliefs.

Do I Stay or Go?

By Lynn Spiro

It was a warm, sunny day in late September, and the heat of Indian summer baked through the front door of my home. As I touched the knob to open the door, I felt a deep warmth emanate through it and sensed that something was about to happen. Little did I know that this brief moment was actually a premonition of a profound moment of clarity that would change my world forever.

At the time, my husband and I were having one of our many arguments. Our marriage had been in decline over the last five years, and communication had become quite sparse, often ending in some kind of disagreement. We were at a point where we both knew our marriage was beyond repair, yet we felt unable to break away after 30 years together. We lived in the same house, on different levels, and were being quite careful not to be in the same room at the same time. It was a sad way to live; however, it was the only way we knew how to cope.

The extreme warmth of the living room that day prompted me to open the front door. As I turned the knob and looked back at my husband, I felt a warm light descend around my body, cocooning me in a bubble where I felt suspended in time. This surrounding light was so bright I could see particles of dust floating through its rays as I squinted to see through it.

It was at the precise moment of turning the knob and looking back that I heard the slowly enunciated words from my husband, "If you don't like it, then YOU leave," followed by a gentle whisper across the air: *It IS time for you to go.*

In the bright light of the bubble and a moment suspended in time, what I needed to do suddenly became crystal clear. My entire life shifted during that profound moment of clarity. I knew that, unequivocally, it *was* time to leave and begin a new life on my own.

Flying with My Flock

By Sharon Rothstein

I experienced a pivotal life shift when a long-standing friendship dissolved unexpectedly. I turned within and obsessed to the point of major discomfort with no relief. I spoke with others regarding my need to be right, not truly understanding the real issue at hand.

I am a student of energy and vibration, yet I could not sort out the seemingly absurd behavior of another until I looked up at the synchronization of birds in a wondrous pattern of flight and thought to myself, *I get it now; I can let this situation go with greater understanding and compassion.*

From my bird's-eye perspective, humans are not so different from a pack of birds that flock together vibrationally. We energetically fly with others in our lives as do birds of a feather. I am the leader of my own flock and attract those of a similar vibration who support me and feel good. We draw in what we have become, in a state of ever-changing expansion.

Over time, formations may change, yet my inner being and I are continually at the leadership position. I am more like-minded with those who create my core pack, some of whom may remain for an entire lifetime. That is the beauty of unconditional friends. We are mostly in sync, in rhythm, in tight formation; we complement each other's lives. Conditional friends can change and may fly farther out of range.

I am no longer challenged by the behavior of others. If we are no longer of similar vibration, I know that we served each other for a time and all is good. It is not always possible to understand the workings of another's mind. What old memories have they stored that are slowing them down? Who am I to judge? Not everyone is meant to thrive at the same pace. It is not my issue.

I now have my own existing core flock. Occasionally, I allow new birds to fly in and join my force. I welcome the changes to this adventurous flight. Higher energy to fly with keeps life exciting and perpetuates motion and joy!

Love = Freedom

By Claire Chew

How much do I love myself? Why did I come? What am I doing here? Questions looped in my monkey mind as I flew from Los Angeles to San Francisco last week to see my father. A month had passed since I called 911 as my father had fallen and could not get up. I felt helpless, separated by hundreds of miles and relying on police dispatch for updates. How many times had I felt helpless growing up? Being scolded for not being "Chinese" enough. Punished for being bold and spirited as a child.

Saving face and honoring family lineage are very important to my father. The man in the family has the last word. My father learned from his father. Even when he was wrong, he was right. I've never met my grandfather, the oppressive patriarch who gave away my aunt because he did not want another girl, but I witnessed patterns continuing in my generation. Being a woman meant you did not have a voice, you were not heard. When it became too much to bear, my mother took her own life.

I made a silent vow to myself right then and there to stop being a victim to my past, to my old feelings of being judged and shamed. I realized that, in any situation, I had a choice over my interpretation of it. When I stopped giving meaning to my father's words, they lost their power.

As I made my way up the steps to the assisted-living facility that day, I was reminded of a Robert Holden quote: "Love brings up everything unlike itself so that you can let go of fear and be the loving person you truly are."

This visit with my father was very different. Instead of seeing with eyes of anger from past hurts, I was present to now. I saw a frail man whose love for me came through in a unique way. His words no longer stung. I held space for him and was able to be who I truly am: bold, spirited, and loving. Unconditionally loving and accepting my father for who he is = freedom.

When Shift Hits the Fan

By Michelle McDonald Vlastnik

One Christmas, I was guided to gift my family readings. My guides had me specifically tell my son to have his reading separate from his wife – I'm not sure whose idea it was to ignore that part!

Shortly thereafter, her insecurities caused her to disrespect me. She had always been one to stir the pot and never be held accountable. My son would always say, "I will let her learn her lesson on her own." But this time, things were not going to proceed as if nothing had happened. A close family meant the world to me, but I am no spiritual doormat! I asked my guides, and they told me to come from a place of love and let her know she crossed the line.

That's when the shift hit the fan!

A giant rift in the family formed, and bridges were burned. Even though I was hurt from being cut off from my grandchildren, I felt as if I were standing within the eye of the storm. It was calm in my space, yet I could see and feel the energetic debris flying everywhere.

Discernment told me that it was not my "stuff" to own and not my lesson to learn. A second reading validated just that. The two of them were repeating a past-life lesson. I was told that it would take two to three years before the relationship could be mended between me and my son, and when it did, we would be closer than before.

As I embraced self-love, my perspective on family shifted. *Family* and *Family Circle* have different definitions and hold different vibrations. I chose *Family Circle*.

Twenty-nine months later, her game was played for the last time. The blinders came off, and my son chose to permanently part ways. His vibration shifted. It was palpable.

Weeks later, he sent me a text photo of a message he read saying that his karmic lesson had finished following his "response-ability" to the chain reaction of events and with the assistance of 2016's vibration of completion.

The Universe will whisper, nudge, speak through others, push you, and at times slap you upside the head. What can I say? Shift happens.

The Dream Team

By Michael Brewer

My beautiful wife, Ann, and I were married at Cape Willoughby Lighthouse, Kangaroo Island, Australia. It was a beautiful setting for the happiest day of my life. It was a day I thought was never going to happen. I had missed many opportunities to open my heart to love due to shyness and a lack of belief in myself.

In my 40th year, I decided I did not want to be a 40-year-old virgin. I moved nearly 2,000 kilometres from my home town to Kangaroo Island. KI was a beautiful, peaceful place where I found the wonder of meditation and learned how to bloom from the stillness within, with faith in myself and love. I knew deep within my heart at the end of 2009 that I was going to meet a beautiful soul. By the end of January 2010, I had met Ann.

Ann and I worked together on Kangaroo Island, and a friend started calling us the "Dream Team." In the early months of our marriage, we were living our dream life. Our dream life suffered a bolt from the blue, though, when Ann found a lump in her breast. I knew when I felt the lump that it was breast cancer. The next couple of months were a blur with doctor's visits, an operation, and the decision to return home to be close to our family.

The next two years of our marriage were a real test of our commitment to each other. I was always there for support, but most of the time I just felt so helpless. Ann suffered numerous side effects from her treatment, which led her to fall into deep depression. On top of this, I was working in a job I hated. Life was hard.

My daily meditation routine kept me connected to my soul. I had a strong belief that a bright future awaited us. Then one day, I received a call out of the blue offering us a job managing a motel. It was an opportunity for the "Dream Team" to be back in business. We grabbed it with both hands.

Our love won.

The Great Teachers

By Karrol Rikka S. Altarejos

The pungent smell of disinfectant and cleaner flooded my nose as monitors sounded a rhythmic beat in the background. For a place of healing, I've never actually found a hospital setting to be a conducive place to center oneself. Sitting in the waiting room, I internally worked to steady my own energy. That much, at least, was in my control.

Retreating into my thoughts, I struggled to understand how such a situation could find me again. Why yet again did I have to experience the sudden suffering of another family member, especially one who's considered the most resilient and healthy out of all of us?

At the time, answers eluded me, so I did what I could: I stayed present, supported my family physically and energetically, and placed trust in the doctors and nursing staff while desperately holding on to my faith. My beliefs were being tested once more, but I didn't want to question Source for fear of placing blame.

The months that followed triggered a myriad of feelings ranging from doubt to relief and finally back to a place of peace, as my heart swelled with gratitude during my family member's recovery process. It took time, but like clouds parting after a storm to reveal the bright rays of the sun, I found the light and the lesson it brought with it.

In my life, many teachers have come and gone. Some more mundane, like mentors I've encountered day to day, and others that are of Spirit from whom I've asked for guidance. Then there are what I have come to call the "Great Teachers" – the patterns in life that have pushed me beyond my limits, forcing a rebirth into the unknown. For me, one of the greatest of these Great Teachers has been the concept of *illness*. In the throes of a moment, illness can create an intense fear, with each experience stripping me into vulnerability. Nonetheless, it has also helped deepen me into my personal power, strength, and spirituality.

As a soul being living a human life, I'm privileged to learn from the intangible. These Great Teachers activate life-affirming shifts that have brought me closer to the love of others and to the love I've found within myself.

My Baby Girl

By Lisa Miles Brady

"UGH."

That was not the reaction I'd anticipated upon seeing my daughter for the first time since she started boarding school. My heart ached during that first month. I missed my "baby girl."

Looking at her, it was clear that her adjustment hadn't included self-care. As she approached in wrinkled clothes, I stood in shock, wondering when her hair had last seen a brush. I feigned a smile and hugged her. She responded with, "You don't approve."

She was right. She wasn't "perfect." I was a failure. Even while receiving glowing reports from her teachers, all I could hear in my head was what a lousy mother I was because she didn't take her appearance seriously.

When I returned home, I sat down to write while looking out at my big oak tree and asked, "What am I doing wrong?"

The message I heard was: *You treat her EXACTLY how your last bosses treated you.* I burst into tears.

My corporate career ended with two of the worst bosses I'd ever known. According to them, my very BEING was "wrong," and they never missed an opportunity to say it. The thought that I was in any way, shape, or form treating my own child that way brought me to my knees.

The message continued: *Accept her. As. She. Is. Stop trying to make her "perfect." It's time you learned from her.*

"Learn from her? She's 14! How could she be a teacher to *me*?"

But I decided to trust the message, and our relationship has never been the same. It hasn't been pretty, nor has she followed any plan I had for her. Some days, it's been difficult to watch and accept. But, in learning to accept all the ways she expresses herself, we've become extremely close. We communicate honestly, directly, and with loving acceptance of the other person's path. She has taught me how to laugh more and reminds me that I am capable and courageous. And she knows, without a doubt, that I will *always* have her back. Even when she doesn't brush her hair.

The Power of Support

By Christine Callahan-Oke

For many years, people viewed me as cheerful, positive, encouraging and goofy. But the picture under the surface was different. Although those traits were (and are) part of me, I overused them to compensate for the fact that I felt deeply lost and disheartened.

From the time I left university until I was 40, I had lost sight of who I was and what I wanted for myself. I had a repetitive sinking feeling that something was missing; something wasn't quite right.

My life was good, and I felt guilty that I couldn't just be content, but I needed *more*. I just had no idea what that "more" was.

I soul-searched for decades, trying to "fix" myself. I was going in circles. Thankfully, my soul is wise, patient, and persistent, and it guided me – when I cared to pay attention.

By the time I was on my second maternity leave, I had reached the breaking point. I knew I wanted to return to work feeling grounded, not drifting even further from my sense of self.

I was guided synchronistically to work with a life coach. I didn't know if she would be able to help me because I hadn't been able to sort it out myself, but I had to try.

Working with a coach changed everything for me. I finally honoured myself enough to stop dismissing my inner nudges. I said yes to my soul. My perspective opened up, and I now live in alignment with who I am.

I can't imagine how different my experience would be today if I hadn't taken that step. Maybe I wouldn't have uncovered my purpose. Maybe I wouldn't know how empowering it can be to work with a coach – and to *be* a coach. (I'm a coach now, too.) And I may not have come to realize that I don't have to figure everything out on my own.

I now know it's empowering to ask for support. Sometimes we truly need a helping hand or a new perspective – and when we're able to receive it with gratitude, it can shift *everything*.

It Was in the Cards

By Elaine Lockard

When I was in 10th grade, I bought my first tarot deck and did my first-ever reading for a male acquaintance. This occurred one ordinary school day when several of my classmates and I were playing cards at lunchtime, which we often did.

Since I knew nothing about tarot readings, I followed the instruction booklet throughout the reading, even the interpretations. Only at the end did I give a short summation of what I thought it all meant.

This quiet, introverted acquaintance barely acknowledged the reading at that time. However, after our shared algebra class that afternoon, he very uncharacteristically pulled me aside and told me something deeply personal about himself. It was important to him that I know just how very accurate I had been.

Over the next two years, we saw very little of each other, nor did we even speak again until we were in ROTC together in our senior year. During that year, we got to know one another and became friends. However, for most of that year, I was going steady with another classmate.

In March of that year (1973), the school turned out to celebrate the homecoming of a fellow classmate's father who had been a POW in Vietnam. While a group of us from ROTC were standing around talking, I happened to mention that my boyfriend and I had recently broken up. The next thing I knew, I felt an arm around my waist. It belonged to my new friend – and I have not been able to get rid of him since, nor have I wanted to!

As it turned out, we are soulmates. We had our first date that night and, four years later, got married. At the time that I am writing this, we have just celebrated our 39th wedding anniversary and have been together over 43 years.

My whole life started to shift in many ways with that reading. I really can say, "It was in the cards!"

Chapter 5
Animals & Nature

One year ago, we moved to the beautiful Oregon coast, where we're surrounded by natural wonders: beaches, rivers, mountains, forests, and more wildlife than we've ever experienced on a regular basis – including sea lions, gray whales, bald eagles, and many species of marine birds (including herons, cormorants, snowy plovers, and many types of seagulls) and underwater creatures (including crabs, sea stars, and multi-colored critters who make their homes in the area's numerous tidepools). Spending so much time in nature – especially at the beach – has reawakened a part of our souls that had been dormant. It's rejuvenated our bodies, nourished our spirits, and shifted our lives.

Although we get to the beach (and other natural areas) as often as possible, we don't have to leave home to enjoy nature. Just looking out our window or sitting in the back yard, we're able to watch hawks landing in nearby pine trees and enjoy the antics of "Maestro," our resident hummingbird, who has claimed our flowering bushes as his own. And inside our house, we find constant amusement and love with our three fluffy kitties.

We're not alone in appreciating the profound effect that animals and nature have on us. In this chapter, many authors share about shifts in their own lives brought about by animals and nature. In the pages that follow, you'll find stories of people whose hearts have been touched by dogs, cats, birds, bunnies, horses, dolphins, spiders, and even a tick! You'll read about inspiration found on a mountaintop, under the moon, and in a garden. And you'll find stories of profound life changes brought about by contact with the natural world.

We hope these stories encourage you to open up and appreciate the natural wonders that are all around you.

Spend Time Every Day Tending Your Web

By Marci Kobayashi

I went upstairs for the night. Dinner was finished, the dishes were done, and my father-in-law was already asleep. I was staying with him while my mother-in-law recuperated from surgery at the local hospital.

It was stuffy upstairs. Back in the city, I would have switched on the air conditioning. Here, in the mountains of Hiroshima, opening the windows was enough. I loved falling asleep with the cool breeze and earthy smells.

As I pushed the curtains aside to open the window, I was startled by a large spider, the size of my fist, right there in the middle of the window. After recovering from my initial surprise, I was thrilled because Spider is my totem. Inching closer, I realized that Spider was building a huge web outside, spanning the full width of the window frame.

In the morning, Spider was gone. I wondered about her all day and, after dark, raced upstairs to check. To my delight, she was there again, tending her web. Three nights in a row, I marveled at how she returned and systematically restored her web through a series of small repairs.

Then the news reported that a typhoon was headed our direction. Like everyone in the area, we closed all the windows and even the metal shutters. I worried about Spider. The window frame had once seemed ideal, but by pulling the shutters out over the window, her web was destroyed. I sent her a warning and prayed that she was listening. The rain poured, and the wind howled.

The next morning was beautiful. We opened the shutters and windows throughout the house. The air was crisp and clean. I wondered what happened to Spider. Assuming she was gone for good, I appreciated how she had shared her work and wished her well into the next life.

Later that evening, I spotted Spider again near the window, building a new web – this time under the eaves. I whooped, laughed, cried, and thanked Spider. Seeing her at work again, I realized her lesson: It's important to spend time every day rebuilding our web and equally important to be mindful of where we build it!

Opening My Heart to a Dolphin

By Marie Spencer-Rowland

A couple of years ago, I flew to the Bahamas in order to swim with wild dolphins. Every day, a guide took a group of us out on a boat to a spot where we always came across wild dolphins.

"You need to let the dolphins into your heart," the guide told us on the first day, but for some reason, I struggled to find any connection to these beautiful creatures. At one point, I even mentioned that I thought my heart wasn't working because the dolphins were swimming straight past me.

By day four, I had resigned myself to the fact that I wasn't going to have any profound experiences, so I just stayed on my own and watched the dolphins interact with everyone else.

At one point, while I was swimming on my own and observing a pod of dolphins playing with the other people in our group, I sent out a heartfelt thought to the dolphins: *Thank you for spending time with us. I'm truly grateful to have you here, and I'm more than happy just to watch you swim; but if you decide that you need a bit of peace and quiet, I'll be right here.*

The very instant I finished my thought, the lead dolphin turned in my direction, swam straight over to me, looked me in the eye, and blinked. That blink was one of the most powerful experiences I have ever felt. I felt my heart open up with a *bang*, and I could actually see and feel light beaming out.

I will never forget that experience or the incredibly powerful connection I had with such a majestic animal. On that day, I learned how to open my heart, and I will forever keep it that way – open to love.

For the Love of Trees

By Sheila Callaham

I fell in love with Indian flute music while visiting the Grand Canyon a decade ago, when I heard the beautiful music just as the sun was setting in an orange sky. When I bought my own flute and learned to play, I loved its haunting, ethereal voice, which summoned in me a communion of heart and soul. I often played when I lived in North Carolina, walking into the woods to sit among the trees, allowing the notes to rise amid the birdsong. Playing my Indian flute was therapeutic, and I always felt better afterward.

Having recently relocated to Texas, I've missed that connection with nature. In truth, I guess I am still in the process of transitioning. One morning when I was feeling low, I decided to play my flute. It was a beautiful Texas day; the azure sky was filled with big marshmallow clouds. I stood on my front porch looking at a stand of live oaks whose wiry branches twisted oddly out and up. I would, I announced to the trees with my thoughts, play a song for them.

I brought the flute up to my lips, scanned the 20 or so trees that stood attentively before me, and inhaled deeply as I closed my eyes to play. The warm air from my lungs moved through the walnut instrument to create an earthy, melodic sound. I allowed my fingers to move as the inspiration took them, and notes floated melodiously into the air. The tune felt heartwarming. Authentic. Spiritual.

After a few minutes, I ended the song and opened my eyes. I listened attentively with all my senses to hear what the trees would say about my offering. Suddenly, I had the strangest sensation. I came to understand, as clearly as if someone standing next to me had told me directly, that it was the trees who had played the tune through me, for me – not the other way around. I felt humbled, and rightly so. After all, is it not always nature that inspires my spirit?

I bowed my head in reverence and gratitude as a warm tear found its way to the corner of my eye. "Thank you," I offered silently to the trees, "for giving me the honor of playing it for you."

Paw Prints on My Soul

By Lisa Rachel Cohen

"Hey, Mom, can I have a dog for my birthday?" asked my soon-to-be six-year-old, Alia.

"I think you're a little too young to take care of a dog," I said.

"Please, Mom. I'll take really good care of him," she persisted.

"I'm sure you would, sweetie. Maybe we can get a dog when you're older."

"How much older do I need to be?"

"Oh, I don't know, Alia. Maybe by the time you're eight you'll be old enough."

Life as we knew it resumed. There were school buses to catch, homework assignments to do, and play dates to schedule. Two years passed. Party planning was underway yet again. Themes, favors, and guest lists were debated. "I know," offered Alia. "Instead of a party this year, let's get a dog! You promised that when I was eight we could get a dog," she reminded.

"Let me talk to Daddy," I said.

And so it was that our family of three morphed into four. Our furry angel, Cholly, graced us with his magnificent presence for 10 years. Although he has since come to pass, I will forever remain changed by his embodied journey. My reservoir for joy has deepened, and my capacity for empathy has expanded exponentially.

Cholly taught us how to: Invite others into our hearts and greet those who arrive with joyful exuberance. Share our food and comfort; there will always be enough for those who share. Be kind – really, *really* kind – to each other. Forgive. Experience the earth beneath our feet. Walk with the wind. Bask in the sun. Bathe in the rain. Wait patiently. Be resilient. Play with reckless abandon. Leave paw prints on one's soul.

Thank you, dear friend, for walking us home.

A Flowering of Insight

By Barbara "Bobbie" Carr

"The glory of gardening: hands in the dirt, head in the sun, heart with nature. To nurture a garden is to feed not just the body, but the soul."
- Alfred Austin

When I was growing up, summers were most welcome except for the periodic weeding of the garden beds. Two of my sisters and I dreaded the weeding; there were beetles, earthworms, and spiders (oh, my!), and we had no garden gloves! Worst of all to weed was the tea-rose garden with thorns the size of golf tees, which pulled at your clothes and scratched your skin indiscriminately. It truly was blood, sweat, and tears at times in that rose garden, with the three of us certainly not appreciating our parents' gardening logic.

If the concept and use of mulch to help minimize the weeds was available at that time, my parents had no knowledge of it. So my sisters and I would unhappily trudge outside, grumbling all the way, to do battle with the garden, wishing we didn't have to perform that onerous task.

Fast-forward some years to my husband and me in a newly erected house with little landscaping. Little by little, we added shrub beds of various plants (with me using gardening gloves), putting down mulch as we went, and eventually we planted (among other types of plants) more than a dozen rosebushes. One day, I realized I actually liked to garden! Being outside in the fresh air among plants and animals (even the bugs!) somehow gave me a serenity not found in any other setting.

Over the years, through these gardening experiences, I learned that sometimes what started out being disliked can become a treasured gift. It is a flowering of insight for which I am truly grateful.

Inspiration from the Moon

By Lacey Dawn Jackson

I wondered if I could take any more abuse. It didn't feel right when he turned the things I said into me being wrong. It made me second-guess what my inner sense was screaming. I had to get out! But how?

The emotional abuse was the worst because it continued to fill me with doubts. One moment, I was confident with a plan to leave. The next moment, I was wondering how I was going to get out of this hell as my confidence took another dive.

One night as I stood around the small campfire I had built in our back yard, I looked up into the sky. It was as if I had just discovered the moon for the first time. It was full and bright. It felt empowering and strong. Something inside me shifted. I heard the moon say she would protect me.

Over the next few weeks, every time I felt low, I remembered the moon. I noticed that the moon followed me wherever I went. My confidence soared. I felt as if I were one with the moon. My spirit stayed strong even during the rough times. I felt as if everything would be okay.

One night, I knew that this was the end of the abuse. I felt strong, like the moon. Later that night, I quietly loaded a few things into the car and drove off. I ended up parking at a marina for the night because I didn't have the money to get a hotel room. I didn't want to bother anyone because it was so late. As I curled up in the back seat of my car, I felt very hopeful. I felt safe for the first time in a long time.

As I drifted off to sleep, I looked up into the sky. I was tickled to see the full moon shining down upon me. It had been a month since the full moon had introduced herself and I had experienced my shift. Everything was going to be alright.

Lessons from a Dog

By Robert D. White

I remember the day I adopted my dog, Julein. I had never been known as an animal lover, at least not to the degree that I would own a dog. However, on this particular Saturday, I was consumed by an inexplicable energy – a softer, gentler person had awakened that morning.

Several days earlier, I had glanced at several adoption sites, but I didn't think anything of it. Apparently, my subconscious was hard at work because, on this day, I knew precisely where to go, though I didn't see the connection at the time. I just assumed I was going to the store for fish food. Little did I know, this would become one of the most important moments in my life.

That day at the pet store, I made the most impulsive decision I had ever made: I adopted a puppy. He was the happiest puppy I'd ever seen! His tail wagged nonstop, and the expression on his face looked as if he were smiling. I didn't know what had come over me; all I knew was that I was now the owner of a dog. It wasn't until later that I would realize the blessings that Julein would bring.

The one overriding insight I have is that the care for a pet is one of our greatest teachers. They rely on us for everything and require constant attention, food and water, a place to live, visits to the vet, and the lists goes on. But our furry friends have only love to offer in return.

I'm constantly reminded that while I have friends and family who I can share laughs with or go to in moments of sadness, our pets are not afforded this same opportunity. They can't just call up their pet pals to see how things are going, or invite them out to chat over kibble, or reminisce about things past – in their eyes, we are all they have. We are their entire world.

After spending the better part of this past year reflecting on the meaning of life, I can undoubtedly see that Julein has entered my life to teach me the true meaning of altruistic love – a love that is always giving without boundaries and asks nothing in return. As the Zen proverb so eloquently puts it: *When the student is ready, the teacher will appear.* Julein is that bearer of selflessness.

A Tick's Wisdom

By Lori Thomas

"So, Theodore, what message do you have for me?" I ask. I'm sitting quietly in meditation.

Theodore is a male tick who has spent the last four days attached to my throat. He is now gifting me with his wisdom.

The impression rolls in of beings with a very strong purpose who know exactly what they must do, and who are desperately trying to get our attention.

"We are here to remind you of how we are all connected," he says. "We collect a microcosm of the essence of every being that we feed on. We take each of our meals from a different creature, and thus the essence of each of you – disease, energy, love – is shared with all others. This allows you to form a deep connection with the animals and is a reminder that we are all one."

I quickly scribble down his words as he continues: "Where we bite you points to stagnation, an energy block, or a need for change. We gravitate toward those areas to help release the blockage and get energy moving. Sometimes, disease is needed to remove that blockage. The symptoms can be cleansing. When symptoms are suppressed, the disease cannot complete its job and exit the body, so it remains trapped – and the blockage remains as well."

I respond, "But the diseases you carry cause many people to fear and hate you. They are afraid of becoming seriously ill or dying."

The connection between us goes quiet. Then, out of the silence, I hear the words, "If the energy fits." More silence. Then, very softly, "Even if we inject pathogens, your soul chooses whether or not they should multiply. Look at the body part that was bitten and make changes in that area of your life. The appropriate changes will shift your energy such that disease is not needed and will not manifest."

I sit there, stunned by Theodore's revelation. My perception of ticks and the nature of disease itself is transformed.

I later realize that the bite on my throat was a call for me to speak my truth. Thank you, Theodore.

The Beam

By Sarah Berkett

The day I met the love of my life is as crystal clear as the words on this page. In my mind's eye, I am back in time, waiting on a clear, crisp October morning for the rescuer to arrive. My heart nearly jumped out of my chest as the SUV pulled into our driveway. I ran out to greet them and was surprised that the dog did not jump out; instead, he lay on the back seat. He could not jump out, as he had been kept in a crate and neglected for at least seven months.

My husband, Jim, carried him up the driveway and gently put him down on our front porch. Obviously, this pup had never been outside! I watched in awe as he walked gingerly around, smelling the world. We named him Beamer, as he was truly a beam of light that had come into our lives.

This is when my life shift started to take place. Watching Beamer grow and overcome his disabilities was so inspiring to me. I also learned to overcome many of my own fears and insecurities in this life. Every day for almost eight years was a learning opportunity with this sweet soul that was sent my way. It was no accident that Beamer came into my life when I needed him and left when it was time; that is the way of the spirit dogs.

My life is always shifting. I am grateful to have been given time with Beamer; it was nothing but a gift. It would have been so sad not to share our lives together. After Beamer transitioned, he sent me another beautiful soul, my Sasha, who is my comfort dog. Even from the other side, Beamer never stops giving.

A Sedona Mountaintop Experience

By Donna S. Priesmeyer

As I sit by a fire, surrounded by the red rocks of Sedona, the natural beauty evokes memories of my first visit to this sacred place. Six years ago, I joined a small band of like-minded spiritual seekers as we embarked on a sacred-sites tour that became the journey of a lifetime.

I considered myself a spiritual person but received a calling to go deeper. This opportunity opened a clear path for me to do so. It required an openness to change, a willingness to face my fears, and rigorous soul-level initiations. I was nervous. It was my first group tour, and I had never met the leader or any of the participants, but their warm, friendly souls quickly put me at ease. It seemed that some mysterious force had brought us together. There was an amazing sense of oneness as we prayed, meditated, and shared our visions.

I lovingly called it the "Magical Mystery Tour" because I didn't know in advance which mountain we would climb or river we would cross. For one who is keen on managing my surroundings, this was a lesson in faith. The experience taught me to relax and trust in the Divine flow. There were mishaps and challenges along the way, just as we face in our day-to-day lives, but also an ever-present sense of being guided and supported by Spirit.

One sun-drenched day, I had an extraordinary mountaintop experience. Our leader shared inspired teachings, followed by a guided meditation. We connected to the earth, the sky, and the elements. I felt a shift in my perception as Spirit spoke to me gently, opening my heart in a most miraculous way. Ideas that had previously seemed elusive became clear, and I was blessed with new revelations. It's amazing what can happen when souls join together with the intention of creating a portal for Spirit to be expressed more fully on Earth.

Our trip came to a close, and a heightened sense of joy, peace, and love accompanied me as I returned home. Refreshed, rejuvenated, and uplifted, I was ready for the next adventure!

My Angel Pet Lives On

By Andrea Bryant

I was in shock. Numb. In disbelief. My soul rabbit, Apple, had passed away. Suddenly. This could NOT be happening. Tears flowed like they had never flowed before.

He was my strength, my calm. He was the reason I still existed here on this earthly plane. In the days that followed his death, I moved from shock, to guilt, to anger and grief. He was gone, completely gone. I needed him. I needed to know he was still with me, supporting me, loving me, calming me.

I got my wish. It started gently, like a butterfly fluttering at the crown of my head. Wisps of hair being moved. I dismissed it at first, but it got stronger. I suddenly realised it was only happening when I was thinking about HIM! It dawned on me: *My Apple IS with me! It's him!!!* Every time I thought of him, it happened! My hair moved. I knew in my soul it was him. I was not alone!

Life changed then. In that moment.

I continued to grieve for my angel Apple in his physical form. His cute little bunny body, his snuggles and affection. His presence by my bed at night.

Eventually, I was able to laugh again. A few months after his passing, I was lying in bed, excited about attending an animal-communication workshop the next day. A workshop where I would learn to communicate telepathically with him! As I lay there in bed, I suddenly felt a huge movement in my hair. I leapt out of bed, convinced I had a huge spider on my head. There was no spider.

It dawned on me. It was Apple. Expressing his excitement about being able to talk to me tomorrow!

I stood there in my bedroom, laughing out loud at Apple and his exciting way of getting my attention!

I had always believed in life after death. But everything changes when you get your own personal proof. There is more to life than just this earthly plane. There IS life after death.

An Unlikely Awakening

By Julie Chan

I graduated from Yale, worked in urban planning, and was at MIT for a master's degree in that field. I thought my life was set. Little did I know that MIT, the most rational of places, would spark a spiritual awakening.

"Why are we in this mess?" my teammate yelled on the phone, questioning my abilities as a project manager. We had worked tirelessly for months on the affordable-housing development proposal. And now, due to last-minute printing issues, we were in danger of missing the deadline. Things seemed out of control.

I felt like I had let down not only my team, but worse, I had let down all low-income people. It was personal because that was my background growing up. As I hung up the phone, I started sobbing, hyperventilating.

Standing alone in my apartment, I noticed the flutter of a bird landing on my windowsill. Surprisingly, it had flown up three stories and under the push-out window. I walked closer, holding my breath. It was a robin. He hopped around, unafraid. *You're so beautiful, so free – I want to be you,* I thought and convulsed into more sobs.

Suddenly, an incredible rush of peace flowed through my body, from head to toe. My mind went blank, and my hyperventilating immediately stopped. If peace could be solid, I was encased in its comforting embrace. For the first time, I knew in my heart, heard in my head, and saw a flash of light in my mind's eye – I just *knew* with every cell in my body – that everything was going to be okay. An instant later, the bird flew away.

Sure enough, we submitted the proposal hours later and ended up winning the competition, funding our non-profit partner.

My newfound intuitive abilities started my discovery of my soul's purpose. Five years later, I launched a social enterprise called Being My Purpose to empower others to know and express their purpose with courage and creativity.

To this day, the robin holds a special place in my heart. It bridged my rational mind and intuitive mind, opening up a world full of unexpected possibilities.

Kandi and Miss Luci

By Catherine M. Laub

I kept hearing messages from God that my husband needed a companion dog at work. Tony ran a small business and very seldom ate lunch or took breaks. I told him about these messages, and he kept saying that the last thing we needed was another dog. We already had Miss Luci, a little Yorkie, and we had just put down another dog a few months earlier.

After three weeks, Tony finally agreed to look at the local shelter. As we walked around, all the dogs were going crazy, barking for attention – all except for Kandi, a very big American Bulldog who was just sitting quietly with a sad look on her face. We spent a while with Kandi, and Tony took an instant liking to her. We then had to bring Miss Luci in to see if they interacted well. They did, and a few days later, we took Kandi home.

While Tony still had his company, Kandi went to the office with him every day and insisted on many daily walks. Kandi loved us immediately and continues to keep us laughing and in good spirits. We usually tell everyone that she adopted *us*, because she rules the house!

She has her own language, which sounds like she is snoring or growling. When people hear her special "words," they sometimes think that she's growling, but we know that she's talking. Someday, I'll learn animal communication so I can understand the messages she gives us.

Kandi and Miss Luci love each other and play well together, but if Luci thinks Kandi is hurting one of us she will jump on Kandi to protect us. I can't believe they are both already six years old!

In addition to all the joy and high spirits that Kandi continues to bring us, she brought another big shift to our family: Tony finally began to believe that I receive helpful messages from God and the angels.

If you think you are receiving a message from God, your angels, or a loved one – about adopting a pet or about anything else – I highly recommend that you listen!

A Shekinah Moment

By Susan Elizabeth Schoemmell

One very sleepy Saturday morning, I awoke and was roused to get up. I resisted as I closed my eyes and tried to fall back into a slumber, my bed feeling so warm and inviting, but the pull to get up would not cease. Something tugged at my consciousness and would not let me go back to dreamland. A voice called for me to dress warmly, take my dog for her early-morning walk, and greet the day.

I stepped out the door and took in a breath of cold, crisp air. Walking down to the lake, I sensed that the sun was just starting to shine its glorious rays. Approaching the water's edge, I noticed a large plastic water bottle that had been cut open to be used as a bailer for a boat. Picking this up and anticipating throwing it away, something caught my eye. I walked closer to the shore and bent down to gaze at a beautiful, peaceful seagull that had succumbed to tragedy and was floating face down at the water's edge.

In what felt like a natural gesture, I scooped up this creature of God to bring it to a safe place of rest. It was as if I was drawn to this very moment of getting out of a warm bed, walking to the lake, and finding a handmade scoop to carry this fallen bird to its final resting place.

I followed a path that paralleled the lakefront and looked for a perfect spot to lay this once alive and graceful bird of flight. Brushing aside a pile of frozen leaves, I hollowed a place in which to lay this peaceful creature and covered it gently with the dry leaves.

Starting my ascent up the gentle slope from the lakeshore, a ray of the sun shone through the morning air, blinding me with its brilliance. In this moment, I felt a shift of perception to the deeper meaning of life – a Shekinah moment of being in God's glory and at peace in His presence.

Keira, My Angel

By Sharon Hickinbotham

Sometimes, words aren't needed. Communicating through our feelings, energy, or intuitive senses, the people and animals who are aware remind those around them that, even if words aren't spoken, you are heard, you are loved, and you don't need to explain how you feel.

I experienced this type of communication the day before making the hardest decision – to have my beautiful baby girl, Keira (a 15-year-old ginger cat), put to sleep. I was already feeding her through a plastic syringe and doing everything I could to keep her hydrated, to save her…or at least give her a decent quality of life for a bit longer. Given her deteriorating health, I knew she was nearing her last breath, but how could I say goodbye to my dear friend/family member?

The decision to let her go was made with the help of Keira. With the little energy that remained, she jumped onto my bed where my *365 Angel Messages* book was open and laid her head on a page. In that moment, I felt a strong pull to read the page she had selected. Tears fell as I read the words, *CHOOSE PEACE.* I knew that Keira was saying, "Mum, it's okay; let me go."

The next day, the vet came to my home so that Keira's last breath could be in the garden she loved. I sat with her under her favorite tree, reading the poem "The Rainbow Bridge." As the vet walked up and sat with us, I held Keira in my arms as the needle entered her paw. I kissed her head as she left her body. We buried her in the flower garden. Moments later, a huge rainbow appeared over my house. Through tears and a smile, I knew that Keira was letting me know, *I'm okay, Mum.*

Exactly one month later, my brother passed. In my grief, I knew that another cat would be a great idea for me. I prayed to God, Keira, and my brother in spirit to help guide me to a cat who's very psychic and special, like Keira, a cat who would help me grieve and heal.

Driving to the pound to rescue a cat, I saw a rainbow over the top of the pound. Inside was a little tiny ginger girl who picked me. I named her Angel, as Keira was my angel. Spirit is amazing.

Take Back the Reins

By Shirley Ann Everingham

Some life shifts are small; others are big. Some arrive as swiftly as storms; others are as gradual as shifting sands. And some happen without us even noticing.

One of my biggest life shifts began when Grace sent me a wonderful horse named Tangles to help me and others overcome our fears. Tangles is an amazing horse. He just settles while you think and feel what it is you want or need to do next.

One day, I was working through an exercise with Tangles that helped to get to the real cause of my fears about horse riding. As I rode, the layers peeled away to reveal the truth.

The shift had begun.

I realized that my real fear was that I thought I wasn't enough or that I wasn't as good a horseman as my dad or my son, Patrick – both of whom were/are AMAZING horsemen. It always came back to one fall – a fall I always assumed *they* would have avoided.

One day, Patrick and I were working horses in the round pen, which is often the place for thought-provoking conversations. Patrick said, "How do you know that Toby [my Dad] or I wouldn't have fallen off that horse, too? You don't remember any of it, and nobody else was there. Stop comparing, and just be *you*!"

The shift was gaining strength.

Wisdom from the young is always powerful because you are never quite sure where it comes from. In this case, I just knew that Patrick was spot on! Ever since that conversation, I have viewed my horse and people skills in a new light. I have stepped out to help others on their own journeys. I will continue to learn, but I will stop and be mindful of the fact that I am enough at this point in time.

Where I am right now is just fine for me and my tribe. I am supposed to be here for a reason. Somebody out there needs me...exactly as I am now. They need to follow my journey in order to start their own.

Watch for the shift in your own life!

A Doggone Reason to Live

By Beverly J. Harvey

Looking into my rearview mirror, I saw a black-and-white scraggly mop staring back at me. It had happened so fast – the urge to bring home a rescue dog from the animal shelter. I wasn't even sure I could take care of a dog. It was a challenge just to tell which end was the front or the back with all the overgrown fur!

I had chosen the name "Ollie" for this sweet dog before I even arrived at the shelter. This was very uncharacteristic of me, since I was never a dog lover. Cats were my thing. But there had been one dog of this breed – a cockapoo – that touched my heart when I was a young adult. I told myself that someday I would have my own little cockapoo.

Many, many cats later, alone and retired early because of poor health, I woke up one day feeling depressed, unwilling to perform the most menial of tasks, and not caring if I lived another day. Somewhere in the deep recesses of my mind, it occurred to me that if I continued in this vein, I would not be alive much longer. I had to find a reason to get up every day, so I began volunteering at an animal shelter. I liked the idea of helping homeless animals because the relationships didn't require an abundance of conversation. Slowly, I felt better and eventually managed to smile at the humans when I arrived.

What drew me to the work was my love of cats. In fact, I would back away from any dog coming to greet me. Imagine my surprise a year later when my black-and-white mop wandered past the welcome desk. I was lying awake that night recalling the incident when I had an epiphany: "That's my dog!" It was the cockapoo I said I had always wanted to have someday. "Someday" had finally arrived.

Ollie completely changed my life with his love and acceptance. I'm a "dog person" now. More importantly, I'm glad to be alive.

Chapter 6
Divine Unfolding

We've both experienced our share of divine unfolding – instances of perfect timing, blessings in disguise, and uncanny "coincidences" that were too amazing to be mere coincidences. When we decided to move to the Oregon coast, we were disappointed as one potential house after another fell through, only to have our current (and ideal) home open up at the first possible moment when we could feasibly move. We've also experienced many frustrating setbacks and roadblocks in our business that greatly benefited us in the long run. Even our meeting depended on an amazing stroke of divine timing.

It started after the 2001 Burning Man festival, when Dan and his friend Jordan found themselves at a literal crossroads. They weren't sure whether to drive west and stay with friends in San Francisco, or northwest, where they could visit Jordan's sister in Oregon. At a roadside diner, they called Jordan's sister, but she wasn't home. (Back in that ancient era, none of them had cell phones – if you can imagine that!) After a quick bite to eat, they gave her one last try…and she was there and said to come on up. During that visit, she connected Dan with a friend of hers who had a house for rent in New Mexico. Sight unseen, Dan agreed to rent it; and two months later, we met outside that house – thanks to perfect timing!

As remarkable as they may seem, experiences such as these abound, as you will see throughout this chapter. In the following pages, you'll read stories of accidents that turned out to be blessings in disguise (as well as accidents averted altogether, thanks to divine delays), seemingly unlikely encounters that changed lives forever, and evidence of a higher power at work in our lives. We hope that these stories amaze and delight you, renew your faith in this magical world, and inspire you to feel awe and gratitude for the divine unfolding of your own life.

Finding My Three-Part Home

By Dan Teck

The biggest shift in my life has been finding my home. This wasn't a one-time event, though; it happened in three parts: first for my heart, then for my spirit, and finally for my physical self.

My heart found its home the day I met Jodi. I had recently moved to a small adobe house at the end of a red-dirt road on the outskirts of Jemez Pueblo, NM – an extremely private location for an extremely private guy who was going out of his way *not* to meet anyone. I didn't hear her coming as I knelt in my driveway, trying to fix my bike (key word: *trying*). I had never felt such an instant connection with anyone. It felt less like a meeting than a *reunion*. Two years later, when we got married (a block away from where we'd met/reconnected), it felt less like a change than a confirmation of the reality of our eternal connection.

Even after I was happily married, however, I still felt like a spiritual "bachelor" – getting to know a wide variety of spiritual paths but never "settling down" with any one of them...until I found Abraham-Hicks. Their teachings – including the Law of Attraction, "downstream" living, and the Emotional Guidance System – not only make sense to me, they *work!* They've changed my life – from small, subtle adjustments (such as shifting toward feelings of relief and appreciation) to major, life-changing events (such as moving to the beach).

And that brings me to the final installment of my three-part home: moving to the Oregon coast one year ago. I've lived in some beautiful places, but I always felt like I was "just stopping by" on my way to somewhere else. Here, though, I've finally found everything I want in one area: beaches, forests, mountains, and a town that's my ideal size, vibe, and location. For the first time, I'm happily putting down roots and envisioning the rest of my life here.

Finding my three-part home means that I'm no longer living with one eye on the exit sign and one foot out the door. I still meet new people, experience new-for-me spiritual paths, and take out-of-town vacations. I use my home(s) as a launchpad for further growth and enrichment, knowing that I always have a solid foundation to return to. And, in a deeper sense, no matter where I travel, my true home – my heart, my soul, my spirit, and my love – is always with me.

Guidance from an Angel

By Bryce Goebel

I said goodbye to my parents and prepared to start the three-hour drive back home. I was leaving later than planned. Normally, I don't mind, but it was hot, the sun was setting, and my drive was due west – straight into the sunset.

Dad had lingered getting his last hugs. It was part of our routine. He'd get me a cold drink from the fridge and walk me out. Then he'd give me a big hug and send me on my way. I put on my sunglasses and prepared to chase the sun.

The next hour went quickly. Traffic was light. I was making great time on the interstate. Suddenly, traffic came to a crawl. Thirty minutes later, the crawl turned into a stop. I was grateful for the drink as I turned off the air conditioner. I didn't want to overheat the engine.

It wasn't long before tempers started to flare. Other drivers got frustrated. Horns were blaring constantly. I knew it was a wreck when rescue vehicles and fire trucks drove by. After another 30-minute wait, the police reopened one lane. We finally started to move. A multi-car accident had blocked all the lanes. Countless cars were now fighting for access to the open lane. It would be at least another two hours of driving to get home, but I couldn't help but wonder what might have been...*if only I'd left five minutes earlier, if Dad hadn't lingered getting that last hug...*

In my work, I receive guidance from angels. They always come with messages for my clients. Today the message was for me. The words were crystal clear: *If you had left five minutes earlier, you would've been in the accident.* I realized I was exactly where I needed to be. Delayed, but safe and alive.

Since that day, I never worry about driving delays. If I'm slowed by traffic or stoplights, there's a reason. I've learned to accept it. I close my eyes and breathe deeply instead of getting angry or frustrated. I offer gratitude, knowing I'm exactly where I'm supposed to be.

Reciprocity of Gratitude

By Rebekah Bernard

It had been three months since I was involved in a severe accident that wrecked my car and my spirit. My physical body was okay, but I felt traumatized. My mind and spirit suffered in an alarming new way. I contemplated and questioned my personal growth and purpose in life. I retreated; turned to my faith; and, after some time, felt well enough to return to my spiritual counseling work in hospice care.

My first day back on the job, I was assigned to visit Mrs. Boone, a woman who did not often respond with words but expressed stories of kindness and love with her gentle presence. I immediately felt warmth embracing the family. Mrs. Boone's daughter-in-law, Jessica, disclosed a deep sadness and existential concerns about her mother-in-law's decline and suffering, but serenity radiated as Jessica ascertained that she could now return the love that her mother-in-law had selflessly given through the years. Jessica mentioned that her son would be dropping by and that he was an essential part of Mrs. Boone's care, despite his demanding schedule. I affirmed the additional support that surrounded Mrs. Boone and thought nothing more of it...until he arrived. I instantly recognized him as the paramedic who had responded to my car accident and compassionately comforted my panic during the ride to the hospital. I'd never had the chance to thank him, but when our eyes met that day at Mrs. Boone's home, there was an immediate kinship and an unspoken "thank you."

A life shift happened in that moment. I was able to reciprocate the incredible care this man had shown me during a terribly difficult event in my life. Demonstrations of gratitude throughout our separate lives seamlessly linked us. Now, I could help bring comfort to his family during his grandmother's final life transition. And I learned how the power of gratitude could change lives.

"Everything happens for a reason," said Jessica when she learned how her son and I had previously met. Truer words have never been spoken.

Magic on the Wings of Prayer

By Angie Maya Campbell

In March 1993, John and I had our hearts set on two particular souvenirs from our road trip: I wanted a shaman's drum, and John wanted a dreamcatcher. I felt sure we'd know the right ones when we saw them. Yet, town after town, nothing was really making itself known to us. As we marveled through the canyons and mountains of Utah, Arizona, New Mexico, and beyond, we were smitten by the skies, the wildlife, and the sunsets – so much so, that we forgot about our search.

After about seven days of adventuring through Colorado and Wyoming, we reached the Badlands of South Dakota and, in particular, Pine Ridge. I had long had a deep affinity with the Lakota Sioux, and I wanted to pay my respects at Wounded Knee. So we drove there, along the potholed roads, and although it took quite some time, it felt like we were being carried. When we arrived, I stood at the memorial and said the Four Directions prayer, although I didn't remember ever having said it before.

As I finished, a man drove up and introduced himself as a local artist. He then told us he had two things we may be interested in. I watched as he produced a bag from the car and out of it he pulled two things: a drum and a dreamcatcher.

I was taken aback, to say the least. Yet, at the same time, there was a part of me that wasn't the slightest bit surprised. Such an incredibly humbling and magical place, combined with a deep connection, literally brings miracles. And as if it weren't magical enough, after we said goodbye, we turned to place them in my bag. Within that time, he had gone – almost as if it had been a dream. Only, it wasn't.

I still have my little Wounded Knee drum to remind me every day how magical this world actually is. When we connect with deep respect, love, and an unwavering faith...that, my friends, is when magic happens.

My Liberation: Starting Anew

By Lynn Spiro

On a crisp, fall day in 2014, I pushed the button on my trunk and watched it slowly descend, closing with a definitive *click*. The car was finally loaded, and I had said my last goodbyes. The day of my liberation had arrived. It was time to journey to my new home and my new life.

As I looked around the neighborhood, my heart was heavy with memories. I had lived here for 31 years surrounded by wonderful neighbors, including many children who had grown up with my sons. This was where I had celebrated each holiday and anniversary for 31 years of marriage. Now I was leaving it all. Suddenly, it didn't feel as wonderfully liberating as it should have.

I went into the house and buried my head in my pooch's silky neck as tears flowed out and doubts flooded in. *Is it a mistake to leave everything I've known? Will I be able to find peace and happiness elsewhere?* The questions swirled in my head as the tears poured down my face.

Slowly, I stood up, walked through the house, and let the memories flow. As I closed the door to each room, I repeated the mantra, "This is what you need to do." By the time I reached the front door, I felt a bit steadier. I quietly whispered, "Thank you for the memories we made." I walked to the car, feeling better for honoring the house in my own way.

Tears clouded my vision as I pulled out of the driveway, and I was forced to pull over. I looked into the rearview mirror to gaze at my home once again. The tears stilled, my breath slowed, and I felt a shift deep within. Hard as it was, I knew I *had* to leave in order to heal and grow.

The last view of my home was of it standing in the sunlight behind the huge maple tree. Blowing each a kiss, I eased onto the road and they disappeared as I turned the corner. The time had come to begin anew.

The Stork Doesn't Make Mistakes

By Laura Young

I felt alone on this planet since the day the stork dropped me off at the wrong house. At least that was my perception of it as a child. I never felt like I fit in. I had different experiences and viewpoints from my family and community. I was not comfortable in my environment and struggled against it for many years. Life was tough.

All of that suddenly changed in 2006, the day a friend brought me the DVD *The Secret*. The film was mostly about the Law of Attraction, which was a wonderful insight, but it was much more than that to me. It was the first time in my life that I found resonance with such a large and diverse group of people and their experiences. I felt like these were my people, that I had finally been found, and that my life had been patiently waiting for me all these years.

The moment I finished the DVD, I was searching the internet and finding all the teachers' websites, programs, workshops, and other offerings. I managed to purchase most of their books and attend a few of their workshops, absorbing all the information like a sponge. It was familiar. In fact, I realized that this information was already inside me just waiting to be remembered. *The Secret* flipped the light switch on!

I realized I was not alone. I was not crazy or the black sheep or whatever else people had said of me since I was a child. I was indeed a part of this Universe, and I undeniably belonged!

That single day in 2006 propelled me into a spiritual journey that has brought me so much insight into who I am and how I can use those uncomfortable earlier years to help serve others. The gratitude I found for the struggles I lived created the compassion I needed to help heal myself, my clients, and the planet as a whole.

I realize that the stork did not make a mistake and drop me at the wrong house; he knew exactly what he was doing!

The Deepest Cry Within

By B. J. Garcia

I had just completed facilitating my first victim/offender mediation, a triple-murder case involving six months' preparation for both victim and offender to meet face to face after 13 years. It was a six-hour mediation with intense emotion and miraculous moments. Witnessing this powerful and sacred process was one of the most life-changing events of my life.

The mediation was taped, and with permission, I shared the video with some of my closest friends as a teaching tool during a weekend retreat at Lake Tahoe. Our time together was held as a sacred space and in confidentiality. Each day, I shared part of the mediation, and it affected each of us on a deeply personal level.

During our last evening together, I discovered that one of the participants shared what we were experiencing with someone outside the group. Feeling that our sacred space had been violated, I went spinning into my own victim/offender experience of feeling a lifetime of betrayal, rejection, and abandonment at the core of my being. I tossed and turned all night.

The next morning, with my heart racing, I asked for one last meeting to process my feelings. We gathered outside by the lake. The space was held by the warmth of the sun and the stillness of the water. I felt the love and support of everyone as they held the space for my anger, pain, and fears to pour out.

In allowing the process, something caught hold of me, and a deep cry, a victim cry, came bellowing out of me that could be heard echoing across the lake: "What about me?"

As this cry released from the depths of my being, a deeper cry, a true prayer followed: "I just want to be."

Giving myself fully to this cry, I was turned inside out. Everything fell away. There was silence, light, love, and awareness that everything coming before was in service to this moment of True Being. My heart is full of love and gratitude for the players in this play and for a true prayer answered.

Rescued

By Meilin Ehlke

"Nooooooo!!!" I yelled, as a large boulder slid farther over me to pin me down into the gravel of the dried riverbed. During this surreal moment, as I slipped while climbing down between two rocks and one of them loosened, I knew that I might not survive. What was happening, I couldn't change. Vividly, I remember this flash of acknowledging that my life could be over in an instant, before I could utter, "I am alive."

"I can breathe," I whispered as I looked down at my legs, realizing that if I moved to rescue myself, the boulder would slip farther and smash my healthy leg. "No! I don't want two disabled legs." Despair began to creep up on me.

"Help!" I screamed cautiously, afraid that if I inhaled too deeply the heavy rock would crush my head. When no one in my group responded, I began to worry that they would think I was shouting out one of my sacred sounds. I knew I needed to make a clear distinction, so I cried out, "S.O.S.! *Hilfe*! Help! S.O.S.!"

I repeated this sequence over and over, although I realized I had no chance against the gushing noise of the mountain creek's tumbling water at the bottom of the valley. *No one can hear me. Nobody can see me. I am hidden from sight*, I concluded. Noticing my lower body turning numb, panic rose within me. *I am not going to see my son, Tilo, again*, I thought, as tears rolled down my cheeks.

In this dark moment, I felt the sun's warmth comforting me, as it had done so often before in my life. My doubt was replaced by surety that one of my fellow shamans would feel me – because we are all connected. Yes, we are One.

Reassured, I shifted into my knowing. I began to explain telepathically my position and called it out loud so I could be better found. Although my body was extremely hurt from the immense weight on my hip and the surrounding rocks pressing into me, I believed in my rescue again – feeling relief followed by calmness flowing in.

My rescue confirmed that my faith was justified, and it remains stronger than ever.

In the Eyes of an Angel

By Janet G. Nestor

I slowed down with traffic at the stoplight before making the turn onto the interstate. A well-groomed young man wearing a white shirt and jeans was standing along the median asking for money. My position in traffic caused me to stop right in front of him. Without thinking, I reached into my purse and gave him all the cash in my wallet – maybe 10 or 15 dollars. I was stunned by this automatic action because I rarely give money when it is solicited in this way, let alone empty my purse.

My spiritual worldview was about to shift. The young man and I looked straight into each other's eyes. He quietly thanked me for my gift and briefly told me about the circumstances that brought him to the intersection. As he was talking, I was thinking, "This man might be an Earth Angel." Our minds touched, and he confirmed his divine identity with kind eyes and a quirky little smile that said, "You got me!"

In an instant, I knew him and understood that there were many other angels living much like him. My heart filled with love so strong that it saturated my entire being. I loved him. I loved what he was doing for his family. I loved life. I loved everything and everyone. Then suddenly the stoplight was green, traffic was moving, and the encounter was over.

His lesson may have only lasted the length of a red light, but it contained enough information to fill a book. I have to wonder how many other people received a similar lesson from this beautiful soul. He shared that some angels are living rather normal lives, but others have assumed identities that we might not recognize as angelic. They are prisoners, refugees, homeless men and women, activists, street-corner musicians, politicians, and from every walk of life and every income group.

We are all loved and cared for according to our needs.

A Shift into New Realms of Possibility

By Nancy Merrill Justice

It was the mid-1980s, and I was a relatively new business owner of an insurance agency. My manager had highly recommended my attendance at this unprecedented three-day seminar where the brother of a fellow top sales agent would be speaking. As I sat, anxiously awaiting his introduction, I wondered how this one man could justify this much time away from my office. Little did I know that I would be riveted and transformed by an inspirational and innovative thought-leader named Bob Proctor.

Bob would inspire and enlighten through entertaining stories that propelled my mind and imagination to new heights through new concepts. He spoke of the Universal Laws of Life, including the Law of Attraction and the Law of Vibration. He explained that acquiring an understanding of these laws and living in harmony or disharmony with them would determine whether we lived a meaningful life or a life of struggle. Bob explained that we were the creators of what showed up in our lives and how crucial it was to master our mind and use it intelligently. Of course, this would require some study and thought on our part to gain a deep understanding of our own internal paradigm of conscious awareness and our subconscious belief systems. Bob suggested that this was a problem because most of us were not trained to *think* in school. As he put it, "2% of people think, 3% of people *think* they think, and 95% of people would rather die than think!" We all laughed, acknowledging this apparent truth.

In those three magical days, Bob Proctor masterfully posed thought-provoking questions as he shifted our minds into the quantum realm of thoughts, emotions, energy, and vibration. My self-perception shifted, I began living with increased awareness, and I created dramatically improved results in my business – deliberately, from a space of unlimited possibilities. I am blessed and forever grateful to Bob Proctor and for the inspired leadership and courage of our Southern California regional vice-president at that time, Roger Tompkins.

Designing a New Life on a Wing and a Prayer

By Rani St. Pucchi

*"I am bewildered by the magnificence of Your beauty, and wish to see
You with a hundred eyes. I am in the house of mercy and my heart is a
place of prayer." - Rumi*

December 8, 2012, is a day that will forever be etched on my mind.
It was the day that changed my life forever. My world came crumbling
down as everything that mattered to me was taken away from me. I was
brought to my knees. I struggled, trying to hold on to straws and to my
identity. I had gone through many challenges in life; heartbreak and
failure were not new to me. But this, this was different.

During the next few months, it felt as if I died a thousand deaths, as
one by one every person in my life walked away from me. I lost my
reason for living and, many times, contemplated leaving this planet. I
prayed like I had never prayed before, imploring the Divine for clear
guidance.

Then, one morning, I received an email from Jack Canfield
regarding an upcoming seminar in Scottsdale. I ignored it. But within 24
hours, I received 10 more of the same, which I thought very strange. It
certainly caught my attention. So I took a leap of faith and flew to
Arizona.

During a guided meditation there, I saw the Divine hand me a
beautifully carved golden box with my initials etched in sparkling crystals
on the lid. I opened it and saw a gilded book sitting on lush lilac velvet.
It read: *Rani's Memoir.*

I came out of the meditation with tears of joy. The message was
clear: I was to write my life story, a story that would help women across
the world – wives, mothers, daughters, and all those who suffer abuse
and have lost hope – so that their lives may be transformed. My life
purpose had shifted.

I've never looked back. I am now a published author, a speaker, and
a coach. My memoir is written. All is well. Moreover, I'm convinced that
everything I thought was done *to* me was actually done *for* me. I feel
blessed.

The Unfolding in Divine Form

By Michelle McDonald Vlastnik

A seed within me initiated the gestation of the Believe Circle project, a combining of energies to manifest financial freedom for our families. "GO! Raise your frequency," my Guides kept saying. "This project is bigger than you could ever imagine. It will have a ripple effect helping masses."

Fruition not arriving fast enough caused a few apples to drop from the tree. Then there were seven. Each person needed to do inner work to raise the frequency; not everyone did. Frustration ate away my joy. I was told a second time to cut the cords; I was being held back. My heart agreed; my head ignored. Why? We needed a group's energy; mine alone was not enough.

In 2015, I was guided to The Angel Abundance Ambassador Club program (AAAC). Perhaps I needed to heal my relationship with money. This bread crumb led to a major shift.

In August, I cut the cords, releasing everyone from my project. *Let go. Let God. Let life unfold.* Now, there is one.

My guides had me clear the energetic lines of the McDonald tree, the seed of Solomon, and the DNA of Mary Magdalene from the injustice, including the land. Archangel Haniel asked me to receive a clearing of my House of Self, from infancy to age 18, from "stuff" that blocked my freedom, including the people who touched those experiences. Melchizedek and several others did a healing on my thyroid, and I cleared all timelines of money issues. It took three hypnotherapy sessions.

Did you know that a project has a birth date? In a 2016 numerology workshop, I asked about my Believe Circle project. Her eyes went big as she did a reading on my project. Never had she seen anything like this. Huge angel wings attached to it. This project will ripple out and help masses of people. It is BIG!

A-ha! The people I had energetically touched in my hypnotherapy sessions *were* the masses! Fruition in "Thy" form. The ripple effect had begun. In that moment, I gave myself credit for a job well done.

I AM Enough.

The Power of Names and Numbers

By Joanne Angel Barry Colon

I was never very good in math; therefore, I did not appreciate numbers until I was introduced to numerology. I had my first reading in 2011, which is when I learned that my life path was a six – the teacher, healer, and supportive friend, the one who values community and family. This makes sense, as I am a personal trainer and healer.

Since learning about numerology, I started to see 1111, 999, and 1024. After reading more about these numbers, I realized that spirit was sending me messages. One of those messages was for me to get a numerology reading on my full married name, Joanne Angel Barry Colon. I was told by the numerologist that my middle name and married name carried much power. I then shared the story of how my middle name came to be:

My dad came home unexpectedly for lunch to find my mother in labor. He quickly called her doctor, then he called 911. By the time the police officers arrived, however, my dad had delivered me. The officers helped my dad clean my mom and me up and then escorted us to the hospital, where they stayed with us to assure that everything was okay. Shortly thereafter, a nurse came in and asked my parents for the baby's name. My parents responded that they had picked out a first name but not a middle name. One of the officers asked if he could give the middle name. Intrigued, my parents agreed and asked what it was. The officer smiled and said "Angel...because she looks like an angel."

Although I've had that middle name all my life, I only started using my full name after that numerology reading. Since then, I've noticed a shift with spirit communication and have opened to intuitive gifts such as clairvoyance, clairaudience, and clairsentience. In addition to being a personal trainer and healer, I am now a spiritual intuitive reader. While I'm still not a math whiz, never again will I doubt the importance of numbers...or names!

The Faith Healer

By Lisa Bartello

The magic that shows up in my life is truly amazing: sitting with Oprah at Oprah's Lifeclass, meeting the Long Island Medium on a boat to go swimming with the dolphins, and the list goes on. Even with all these blessings, one of my favourites has been watching divinity unfold for a friend who desperately wanted to be a mother.

One day, after my friend had been to a birthday party where she discovered that *three* of her friends were pregnant, she asked me to pray for her to get pregnant. I didn't want to sacrifice our nights out on the town, yet I prayed. Another evening, I found myself telling her that it would happen when God decided, and all the painful, rigorous testing would have nothing to do with divine timing. Driving home that night, I wondered where my words had come from.

Then, one morning just after I'd read a chapter on God in the Long Island Medium's book, I received a random email about a faith healer. It told the story of two women talking in a doctor's waiting room. The first one desperately wanted a baby but didn't think that it was possible for her. "I used to feel the same way," said the second woman. "But then everything changed. That's why I'm here. I'm going to have a baby in three months." The woman then revealed that the pregnancy had come after she went to a faith healer.

With continued faith and prayers, I forwarded the email to my friend. On that *exact* same day, I learned that she had gone to the doctor, who confirmed that she was pregnant. Knowing that she'd already had two miscarriages, I told her that this baby *was* going full term. Mission accomplished! She now has *two* beautiful baby girls.

The experience was certainly a blessing for my friend, and it was for me as well. It was the first time that I acknowledged the power of prayer…and put it to use! Up to that point, despite my spiritual beliefs and blessings, this had been a void in my life. Now, I will never forget the power of prayer and the magic of faith.

The Car from Heaven

By Helen Ferrara

I was looking forward to having a new car; my current one was unreliable despite ongoing, expensive maintenance. However, not having had good experiences in finding and buying cars, I was anxious and kept putting it off.

Deciding to face my fear, I finally asked for divine guidance. As soon as I'd made that decision, I found out that my husband's older brother, Tom, who lived on the other side of the country, had been hit by a car. He was in intensive care with two broken ribs, which they thought might cause pneumonia due to his lungs' condition as a heavy ex-smoker.

While praying for Tom, sending love and light, a friend's young grandchild, Nathan, was admitted to the hospital with meningitis. As my prayers opened to include this, I abandoned all thoughts of the car. A day later, Tom's condition seemed to be worsening, yet I had a strong sense that all would be well and kept praying for him and Nathan.

Within a week, Tom went home, fully recovered; the next day, so did Nathan. Although I'd been quite certain of this outcome, I was still very grateful. I was reluctant, however, to return to finding a car. I'd grown up believing that I should sacrifice personal gratification for more important things. In this case, a new car seemed very unimportant compared to human lives, so I couldn't resume asking for help.

That evening, I sensed my late sister (who used to be very into cars) close to me. I felt reassured by her that I could ask for a positive outcome, as I was clearly shown that the Love that cares for us and guides us is infinite and unconditional. When motivated by love, I could ask for all I needed or wanted, and much could be motivated by love, as long as I asked.

With this reassurance, I went online and, within minutes, found the exact car I'd hoped for, down to the colour – the only one available – and bought it the very next day.

The Why of Synchronicity

By Sheila Callaham

I met 20-year-old Carlos when I traveled to San Diego for business. He picked me up at the airport to drive me to my conference destination on Coronado Bay. During our trip, we struck up a conversation about the high cost of living in the city. Carlos told me he was to be married in six months and worried about finding an affordable apartment. With the average monthly rent for a one-bedroom more than $1,400, it's no wonder.

I asked Carlos if he'd ever considered applying for a job at UPS. My twin sons worked there, and I knew it to be a good company with a competitive salary and benefits. Carlos explained that he had visited the UPS website but didn't think they would consider him. The company required drivers to have two years of driving experience, and he only had 18 months.

Having spent 15 years in Human Resources for a global company, I knew that company policies are guidelines, offering flexibility as needed. Carlos looked skeptical, but I assured him that my experience proved that policies are not etched in stone. As if the Universe wanted to emphasize my point, when we came to a stop sign, Carlos spotted a UPS truck parked in front of a residence just down the road from us!

I knew it to be a beautiful moment of synchronicity, and I could tell by the changed expression on Carlos's face that he recognized it too. When I asked what seeing the truck meant to him, he didn't hesitate telling me it was his sign to call UPS!

Synchronistic moments like this make my heart sing with joy. More than ever before, I understood that synchronicity shows up as an affirmation of a higher power to support our intentions. For Carlos, it showed up to encourage him to pursue a new opportunity offering better income, job security, and benefits. It showed up to encourage him to think big, keep the faith, and believe that everything happens for a reason.

Love Was with Me

By Davalynn Kim

I begged for a scarlet letter. I apologized a million times for my transgressions. I was in a prison of my own guilt and couldn't break free. I was a pregnant single mother of two, and the shame I felt was staggering. How was I going to face my children?

I had an idyllic childhood. My parents were supportive and kind. My father was an amazing example of a human being. While I felt loved at home, I never felt as though anyone really knew me. I didn't even know myself!

I had been on an endless quest for love. All that was important to me was to love and be loved in return. I spent years dancing my way through relationships, searching for "The One." I suppose you could say I was in love with love itself. I craved intimacy. I had not learned any other way to request it, so I used my sexuality. Over time, promiscuity needled its way into my life.

After two failed marriages and a child from each, my soul was desperate for a change. That change came about on Halloween 2002, when I dressed as a "social butterfly" – complete with sparkling wings – and my own metamorphosis began.

The man I met was largely irrelevant to me, aside from being the catalyst who set off a chain reaction of events that would change my life forever. Two months after meeting him, I found myself with child. This was not part of his plan, so he disappeared. It was, however, part of my own life's Great Design.

I cried. I prayed! I endlessly asked for forgiveness. I felt like an embarrassment to my children. It seemed to be an impossible situation until one evening when He directed me to a verse in Timothy. The verse explained that a woman is saved in childbearing if she continues in faith and love.

That powerful message delivered from Above caused a magical shift in my life that would never be reversed. I knew I was everything I needed to be. The search was over. Love was with me all the while.

A Greater Power

By Julie Jones

As a young critical-care nurse, I had an attitude that death was a "failure" on my part. I thought that I should be able to save every patient, regardless of the circumstances, and I fought hard to do just that. That was my job. Early in my career, however, I had an experience that completely changed how I view death, how I talk to the dying, and how I care for them. Sometimes it takes years to alter how you approach death, but my experience took only one moment.

I was on an afternoon shift at a small community hospital when a man in his 40s came into the emergency department with a heart attack. Upon being admitted to the coronary-care unit, his heart stopped altogether. He needed electrical defibrillation.

As critical-care nurses, we are trained for emergencies like this – our adrenaline kicks in, and we work! And that's just what we did. The emergency cart was brought to the bedside, and all the nurses worked as a team. We hooked up the defibrillator and stood back for the "all clear" – but the defibrillator wouldn't send the electricity needed to restart his heart. Immediately, we checked the machine, double-checked settings and batteries – again, nothing. The team brought a backup cart – again, it didn't work. It was as if there were a shield around the machines preventing them from working.

After numerous unsuccessful attempts to revive this patient, he was pronounced dead.

Afterward, I noticed that the defibrillator's lights had come back on. I couldn't believe it – all the lights were on, and the machine was functioning normally. It was as if the shield had been lifted.

In that moment, I understood that there was a higher power. I experienced that death could not always be prevented, nor was it always a failure.

On that day, I witnessed a power that forever changed how I dealt with death. I no longer saw death as the enemy. I began to be open to the mystery. This experience strongly influenced how I view health, healing, life, and death. It made me a more gentle and caring nurse and a more compassionate human being.

Heaven's Connection

By Brian D. Calhoun

Life sometimes takes an unexpected turn. Such was the case when I decided to learn to run. Over the course of the "Learn to Run" clinics, I was one of the leaders of the pack when running, most times. And then it began: my knees started hurting. Once I stopped running, though, the pain stopped within the day, so I felt relaxed about it.

Ten weeks into the training, I completed a five-kilometre race, which was the clinic's goal. After the run, later in the day, I went for a 50-kilometre bicycle ride. Within minutes of arriving home and relaxing, my knees began to ache. Over the next few days, the pain got progressively worse, especially when having to deal with stairs. So I went to a doctor who diagnosed me with runner's knee.

Something about that diagnosis didn't sit well with me, though, so I visited other types of doctors to get to the root of what was truly going on. Each doctor gave me a different diagnosis. It was on the last visit, while I was waiting to see a sports medicine doctor, that something clicked. My friend, who worked at the clinic, told me about an angel reader she had gone to see. While my friend was speaking, I somehow knew that this was the answer I was looking for, and I immediately felt a shift in the pain for the better on one level.

Once I arrived home, I made an appointment with this reader, and a couple of days later, I went to see her. While she was relaying information and doing energy work with me, I felt that I had found the next step in my life purpose. It wasn't through anything the reader said; it was from my soul *knowing*.

I knew then that the next step was for me to connect others to their divine spiritual team of angels, guides, and departed loved ones, which I now do daily as a psychic medium and spiritual teacher.

The Wake-Up Call

By Janice Littler

Bang! The plane shuddered as it hit the ground at an angle and suddenly lurched back into the air. What happened? Slowly, the plane gained altitude. We'd flown through a storm and attempted to land for the third time. A voice over the loudspeaker reassured us that everything was alright and we were returning to Madras. My heart was racing, and images flashed through my mind of what I still wanted to do in my life. *I'm too young to die*, I thought as I looked out the window, horrified to see that the wing was bent halfway, pointing upwards.

For several hours, we wobbled back to the airport, where we finally landed safely. Later, we boarded another plane and arrived at our destination without further incident.

As we sat around the hotel pool that afternoon, I overheard a conversation between two Air Force men.

"You know that plane that came in today?"

"Yeah."

"Well, they're lucky to be alive!"

I felt very weak, and slowly walked to my room. Shaking and crying, I pulled out the Bible, prayed, and thanked God for keeping us safe. We had come within a whisker's breadth of losing our lives.

Even today, 30 years later, when I think about this incident, I can still feel the sensation as the plane shook when it hit the tarmac. How the pilot managed to get it off the ground was nothing short of a miracle. As we exited the plane in Madras, I remember seeing the pilot exhausted, slumped over the controls. He saved 122 lives that day.

This was a wake-up call. The Universe nudged me to read personal-development books, which in turn opened up a world of new possibilities. My journey led me to run a business and then complete a diploma in Life Coaching. Slowly, I realized that one of my life purposes was to serve others, in particular mums. My mission now is to help mums create monumental shifts in their hearts, regain their sparkle, and give themselves permission to blossom.

I'm immensely grateful for this second chance in life.

Wind Beneath My Wings

By Tania Smith

I was in the process of ending a relationship and was feeling very frustrated, so I decided to choose an affirmation, repeat it every night for a month, and trust that something life changing would happen. And it did – almost to the day!

I had recently come back from a European tour with Australian popstar Kylie Minogue and was playing keyboards in a club in Sydney when a famous Australian country artist stumbled in and asked me to sing on his next CD. The producer, Rafe Van Hoy, was from Nashville, and we became friends and started writing songs.

This meeting occurred several years after the death of my maternal grandfather, who was my first spiritual mentor. A Mason and Rosicrucian, he was into all things metaphysical and taught me about energy. He also loved the music of New Orleans and said that one day he would take me there. The day before he died, he said, "I've had a good life, but I wish I could've taken you to America. When it's time for you to go, I'll send you an angel and he will take you there."

I smiled and said, "Okay, Pop. I love you." He died soon afterwards.

This final conversation came rushing back to me when, shortly after meeting Rafe, I asked him about his name. "It's a derivative of Raphael," he said.

Oh my God, I thought. *That's an angel's name!*

Later that night, I told Rafe what my grandfather had said about sending me an angel to take me to the U.S. I also told him about the night my grandfather had a heart attack: I was watching the movie *Beaches*, and when I heard Bette Midler sing "Wind Beneath My Wings," I knew that if I didn't get on a plane the next day, I would never see him again.

Rafe looked at me stunned and said, "My best friend wrote that song!"

To which I replied, "When are we going to America?"

As it turned out, Rafe is not only the angel who took me to America; he's also the angel who became my husband!

Chapter 7
Everyday Shifts

Throughout this book, you'll find amazing stories of dramatic shifts and life-altering moments: astonishing coincidences, once-in-a-lifetime encounters, and experiences that are nothing short of miraculous. But not every life-changing experience begins with fireworks. Sometimes, small, subtle shifts ultimately lead to some of the most significant transformations in your life.

In this chapter, you'll read about powerful shifts that grew from humble origins:

- Taking a new route home from work...and opening to new realms of possibilities in all areas of life.
- Appreciating a tiny flower...and finding the courage to rise above fear.
- Responding to a tapping on the window...and being led to life-saving medication; a reunion with family; and a restoration of mind, body, and spirit.
- Getting a new car...and rediscovering joy.
- Watching a movie...and opening up to newfound faith.
- Reading a book...and deciding to follow a dream.

Sometimes the shift begins with something as simple as a momentary smile, meeting someone's eyes, and connecting with their soul. Sometimes it begins with a decision to take action. And sometimes it starts with a moment of clarity. But all of these everyday experiences have one thing in common: they're seemingly ordinary moments that led to extraordinary life shifts. We hope that through the simple act of reading these pieces, you'll open up to soulful shifts in your own life.

Meeting David

By Karen L. Wythe

"Happiness resides not in possessions and not in gold;
happiness dwells in the soul." - Democritus

Years ago, while working at the Cantalician for Learning in Buffalo, New York, I had one of my greatest life-shifting experiences. I was working as a teacher's assistant in a room of severely autistic teenagers. Every day was a new learning experience for me, as well as for the students.

One by one, the students were escorted to the classroom. At first, it seemed like an ordinary day; however, it quickly became clear that this was going to be one of those days when listening skills were very lacking. There was an extra bit of morning chaos, and it was difficult for us to get the normal school routine started. Finally, all of the students were settled and ready to begin the day, except for David.

As he often did, David, was hanging around the classroom's large window – facing it, but seemingly not looking out of it. When he was called on that morning, he did not respond. He just stared at the large plane of glass.

I walked over to him by the window and leaned down to be at eye level with him. Looking into his eyes, which had their usual vacant stare, I said, "David, come sit down. Let's start a happy day!"

Then, all of a sudden, his eyes met mine. The window to his soul opened. Being fully present, he smiled a heartfelt smile. He held my gaze for a good 30 seconds, and in that time, I felt a great joy.

Though I had worked with this young man for years, this was the very first time I had met the true essence of David. He opened his soul to me. I felt honored for that brief encounter. It never occurred again in the time I worked with him, but to this day, I recall that moment. In less than a minute, he taught me that there is a joyful Higher Self residing within each person we meet. And he taught me that just because we cannot always see that essence, it does not mean it is not always there.

Taking a Risk on a New Route

By Felicia D'Haiti

The drive home from my new job had become painful on a daily basis. During the summer, the drive took about 60 minutes. In the fall, with schools and congress in session and everyone back from vacation, there were more cars everywhere, and if I was lucky, I'd get home in 90 minutes. Every day, I would check the traffic reports and mapping directions to get the most direct route home. Well, it must've been the most direct route for everyone because we were all sitting there together...car after car after car. There was no point in considering public transportation either, as many of those routes were closed down for emergency repairs and long-overdue maintenance.

A few times I noticed that my mapping directions would suggest that I cross a bridge near my job into Virginia and drive south until I reached another major bridge to cross into Maryland. I ignored these directions, wondering how driving through three different jurisdictions to get home would be faster than my current route.

Then one day, out of curiosity and desperation, I decided to take the suggested route. I followed the route from Washington, D.C., to Virginia, then back to Maryland. Amazingly, it took just under 60 minutes. I thought it must've been a fluke. That would never happen again! I tried it the next day. It took a bit longer, but still, it was only about a 60-minute drive. This new route was much less stressful, too. I made fewer turns, and the drivers even seemed less aggressive.

What amazed me as well was the way I felt when I arrived home. With the new drive, I was less stressed and had more energy. I wondered why it had taken me so long to take a chance on that new route. I now realize that powerful changes can be made by just trying something new – even something as simple as a drive home. How I drive home has changed my willingness to take chances in other areas of my life. There could be better things waiting in the unexplored.

Transforming Life Through Art

By Polina Ivanova

On June 17, 2014, I walked into the classroom of Kyoto artist Yasuo Imai for a Japanese painting experience. Disappointed in my studies, anxious about my career transition, and stuck in my personal life, I didn't think of that moment as pivotal. Nor did I have high expectations for the class. I was just trying out random activities and workshops to distract myself for a while.

I soon discovered the soothing effect of painting. The process reminded me of an art class in elementary school. I enjoyed painting so much that I started singing quietly without realizing it. Those years were a nightmare of constant bullying and sickness, during which time I developed numerous compensatory strategies and limiting beliefs. Art was my only getaway, and I find that it still helps release tension and anxiety.

I went back to the same Japanese painting class again and again, and gradually discovered the healing properties of art. The class ignited my creativity and brought back my faith in myself. I started drawing doodles and writing stories that revealed old issues with my parents. I discussed them with a counselor and felt better afterward.

I found that art also helps me be authentic and connect with people on a deeper level. It overcomes the cultural and linguistic barriers that I often experience living in a foreign country without mastering the language. Art helps me find my new community.

Now, I have many art-related ideas and plans that I am enthusiastic about, which feels great after a year of inertia. But the most important part for me is that art gets me into the state of flow and gives meaning to my life. However, as soon as I apply old strategies – such as focusing too much on results instead of process, or comparing myself to others – the magic of art stops working and the activity becomes a chore. I believe that authenticity and balance are the keys to living the art experience to the fullest and maximizing its positive effect on all areas of our life.

The Period to the Sentence

By Monica Laws

Hapuna Beach on the Big Island of Hawaii. The large man in his flowery shirt at the edge of the pool with his ukulele looks like he stepped out of a travel brochure. But he is real. The hula dancer is real. This is my life. I manifested this. I am grateful. Aloha.

It is time on this journey in Hawaii to release the Grand Bend rocks into the ocean. Memories of a place where I feel at home, a special place on Lake Huron in Canada. I will leave a little part of myself here on this island where I have changed and grown so much.

The sun is setting. Pinks. Purples. Reds. Oranges. Twilight. I walk to the water. Mesmerized and at peace. The waves lap over my legs and onto the shore, calming and rejuvenating my soul. I throw my rocks into the ocean.

Present in that moment, I raise my arms high at my sides, like a bird in flight. Freedom. To just be. I laugh out loud. And I feel utter peace. I dance with my arms out, in a circle. Almost getting dizzy. Childlike but not childish.

Then I watch my friend, Diana, go to the water and stare at its beauty. Just for a minute or two. I run to her and pick her up and twirl her around. We both dance and twirl and laugh and laugh.

And then: "Do you hear it? The song!" I pick up my things. Diana looks at me knowingly and smiles and nods as if to say, "Go ahead. I'll catch up. Go. Go."

I reach the patio and sit close to the music. "Somewhere over the rainbow…and the dreams that you dare to dream really do come true."

Diana joins me and snuggles close. She asks me, "Are you crying?"

I can barely reply. "Yes. I am. I am happy."

And she says, "This. This is the period to the sentence."

Awakened: My Newfound Faith

By Linsey Fischer

One relaxing summer night a few years ago, I was snuggled up in my living room and decided to put on a new movie I had heard so much about, *Heaven Is for Real*.

Movies based on true stories have always been one of my favourite genres. An empathetic person to the core, I love hearing and connecting with others' life stories. It can be truly eye opening and inspiring, and it allows you to reflect, connect, and feel motivated to take action in your own life.

This particular movie not only did just that, it did something I didn't expect: It awakened my soul and set me on the path to my newfound faith.

Growing up, I didn't identify with one type of religion. My family always encouraged me to make up my own mind about what I believed, but I was unsure of what that was.

I was open to learning about different religions throughout the years, but I never gravitated to one in particular. I believed there was something more than life on Earth, but I didn't have faith in what that might be, until I had the opportunity to see this beautiful movie.

The little boy's story in the movie was so intriguing. I felt extremely connected to it and wanted to learn more. I went on to buy the book, started reading scriptures, communicated more with my Christian friends, and completely opened my heart to the possibility of identifying with one particular religion: Christianity.

The more I learned about what it means to be a Christian, the more I realized that I had been one all along; I just hadn't opened up to it yet.

Once I embraced my newfound faith, my soul and my life shifted tremendously. Amazing things started happening. I was at peace, happier, and I felt like I had something important to live for.

This was a major shift in my life. It set me on the path to being a better version of myself, a believer, a girl of faith.

My Shift Back to Absolute Joy

By Carolyn McGee

A few years ago, my life was going through a major transition: my daughter had gotten her driver's license! She was entering her senior year of high school, had a job, and wanted her independence. This emotional and physical separation allowed me to start looking at who I was and who I wanted to be. My job as a mom was getting an overhaul.

We looked at reasonably priced cars and realized that the cars that fit our budget were small and unreliable, and I worried about putting my new driver in that type of car. The car I currently had was a midsized SUV, and I loved the fact that she had learned to drive on it. So I shifted my thinking into letting my daughter drive what she knew, and *I* got the new car.

One of my all-time favorite cars is a VW Bug, and I fantasized about owning one. I once worked for a startup company where we all had our dream cars on a vision board; mine was a red VW Bug!

I decided to look for one, and the stars aligned: I found a standard red Bug, and with divine support, it waited on the lot for two months while I worked out the details.

My maiden voyage was exhilarating. I had to relearn how to shift, but I quickly adapted and loved my car! She brought back memories of having fun with childhood friends while learning how to drive on a Bug. I was excited every time I got to drive. Work was fun as I loved driving my Bug, named "Rosalita" (after a favorite Springsteen song).

Miss Rosie and I have had many adventures, and still, every time I get behind her wheel, I experience joyous exhilaration. The shift in my attitude from ho-hum to excitement, joy, and being authentically myself has been so fun. I love the attention, seeing the "Punch Buggy" game, knowing that I am completely myself, and feeling happy to be seen and different when I drive my Bug and in daily life!

On the Edge of Fear

By Mauri Barnes

If you stay at the Belmond Sanctuary Lodge outside the park gates, there is time to wander around the majestic ruins after the trains depart, carrying the masses back to Cuzco. It is a magical time to explore, watching condors soar in the sunset skies and llamas that come out to graze with the Urubamba River roaring below.

I joined a small group early in the morning to hike the Inca Trail from the park up to Inti Punku, the Sun Gate. We had hoped to capture sunrise photographs of the ancient city of Machu Picchu, but clouds covered the mountain. Our visibility limited, we breathed heavily in the moist air and climbed higher. Chants of celebration filtered down as trekkers began the final ascent to their destination. The sun was just a small white dot shining through the fog.

We took our break at the Gate, resting from the climb. When we began our descent, clouds were thinning in the heat, and the entire city was breathtakingly illuminated by the sun's rays.

Suddenly, I felt as if I were falling and sank to my knees, backed tight against the mountain's wall. I was paralyzed by overwhelming fear and could not breathe. The trail seemed impossibly narrow, with over a 1000-foot drop to the river below. Too frightened to stand, I crouched there, looking toward the edge, thinking, *If I have to, I'll scoot back down the mountain on my butt.*

I noticed a small, yellow flower clinging to the rocky edge and focused on that, so pretty in this grey mountainous place. Everything faded into the background as I forced myself to look away from fear, looking instead at that beautiful mountain orchid. My breathing eased as I shifted my attention to something that I loved and took a picture.

Click.

The spell was broken. Shakily, I reached for the hands of my companions, lifting me out of my panic. I rose, feeling victorious, wanting to skip down the Inca Trail, no longer afraid.

Send Them off with Love and Light

By Shannon L. Brokaw

I had always held an innate feistiness inside, a deep longing for being right and making sure that people knew it. I chalked it up to being a Scorpio. I was an independent and strong-willed girl who wanted her way, but I was also an extremely sensitive being who didn't like to be hurt. I thought that if someone was cruel enough to do something bad to me, then I must hold on to a grudge like nobody's business because I needed to protect myself from any further possible damage. I held no love for anybody who hurt me, and I wouldn't let things go. I hid my feelings well, but I would hurt nonetheless.

After many years of being stoic yet dealing with a shameful anxiety, I stumbled upon a book by Dr. Wayne Dyer. At the time, I had no idea who this guy was, and I was over self-help books; I already had more than I cared for. But there was something appealing about this particular book, *Change Your Thoughts – Change Your Life: Living the Wisdom of the Tao.*

I decided to buy a copy and pick a verse each day to focus upon and put to practical use. Verse by verse, I started to feel lighter, but when I came across a verse that talked about sending people off with love and light, no matter what, everything started to change for the better. In a nutshell, this teaching encourages you to cut your karmic ties and let them go – to realize that whatever battle the person who hurt you is going through has nothing to do with you and should have no bearing on how you go about treating others.

I kept putting this into practice, repeating: "love and light, love and light." It wasn't easy at first, as I really didn't know exactly what it meant, but one day, I finally *felt* it: I felt at peace – not just with the outside world, but at peace with myself.

Life Is for Living

By Karen L. Wythe

"If you correct your mind, the rest of your life will fall into place." - Lao Tzu

It was a beautiful fall day as I drove home from running errands. Looking over to the right, I noticed the shooting range. *Oh, it's such a beautiful day,* I thought. *I think I'll stop and watch the skeet shooters for a while.*

Pulling into the lot, I parked. As fate would have it, there just happened to be a group of shooters right in front of me. I watched as the first man yelled, "Pull!" and shot his skeet. He wasn't a bad shot. I noticed that his form was good – elbows up, nice and sharp. He quickly tracked the clay pigeon, hitting it with no problem.

The second man took his turn. His form wasn't nearly as good. He yelled, "Pull!" and a little clay bird flew into the sky and down again. He missed. The third man came up for his shot and yelled, "Pull!" His form was completely different from the first two shooters: he threw his body forward, his gun flew into the air, and he one-handedly hit his mark! The clay pigeon exploded into tiny pieces. I was mystified. I wondered why he shot so oddly.

Together, the three men started walking toward the next shooting station. It was then that I noticed that the last man limped along, dragging his left side.

This was such an eye-opener for me – seeing a man pursuing something he loved in the face of physical challenges. Not only did he pursue it, but he excelled at it. I went home a changed person. This stranger was living proof to me that there are no physical challenges that we cannot overcome if we choose to. Indeed, he taught me that life is for living. I became aware that there are extraordinary ordinary people living life to the fullest. And I learned that my perspective not only changes everything, but it makes everything possible.

The Essence of Giving

By JoBeth Hitt

All my life I have heard how important it is to help others. As a child of a middle-class American family, I never worried about where my next meal would come from or where I would sleep at night. My parents explained that most people in the world did not live as we lived and our Christian faith called us to give to people in need.

My church and school provided opportunities for my family to give to others. As we collected money for various charities, we felt we were doing our duty. We counted the change in our little boxes and turned the money over to the organization that would help someone, somewhere in the world. However, we rarely connected with the people we served.

Years later, a group from our church had an opportunity to go to Baja California, where we would help build a house for a struggling family…in one day! As we worked, we got to know the family of five. We saw how they cared for each other and for their neighbors. We laughed with them as we struggled with our Spanish and listened as they described the difficulty of raising young children in a structure that consisted of a tarp roof and newspaper-stuffed chicken-wire walls. The work was exhausting, but the organization, Corazon, had an efficient process, and by late afternoon, sore and hungry, we finished the house.

Before we prepared to return to the United States, we gathered in a circle to say a prayer and hand the house keys to the new owners. When the prayer began, I suddenly felt an overwhelming connection not only to this family but to the human family. The feeling was so powerful that I actually lost my breath for a second and fought to hold back tears. The tears were tears of gratitude for being given this extraordinarily transforming experience. For the first time in my life, I realized the essence of giving: when we wholly give of ourselves and mindfully connect to those we care for, we are all transformed.

A Life Shift in the Snow

By David J. Dunworth

It was late March of the new millennium. More than eight inches of snow had fallen unexpectedly the night before. I awoke to the sound of knocking on the front window – unusual to say the least. I wasn't accustomed to having contact with the world so early in the morning; the sun was just peeking over the horizon. I wasn't sure how to feel about all of this.

As a lifelong sufferer of manic-depression, this morning was my all-time low. In the last quarter of 1999, my home got foreclosed by the bank, my wife of 30 years had moved to Chicago for a job, my kids thought I had fallen off the deep end, and the judge had ordered the premises vacated by January 4th. This same thing had happened to me 10 years earlier, almost to the day.

"What? What? What do you want?" I muttered with a rather gravelly voice and a negative tone. (Sleeping in a '92 Ford Thunderbird in the middle of a Detroit snowstorm can do that to a guy.)

"You can't sleep in your car in the parking lot. It's just not allowed," was the greeting I received from two men in security-guard uniforms. I knew these fellows; we shared the same employer. I worked for United Airlines at the reservations facility, serving on the international travel desk for frequent flyers. The job was not exactly executive status, just low-paid hourly. I was now one of the working homeless.

Somehow, I knew that this fateful day would come, but I didn't expect it to hit me emotionally as hard as it did. I was a physical and mental mess. I hit the proverbial bottom.

In retrospect, I credit that train wreck of a day for my dramatic shift toward a new life. As a result of the encounter, I received help addressing my depression, was transferred to be closer to my family, and was placed on medication that is saving my life. Today, I am happy, healthy, and with family. I've experienced a shift in mind, body, spirit, and nearly every aspect of my life.

The Interruption

By Claire Bunker

On the last night of vacation, my son and I were enjoying dinner at a restaurant in Lexington, Kentucky. It grew dark as we were talking and leisurely finishing our meal at an outside table. An elderly woman approached our table and asked, "Can I draw you a picture?"

My son politely responded, "No, thank you."

The woman, not offended in the least, replied, "I could draw you both on a two-headed dinosaur eating birthday cake." Well, *that* was an offer I couldn't refuse! My son shot me a huge grin, as if reading my mind.

The woman sat at our table in silence and worked diligently, repeatedly looking at us, studying every feature. The waiter soon approached, motioning that he could move her along if she was bothering us. I smiled and said, "No, we are doing just fine."

When the picture was finished, the woman said, "I hope you like it. Sorry it took so long." My son and I told her we loved it.

When she left, my son turned to me, still grinning. "She reminded you of Grandma, didn't she?"

With a tear in my eye, I said, "Yes, she did." You see, my parents met at the University of Kentucky in the early 1950s. My dad died of cancer at the age of 42, leaving my mother and three children behind. My mother, who suffered from depression, could no longer bear to hang on and went deeper and deeper into a tailspin. (This was in the 1970s, when there was little or no effective help available for people with mental illness.) Thankfully, 15 years later, she finally got the help she so desperately needed. She was able to live out the remainder of her life in peaceful solitude, although often regretting those lost years. That lady on the street could very well have been my mother.

People often stereotype the homeless as lazy, dirty, dimwitted, and dangerous, but I know in my heart that this lady was brilliant, caring, and beautiful! Thank you, sweet lady, for "The Interruption." You remind us that we all have the power to transform the stigmas of homelessness.

A Life-Changing Read

By Janice Littler

There are times in our life's journey when people and information come to us for specific reasons. One such time for me was when I read a book that had a profound effect on my heart and soul: *Awaken the Giant Within* by Anthony Robbins.

In this book, Tony shows us that anybody can change the way they think and respond in different situations. He shows that change does not happen on its own. We can be aware of our need to alter our path and take specific action steps so that, ultimately, different results occur. And he shows us that the actual processes used are not difficult to carry out; we just need to have the willingness to get started, maintain our momentum, and consistently take small steps towards our goals.

From reading this book, I realised that we all have something to offer others during our time on Earth – to make our world a better place and to leave a legacy. I realised that it is okay for me to step outside my safety net of certainty and explore new options that lead to variety, sparkle, and fulfillment.

As a result of reading this book, I left a permanent, secure job and started my own business. While the business did not pan out the way I had expected, I received many lessons along the way about how to run a business and the ways in which people reacted to situations. Most of all, I discovered new aspects of myself.

Twenty years later, I reread this book at a time when I was undergoing life-coach training. I saw there were other ways I could take action. It was like unpeeling the layers of an onion, going deeper, becoming increasingly personal and more meaningful. I am now purposeful in chasing my dreams and increasingly aware of my actions and the resulting consequences.

One great takeaway from this reading is that age is only a number. I am a lifelong learner and am keen to explore further possibilities and embrace freedom.

I highly recommend that you read this book. Perhaps it will affect your perceptions, thinking, and future actions – just as it did for me.

Eaten Up by Anger
By J. L. Eck

Growing up, I constantly acted out in anger – slamming doors, throwing things, telling people off. In my teen years, I developed alopecia, a rare autoimmune hair-loss disorder. At first, I just had thinning hair and bald spots that were easily treated. But in March of my senior year of high school, my world came crashing down around me as all the hair on my head fell out within the month. Nothing worked to stop the hair loss or bring my hair back. I stopped going to school and just lay in bed all day, every day. I had no desire to do anything, but my mom talked me into buying a wig and going on with life.

College brought on more difficulties. My best friend/roommate decided halfway through freshman year that she couldn't live with me anymore. I tried to date, but nothing ever went anywhere. The older I got, the angrier I got and the more I shut myself off from the world.

By the time I was in my late 30s, I was in crisis mode. I was desperate to find true love. I thought that if I could just find my soulmate then I would find happiness. I didn't understand that I had to find happiness by myself first.

I was guided to read the book *Eat, Pray, Love*. I didn't normally read self-help books, but I reluctantly decided to try it. As I read, a spark was ignited deep within me! I learned that Elizabeth Gilbert recommended the works of Pema Chödrön – a down-to-earth, humorous, American Buddhist nun – so I bought all of Pema's books.

Pema turned my spark into a bonfire! I started meditating and seeing myself more clearly – including realizing why I always turned to anger as a coping mechanism and why it never helped. As a result, I was able to stop the pattern.

Soon after that, I met my husband, and we now have a beautiful daughter. I know I wouldn't be where I am today if I hadn't had that breakthrough and stopped acting out in anger.

Sew On and So Forth

By Karen L. Wythe

"Life is a series of natural and spontaneous changes.
Don't resist them; that only creates sorrow. Let reality be reality.
Let things flow naturally forward in whatever way they like." - Lao Tzu

Making my rounds in a nursing home as an ombudsman for the local branch of American Red Cross had many rewards. I met so many interesting people and learned many life lessons on any given day.

One day that really stands out to me is when, as I routinely stopped into an activity room to speak with the residents, I observed a woman sitting in a wheelchair pulled up to a sewing machine. She had piles of finished items that looked to be square pillows and small fabric Kleenex covers. There were other piles of cut fabric ready to stitch. She glanced up at me and went right back to her feverish stitching.

I introduced myself over the hum of the machine as she continued her work with no response. After watching for a few moments, I said to her inquisitively, "You must have been sewing for a long time?"

She abruptly stopped her sewing and looked me straight in the eyes, responding with such joy: "Oh no, honey! I just learned to sew. Every five years I learn something new!"

Never have I forgotten that pivotal moment. That joyful woman taught me that learning is a lifelong source of joy. I've heard it said that learning and mastery of things takes five years; however, this brief encounter reminded me not to get stuck and not to be afraid to learn something new. Moreover, I was reminded that variety truly is the spice of life.

Over the years, I have often thought of this woman with gratitude for sharing her wisdom. To this day, I remain open to learning new things and embracing the learning process with a joyful heart.

The Missing Ingredient

By Marci Kobayashi

My father-in-law lives with us. He is an easygoing guy who likes to please others. Even so, he is dealing with Alzheimer's and sometimes becomes ornery and uncooperative.

Getting him to drink enough fluids during the day is my current challenge. It's hot, and reports of new deaths caused by dehydration are on the news daily. He watches the morning news with me, and we comment on it. Then he takes one sip of water with his pills and leaves the glass still full on the table.

I get it. My father-in-law is worried about having to pee. He had a few near-accidents when we were out together and one or two real accidents he hid from us, or so he thinks. It's a real concern and one he thinks is easy to fix. No fluids going in, no fluids coming out.

How can I make this man do what he doesn't want to do?

A few days ago, I got a bottle of Calpis, a sweet milky syrup popular in Japan since the early 1900s. When added to ice water, it makes a refreshing, uncarbonated soft drink. My father-in-law is Japanese and grew up with this tasty treat.

I grabbed our biggest water glass, filled it with ice water, and added the syrup. I set it on the table in front of him and stood back to watch. He downed it and has done the same thing every morning since.

It feels sneaky. I am giving him a full glass of water, and he will need to pee. But it doesn't seem to bother him. It is no longer in the same category as water. By adding one ingredient, his nemesis transformed into something he loves to consume.

I am deeply relieved. He is now taking in fluids, and thanks to his delight, I discovered another secret to life. I've tried masking the dreaded tasks we can't avoid. It doesn't work. Instead, I now look for the missing ingredient. What if our life, *all* of it, were something we loved to consume?

Chapter 8
Physical Healing & Self-Care

We believe that our body is always talking to us, letting us know exactly what it needs. When it needs water, we feel thirsty. When it needs rest, we feel sleepy. As long as our lives are flowing smoothly, we generally respond to our body's messages – we make time to stop what we're doing and drink, sleep, or do whatever our body is asking of us. But oftentimes, we get busy and ignore its whispers. We feel that we don't have time to listen and take care of ourselves. When that happens over a period of time, our body often gets louder with its suggestions – begging us to stop and heed its wisdom. And if we continue to ignore it, we may find ourselves faced with an injury or an illness that is so serious that we have no choice but to listen. The story doesn't have to end here, though. This is where the potential to shift begins – where we get to decide to listen, make changes, and remember that we're not at odds with our body but instead are a team.

Throughout this chapter, you'll find many such stories from those who have been through physically painful moments – who found themselves out of balance in some way and were able to find their way back to their healthy center again. You'll read about people who rediscovered the importance of self-care. And you'll read moving stories from some who were at death's door and found their way back to complete well-being. We hope these pieces inspire you to listen to your body's wisdom – to pay attention and remember that it's here to help you. If you're currently in the midst of physical healing, know that much wisdom can be found in this period of your life. It's our hope that you'll emerge from this experience with a newfound trust in your body and in your inner wisdom – knowing that when you take care of your whole self, your life has the potential to flow beautifully.

As I Lay Dying

By Amethyst Mahoney

Looking up from the hospital bed, I knew I was about to die.

My husband sat beside me, holding my hand, trying to smile through the grimness and holding back tears. For the past two weeks, I had been in pain but thought it was one of the usual suspects: a burst cyst, PCOS, endometriosis. I had ticked off each possibility over the days, remembering past episodes from living with severe pain for over two decades.

But this time I had waited until it was too late.

As I lay dying, I expected my life to flash before my eyes. I expected to think about all the good times and all the bad. I expected to experience my deepest regrets.

A few years earlier, I had read an article by a hospice worker named Bronnie Ware who interviewed her patients about their end-of-life thoughts and regrets. She identified five common themes, including being more authentic, working less, and spending more time with friends and family. Little things. Everyday things. Things that we often take for granted.

I looked at my husband and thought about how we said we'd go to Greece someday. I thought about the times we'd moved from one state to another, then across the country, how he'd gotten laid off from work for six months. I expected a crushing wave of guilt and pain and regret, but I felt none of that. I realized that my husband and I had worked very hard to love one another, pay attention to each other, and spend time together.

Maybe it was the influence of Bronnie's work, but I had significantly changed my life in recent years – turning down a good job in order to start my own business, spending more time with friends, traveling to do what I love. Yet there was one regret that still lingered – one thing I wish I'd done more of, or better: I wished I had spent more time sharing my work with others. I wished I hadn't been afraid or turned people away.

One adept doctor and one miracle later, I walked out of that hospital. I was given a second chance. I had more time to live – *truly* live – and I don't want to waste a second of it!

Time to Trust

By Bryce Goebel

I'd never hiked around Sedona's Airport Mesa before, but it looked like a leisurely trail that would take a few hours. Armed with sunscreen, water, and trusty hiking shoes, I was prepared for anything. Or so I thought.

The hike was an opportunity to reclaim lost confidence. Since knee surgery, I'd been unable to completely straighten my leg. I learned to live with fewer degrees of knee bend, the occasional catch in the joint, and lots of anger toward the surgeon – all of which had become my "new normal."

The first hour passed quickly. Lost in the rugged beauty of my surroundings, I barely noticed that the trail had changed. And then it happened: There was no more trail – only a sheer cliff face. I couldn't move forward, turn back, or sit. I'd gotten myself stuck.

I calculated how far I'd fall. I wondered if I could call 911 from my phone. Would they send a rescue helicopter to pluck me from the mountain after I fell a few hundred feet? Would I die?

The voice was a whisper on the wind: "You must trust fully, right here, right now. If you do, you'll be fine." Where was the voice coming from? In that moment, reality came crashing down. I'd allowed myself to be a victim. I'd been afraid to trust my knee. Deep inside, I knew it was time to trust.

I began walking forward, scrambling over rocks and broken limbs, no longer compensating or leading with the "good" leg. My steps became confident and powerful. Thirty minutes later, I was off the cliff, back on the trail, and full of gratitude.

In the last half mile, I found a new sign marker showing that the trail was "Advanced." (I'm a "Beginner" hiker – or so I thought!) Why wasn't the sign where I started? Because being on the trail was divine guidance. I needed to learn that my knee didn't have to "work right" in order for me to live! I simply needed to trust, stop being a victim, and set myself free.

Unforeseen Blessings

By Karen Hill

It started out as a typical morning for me: I woke up, took a shower, got all prettied up for work, fed the dogs, and took them outside where they played and did their business. I grabbed my cup of coffee, headed out the door, got in my car, and said my prayers.

This particular morning before work, however, I went to the hospital for further testing to follow up on a recent mammogram. This did not worry me until the doctor came into the room to look at my ultrasound. I could see a measurement on the monitor, which looked really big to me. The doctor and nurse took me to a private room, and the doctor said, "I am 99% sure you have breast cancer."

I cried on and off. My husband and I really didn't know what to think about the whole situation. I was so full of fear, and many thoughts ran through my head: *What's going to happen to my life, my job, my income, my body, my hair?*

All of my fears became clearer while doing radiation. I had to resign from employment after 11 years of service because I now had nerve damage. It grew worse over time. I no longer could get up to feed my dogs or take them outside. There was no more getting in and out of the shower with ease. Depression set in, and my prayers changed – partly because I couldn't even remember some of the ones I had said regularly in the past.

My health has become a priority. I am fighting every day as I am learning to live with a "new normal." Although I am still suffering from nerve damage and other newly diagnosed medical problems, I am two years in remission.

During this last year of my healing journey, I've experienced many blessings. I'm blessed with spending time with my family. I've joined forces with social media that led me to writing in this *365 Book Series*. I've discovered Archangel Michael and many other angels to call upon to guide me. And I am very excited to see what will come next in my life during my time of healing.

Love of Yoga, Love for Life

By Tracy Ryan

I've heard that most people who find religion or spirituality do so while they are in pain. Heartbreak, illness, and loss often make us look for some external and almighty force to beg or to blame. I'm guilty of this myself. Although I was raised Christian, the church held little interest for me, and the dogma...well, let's just say I don't believe that truly holy men can also be misogynists. Regardless, I've been there. Many times. Praying to this Christian God for a miracle, for the answers, for forgiveness.

I never felt like I had any power over it, though – neither the prayer nor the outcome – until I found yoga.

I began studying yoga seriously just after my 40th birthday. After many years of playing sports and running, my body finally said, *no, nope, no more of that – these knees will not stand for it!* Yoga seemed like it was going to be more my speed at that point in my life.

The more I learned to incorporate the mindfulness of meditation with the postures, the closer I felt to joy with every twist and fold. When I started yoga teacher training, I hadn't really had the intention of having a spiritual awakening. In fact, I had little intention of any kind. I just felt compelled to learn the art behind the practice. What I found was the art inside my soul – the godliness within me. I felt the power and connection to creating my own miracles because source connects all things to me. This is where joy lives.

I still have pain. I feel sorrow. Sometimes I get so frustrated I want to hit something. Every shift has its shadow. My shadows are now shifted through the divine light and guidance I've found through the love of yoga.

Fighting for Me

By Holly Wade

"You're one lucky woman. You got here just in time. You need to thank The Man Upstairs."

These were the words directly from my doctor. I entered the hospital completely emaciated, at the lowest weight of my adult life – not much more than a skeleton. What had once been strong, athletic legs could now barely hold me up. My eyes were sunken in and sallow. My ribs protruded. My skin was gray and dull. I had always been known for my thick, curly mane; now, over half of it was gone.

I'd lived with Crohn's disease for over a decade and knew that it was the culprit. I couldn't keep food down. It was so painful to eat that I became anxious about *any* food.

I felt that my body had been betraying me for years. After all, I had taken good care of it: I don't drink or smoke. I'm a fitness person. I meditate. Pray. Do yoga. I've sought all kinds of treatments and followed strict food guidelines to strengthen my gut. Why hadn't they worked? How can I contribute to this world when I'm sick?

For my entire adult life, I'd seen the Crohn's as a reminder that I was somehow flawed. I wasn't smart enough. Pretty enough. Successful enough. Skinny enough. Rich enough. I wasn't enough, period. Although I was quite accomplished, I couldn't come to a place of peace within myself.

After running every test imaginable, my medical team decided that surgery was the only option to give me any kind of life. My biggest fear was becoming reality.

As the scar on my belly healed, I understood that my body had actually done everything possible to keep me alive. Rather than fighting against me, my body was fighting *for* me.

As I reflected, I realized how I had abused my body: Teaching up to five times a day. Not getting enough sleep. Pushing through emotionally and physically. Disordered eating. My body hadn't betrayed me; *I* had betrayed my body.

Now this beautiful scar on my belly reminds me of this miracle called my life.

The Gifts of Cancer

By Mary Lunnen

On May 12, 1994, while I was recovering from a procedure following an abnormal cervical smear test, the phone rang: my doctor wanted to see me right away. My stomach lurched; so did my world.

Somehow, I drove myself to the health centre, where my doctor told me I had cancer and would need surgery and maybe radiotherapy or chemotherapy. My world shifted some more.

In a daze, I began telling people: my husband, my employer, my mother. That day, a bouquet of flowers from colleagues appeared – a lovely gesture, but one that made my change from "Mary" to "cancer patient" very real.

In the years since, living with long-lasting pain from the surgery but fortunately needing no further cancer treatment, I have been along a bumpy journey. Along the way, I've learned a lot about myself. Ultimately, this huge earthquake-like shock led me to my true vocation and to a new outlook on life.

This happened in small steps: After an uncomfortable pre-surgery experience with a community nurse who encouraged me to prepare for the worst, I later found counselling to be useful. I began training as a counsellor but then, while going through redundancy, found the services of a life coach a huge support. That was when I knew that this profession was for me.

Another step of my healing journey was to receive acupuncture treatment for pain relief. This opened my eyes to complementary therapies and, later, to becoming attuned as a Reiki master.

And, perhaps most importantly of all, this whole experience has helped me to simply appreciate life – to enjoy the wonders of nature all around me and the gift of each new day.

Twenty-two years later, I can look back and feel that the wake-up call I received back then was, although unpleasant, a chance to choose. To follow my heart, however long or short my life was to be. To choose to rediscover my true self and to allow that to shine in the world. To dare to blossom.

Shifting Illness with Self-Acceptance and Love

By Tanya Penny

Looking back, I believe that my diagnosis of Multiple Sclerosis was really a wake-up call to heal the part of me that allowed myself and others to treat me poorly and even abusively. From a mind-body healing philosophy, autoimmune disorders (including MS) have to do with attacking yourself versus accepting, loving, and honoring yourself.

I noticed that I was attacking myself in many ways: I judged, blamed, and shamed myself for what I did or didn't do. I pushed myself to physically work or do too much (in order to feel worthwhile and safe, and to receive love/attention from others). I stayed in relationships and jobs that were abusive, not loving or truly fulfilling. I abused myself with food, alcohol, sex, and exercise. And I often found myself not speaking/standing up for myself and my needs or desires.

So why would I (or anyone) have these patterns? Like most of our behaviors and patterns, I carried forward what was modeled for me while growing up – especially how my parents treated me and one another. Shifting these conditioned patterns of behavior and the deep-rooted beliefs that held them in place wasn't always easy. I had a lot of fear and doubt. It took awareness, tools, time, courage, patience, practice, support, and loads of compassion. But I realized that when I truly accepted, loved, and honored myself that I would no longer attack myself in these ways or allow others to do so.

One of the shifts I began to make daily was to practice what I now call Compassionate Self-Talk. Anytime I caught myself saying something critical, I would acknowledge it and replace it with a kind thought. I also recorded guided-meditation practices that instilled beliefs of self-acceptance and love that I listened to midday and at bedtime.

If someone treated me in a way that was not honoring, I would clearly state that it was not okay and that I would not allow it. If they continued, I would leave, hang up, or eventually end the relationship.

With my boost of self-acceptance and love, I began to see positive shifts in my health. As of September 2010, the MS is healed. Gone. Now, my passion and purpose is to support others to make these shifts and heal, too.

Gratitude Is the Attitude

By Alison M. Stokes

Often when something "bad" happens to us, we fail to recognize it as a blessing in disguise. I'm no different. In September 2009, I ended up in the hospital for three months with nerve damage, in constant pain, and unable to move from the neck down.

In the hospital, I had to completely rely on the staff for my every need: bathing, feeding, dressing, trips to the gym, and even going to the bathroom. I hated not being in control, and I resented being so completely reliant on others. It was often humiliating, yet it taught me some valuable lessons: patience, appreciation, and total gratitude for all the little things in life that I could still enjoy.

When the doctors told me that I might never walk again, I instantly refuted them. Somehow, I knew they were wrong, and an inner voice strongly insisted that I would someday move and walk unaided. The doctors said I was in denial, but this inner voice was making its presence felt; it urged me to work harder in the gym, to focus, and to change my mental attitude.

Slowly, I mastered holding a fork to feed myself again, a pencil to learn to write again, and a wheelchair to become mobile again. Just before Christmas, I was discharged from the hospital, and I left the ward with the aid of a walker. I had done it! I felt wonderful and alive!

After this experience, my outlook on life was different. I learned to appreciate the goodness I had previously taken for granted, such as the unconditional support from family and friends, the affection of pets, a walk in the park, or sharing cake and ice cream with my nieces.

To this day, I am grateful for that time in the hospital. It gave me a new perspective on my life, an appreciation for my body, and an unwavering attitude of gratitude.

Going Back to School

By Jenna Kelland

Your first day of grade one:

I'm nervous, scared, and overwhelmed. I hold tight to your hand, hoping your touch will ground me and calm me. I make sure that you find your classroom and that you are settled at your desk. I try to focus on you, but all I can think about is getting out of the school.

I don't know what you feel or what you need to feel ready for the next year. I showed up. I did my duty. I go home and collapse. The day is a blur – calling attention to my poor health and my inability to be present, a reflection of how I push myself to meet your needs and ignore my own.

Your first day of grade two:

We hold hands. You're so grown up in your new back-to-school outfit. I see and feel your excitement as you greet your friends. You offer hugs and kisses and wave me away. You can do this.

I can do this, too. I can let go of my challenges – the guilt, fear, and struggle of the last 12 months. I can focus on the fresh start that comes with a new year. Through medication (with its side effects and stigma) and meditation (with its practice of mindfulness and being present), I now know how to look after myself.

I'm able to support you, to see your needs, to be present in your joy and excitement. I'm more grounded, more connected to myself. I know what I need and what I want – for you and for myself. My decisions are more conscious. I know when to return to my calm centre through meditation, yoga, exercise, and quiet. I connect to the part of me that provides energy and focus for my life.

Last year, you learned to read and write, and I learned who I am and how I want to be in my life. You're ready for a new year, and I'm excited to share the adventure with you.

Living Sober

By Nadean Ollech

Giving up drinking was one of the hardest things I had ever done in my 24 years of life. Now, at 43, hindsight shows me the things that would not have been possible had I not made the decision to become sober, commit to that decision, and follow through with it. Without stepping away from this drug, my years of travel, self-discovery, and blossoming could not have taken place. How could they have? Between the ages of 17 and 24, survival was my existing mode.

This life shift means that everything I have experienced, decided to do, and was put through, I did it sober. For the past 19 years, there has been no liquid courage to help me travel alone, face cancer, deal with deaths, have a fling, get dumped, stand up for myself, or make life-changing decisions. Living a sober life can be challenging. There's nothing to blame or even lean on when I want to do something difficult or out of my comfort zone. I just have to gather my courage and do it.

Meeting a 92-year old Buddhist monk and starting my meditation practice, getting my degree in Religion, and leaving everything and heading to Europe for a year to learn how to follow my heart and connect to my higher self – I never would have even *considered* (let alone achieved) these dreams before I stopped drinking.

Life is not perfect. Once I was completely consumed by when, where, and how I would get my next drink. Now, my life has turned into one that is as genuine, as open, and as involved as I am possibly able to live.

Health Restored

By Sharon Rothstein

My health scare changed everything. My thyroid was no longer serving me – or perhaps *I* was no longer serving my thyroid. In either case, this experience proved to be a pivotal moment, a catalyst that led me to reflect upon my lifestyle and thoughts: *Why me? What have I created to support or denature my health to date? What happened to my energy? What works for me and what no longer does?*

It was time to consider myself and my needs, a practice that was as alien to me as landing on Mars. I thought I was put here to take care of and nurture everyone else. I had always been able to serve others with the greatest of ease – family, friends, employers, co-workers, even strangers – but what about *me?*

My body was out of balance. How would I regain my equilibrium? Where might I begin? Would it even be possible? How could I slow down this merry-go-round that was moving too fast on this ride toward my well-being?

Fortunately, I have always considered myself to be a researcher by nature, a Sherlock Holmes of health. What about my internal flow? Were my thoughts supporting peace of mind or chaos? Was I allowing my cells to correct and enhance themselves? My body was crying out to let go of past hurts and my very own erroneous belief system.

Self-love and self-care to the rescue! I began tending to my own needs, both physically and spiritually. I reminded myself to pay attention to my healthful eating and to my thoughts.

My greatest lessons through this health journey have been to quiet my mind, find peace, and always seek solutions that support my own wellness.

In this wonderful present, all is well and shall remain so. I am now a full package. I put my own precious self first, still with room to guide and assist others. After all, what fun is it to serve a pie I baked for others and not enjoy a slice myself?

From Body Loather to Body Warrior

By Kellie McGarry

My heart raced as the doctor walked in. "You will be so happy with the result," he declared. The "result" I had obsessed about for years was to obtain a perfectly flat stomach. I thought a tummy tuck would make me happy and confident. I'd recently had two (big) babies via C-section, and like most new moms, I wanted to "get my body back," which is funny because I never *lost* it! However, when two people asked me, "Are you pregnant?" when I was not, I felt like a brick of shame just crushed me. I hated the loose skin and felt like a fat blob.

My days at that time were spent comparing my body to other women and worrying what others thought of me. Wearing a swimsuit and making love with the lights on were out of the question.

Imagine my elation when, after years of hating my body, my husband agreed to let me have the surgery. Looking back, he just wanted his wife to feel happy again.

Everything changed on a fall day in 2010 when I was diagnosed with fibromyalgia. If feeling fat wasn't depressing enough, I was also struggling with chronic pain. However, I was in denial, and all I could focus on was finally feeling sexy once my surgery was complete.

One day, I was at home playing with my young daughter when memories flooded me about how I suffered from anorexia and bulimia in college (and thankfully am in recovery). I feared for my daughter, and I wanted her to know that she will always be beautiful no matter what her size. And then it hit me – *BAM!* This was a message from the Universe for ME!

I resolved that day to make the health of my body (and soul) more important than the shape of my body. I canceled the surgery and became a body-loving warrior, defending my body from the negative darts society throws at us to be perfect. Today, my passion is to encourage other body-loathing women to learn to love and accept their body, loose skin and all.

On the Gurney

By Jenny McKaig

"Please, God, keep us safe."

I was curled over, head toward my stomach, hugging that massive mound that had grown beautifully those past six months. I was 28-weeks pregnant, and I had never felt so scared in all my life.

I didn't know I could love someone so much, let alone someone I didn't yet know. I knew her though. My husband and I had made her; I was growing her, and I loved her more, or perhaps more deeply, than I had ever loved anything or anyone, ever.

"Please keep her safe." I spoke the words aloud, a quiet whisper but firm so God could hear me. Tears welled in my eyes. "Please keep me safe so I can meet my daughter. Please, God, keep us safe."

Plastic tubes and metal equipment lined shelves in a cold, sterile room. I could see through a tiny window, gleaming fluorescent lights where I was about to have surgery.

I had never prayed to God in this way. I didn't even know what to call him at most points in my life – He, She, It, or in later years, a supernatural power that was Universe, Life, God, or god.

"Please keep us safe."

I was petrified to go into surgery after two of the most menacing days of pain in my life. The doctors explained that the pain was from a nine millimeter stone lodged in a tube only three millimeters wide, hence what felt like knives on my insides splitting me open.

In a way, I *was* being split open. That's why moments before surgery, after raking the doctor over the coals of odds and percentages of risks and what-might-happen-if and how-would-she-be and...

I prayed, "God, please keep us safe."

It was the start of not only calling on and trusting God in that way but also a level of love I had never known, one that grows every day as I get to know my growing daughter.

Forgiveness

By Tiffany Andersen

Have you ever been crushed by a loved one or a friend to a degree that you didn't know how to forgive? I have experienced this several times in my life. Crushing as these experiences have been, somehow I've used them for fuel to rise again to the top. This "fuel" didn't always take the form of forgiveness, though. I am also guilty of using anger to get me through some difficult times.

Anger can be a great source of energy. It can push you to great success. But it also burns a hole in your soul, leaving you feeling empty. For me, anger resulted in a battle with stage-IV cancer at the age of 33.

Beyond the shadow of a doubt, I believe that all the toxic energy I held in and used for fuel was killing me inside. It was only when I fell into the Light of Christ that I found my true purpose in life. Giving all my pain over to the winds of forever is how I gained a mission with a higher meaning to life.

Forgiveness is the key, and it's not just for others; it's for myself as much as it is for the person I'm forgiving. I no longer wish to hold hatred in my heart. I choose to give back the same love that was given to me from something so sweet that it could only have come from Christ.

If you feel betrayed or hold anger in your heart, I pray that you can find the same Light that can break you free from being locked in the dark. If you can't learn to walk free of the pain and forgive...well then, in the end, the betrayal remains only in your own heart.

The journey you walk is *your* life. Don't let anyone or anything steal your true beauty from the radiant life force in your eyes.

Be Still

By Katy Beaumont

Two years ago, I was a supervisor on a huge project. We were way behind, and our daily hours kept growing. Eleven hours a day, seven days a week of being "on" and ready to help my team was taking its toll. I could feel the stress. Giant knots took up residence in my shoulder blades. A permanent lump clutched my throat, and headaches lasted for days.

Something had to change.

A small, seemingly insignificant thought flitted through my mind: *Be still.*

But I didn't have time to be still – I was busy being *busy!*

Still, the thought came and grew: *Be still. Settle down.*

I couldn't just sit still, and even if I was physically still, my mind continued racing.

I found a guided meditation online. I didn't like the music. I found another. The voice was grating. I almost gave up.

I finally found one I liked. And it was less than 15 minutes. I could carve out 15 minutes. Totally doable.

I decided to try that meditation every day for a week. I squeezed it in at night as part of my bedtime routine.

After a week, I began to sleep a little better. I didn't toss and turn as much.

I then set a new goal to meditate every day for a month. I missed days each week, nights when I was too exhausted to even eat dinner; still, for me it, was a success.

Since then, I've kept meditation as a part of my normal routine. Sometimes, to give my mind a break from the chaos, I just have a guided meditation playing while I get ready for the day.

I've taken on more responsibility at work and have begun pursuing my dream of writing a novel. Even with the extra work, I feel less stressed and more balanced.

The most exciting benefit for me has been the drop in headaches – from nearly every other day to just a couple of times a month. I actually feel like a normal person again!

Healing Through Writing

By Linsey Fischer

Could have, would have, should have. These three short thoughts replayed in my mind for many years. I had so many regrets, so much anger, and so much left unresolved. My extreme emotions were having a major impact on my life.

I've always been a sensitive person, but I found that the more I lived in the past and didn't resolve the things I knew I needed to, the more intense my moods would become. I wasn't being my best self, my true self. I recognized this, but for the longest time, I didn't know how to change it.

I went through some things in my teenage years that I needed to get past. I also had some health scares in my 20s, followed by getting over an unhealthy relationship. I put my career on hold for years because of being consumed by that relationship, which was something I regretted. I was also dealing with a brother with a mental-health condition.

Consumed by regret and stress, I fought to work through these issues, frequently asking myself, *Why didn't I do things this way? Why didn't I see that then?*

I tried to heal my mind through counseling. Although I think it's a great tool that works for many people, it wasn't for me. I also tried exercise as a form of working through my emotions, which was great temporarily but didn't resolve the deeply rooted emotions that I needed to work through.

Then, my soul spoke to me: *Use your passion! Write!*

Writing, one of my great comforts since I was a little girl, would be the ticket to healing my mind. Using this passion would be the shift, the way to evaluate my emotions.

Through writing, I was able to reflect and learn about myself. I learned to problem-solve through that reflection and discovered what worked for me in letting my best self shine through. It was like studying my own life and meeting myself, and I started to love the person I was meeting.

Surgical Cure for Smoking

By Mary Ann Reel Bouttu

I smoked two packs of cigarettes a day, but I wanted to quit. I had brief periods of success, but they didn't last.

During a visit with my gynecologist, he informed me that my recent ultrasound showed a large mass on my ovary, which he thought could be ovarian cancer. As we set a date for exploratory surgery to verify his suspicions, I became numb with shock.

On my way home, I pulled into a parking lot as the reality of what ovarian cancer would mean to my life set in, and I began to cry. Through my sobs, I begged God to let me live. I was a single mother with a 16-year-old daughter at home. When my tears stopped, I drove home and discussed with my daughter the facts of the visit and the planned course of action.

On the morning of my surgery, my daughter sat in the waiting area with her great-aunt while I was wheeled into an operating room. The course of the surgery was unknown, but I knew that my daughter would hear the news before me, so I had asked my aunt to wait with her. In the event that my diagnosis was cancer, I did not want my daughter to be alone while receiving bad news.

When I awoke in the recovery room, I was greatly relieved to learn I did not have cancer. As my beautiful daughter entered the room, my tears welled up. No words were spoken as we wrapped our arms around each other and cried in relief and gratitude!

What does my story have to do with smoking? When I saw my daughter, I knew I wanted to live and vowed to myself I would quit smoking. "Cold turkey" didn't work for me, but in the following months, I reduced my nicotine intake and the hold it had on me. Twenty-six years have passed since that moment in the recovery room, and I am still an ex-smoker.

Love: The Ultimate Expression

By Tami McConnell-Finseth

"Love is the ultimate expression of the will to live." - Thomas Wolfe

I stood up, as if already weary from battle, and feebly removed the photo of my children from the desk. *Cancer? That can't possibly be! Were they actually referring to my life in percentages?*

"We'll take you to death's doorstep, ring the bell, and hopefully pull you back before death takes you in," they said.

I felt dizzy. My heart shattered into a billion tiny pieces. It was then that I embraced the meaning of life, love, and the will to live.

As parents, we are wired to protect our children from harm, yet we never anticipate the nightmarish possibility that we could be the catalyst of that pain. How, as a single mom, do you look into the eyes of your babies and say, "Mommy has cancer"?

Those three words began my five-year battle for life.

I had no one to hold me and tell me we'd be okay; no spouse to fall apart on; and no safe house where I could bleed out my heart, terror, and sadness. My only choice was to turn gut-wrenching agony into courage.

In those three words, I found my power. Defeat was not an option. This demon named cancer would not destroy us. I had children who depended on me; I was their world, and they were mine. This battle was real, and it was for my life.

In my darkest hours, I found light. I learned that in being strong for others, I grew stronger in myself. I took what was meant to kill me and used it to bless others. I trusted that God didn't gift me these two precious souls to leave them orphaned. I fought with a vengeance that felt otherworldly.

I'm alive today because my heart is not my own; it beats loudly and boldly in the chests of my most cherished. For in a mother's love lies the power of life. I will forever and always remember how fragile and how precious life truly is.

Water Is Magical

By Lindsay S. Godfree

Who would have thought that drinking water would be a key component for a shift in consciousness? When you realize that your body is 75% water and the brain is 85%, it makes sense that the body needs plenty of hydration to function properly. Dr. Masaru Emoto's ground-breaking scientific research with water implies that water is conscious and receptive to human energy, vibration, and intention. Since we are made primarily of water, our relationship with it is central to our relationship with ourselves.

Every cell needs water to transmit energetic and mental signals throughout the body. No matter whether your focus is upon your emotional, mental, or spiritual life, you just can't get anything to work well if your body is not fully hydrated. Good health is ultimately based on the body's ability to move nutrients into and eliminate waste out of trillions of cells.

What does this have to do with my personal shift? I am one of those people who hated drinking water. It just didn't taste good, and tap water isn't safe to drink in many places. Through family and friends, I was introduced to a water ionizer that makes alkaline, antioxidant, and restructured water. In fact, it makes seven kinds of water. It produces the best water on the planet!

I've determined that, because I have to drink water for my health, this is the only kind worth drinking. It is convenient, too, because the machine hooks up to your kitchen sink. I began replacing all my soda and other beverages with pure, clean, alkaline water and lots of it. Since doing so, my mind has become clearer, my systems run more smoothly, and I have more energy. The shift has been most apparent in my improved attitude toward life and greater clarity in my thinking.

I believe that I can now hold more light energy with higher vibration within my cells, thus increasing my consciousness. Hydration at the elementary level is the most important thing you can do for yourself. Drink more water! Drink the BEST water: alkaline, antioxidant, restructured water. Make the shift.

Go Within or Go Without

By Jody Vehr

If you feel stuck, lost, or doomed to a less-than-desirable lot in life, I am happy to share good news: *You're not stuck!* No matter what you may be going through, know that you have the power to change.

There was a time when I found myself standing in a shattered world, hardly able to recognize myself. I was unknowingly amidst a tremendous blessing, an answer to my prayers; but, blinded by my humanness, I was unable to see it. At the time, I bemoaned everything that was happening to me, but now I see that it was all happening *for* me. Life is always for us. All of it. Without those darkest hours, I never would have been drawn inward to discover the most important person in my world: *me*!

I don't mean this in a narcissistic manner; I mean it in the most fundamental way of nature. The same is true for everyone. It is everyone's purpose to discover who they are. The most important person is ourselves. If we do not go within and love ourselves unconditionally, we go without. Our inner reality is truly reflected outwardly. A reality filled with unresolved issues creates an outer world with ample opportunities to heal.

Prior to my perceived "shattered" world, my life was filled with no self-esteem or self-love. This was reflected in abusive relationships and a run-in with drugs. But once I turned inward, surrendered to healing, and opened my heart to receiving, miracles happened. Once inward, I learned to walk with courage, loving myself enough to forgive the false truths I had placed on myself and others. Through forgiveness and the healing of my negative beliefs, layers of false identity were set free through the doors of my liberation. I fell in love – with myself and with life – and beautiful things happened: my inner reality of light was reflected outwardly.

I encourage you to go within and love who you are, too. Believe in your highest potential and be open to receiving the many blessings that await you. You are adored and loved beyond your wild imagination.

The Unexpected Gift

By Brian D. Calhoun

On a glorious September day in 2014, my life took an unexpected turn. I had just finished running my first half-marathon and had been working as a personal trainer helping clients and myself improve the quality of our health for the last few years. So far, my change in lifestyle seemed to be working. I'd been a healthy raw vegan for four years, lost 200 pounds, and significantly improved my health and fitness.

On that fateful day, however, I felt some side stitches that wouldn't clear up. I didn't think much of it, though, because for the last couple of years I'd been having attacks after I ate heavier or denser food. So I just assumed that my body didn't agree with my choice of breakfast that day (even though it was something I often had before going out for my morning runs).

A week later, it was difficult to get my mojo going for my runs; it felt like something was missing. When I asked my guides why I was having heartburn, I had a flash of a hole in an organ. But the pain had left, so I thought I would get things checked out only if other issues continued.

Fast-forward three and a half weeks: I am lying in the hospital bed after going septic, finding out that I had been running the race (and doing everything else for the past month) with a ruptured gallbladder. I also found out that I had pancreatitis and a blood clot, and there was something wrong with my liver.

This health crisis was the first step in a chain of events that would pave the way for the next step of my life purpose and have a profound effect on the lives of others. Sharing my journey has helped others to go get their symptoms checked, and lives have been saved in the process. Not only that, the information has helped many after their surgeries make peace with their body as it finds its new normal. It's the gift that keeps on giving.

The Ultimate Wake-Up Call

By Jody Doty

Many twists and turns have transformed the course of my life and altered my path, but by far the biggest catalyst for change has been my on-again/off-again relationship with cancer. It needed my attention so much that I experienced two types: skin cancer and breast cancer.

There's nothing like cancer to turn your life upside down, yet cancer has also taught me some profound lessons. Cancer taught me that bodies need attention and love – that it's not only okay to ask for help from others, it's essential. It opened my heart to the kindness of strangers and gave me permission to share pieces of my soul. Cancer reminded me that I can't control all of life's circumstances, but I can respond in the best way possible.

Thanks in part to cancer, I'm now kinder to myself. I listen to my body, pay attention to my feelings, forgive, and make changes. I appreciate the simple beauty of living, and I appreciate that life is a process.

There are good days and bad, triumphs and challenges. Through them, I have learned about the depth of compassion. Cancer taught me that I am not limited to the color pink; I can use all the colors in life's crayon box to heal myself. Cancer reassured me that I am resilient, courageous, and strong. It strengthened my faith and encouraged me to release fear.

Cancer is the wake-up call I wasn't expecting, my inner alarm for change, patience, and persistence. To all areas of my body that cancer has touched, I send healing, love, hope, and beauty.

The lessons have not been easy – they have involved emotional and physical pain, disfigurement, and years of healing. Through it all, cancer has been a powerful teacher. I'm living its lessons. I value my moments, love my body, and honor what makes my soul sing. No longer a student, I am a survivor, a thriver of life, and I couldn't be more grateful to be here.

The Awakening of a Healer

By Atiya Ahmed

A deep cloud of depression encompassed me; I had become this lifeless, depressed, scared, anxious being. Months dragged on, and sleepless nights filled with anxious thoughts about the future became the norm. Life was a struggle. Life had no purpose. Life was not meant to be this way. Things had to change.

A voice inside me beckoned me to wake up, to open up to new possibilities. *There has to be a way out of this,* I thought, as I stared at the newspaper in front of me. Suddenly, an advert for alternative healing caught my eye, and I dialed the number.

The morning of the first session, it was raining and the sky was a dull grey. I made my way there with my usual mantra in my head – *You are going to be fine* – but I didn't quite believe it.

After I arrived, I sat in a chair while the practitioner placed his hands over my head. I felt as though something heavy were being pulled out of me. As the session drew to an end, I looked around the room in amazement. It seemed so much more inviting than when I first walked into it. It felt like a shroud of darkness had been lifted from me. Something inside me had changed. It was as though I were looking at the world with new eyes. As I left, I noticed that the sun was shining, the sky was a beautiful calm blue, and the birds were singing cheerfully. This was the start of a new healing journey.

Over the coming weeks, I began to sleep better. My problems had not disappeared, but my outlook on life had changed for the better. I knew that my life had a deeper meaning. My own experience had awakened the healer inside me. I wanted to help others experience the joy and power of natural healing. I wanted to let the world know that healing is possible...we just have to open up to it.

Learning to Love My Body and Myself

By Vicky Mitchell

In February 2016, I noticed a small, red flaky spot on my lower right arm. Since it didn't itch or spread, I chose to ignore it until the first week of March when, before going into a 35-minute infrared sauna session, I placed two drops of oregano essential oil on the spot. Later that afternoon my arms, torso, and legs became inflamed, bumpy, and extremely itchy.

I wondered if this was connected to something I had recently noticed: my emotional and spiritual negative self-talk had been surfacing in explosions of angry inflammation. Four to six hours after each meal, my volcanic self-blaming anger, pain, and frustration would peak and erupt with self-loathing.

Intuitively, I ordered food-sensitivity tests. After reviewing the results, I realized that my bubbling, boiling skin was a reaction to some of the foods I had consumed. I also felt the emotional connection as my inflammation began to cool after my perception shifted from anger to forgiveness and gratitude.

If not for this crisis, I would still be fueling my body with reactive foods. Instead, I made feeding my body and cooking my food with love and appreciation a priority. By listening to my body, my itch and rash began to heal.

In addition to fueling my physical body, I slowly reincorporated prayer, gratitude, meditation, and movement into my daily spiritual practice. As my skin cooled, I felt the stress flow from my body and my negative emotional reactions recede. In late July, I was able to identify the main "undigested" spiritual and emotional issue that was still consuming me. As soon as I voiced it and set my boundaries, the true healing shift occurred.

By listening to my body and making loving myself a priority, I gave myself the gift of courage to be vulnerable and share my journey. My final shift was my evolution from a holistic health coach into a healing coach who empowers others to improve their health and joy by reducing stress the easy way.

Breaking My Humerus, Finding My Humor

By Donna Kater

There I was, cruising along in my life. Admittedly, I was ridiculously busy taking care of my aging mom and running a successful healing clinic, but I was living a very fulfilling life.

My mother was very dear to me. Mama was happy, articulate, and engaging, even at 90 years old. Her smile could melt even the most hardened heart. It felt like an angel lived in our midst.

I loved my work. My patients were getting great results. Using the techniques I had spent years learning and honing, I was able to alleviate much suffering. The clinic was described as a "bit of Heaven on Earth."

Then came the crash. I fell, breaking my humerus bone in the process. Within a few days, Mama passed. Neither were very humorous events, to be sure; to have the two happen so closely in time was almost unbearable. I lost physical well-being, which led to losing my livelihood. I lost my mom, a driving positive force in my life. And somewhere along the way, I lost my joy and sense of humor. However, I did not lose my perspective. I just *knew* that something good would come out of this.

Recovering took time. I had surgery, therapy, and lots of time to think deeply. I started listening inside. Inwardly, I heard the title of my book, *I'm Still Alive, Now What?!?*, which I proceeded to write and publish. The whole process of successfully surviving a life-changing event revealed itself to me, and I began to find my humor again. My life purpose was revealed in a new light. I found a wonderful pathway of healing that I now share with others.

My joy comes from helping people in person as well as through writing. I now spend my days writing, traveling, speaking, and encouraging others as they struggle with difficult times. I am able to reach more people than I could possibly have done before.

I assist people in embracing *all* of life. Above all, I assist others in finding their joy and humor again, just as I found mine.

Through the Darkness and Back into the Light

By Karen Hill

I come from a family of loving, upstanding, respectful individuals with tremendous integrity. They instilled many positive values and beliefs in me, including hard work, structure, responsibility, honesty, and respect for others. As a child, I enjoyed playing and riding my bicycle on trails back in the woods, working in (and eating fruit from) my grandparents' garden, and riding horses with my friend. At school, I got good grades and enjoyed being a cheerleader and playing basketball. I never dreamed that my life would take such a negative shift.

It began when I decided to smoke pot with my next-door neighbor. Then I decided to steal a beer out of my grandparents' cooler to see what it tasted like. Shortly after that, I started hanging out with friends whose parents did not have any structure, and we could drink alcohol and smoke pot easily. My life became very dark, and by the young age of 19, I became addicted to smoking crack-cocaine.

I began hanging out in Over-the-Rhine in the downtown Cincinnati, Ohio, area where drugs were easy for me to obtain. I was intrigued by city life, all the people hanging out on the streets, and all the beautiful lights. Eventually, I began getting into legal trouble, but by then I was so insane that I thought I was having fun, and jail became just a place to get some rest and food.

My family was so baffled by my behavior. They tried everything in their power to help me act right. At the age of 26, by God's Grace, a loving family, uplifting support groups, the legal system, and social-service workers, I began to turn my life around.

I am very fortunate to have lived through that dark period and shifted back to the woman I was meant to be. I entered college, attained my bachelor's degree, and became a Certified Alcohol and Drug Counselor. I am so blessed today for my upbringing and for those who loved me until I could love myself.

Inverted Beauty

By Angela B. Simmons

Today, I nurture my body, mind, and soul; I feel good being in my own skin. But this was not always the case.

I was raised in the South, an overweight, introverted child, and I didn't feel comfortable in my own body. While 99% of the women in my life had hourglass figures, my body looked like an inverted pyramid. From little girls to very old women, everyone else seemed to have a tiny waist and a fairly large bottom. I, on the other hand, had broad shoulders, no waistline, and a flat tush. I was always made conscious of my figure. I was teased relentlessly by my peers, and at the age of 11, I was molested. The combination of these experiences caused me many years of body shame and depression.

When I turned 39, I experienced a wake-up call that made me shift the way I cared for my body. I began a walking regimen, and I used affirmations and chanting as a way to heal the way I saw my body. I began to realize that I was not a victim and that if I did not love and respect my body, no one else would. I started to feel good in my own skin.

As I continue my journey of self-acceptance and self-nurturing, I often repeat this simple but effective affirmative prayer:

All judgment about my body's shape or size is totally lifted from me. All patterns of eating for comfort are transmuted. I establish daily routines that allow me to exercise in a way that nurtures my body and soul. When I feel pain, sadness, or boredom, I allow these feelings to teach me and to guide me into what my soul is truly craving. I am strong and flexible. My body is the temple of the Holy Spirit, and I treat her well. I am beautifully and wonderfully made, and I accept my size and my figure. I love, embrace, and care for my body. Today, I nurture my body, my mind, and my soul!

The Invitation

By Jessica Robinson

My purest love and my true north will always be my grandma. Just after the year anniversary of her passing, I received an unforgettable invitation.

The sun shined its light in stark contrast to the heaviness I felt inside. I dismissed my appearance in the mirror. Unsure of when I had stopped recognizing my reflection or when the void within me had become apparent in my eyes, I vaguely wondered if anyone else had noticed.

I sat on my couch with self-loathing curled tightly to my chest; the emptiness I felt was almost unbearable. I was unhealthy, extremely overweight, and excruciatingly miserable.

For years, I had wanted to change – to do something more and be someone better. But I was becoming *less* – less motivated, less happy, less of who I really was – and I kept abusing my body with processed food and a sedentary lifestyle. My self-worth was buried under despair.

My heart remembered my grandma's voice saying, "Be happy." I realized then that she had seen the void within me, and the pain of her loss took my breath away.

Though I was consumed by emotions, my awareness shifted to background noise coming from the television. I heard these three questions: "Do you know who you are? Do you know what's happened to you? Do you want to live this way?"

It was an invitation to my turning point, and I allowed the impact of the moment to move me. I realized I had been destroying myself by denying my truth, and doing so had made me powerless. I set out to transform my body and reclaim my power.

The journey of learning my capacity for self-care has been nothing like I imagined. I learned that my physical state was only a symptom, not the source of my despair. Owning my truth and accepting responsibility for my story resulted in healing my soul, which has since opened many doors to the path of my highest potential. I now realize the most profound wisdom my grandmother shared: the way someone loves you *changes* you – especially the way you love yourself.

What Cancer Taught Me About Love

By Tandy Elisala

When we don't learn the lesson or receive the blessing in an experience, the "thing" often leaves the room, changes clothes, and comes back into our life posed as something else. In my case, it came back as the same thing...FOUR TIMES! I consider myself a quick learner, yet I was clearly missing something.

After my fourth and final cancer diagnosis, I wrote down my life vision. One of the things on my list was to find my divine male complement in physical form. I went on to write down that when I released the rest of the excess weight, I'd be ready for this relationship. The next thing I knew, something came over me, and my pen scratched that sentence out...and kept on scratching like my life depended on it.

In that moment, I knew I was the same person I had been 85 pounds ago and would be the same person when I reached my ideal weight. I knew I deserved to be in a relationship – whether it would be the next day, the next month, or the next year.

This doesn't mean I no longer want to gain completely restored health and fitness. It means I accept myself exactly as I am, and I open myself up for infinite abundance in all life areas. It means that I feel love...self-love.

On the fourth try, cancer finally taught me to be my own best friend. It taught me to totally love and accept myself with all my stretch marks, scars, and wrinkles. It taught me to let go of caring what others think of me. It taught me to stop waiting for the "perfect" time to open that nice bottle of wine or wear that gorgeous outfit. It taught me that all the answers are within me and that self-love is the best love.

This time around, I've finally gotten the message! I now feel, believe, and *know* I am perfect in all my imperfections. I am so grateful for my life experiences. They have served me well, and I know that my future is bright as I shine my beautiful light out into the world

Learning to Live Without Fear

By Mark Semple

One of the greatest blessings in my life today is my space of peace and serenity where fear no longer exists. It wasn't always that way, and some shifts were necessary to bring this transformation about.

I had lived with fear the majority of my life – as far back in my childhood as I can remember, throughout my early adult years, and again in my 30s. I had discovered that alcohol nullified emotions, and I became a little too involved with it for several years.

In 1991, after my son was born, I woke up to the fact that I was slowly killing myself and that a major life change was required. As soon as I took alcohol out of the equation, the fear came back full force, and I found myself on medication for anxiety and panic attacks.

The medications were a blessing at that time in my life, as they enabled me to maintain my job and be somewhat present for my family. Then the day came when I wanted the medications to cease also, and I opted to stop taking them.

Thankfully, I was no longer in the panic zone, although I did experience constant fear around way too many aspects of my life. This was extremely draining energetically and caused additional discomfort and conflict with my family.

The significant shift for me was that I made the simple decision that I wanted peace to be the foundation of my life. Being an IT analyst by profession, I resisted the urge to get logical and work a project plan on achieving it, instead opting to hold the awareness of the desire for peace and the willingness to do whatever is necessary to achieve it.

Trusting that you receive what you focus on, I began to experience more peace, and that which was incompatible simply ceased to be present. This brought certain books, tools, processes, and teachers into my life, all of whom contributed to my life of peace and, thus, the elimination of my fear.

Waking up free from fear is a truly sublime – and achievable – experience.

The Long Road to Self-Care

By Tanya Levy

I went to see my doctor with symptoms of dizziness, blurry vision, headache, poor balance, and nausea. At the time, getting dressed was like sitting on a boat – it felt like the room was swaying. Walking through the hospital, the floor seemed like it was moving up to meet me.

The doctor said it could be an inner-ear virus and prescribed me antibiotics. She also told me she thought I may have a brain tumour or MS, like my dad, and sent me for an MRI and to see a neurologist. As a single parent of a two-year-old, I was very worried. I went on leave from my new job and moved home with my young son.

Fortunately, when I went for my MRI, I learned that there was nothing of concern. I continued on the antibiotics. I rested. I learned and started doing exercises to help with balance. I also spent a lot of time in prayer asking for guidance.

I healed slowly and was able to return to work after three months, though the symptoms continued for almost a year. When I returned to work, the real healing began. My doctor told me I needed to make my health a priority and focus on self-care.

As a counsellor, self-care was something I taught *others* to do; however, practicing self-care for *myself* was altogether different. I needed to walk the talk.

I began carving out time in my schedule for myself. I would go for a walk, play with my son, or meet up with a friend. I wrote out my feelings. I started drinking more water and eating food that nourished my body. I decluttered and cleared out things I no longer needed. I spent time learning what my needs were. I learned to talk more kindly to myself and let things go. Most importantly, I learned that self-care is not a luxury; it is a necessity. Each day, I commit to self-care. I am worth it, and so are you.

Bigger Than a Grapefruit

By Ayeesha S. Kanji

I woke up with a jolt. I had been dreaming about waking up out of surgery, and now an actual nurse was asking me if I remembered where I was. I said "yes," as it dawned on me that I really was in a hospital bed. I had just come out of an abdominal myomectomy. My fibroid had finally been removed.

As I was wheeled into another room, I could feel the pain in my lower abdomen. It got worse every time I coughed, laughed, or even used the bathroom. My mom came to see me and showed me a picture of my fibroid. The doctor had mentioned to my mom that my fibroid was bigger than a grapefruit. The picture of it blew my mind. I was so happy it was removed!

That fibroid was like the past year and a half of busyness that had weighed so heavily on me. I had just finished my job at NYU and my third semester of school a week before my surgery. I rode myself hard before my surgery, keeping up a non-stop routine of studying, working, class time, or writing papers. I was so caught up in the disease of "being busy" that I hardly gave myself time to breathe.

All of that was about to change. The doctor ordered six weeks of taking it easy, and my mom packed me to Toronto for a month to look after me. For the first time in a long time, I actually was nice to myself. I slept more than I had in months. It was a sigh of relief to not have to do anything.

As I finally took the time to breathe and heal, my priorities shifted. I realized that I didn't want to be busy all the time, and I began taking care of myself...no matter what was written on my to-do list!

Upon coming back to New York, I changed everything. I started saying no more often and didn't try to cram as much into each day as I had done before my surgery. I was nice to myself, I took care of myself, and I always remembered to give myself space to breathe.

Revealing My True Self

By Ellouise Heather

While recovering from Chronic Fatigue Syndrome, I woke up to the fact that I'd lost touch with the real me. Up until that point, I was living the way I thought I was supposed to. I measured myself against mainstream society's standards, and I fell short of the mark. I held beliefs about how my family expected me to be, and I longed to please them, yet most of these beliefs had shaky foundations. It wasn't until I was recovering my health that this began to dawn on me.

With this new light, I saw the many restrictions I'd been placing on myself. The cracks in my belief system were now illuminated. As the light grew brighter, it consumed my vision and I began to lose sight of these constraints. As a result, they loosened their grip on me. Instead, what became important to me was rediscovering who I was without the convalescent's cocoon of "shoulds."

Like a moth finding itself beckoned to a light in a newly lit room, I was drawn closer. But it wasn't a solitary bulb above me that I felt obliged to ascend towards. It was pulling me from within. I began to intuitively sense what made my light stronger and what diminished its gleam. Its magnetic attraction affirmed my need to act on it.

This inner light was my truth. I'd spent much of my life looking to others to light my path and, in doing so, had unwittingly given away my power. Now I see that I had the power to light my own way the whole time – using the most reliable source I could ask for.

The Beauty of My Present Reality

By Felicia D'Haiti

I clearly remember the day I had my first post-chemotherapy scan and the doctor told me the scan was clear. I quickly spread the news, "I am clear!" I rejoiced, and everyone I knew rejoiced with me. Soon after, many people stopped checking on me as regularly. The energy of worry was gone. Everyone knew I was fine.

Little did I expect, however, that I would still struggle with low energy and some other annoying side effects. When I was going through my cancer treatments, I was so focused on the day I would be finished and everything would be back to normal; it never occurred to me that my pre-cancer normal would not be the same as my post-cancer normal.

I immediately tried to jump back into my old and very full schedule. I quickly became disappointed when I couldn't accomplish all the things I planned in my daily routine. I spent months struggling against my new reality of lower energy and body aches until I started getting messages in many forms, especially from friends, to slow down. It took multiple reminders and me physically not feeling well for me to stop and realize that I needed to focus on being present and not wishing or pretending that things were the way they used to be.

From that point on, I began to focus more on living in the present moment – not wishing for what I thought were the good times of the past. I am learning to ride the wave of uncertainty, not locking myself into preconceived notions of what I "should" be able to do or what I used to be able to do. I am now able to better prioritize what I want to accomplish, knowing that my energy level is different from what it used to be. I have learned to appreciate more what I *am* able to accomplish and celebrate myself for everything that I do.

The Art of Acceptance

By B. G. Friedman

I used to think that accepting a bad situation was a way of buying into victimhood – if you validated the problem, you were giving up by giving in. Now I believe the opposite.

Five years ago, I was diagnosed with Parkinson's (PD), an incurable degenerative neurological disease. The very name of it made me cringe in fear. I was terrified and thought that if I accepted this as my reality, it would give the disease more power. When I thought, *I have Parkinson's*, it felt like I was creating that reality. So I called it a condition rather than a disease, and I refused to take medication, opting instead for holistic and alternative treatment.

Even though my mental abilities were just fine, over time, daily life became harder and physical functioning more limited. Then a friend told me about a consciousness coach who did phone sessions. She is wonderful, and I still work with her. In one of our early calls, she encouraged me to fully accept that I had PD, but that it was my mind/body self that had it, not the Essence of who I truly am. Furthermore, she explained that until I fully embraced it, I couldn't really do anything effective about it. After a little objecting, I got it: All my energy was going into the refusal to accept my situation rather than addressing it.

As soon as I surrendered to the idea that my physical body had PD but my True Self was apart from that, things began to change. I felt more empowered, more focused, and more relaxed. I even began taking medication, which is surprisingly effective. There is still more transformation ahead for me, and I feel I need the challenge of PD to keep me on track for now, but the fundamental shift from non-acceptance to acceptance of my physical reality literally changed my life!

Finding the Power Within

By Robin Chellis

It had been a long road to recovery from lupus, chronic fatigue syndrome, and fibromyalgia. I had been through over 10 years of debilitating symptoms. At times, I wondered if I would ever get better, but I knew in my heart that someday I would be healthy and pain free.

During the worst of my pain, my doctors said I was one of the worst cases they had seen. I was sleeping over 20 hours a day, and the pain was so intense that the strongest medications didn't help at all. This was no way to live. I could barely function.

At one point, I was on over 12 medications, but none of them helped. Instead, they caused more symptoms (a.k.a. side effects). Since the medications were only making me worse, I slowly went off all of them. This helped a bit, but I still couldn't function well.

Doctors recommended moving to a warm, dry climate to help my symptoms. I was willing to do anything to feel better, so I moved away from family and friends to see if it made a difference. I was alone in a new city, and it felt like a new start. I explored new things and opened up to new experiences. I tried many natural healing methods and started eating a super-healthy diet. Then I tried energy healing.

It was powerful. It was incredible. It was life changing.

Even though I had felt some shifts after going off all medications, using natural methods, and eating healthy foods, none of that compared to my first energy-healing session. That session opened me up to the amazing possibilities of energy healing. It was one of the only things that helped the pain and gave me energy.

At that point, it became my mission to learn everything I could about energy healing and heal myself. I became certified in several modalities and completely overcame my health problems. I was a different person. Energy healing changed my life, and now I also love helping others tap into their own healing powers.

October 5

A Heart-Opening Healing

By Cynthia Helbig

My life had reached a crossroads. My old path no longer felt right, but a new way forward had yet to reveal itself. I was waiting, marking time, unsure of where to move next.

In my earlier years, I had searched religion for the answers to life's big questions: *Why am I here? Do I have a purpose? What is God calling me to do?* But the answers did not flow, and I became disillusioned and disheartened. I started wondering if life simply held no meaning at all.

Then I began to feel a gentle tug to explore something new, even as a deep-seated fear of moving away from what I had always known kept me trapped. The inner pull grew overwhelmingly strong. I was guided by a friend I deeply trusted to visit an energy healer, which was not something I felt comfortable with. My trepidation and fear were intense, but I went ahead and tried it anyway.

As I lay on the bed, eyes closed, I could sense the energies moving in my body as the woman worked – sometimes touching me, sometimes not. Gradually, I felt my fear dissipate, the barriers drop, and my heart open. I began to sob, first gently and then in great heaves as wave after wave of release hit me. I felt lighter. I intuitively knew that a major shift had taken place.

I cried a lot over the next three days. I was surprised at the strength of my emotions but accepted these tears as healing and cleansing. And I noticed something within me completely change. Before the healing, I had lived in a world of noise, morning to night: TV, radio – anything to drown out my thoughts. Afterward, for about a year, I could barely tolerate noise at all. My energies were realigning, and silence was all my body and spirit could endure.

I now regularly incorporate energy healing into my life. I love it, and while the effects are seemingly more subtle than my first experience, I know that it restores balance, realigns me to my divine nature, and supports me to live an empowered life.

How Gratitude, Kindness, and Love Helped Me Heal

By Giuliana Melo

I have been on a healing journey since a cancer diagnosis in 2011. Up until that point, I realize now, I was just existing and not really living. I learned to listen to my intuition and my internal guidance – that voice within me that is God. I changed my thoughts by doing positive affirmations and by setting intentions. I learned to practice being kind and compassionate by performing daily random acts of kindness. I began to work with angels and, with their help, have learned to forgive myself for all the wounds of the past. I learned to practice gratitude and count my blessings. I chose to live each day with love and purpose and not in intense fear and old wounds. I learned to trust in the Divine Wisdom and, in turn, have strengthened my faith in God.

Everything shifted for me when I released the victim mentality of my cancer diagnosis. Instead, I embraced my inner warrior! I learned of the Goddesses and their healing energies available to us all. I'd had a continuous connection to Mother Mary, but when I learned that she was not only the mother of Jesus but a Goddess as well, that information initiated courage to explore the Divine Feminine energy that also helps us heal our human selves.

The biggest shift, though, came when I realized that we are all truly connected. We are one heart – one love. When you tap into that, there is no going back into the loneliness of separation. The reality for me was to come to grips with the fact that my life wasn't going as I had planned, and that was a-okay because my life was going in the direction of God's plan. Now, I thank God and spend time in prayer, contemplation, and gratitude each day. It grounds me, connects me, and soothes me, and I am ever so thankful.

My Illness Became My Greatest Blessing

By Sheila Sutherland

My whole life, I was known for my intellect, having a sharp wit, and always having an answer for everything. Then one day I woke up and everything was different. I couldn't think. I couldn't concentrate. I couldn't sit and watch a TV show. I had to read every page of a book several times before I could retain what I'd read. Conversations became stressful. I would mix up my words, and people would often catch it and make fun of it. This led me to start withdrawing socially. I felt SO stupid!

I knew that something was wrong. I started feeling a level of tiredness that was impossible to explain, and chronic pain took over every part of my body. I felt like I was falling apart, bit by bit. I could deal with the pain and the exhaustion, but not being able to depend on my brain, I felt like my identity had been stripped from me. I ended up having to leave my career. Everything that I had worked so hard for was now gone.

It would have been easy to stay a victim of circumstance, but something deep inside told me I was meant for something greater. My old identity was gone, and a new path had to be forged.

For the first time in my life, I put myself at the top of my priority list. Some people called me selfish for setting firm boundaries and thinking about myself first, but in this time of major life shift, I came to realize that if I didn't take care of me, no one else would. I am no good to anyone if I am not full and at my best.

I discovered a strength and resilience that I didn't know I had. I found my own self-worth and finally understood what self-love and self-care truly mean. None of this would have happened had my illness not shown me that there was a better way. My illness became my biggest blessing as it brought me back to ME!

Mirror of the Soul

By Pauline Hosie Robinson

Do you love mirrors? I certainly do! Mirrors brighten the dullest of areas, adding another dimension to any room. At one time, however, I dreaded mirrors. During that time, I felt defeated by life, unable to feel any joy. Mirrors reflected that brokenness, reminding me continually that my mentally ill husband saw me as the *enemy* and my life had been a battlefield of despair. The years of emotional abuse prior to my husband's traumatic death had left me feeling numb. In truth, I didn't *want* to feel.

To prevent painful memories from seeping into my consciousness, I spun a tight cocoon around myself. Unable to face the world, I refused to acknowledge that the woman in the mirror was me! She was drained of life, sucked dry. Sleep eased the burden of remembering, yet even in sleep, painful memories tore at my heart. Each day became a nightmare until I found the courage to face the feared mirror.

The day I dared to look directly into the mirror changed my life forever. Willing myself to face the truth, I beheld my reflection and focused on the lifeless, blue eyes. To my surprise, the eyes contained a deep pool of compassion and understanding. Soothing me with their warmth, they bore witness to the pain of rejection, never-ending emotional abuse, sleep deprivation, traumatic death, and the stabbing pain of lost love.

Tears flowed freely for the vital young woman I had been. Embracing pain, I wept for the brutality of war and the sense of helplessness when someone you love is beyond reach. Compassion filled my veins as truth warmed my heart. Yes, I had chosen to stand by my man. No one had made me stay! In that precious moment, as I took responsibility for my own pain, I understood that I was free. The gift of life pulsed through me, did it not? What was I to do with that gift? By choosing to honour life, I was ready to forgive, heal, and reclaim my true self!

The eyes in the mirror glistened with joy.

Painting the Fabric of My Life

By H. Michelle Spaulding

For the past several years, I have been challenged with chronic illnesses, fighting lengthy legal battles, and grieving the deaths of most of my family and friends. One day, as I was feeling all alone and abandoned, I realized that the only person who could rescue me was *me*.

I believe in and teach the power of healing and self-care through creative expression, so I decided to use this practice myself. To deal with my unexpressed emotions, I got white cloth, paints, brushes, and resist (a fabric-printing method) and started drawing and painting. I wrapped myself in a cocoon of creativity.

The following morning, as I was washing out the resist to reveal the designs underneath, my heart and soul burst with joy. I was ecstatic and full of delightful whimsy. Seeing the designs, the vibrant color, and the textures that had been in my head manifest themselves in the physical excited me. My body, mind, and spirit were filled with so much comfort and joy. I hung these fabric panels all around my house like prayer flags to dry.

At the time, I didn't realize that this creative outlet was also a metaphor for my life. The resist that I was drawing and designing with represented the "resist" in my life. The color I was painting on top of the resist represented my healing energy. Rinsing the resist out revealed the gorgeous vibrant fabric of my life unveiled.

Later, I received unsettling news from my lawyer. Then, the following day, a hurricane hit the island where I live, causing flooding and power outages. Yet, even in the path of all this chaos, I knew I would be okay. I was protected from harm because I had intuitively taken care of myself by creating this healing vortex of color. This artwork created an opening for me to protect myself and release past trauma. Painting this fabric allowed me to shift from victimhood and suffering to empowerment and safety.

Shocked into a Life Shift

By Lori Thiessen

Several years ago, I took my two teenage boys to a sports development clinic. The boys easily jogged up the stairs to the second-floor meeting room while I lagged behind. By the time I reached the top of the stairs, I was completely winded, gasping for breath, and my leg muscles were burning.

I was horrified. Astounded.

How did this dramatic decline in fitness happen? Here I was, the mom of two high-performance athletes, unable to manage one flight of stairs! AACKK!!!

I always considered myself in good shape. I'm not a smoker, I'm not overweight, and I'm not elderly. There was no reason for my struggle with those steps! I thought, *What's wrong with me?*

WAKE-UP CALL!

That was it. Fitness mattered to me. I was going to start running again and get into shape.

The next day, I laced on my old running shoes and took to the trails. I managed about one minute before I nearly collapsed. So instead, I walked.

I walked on the trails for months and months and months until finally I was able to manage running for five minutes. Then 10 minutes. I continued to build up my strength, speed, and stamina until I was able to run my first five-kilometer race. It took me 47 minutes, and when I finished, I thought I had conquered the world!

Looking back, I realize that it all began that day on the staircase. Because of my one decision in that moment, I have now achieved a level of fitness that has changed my life, brought new friends, and opened opportunities. I allowed that shock to jump-start my motivation and make some big, necessary changes.

Today, I continue to run, and I still build on those friendships and take advantage of new opportunities for growth, fitness, and fun.

Remembering Me

By Stella Tassone

Somewhere along my journey, I truly forgot who I was. I was a mother, wife, daughter, sister, friend, and someone who always said "yes." I was a people pleaser, yet I had forgotten to please myself. I no longer knew what my dreams were. I went about my day in a routine of thinking of others and making them happy, forgetting to think about myself.

When my marriage ended and my life was just me and my children, it was a daunting but exciting time. Over time – I'm not sure when, where, or how – a little spark ignited inside me. It was time to remember and rediscover who I was.

I stopped watching TV and began reading self-help books and watching life-changing movies. Synchronicities began occurring (or perhaps they always had been, but now I was more *aware* of them). In one such synchronicity, I learned that the authors of the life-changing books I'd recently read were heading to Australia. I knew it was a sign that I had to go.

I not only got to watch and listen, but I also got to meet these amazing souls who had helped me transform my thinking and return to who I was: Louise Hay, Gregg Braden, Wayne Dyer, Doreen Virtue, Neale Donald Walsch, Don Miguel Ruiz, and others. Listening to their messages in real life was overwhelming. As I sat in the room with these greats, I knew I was meant to be there.

Even though each day is still a new discovery, I am grateful that the little spark ignited inside and reminded me of who I am. Once I rediscovered myself and remembered the fun, loving, caring, compassionate person I am, I began to let go of what no longer served me. It took time. I had to go back to my past, remember, forgive, and heal. But when I did, my life took a new turn. I remembered that I was worthy. I was authentic. I was me.

Social Healing

By Suzanne M. Fortino

In 2015, I received the devastating news that my mama, the woman who took me in when I was 13, was diagnosed with cancer. I remember thinking, *Oh, God, not another one! Please, I can't lose another to this disease.*

I immediately set out to see her. Once I arrived, she embraced me and explained that she knew she was in God's hands and that if her work was done here, she'd accept it. However, she stated, "I don't feel like I have cancer, and I don't feel like I'm done on Earth."

She began posting her diagnosis and updates on social media, and the response she received was amazing: prayers and blessings were shared from hundreds of people all over the world.

She was referred to cancer specialists for blood work, scans, and biopsies. Every time we went to the doctor, cancer was found on scans; however, cancer was not her reality. She'd often say, "Well, *if* I have cancer…" and I began to worry that she was "the Queen of Denial"!

During our final visit for her biopsy results, the doctor told her it was a miracle. "You do not have cancer!"

The first words out of her mouth were, "See, I told you I don't have cancer!"

I believe that through her acceptance of God's will, the blessings and prayers given from so many, and her denial, this cancer miraculously became not real.

This experience forever changed me and the way I see things. I now embrace my healing journey and take the path of sharing love, light, and healing. I realize the healing power of social media. This new vision has allowed me to connect with such beautiful people and communities all over the world.

I Chose Life

By Judy N. Green

The breath caught in my lungs. My heart stopped beating. As the seconds ticked by, the truth slowly sank in. I had cancer.

In September 2009, I developed a lump and angry red fingers radiating out from my left breast. My physician thought it might be "mastitis or something worse." I was 47, and my only son was 26. Mastitis was highly unlikely.

After two courses of antibiotics, the crimson fingers crept across my chest and threatened to encircle my throat. I was sent for a mammogram, after which they immediately performed an ultrasound. I could see the lump on the screen. It was HUGE. I was informed that the results would be available within two weeks.

They called me into the clinic the very next day.

My young physician was visibly distressed as she told me that the results were highly disturbing and indicative of inflammatory breast disease, a fairly rare form of cancer.

I had watched my mother-in-law die of cancer within six months of her diagnosis. She was a "cancer survivor," having survived stomach cancer, only to succumb to lymphoma some 20 years later. My sister-in-law had been battling breast cancer for years. My maternal great-grandmother had succumbed to cancer before I was born.

Cancer was all around me, but I never expected it to be *in* me.

Soul-crushing fear threatened to consume me. I could feel myself being dragged down into a black hole of fear and despair. I knew I had to do something. I had to embrace my power before the cancer stripped me of it. As I left the clinic, I made a decision. I was fighting this *my* way, on my terms. I would not choose conventional treatment.

It's been said that the definition of insanity is doing the same thing over and over again and expecting different results. Well, I chose to stop the insanity. I chose to stop feeding the cancer and start giving my body what it needed in order to fight.

I researched. I learned. I changed. I lived.

Back to Me: Honoring My Limits

By Lisa Hutchison

Here I was, frustrated, stuck, and confused, with my back reinjured. As a highly intuitive empath, I had learned how to separate others' energy from my own, yet I still lacked awareness of my own body.

I had prided myself on being tough and pushing beyond my five-foot, two-inch limits. I was the type to bring in all the grocery bags in one trip from the car to the house – it didn't matter how heavy they were; I could grin and bear it.

It was no different on this snowy, New England, January day. After my dental appointment got canceled, I decided to help out with snow removal. (Here's another confession: I don't know how to help out; I only know how to overdo.) I didn't remove the snow in layers but rather pushed an entire foot across the windshield in one swipe. That's how I injured my back the first time. Within three months, I injured myself a second time. (Old habits are hard to break.)

At this point, physical therapy had failed, and I was labeled with a chronic injury and offered pain medication. After a couple of weeks, though, I could no longer accept this diagnosis or the side effects of the medication. Intuitively, I found a chiropractor to work on the trigger points in these muscles.

My chiropractor worked on the outer muscles while I healed the insides. Over the years, I had tied myself up in knots, trying to do it all. It took me many years to slow down and admit that I have a limitation, which I hated. At first, I felt weak and useless saying I couldn't lift this or do that task. Over time, however, I came to see it as a strength every time I acknowledged and supported myself emotionally, physically, and spiritually.

From these experiences, I learned to be flexible with my thoughts, supporting myself in healthy ways without overextending. While I still find myself compelled to jump in and help others, I now acknowledge and respect my limitations. Today, I can honestly say I have my own back!

Lifestyle Check

By Linsey Fischer

"Hey, Miss Linsey, we reviewed all of your test results, and nothing came up. You seem to be just fine!"

After several health scares over the years, you would think that this would be great news to hear, but that answer didn't give me the relief I was looking for because I did not feel fine. I needed an answer, a solution, and in my mind, it was up to the doctors to give me that.

I thought it could have been from previous injuries I'd sustained in a car accident, but doctors kept reassuring me that I had healed just fine. So why was I having constant aches, pains, and fatigue? As we ran through more and more questions, one came up that I'd never given much thought to: "What are your diet and lifestyle habits like?"

A sudden montage of all the unhealthy habits I had been indulging in over the years flashed through my mind, and it hit me like a ton of bricks: *Wow, I need to make some changes!*

I went home and did research. At the top of my priority list was healthy eating habits. To be honest, following recipes and cooking wasn't my thing. So I dove into juicing and enjoyed the simplicity of it. I also started looking into modern medicine and natural remedies, and I made the decision to become a vegetarian.

The change in me was liberating. Within the first month, I felt a sense of healing, physically and mentally. My skin looked better, and my mindset was clearer – it was an incredible transformation!

That pivotal moment – when the doctors had no direct answers for me but in turn asked me a simple question – forced me to reflect and realize that the solution to my issues had been within me all along; I just needed to discover it.

I call this experience my "lifestyle check." It has enriched my life in so many ways. I now focus on putting the proper things into my body. I am healthy, happy, and in love with my new lifestyle.

Inspiring Pain

By Tiffany Andersen

What does it mean to find inspiration through pain?

Sadly, I think that many, like me, have had to search deep to find the meaning behind the beauty that some might call pain. I sometimes think that only those who have suffered a great deal in life can truly appreciate the beauty that comes from chronic pain. Living with it daily and thriving is a challenge that requires much passion for life.

After suffering for 30 years with injuries from a catastrophic accident that nearly paralyzed me for life, I know that each day I can walk is a gift from above. I appreciate my life. And though each day it's difficult to take that first step, the fact is, I am a free soul who can walk. My heart bleeds for those who are trapped in bodies unable to move; they are my inspiration to get my ass out of bed and move and not take my freedom for granted!

When the pain is too much, I just remember the days when I was unable to tie my own shoes. Then the true beauty in life comes shining through. The pain I feel pushes me to rise and begin a new day with the hope to continue my life with a spirit that is soaring and stepping into the Light. Being able to gently kiss my true love goodnight is an added bonus that helps me continue to fight.

Thank you, Lord, for helping me see past the pain and for giving me a blessed life.

Shift to Spiritual Awakening

By Nikki Ackerman

Ever since I was a young girl, I have been spiritual – not always in a dogmatic, religious sense, but connected to something beyond our human existence. I've experienced many stages of spiritual growth, both intended and unintended.

In 2009, I became a practitioner and teacher of holistic Reiki (a modality of energy work for relaxation and healing). This has opened many doors and awakened ways for me to lead a more fulfilling life.

Last year, I was introduced to dōTERRA's therapeutic-grade essential oils and started using them on a daily basis. This has made a significant improvement in my health, helping me live a more natural life. The use of the oils led me to learning an oil technique to help others with relaxing, healing, and rejuvenating. I knew that the oils were a perfect fit with my holistic practice, so I have incorporated them into my work.

I also recently became aware, after all these years, that I'm an empath (someone who is sensitive to others' energy and emotions). I have been learning how to protect myself from others' energy invading my own by creating boundaries that are more supportive and empowering. I'm no longer using food to create boundaries, and I'm finding an aversion to fast food, which had been my daily staple for years. I have learned that I require quiet time alone to "download" the energy I have picked up and release it to the earth. This replenishes my mind, body, and spirit.

All of these experiences have been leading to a major shift with who I am. I've been experiencing moments of serendipity and, unfortunately, physical issues that have been teachers for me, helping me do what is best for me. I'm clearing out the old and evolving to an elevated spirit, entering a new world of love for all human existence.

A Nightly Ritual for Daily Blooming

By Cindy Hively

In the 1800s, French aristocrats would dress elegantly – with the ladies wearing their gowns from the famous House of Worth – and promenade to the garden. When the four o'clocks began to bloom, they would shout, "*Mon Dieu!*" and toast them with Champagne.

Here in my home, in the Blue Ridge Mountains of Virginia, I have my own early-morning ritual in the garden – although mine doesn't involve Champagne or elegant dress, and instead of aristocrats, I'm accompanied by my tail-wagging boys. Together, we stroll through our garden each day – the boys barking at anything that moves while I appreciate the garden's beauty and see what new blossoms have awakened since our last walk.

I recently had an awakening of my own in this garden. In mid-March, as winter transitioned to spring, I saw that the Japanese cherry trees and the dogwoods had burst into full bloom overnight. As I admired these trees and the other night-bloomers in my garden – including the aptly named moonflower, evening primrose, and flowering night shift – I realized that I, too, need the night and darkness for my body to blossom and shine, and I was inspired to take steps to assure a better night's rest.

I now practice the following nightly ritual: I have a set bedtime of 11:00–11:30 p.m. I get 7–8 hours of sleep every night. An hour before bed, I turn off all electronics and don't watch the news or allow negativity to enter my body. I wash my face, put on luscious lotions and oils, and turn on my essential-oil diffuser. I drink eight ounces of water before going to bed. I have a blessing, prayer, and candle ritual. I make sure I am in love with my sheets, blankets, and pillows. Before I lay my head down on my pillow, all upsets are resolved and I am in a state of peace and ease. I offer my gratitude to God.

Since starting this routine, I've been feeling amazing. My health is great, and I'm in remission from a chronic illness I'd been suffering with for eight years! By taking better care of myself each night, I'm better able to heal, grow, and thrive each day…just like the beautiful blossoms in my garden.

Reflection in Her Eyes

By Janet Dhaenens

I looked into her eyes and shut down immediately! I was doing massage and reached to give my client's shoulder a stretch, totally forgetting she had warned me to be careful of it. She cried out, breathing heavily in her effort to get through the pain. I felt TERRIBLE!

The next morning when I woke up with an intense headache, I knew I had to address the fear I had shut down against, the fear that I am different and wrong and would never be able to do things right. The terror I saw in her eyes was a match to the terror that lived in me. Seeing it in her instantly dropped me into that emotion, and I felt overwhelmed by the underlying belief that I could never be good enough.

My client wanted me to help her body make changes, and I was doing my best to meet her and be a fix-it person, but in my effort to be helpful, I disconnected from parts of myself. One of the parts left behind would have remembered to be careful of her shoulder. I could feel there was a big difference between pushing to make something change and being present with and honoring what is while listening for what is needed.

I determined at that moment that to be the healer I wanted to be, I could not let my own or another's desire or expectation cause me to disconnect from parts of myself. The part that spontaneously receives information, and feels things my mind may not understand, is especially important to stay connected to.

Now I have practiced enough that when I disconnect from parts of myself, I am aware of it quickly and can usually reconnect within a few minutes. I no longer live with an inner terror of doing things wrong. I trust myself to slow down, stay present in the uncomfortable feelings, and explore what is possible. My mind may not know how to be helpful, but when I stay with and feel what is occurring, I can learn something new in each moment.

Honoring Self

By Jen Salstrom

I looked around with a sinking feeling in my heart. I was trying so hard to figure out what everyone wanted me to be that I had forgotten what I wanted myself, or if that even mattered. I thought I had to accomplish everything perfectly before deserving happiness or connection.

One day, I woke up and realized I just couldn't go on like this anymore. I was broke, unhappy, and dimmed out by too much alcohol and not enough self-care. I had lost my way. I remembered that once, when I was much younger, I used to wake up with excitement. I had lost some intangible quality of life that I could only explain as *joie de vivre*.

I did the only thing I knew to do: I went on a quest for that simple excitement that had somehow been squelched. I found that much of it had been lost when I forgot how to honor who I was inside.

After this realization, I shifted from a space of "I want to please you," into a deeper resonance of "How do I please myself, and how do I serve my highest purpose?" No longer seeking outward, the process of bringing out what was within empowered me to live to my highest potential. And instead of being afraid to take action, I was now inspired by my greater purpose.

From this perspective, everything changed. My relationships to friends, family, career, and self transformed. Coming from a place of authenticity, true connections were born.

Savasana Shifts

By Heather Wiest

In 2001, I stepped into my first yoga class at a local gym. I was faithful at working out to stay in shape and to relieve stress from my social-work career, but something about the dimly lit yoga room drew me. I was feeling a shift at 30 years old. Priorities were changing as I thought about starting a family. I longed to try something new, and willingly said "YES" to the still, small voice inside.

The yoga class was powerful, sweaty, and challenging. I totally felt at home! As I focused inward and tuned in to my breath, every unnecessary layer of the outside world vanished. During the final resting pose (or "corpse pose"), savasana, I felt so alive, calm, clear, and balanced. I experienced the true me, unmasked and unbound. It was love at first savasana!

As we participate in savasana at the end of each practice, the body is heavy, but the heart space is light and buoyant, always ready to receive. Savasana symbolizes our death as we lie down, and new life as we arise, perceiving fresh insights about our connection with body, mind, and spirit. It reminds us to make time to just *be* and listen to the still, small voice inside – to accept ourselves for who we are outside of our life roles, responsibilities, and contributions. Moments of rest invite momentous breakthroughs. They allow us to put to death what no longer serves us, creating space to fully experience the joy and liberation of new life – affirming: *I release all that no longer serves me to embrace positive change in my life; I am grounded, yet free!*

Now, as a yoga teacher and a mother of two amazing daughters, yoga continues to be my moving meditation as I center, connect, and receive daily on the mat. My life reflects this expanding inner experience as I encourage others to say Y.E.S. – *Yield, Experience, Shift* – to savasana. Let intrigue guide you to something new. Embrace change with joyful anticipation, and most importantly, always trust that still, small voice inside.

Fun Is Fuel!

By Lisa Anna Palmer

Illness can be a great teacher. Eleven years ago, after a decade of overwork, I burned out and was diagnosed with fibromyalgia – in fact, the rheumatologist called me "the poster child for fibromyalgia." I was doing less and less physically to try to alleviate my symptoms, but chronic pain and fatigue still hung over me like a dark cloud. I felt awful, and I wondered if I would ever feel good again.

Then, six months later, came a big a-ha moment: I was sitting slumped in my chair at a wedding reception, feeling depressed and despondent. Suddenly, out of the corner of my eye, I spotted a whirl of a woman in her 70s with arthritis so bad that her fingers were bent at a 45-degree angle. She was dancing up a storm, twirling and kicking up her feet! Despite her pain, she was still enjoying herself! She out-danced people half her age, and her big, bright smile was simply radiant!

In that millisecond, a powerful realization sparked my heart and I was deeply inspired. I made a choice that night that changed my life: I decided to follow in the dancing woman's footsteps; I got up from my chair and danced!

Yes, the next day, my back hurt and my legs were stiff, and it took me a week to recover – but it was so worth it to be able to experience pure joy once again! That moment of truth was very liberating for me, and I jumped back into the driver's seat of my life.

More than all the treatments I had tried, this major life shift is what saved me. Now, I am committed to having fun every day and making it a priority. I went from being barely able to walk at 34 to today, at 45, being able to swim, walk a 5-mile race, kayak, play touch football with my son, stay out late with my husband, and run my own business. I dance the night away at weddings, and I love life!

Thanks to illness, I learned that fun is fuel!

Chapter 9
Transitions

One of the hardest parts of being here on Earth is having to say goodbye to our loved ones when they pass away. Even though we believe that life goes on in another realm and that we will see them again, there's just no getting around the emptiness and sadness that can feel all consuming when their soul leaves this plane. That moment they take their final breath and we feel their spirit drift away remains with us forever.

However, even with this harsh reality and the finality of death, we've found that being a witness to it can be both life affirming and life shifting. In fact, while extremely heartbreaking at the time, some of our greatest personal shifts have come about as a result of saying goodbye to our loved ones. Through the process of grieving, we have been able to learn more about ourselves and deepen our connection to all that is. We've learned to lean on each other, to be more loving with ourselves, and to open up to love that truly is forever – whether someone is here on Earth or in another realm.

Throughout this chapter, you'll find moving stories where the authors share beautiful moments of being able to take care of their loved ones who were in the process of dying and heal old wounds in the process. You'll also read about how their lives were forever changed after a loved one passed away – how their hearts broke open to reveal an inner strength they never realized they had.

We will all say goodbye to loved ones at some point in our lives. And it's our hope that the pieces in this chapter will help each of us feel more connected – through our love and our grief – and know that, even from the most painful transitions, great beauty can emerge.

Mommy Just Moved

By Norma L. Gunner

Today, as always, I arrived at 8 a.m. As usual, I closed the garage door and announced, "Lizzy, I'm here." Normally, the response would be the sound of four-year-old Molly giggling as, with a bounce, she would leap into my arms. I'd swing her around, hugging her ever so tight, and we would head upstairs to see about Liz.

But today was different.

Today began with a telephone ringing at 6 a.m. My feet couldn't seem to find the floor as I reached to answer, taking in the news through my inner fog.

A soft mist seemed to mix with my tears as I traveled those few miles. When I reached the house, I held back for a moment before entering through the garage – pausing to tell my heart to be still, telling myself that today was different.

But, just like clockwork, Molly bounced down the stairs and leaped into my arms. Cupping my face into her little hands, she looked me squarely in my watering eyes, taking on the face of an old soul, a sage, or a prophet. "Ms. Norma, there's no need for tears. Mommy just moved to a city called 'Heaven.' It's okay." Patting my face, she proclaimed, "We can't call her; she'll be having so much fun she won't hear the ring. We can't write; the postman doesn't deliver there. And we can't visit her because there are no cars there on the streets of gold. But we'll see her again – we must simply wait our turn."

That moment has forever changed me. I still visit Molly often, and each time, I am comforted by the memory of a special child who, smiling through her pain, comforted and left us all better. I now look at life differently. I walk and talk differently. Mostly, I listen and I pray: *Lord, make me an instrument working in concert with your divine plan.*

Lessons from Dion

By Michelle R. Terry

In October 2004, my husband's best friend, Dion, was diagnosed with leukemia. When my husband told me, my normally positive inner voice said, *At his young age, leukemia is a death sentence.* I'd been working in healthcare for almost 15 years and knew the morbid statistics. I didn't speak these thoughts, but my face betrayed everything my heart refused to believe. I told Dion, "You are going to beat the numbers." I tried to give hope to everyone – myself included.

After less than two years of chemo, experimental drugs, and a bone-marrow transplant, we were standing around Dion's bed. I was holding his hand when he took his last breath.

The aftermath swallowed us up, and we weren't ready for gratitude or life lessons. But, with time and reliance on each other, my husband and I realized that sometimes there are no answers. There wasn't anybody to blame or be angry at, and we'd had so many good years with him. Ultimately, forgiveness and healing trumped bitter regret, and we now try to embody these three lessons that Dion taught us:

You can't control everything. The weekend before Dion went to the hospital for the last time, skin cells from a graft glued his eyes shut and he needed me to pry them open. Though he ached for human contact, he sobbed in pain when I touched him. As I worked, my inner voice screamed at me to *do something!* Afterward, in a private moment, I crawled onto my husband's lap and said, "Honey, he's dying." In writing this, I have accepted that there was nothing else we could have done. Because of this, I fight the urge to control everything, and I've found that there's freedom in letting go and letting be.

Don't sweat the small stuff. We are now less selfish and have zero tolerance for people who complain. "You're whining? Dion would've traded places with you in a minute!" Without him, I may have remained an ungrateful, self-centered person focused on insignificant minutiae.

Life is short. Take the trip, always be kind, say the words, and spend time with the people who matter. We've all weathered losses. It's how we survive that scores our legacy and makes it worth the scars.

Return to Living After Loss

By Lisa Miller

Burying a child is life altering; the thought of continuing on with life is unimaginable.

My world was turned upside down on November 28, 2008, when my 16-year old daughter, Tasia, was killed by a drunk driver, leaving me stumbling through this world without her. I could not imagine ever taking another family vacation, celebrating another holiday, or making a new memory without her.

Charges were brought against the young woman who was responsible for my daughter's death, and I found myself obsessing over her life as she continued on without a care in the world. How dare she continue living when she stopped my daughter's life so abruptly! A six-month jail and probation sentence was handed down, which she violated after her release, and she served the remaining probation period in federal jail. As I watched her shackled, handcuffed, and led out of the court, I could finally breathe. Although forgiveness has not yet come, this young woman who took my daughter from my family could now be completely out of my life, my thoughts, and my mind.

One day while visiting my daughter's gravesite, the most beautiful butterflies appeared. I thanked Tasia for sending me a sign that she was near. A peaceful calm came over me as tears stained my face and loving memories flooded my mind. I found myself reading aloud the words so boldly imprinted on her headstone, "Live Your Life," just as another butterfly gracefully landed on her headstone. I thought how sad my angel would be for me putting my life on pause and not embracing it. At that moment, I looked to the skies and declared, "I'm going home now and planning a trip, baby girl!"

I'm always saddened when doing things that Tasia is missing out on, but I truly believe she wants me to love and LIVE every second of my life. I know she's always with me in spirit, and what a celebration it will be when we reunite eternally! Until we meet again, my sweet girl. Until we meet again.

The Whisper from the Ocean

By Monica Laws

On February 24, 2012, I got the call. That dreaded phone call. The one where people say, "This is supposed to happen to someone else." The one where your entire life changes in a heartbeat. His best friend prepared me by asking me to sit down. His voice quivered. "He's gone. He died."

I fell apart. I utterly fell apart. I took a week off work. When I returned, I could only go through the motions. I ended up taking more time off because my grief and my loss of zest for life left me unable to function.

A few months later, I found myself on Long Island, in the town of Montauk. I lay on the beach at the Atlantic Ocean. I was alone. The sky was blue. Just a few clouds speckled here and there. The sun sparkled on the water as the waves rolled in. The water glistened with dancing light. Magic. Mesmerizing.

I heard a whisper. My soul whispering to me? My heart? An angel? It was time to let the anger go. To let go of the hurt, the self-pity. Time to live again. I removed the beautiful diamond and sapphire ring from my left hand. I held it and remembered good things. I put it on the fourth finger on my right hand to remind me every day that love is possible. That there can be something special. I have had that. And at that time I knew that, whether or not it came again, I had so many things to be grateful for. It was time to choose life. And choose to live with love in my heart – not fear, love.

There continue to be challenges and issues in life. But every day I am grateful. Every morning I say, "I am on an adventure." My children are the greatest joy of my life. I have wonderful friends. And today I have love in my life again, a beautiful true love. I cherish every moment. Life is precious. Each and every moment.

Love Reveals Who We Really Are

By Sheila Jenkins

The journey into my soul began after the sudden death of my boyfriend Sam. For the first time in my life, I fell into unbearable grief – the kind of grief that transforms you or, as I like to put it, "reveals" you. As the grief grew deeper and deeper, so did my infinite love for him. I had never experienced such profound pain and deep yearning for anyone like this in my life. I felt compelled to unravel the mystery as to why I would go into such deep grief for a man I had dated for only one day. In my quest to uncover the answers my heart desperately needed, I found out who I was as well.

I started the painstaking journey into my soul to emotionally declutter what no longer served me. I began by shining a light in the darkest corners where I had hidden resentment, anger, guilt, and fear. I needed to forgive those I thought had done wrong by me, and I also had to forgive myself to make room for peace and joy to enter so that love could prevail. I knew I had to love myself first in order to love others freely, unconditionally, and without judgment.

There was no longer room for negativity in my life, and gratitude took center stage. I found the courage to become the author of my own life without any conforming, restraints, or fears that I had allowed to rob me of fully living, loving, and experiencing the present moment.

Shortly after his death, Sam began communicating with me from the other side with the hope of helping me and others. I felt I had quite a story to tell about love, loss, self-enlightenment, and the continuity of the soul, so I sat down and penned the book *The Day Before: Eternal Bonds into the Afterlife*.

Through my experiences with Sam, I've come to believe that grief makes us look within so that we can live the life God/Source/Divine intended us to live. I've also come to believe that love is eternal…and so are we.

Love, Loss, and the Blue Light

By Mary Lunnen

The moment my mother died I became an orphan – in the sense of a person with no living parents. That day was a mixture of sadness and joy. Since her stroke, over five years earlier, she had been paralysed on her left side and dependent on caregivers in a nursing home.

In spite of this, her spirit and love were inspiring: she became an "agony aunt" for many of the staff, always interested in their lives. Although she was able to stay positive, she often said she wished she had died when she first had the stroke. I was able to tell her how grateful I was for the time we had together.

When the end came, I was alone with her before my brother arrived. I was able to say goodbye, to sing to her the simple lullaby she soothed me to sleep with as a child, to know she felt me with her.

One of the tales she told me was this: one evening on holiday, she sat outside holding me, a small baby, in her arms. She saw a globe of blue light circle over us and then fly off down the valley towards the sea and disappear. There was no logical explanation, but that blue light is a constant connection to spirit for me.

Since she died in 2005, I have felt her presence very strongly in my life, although even now there are still times when I go to tell her something and realise I can't physically do so. I see her surrounded in blue – her favourite colour – a blue light of her own. The colour for me is associated with clarity and healing, something I work with all the time now. I now believe absolutely that death is not the end, that something of the soul endures – a love that can be felt by those still living.

Even though I have experienced that life shift of loss and am now an orphan, my mother is still with me, connected through love and the blue light.

Learning from Loss

By Fiona Louise

I vividly remember that day in March, nearly 20 years ago, which altered my life forever. He has now been gone for almost as long as he was alive. Although I know that his energy and essence live on in my heart and in universal consciousness, I still miss him every day.

It took me a long time to grieve, heal, and feel happiness again. But I do so to honour him, to honour my part in his journey and his part in mine. To remember him as my beautiful, sensitive, courageous, and cheeky brother – the one who would jump out from behind doors, rugby-tackle me to the ground, shout "think fast" while throwing a soccer ball at my head, and endlessly tease me the way only big brothers can. I remember bike rides and walks around the lake, his crazy hacky-sack skills and rain dances, his beautiful handwriting and amazing drawings, and that school holiday when we had coffee and spaghetti buns while watching *Aliens* every day for a week!

For many years, his death defined me. It was too painful to have these memories or even to talk about him. He is my greatest loss and my greatest lesson. I was in the dark abyss for too many years, and it was a slow, arduous, uphill journey back to the light. However, his life and death and the experiences since have taught me that our life is what we make it. We have the power to shape our reality, to wallow or to truly live. We can make changes for the better. We can discard the relationships, habits, and attitudes that harm us. This is what I did, learning to believe in my inner strength and wisdom, gaining a resilience that no one can ever again take from me. I have learned to prioritise myself and my dreams; respect my space and place in the world; embrace the unexpected; and accept love, hope, and miracles into my life. I now have purpose to show others how to see their value and find their worth, to release and heal, and to discover meaning in their life. I have learned so much from such profound loss, and for that I am grateful.

From Loss to My Gift and My Life Purpose

By Debbie Labinski

My life shift began at 19 when I found out I was pregnant with twins. Even though I had no plan and wasn't married, I fell in love with the thought of being a wonderful mom. I had faith that God had a plan for me.

I became devastated when I found out that my body miscarried one baby seven weeks along, and then at 22 weeks the second baby was stillborn. I did not understand why, and my outlook on life changed. I would cry every day in hiding, and then I would put on my happy mask when I went out. I always thought this was my fault and that I did something wrong. It was easier to blame myself than God.

Even after I had my three boys, I carried these feelings of guilt for 21 years until spirit guided me to a social-media post by a medium who invited me to her energy circle. I showed up and followed her guidance. She turned to me and asked, "Have you lost any children?"

I was surprised and tentatively responded, "Yes."

She then relayed, "Mom, we are here. Please stop carrying the guilt of our loss. We were not taken from you; we were gifted to you from God. We are always with you."

I softly cried and felt the shift in my heart. They were giving me permission to be free from the guilt because I had done nothing wrong. It was all part of my life path.

I was so grateful for this message that I decided to study and open myself up to the angelic and spiritual realm. I am now an angel communicator, spiritual teacher, and coach. My passion is to pay it forward to other women who have experienced loss and are carrying grief in their hearts. I teach that we are all survivors with gifts and stories to share with open hearts – a process that brings about deep healing and helps us fill our lives with joy.

Losing a Parent

By Catherine M. Laub

My father, Michael Luciano, was a great person, and everyone loved him. He had a heart attack early in life and never returned to full health. It never really got him down, though. He attended every family function and loved being the patriarch of a large family. Every Christmas, we would gather, and he would make a speech about how proud he was of his six children and the extended family.

On December 15, 2012, my husband, Tony, and I joined 21 members of our family in the hospital with my father. Four days earlier, he had died from a massive heart attack and had been revived, but was in a coma. There was no hope of recovery, so my mother agreed to remove him from life support. We were all by his side when he passed peacefully.

It was hard on me because I had had a major surgery in October and was still healing. I refused to go home after the first night because I knew he was going to die. So I stayed in the hospital every night, sleeping in the lobby. I am a psychic, and he had told me twice that year: In January he came to me in a dream and said he wasn't going to make it to the end of 2012, and in December, again in a dream, he looked me in the eye and said, "Please just let me die."

Soon after his passing, he came to me in spirit to let me know he was okay. For the next six months, he sat close by as I slept. He still comes to me in my dreams and lets me know he is proud of what I am doing with my psychic skills, guiding people to be their best selves. This makes me happy because earlier in 2012, he expressed disapproval of me. I am at peace knowing that he supports me now.

She Spoke with No Words

By Rhonda Lee

I heard the reverberating sound of the gunshot just as I peered through a thick fog. Slowly, the fog lifted as I walked closer to the casket before me. I startled awake. It was the same nightmare that had haunted me almost every single night for two years.

When I was nine years old, my grandmother took her life in a very dramatic way. After ages of severe back pain and depression that came with it, she was put on an experimental medication that did not sit well with her system. Ultimately, she succumbed and shot herself.

To say that my grandma's death was a pivotal point in my life would be an understatement. I remember when my father got the phone call, he went running out of the house. I didn't know what was going on, but I knew it was a catastrophe. Hours later, he came home and told me that grandma had shot herself in the head. My shock was immediate, as was my guilt. In my child's mind, I should've been able to take away everyone's pain.

The nightmare started just a few days after grandma's burial. Night after night, it was always the same. After two years, my dream changed. In my new dream, I was at my grandmother's house. I stepped out onto the back steps and saw her about 20 feet away, looking beautiful in a flowing, white dress. Her skin was like flawless, creamy velvet, and she hovered just above the ground. Although her lips never moved and there was no sound, I *felt* her voice when she looked at me. I felt her peace. I felt her saying she was okay. I felt her complete love flowing into me.

I awoke from that dream a completely different person. I never had another nightmare about my grandmother. I understood love and peace unlike any I had ever known, all spoken to me without a single word.

Mothering the Mother

By Shari Sorbo

I was my mother's caregiver. It wasn't an easy job because my mother was not easy to be around. I grew up in a dysfunctional family with an alcoholic father and rageaholic mother, yet when my mother took ill, I was the one who stepped up to take care of her.

My mother was a mean and nasty person, and growing up with a person like that left many open wounds that were triggered when I became her caretaker. Yet somehow I knew in my heart that there was healing that could happen.

The more decrepit she became, the meaner she got and the more she lashed out. Then one day, I decided that I would begin to see her differently.

I began to see a woman named "Louise" rather than the label "mother." There was so much baggage attached to the words "mom" and "mother," and no baggage attached to the name "Louise." That day, I began to see her as a human being in need of love and caring, something she had neglected to give to her own children.

As I sat with her as Louise, I heard her stories of her own childhood and the struggles she had growing up. As she talked more, her barriers of protection began to come down, and as I listened intently to her stories, the armor around my own heart began to drop away as well.

Thus began a deep healing in our relationship. We began to see each other without the labels of "mother" and "daughter." We began to see each other as two women enjoying each other's company.

Before she passed, Louise said to my granddaughter, "Shari is my angel. I don't know what I would do without her." When I heard that, I knew our relationship was healed.

She passed at 97 years old, seven years after I became her caregiver and she became my dear Louise.

Shifting Sorrow and Sadness into Soulful Spirit

By Gina Karas

July 19, 2003, was the day that my life drastically changed. My father was killed in a car accident. I lost the man who taught me to love baseball. I lost the man who always reassured me that things would be okay. How was I going to live without him?

The tears are rolling down my face as I write this. The void is unbearable. The relationship between a father and a daughter is a special one. He was so proud of everything I accomplished and bragged to everyone he could. I was his firstborn, and he let the world know it. Thirteen years later, my heart still aches. That hole will never go away.

My mom was the one who told me that he had been in an accident. Then she said the words that changed my life forever: "…and he died." I couldn't breathe. My world spun out of control. I bent over in pain and sobbed uncontrollably. This couldn't be happening. My dad wasn't gone.

Yet the reality soon set in. The sorrow and the sadness of that realization were so heavy. He was my dad. Who was going to protect my heart now?

They say that parents and children have a bond that can be felt when the life forces are torn apart. I felt that void that night. I had to learn to grow up really quickly. My world had shifted immensely.

I still don't know how I get through trying times without him. But there's a voice of reason that comes to me sometimes, and I know it's him telling me what to do. He's still there for me in those moments as my protector – just in another way.

I'll never understand why he's gone. I'll never hear his contagious laugh again. I'll never hear him talk about baseball with that energy in his voice. But I will keep his generous spirit alive and carry on his legacy of kindness. I'm still looking for the lesson, but I might just be getting a little closer by sharing my story with you.

My Unborn Mentor

By Jane Francis

In 1972, I was suddenly aware that I had just conceived, and I knew that it was a boy. Immature and unmarried, it was a devastating decision, yet the right one, to place my son for adoption.

Four years later, at the moment of conception, I knew that my husband and I were going to have a boy just a few months after our first anniversary. We were elated.

A year later, I became pregnant again – this time with a girl. I cherished my about-to-be daughter from day one. Eric would nurse, lying just above his soon-to-be sister, and I would imagine them growing up together. Two months later, however, those dreams were dashed when I miscarried. I was distraught by the loss, and although we tried for years afterwards, I was unable to conceive again. Three pregnancies resulted in only one child to nurture.

When Eric was 18 years old, I sat with spiritual medium Roy Waite. My session began, "You have three children – two boys, one girl."

I shook my head no, thinking of the miscarriage as an unfulfilled potential, but Roy insisted, "Yes! Your daughter is in spirit from abortion or miscarriage; she is 17 now."

I gasped, stunned because that baby would have been 17!

"You named her Margaret."

"No, not Margaret," I blurted. "I thought, maybe Megan."

Roy reprimanded sharply, "She chose her own name then!" He shared many more messages from Margaret, then said, "She came through you to connect as your family angel."

Amazed and delighted that our almost-baby was alive on the Other Side, I longed to talk with her myself. Roy told me Margaret could use Angel Cards to communicate, so I bought some that very day!

Discovering Margaret's ongoing existence sparked my interest in learning about the afterlife and spirit communication. My life moved in a whole new direction with Margaret as my mentor and coach. In fact, all three of my children are my greatest teachers, and I am forever grateful for them all! (P.S. Megan is a derivative of Margaret!)

A Mother's Love Never Dies

By Diane Marie Ford

On December 16, 1995, my mother, Leah, died in a tragic car accident. Her neck broke. My heart broke. I was not prepared to live without my mother's unconditional love and deep friendship. We were the only women in our family, and we shared a tight, unbreakable bond.

Her accident changed the trajectory of my life. I did not believe I could live without her presence in my life. Little did I know at the time, I would not have to.

We had always been close, psychically connected. It wasn't until several years later, well after she transitioned into spirit, that I realized my powerful connection to the spirit realm. For reasons unknown to me, I developed a gift of communication with spirit and began offering my services to others.

One evening, as I meditated in preparation for a spirit circle, my mother came through to me and asked one question: "What if I were to tell you that the reason I brought you onto this Earth plane was so I could help you from the other side?"

Bewildered yet curious, I shook my head and asked, "What?" (As in, "What am I hearing?" – *not* "What is your question?")

She repeated: "What if I were to tell you the reason I brought you onto this Earth plane was so I could help you from the other side?"

My response was, "How do I know I'm not crazy right now? How do I know I'm not just hearing voices?"

My mother replied: "Do you trust me?"

Without missing a beat, I said, "Of course I do, Ma."

She comforted me with the words, "Well then, you know what I did for you when we walked the Earth plane together; imagine what I can do for you from this vantage point."

Twenty-one years have passed. Our relationship grows deeper every day. There is no doubt in my heart that a mother's love never dies; it simply changes form.

With Death Comes Life, More Abundantly

By Freda Durden

And just like that, he was dead. My father had been the missing piece in my life – or so I had thought – for 18 years. During a casual talk with my mother, I heard about his passing. My longtime search for a part of me – what felt like the key to understanding who I really was – had come to an abrupt end during a 10-minute conversation.

I was detached in the moment, but later on that evening the emotion came streaming in as I wondered, *That's it?!* My head felt like a ton of bricks, and I could feel the tears welling up from deep inside my being. The little girl who had been abandoned felt left behind all over again.

That's it?!

The feeling became more desperate and angry. The injustice was overwhelming. I analyzed all the decisions I'd made about myself and my life based on this one person, and now his existence was no more. There were so many details swimming around within me, each one triggering a deeper pain than the one before.

In all the *why*s that had been unanswered, there was one that flashed bright red in my mind: *Why me?* Life had brought me the lesson many times that within my pain was purpose. Sitting with the *why* (and a libation or two), I discovered that this was the end of that story. With the passing of my absent father, I had been set free to rewrite my life in a way that fit who I knew I was.

On that day, I decided, *That's it! No more searching for missing pieces.* I gathered up the parts of myself that I had and decided that I *AM* all that I need to be: *ME.*

This experience confirmed that no matter what happens, it is our perception that determines how we overcome and thrive beyond pain. I chose to see death as an opportunity to have life, and to have it more abundantly.

Kaarina, My Little Angel

By Ingrid Koivukangas

I rarely share this part of my life – it makes people uncomfortable, which then makes me uncomfortable. But I keep feeling that someone is waiting for these words so they can begin to share and acknowledge their loss.

I was 19 years old and a new mom. After a few scares and a long bed-rest hospital stay, my daughter, Kaarina, had arrived safely. I'd always been intuitive and had had a couple of disturbing dreams while pregnant, but in the light of day, they soon disappeared to the hazy place dreams go. I told myself I was just having new-mom jitters. I had never been so happy in my life. I was completely in love with Kaarina and with being a mom.

One day, not long after Kaarina's birth, I woke up to the early-morning sun soft on my window. I looked at the clock, surprised to see that it was a little later than usual. Kaarina must have slept through the night. I got up, singing softly as I entered her room. Leaning over her crib to pick her up, I immediately sensed that something was terribly wrong. Her soul had somehow slipped away as I slept. And I entered a nightmare.

I heard myself screaming and screaming. Someone was on the phone talking to 911, then the sound of sirens: ambulances, police cars, fire trucks. Strangers crowded into my home, talking in hushed voices.

I sat on the couch. I couldn't comprehend what was happening. I felt like I was underwater, suffocating. My heart was breaking. I wanted to hold my baby. I wanted to ask the police officer to bring her to me so I could rock her and sing to her. I wanted to wake up from this nightmare.

In that moment, my soul recognized that my mind was nearing a place that if I entered I would not be able to leave. I was on a precipice: go mad or somehow find the strength to move forward without leaving her behind.

I chose to live, to find a way through my grief, to carry Kaarina with me always, in spirit and in my heart.

All I Ever Felt from You Was Love

By Tanya Levy

On St. Patrick's Day, 1992, my mother became paralyzed. I lost a part of her that day that never came back. She was a super mom: organized, always on top of things, ready with a wise crack that would make me smile. Never one to give up, Mom continued to devote herself to her family. She would make meals, join me to shop at the mall, crochet in bed, and write notes to family and friends.

Little by little, she became more frail, and in the last years of her life, she was bedridden. Because I lived 90 minutes away and didn't get to see her all the time, I called her every night at 7 p.m. I didn't know if this mattered, but I wanted to talk to her as often as I could. In the last letter she was able to write to me, she wrote, "Thank you for your daily calls; they break the monotony."

My fondest memory of my mom is when I sat by her bed and held her hand. During our chats, her eyes would sparkle. She would ask how my life was and share snippets of wisdom about marriage, parenting, and life. She would also tell me to put my phone away if I checked it too much.

It became clear that Mom's condition was worsening as she was in and out of the hospital. Before she left this world, there were some things my heart needed to know. I asked her if I had let her down. She said, "never." I asked her if she was angry with me. She said, "never." Then she looked at me and said, "All I ever felt from you was love." Then I finally understood my mom. I was not able to remove her paralysis, her suffering, or her pain; however, I was able to show her love. Those eight words got me through her death in March 2015, and through the tough days of grief that followed. Love is what matters.

Letting Go of My Plans

By Lore Raymond

Thirteen years ago, the phone rang at 4:00 a.m., piercing my peaceful dreamtime. Panic seized me. It was Dad calling from Florida to ask my permission to die. *WHAT?! Could I let him go?* His cancer had returned. No more options.

"I love you, Lo," would be his final words.

"Love you, too," I blubbered.

Grief's flu-like symptoms left me aching to be stateside with him and Mom. Could I magically crawl through the phone line from my home in La Ceiba, Honduras?! I had just started teaching fifth grade. Imagine making indefinite plans for the care of my students, home, dog, *and* seventh-grade daughter. Setting a return travel date would mean that *he died.* An unbearable thought.

I zoomed back to Florida for this final Earth journey with him – all possible because of friends like Deni and the Alvarados. Waking early, I wondered why he hadn't yet left his Earth suit; he'd been in a coma for two days. "Open the sliding glass doors so his spirit can leave," came the whisper. I got out of bed to find them already opened. My sister had heard the same whisper.

Mom had stepped out, so it was just Dad and me. I sat beside the bed, holding his frail, ink-veined hand and started matching his breaths…inhaling…exhaling…the crisp morning air of October. I lovingly and firmly said, "You need to go now. We three kids will take care of Mom."

Minutes later, my forever fierce, fighter-pilot Daddy zoomed off into a new sky. This favorite son and 30-year veteran from New Hampshire was now "living free" from all disease.

While flying back to resume life as a single mom and teacher, I decided something: Nazlie and I would return to Florida at the end of the school year to join Mom. Dad's early death at 75 jolted me into remembering that family was everything. Sure, I wanted to teach my next four years in Guatemala. But it was time to return home. It was time to say yes to letting go of my plans.

Broken Open

By Amanda Hendricks

I was 14 when Heather came to live with my family. She was five months old, born with HIV, and projected to live only two years. She clearly had other plans and grew to be a healthy, capable child with a beautiful brightness about her and a gorgeous smile. Heather, like seven of my nine siblings, became a permanent part of our family. Her teenage years were marked with many of the typical familial challenges, as well as shame and anger from having HIV. During her time as a young adult, Heather had many visits to the hospital for a variety of health issues related to HIV. A few months before she turned 25, she entered the hospital for the last time. She spent a little over two months there, her body weak and trying to fight several infections, before her pleas of "Help me" were answered with pain management in hospice and, ultimately, her death.

I am grateful that I was able to be with her in the hospital often during her last months alive, simply BEing with her – listening, loving, grieving, and celebrating her life with our loved ones.

My life experiences prepared me to hold space for Heather and my family during her transition. My commitment to being healthy and honoring my body led to infinite self-love. I experienced heart-wrenching pain when my relationship with my beloved ended. I can still feel the exquisite bliss of my first experience of connecting with Spirit. Each of these experiences were vital to supporting me during and after Heather's transition.

I know there is not just one "good" or "right" way to grieve. Some of us get angry or withdraw. Some of us feel into the beauty of death and the afterlife. Some of us curse reality and hold on to our departed loved ones tightly. All responses to death are valid.

My sister's death gifted me by breaking my heart open, allowing more space for love and acceptance. It deepened my connection to mySelf, my family, and Spirit. It created opportunities to ask for and receive support from others, and to honor the ways I love. The most amazing gift of all the gems Heather has gifted me is that I *feel* her here with me.

For the Love of Friendship

By Malcolm James Kutner

"I awoke this morning with devout thanksgiving for my friends, the old and the new." - Ralph Waldo Emerson

I was up early on the day of Mom's memorial service. Numbed by exhaustion, I went through the motions of prayer, meditation, and checking in with family and friends. Looking over the service notes, I remembered to expect over 500 people to honor Mom's life. Yellow roses – the flower of friendship – were everywhere, as were loved ones from near and far. We would focus mostly on friends, family, and faith – cornerstones of her life, and foundations for a future without her.

I drove myself to the church, where loved ones were holding space before the service. Everything was in order; everyone was ready. Except me. I was crashing inside.

I had spent most of the past two years in emotional limbo, going back and forth between Mom's home and hospitals in Texas while maintaining a life of my own in New York. Endless days and sleepless nights were accompanied by confusion and consternation, along with an emotional rotation of anger, fear, and sadness. Now, overcome by sensations of weightlessness and desolation, I felt alone and abandoned, detached from the present and consumed by the loss and absence of my mom.

I delayed the start of the service and took a few minutes to collect myself in the restroom. As I went to leave, the door wouldn't open. Catastrophizing panic set in. I pushed again and again, but it would not budge. When I finally let go, the door opened toward me, and there was my friend. Behind him were three other friends, all of them just arrived from the airport to be there for me. Inside the sanctuary were countless more friends from near and far. Everywhere I looked that day, I saw a friend who was there for me, and I realized that I am here for them, too.

On that day, my life shifted as the loss of my mother gracefully opened me up to the deeper exchange of love and life with my friends, my treasured family of choice, for whom I am grateful beyond words.

Remembering a Friend

By Margo Kirzinger

I recently lost an old childhood friend. She passed away suddenly from a heart attack at the age of 51. As my friend and I were approximately the same age, the news came as quite a shock. During the past week, while the reality of her death sank into my consciousness, many memories floated across my mind.

We met when I was just seven years old. My memories revolve around two young girls playing with Barbies; dressing up our paper dolls; and, later, sitting in her bedroom listening to ABBA records and swooning over our current teen idols.

As I reminisce, I also find myself in the midst of other more painful childhood recollections. Within two short years, my home life became a place of chaos, instability, and fear. More than once, I ran to my friend's house for shelter when it was unsafe at home. Her parents always opened their door to me, and for this kindness alone, I am forever grateful.

Many years later, my friend married my uncle and became a part of our family. For some, this union may have provided an opportunity to deepen the existing bond of friendship, but that was not the case for us.

Instead, we became two stubborn, strong-willed women who would rather break than bend to accommodate one another. This truth saddens me as I realize there will never be another chance to repair the damage to our relationship.

I will now strive to curb a critical tongue, tell my family and friends I love them, apologize when I should, and mend broken fences quickly, as you never truly know what each day will bring you – or take away from you.

When the Sky Crashes In

By Sam Ritchie

My phone's caller ID said "Dad," so I happily answered: "Hi, Dad."

The voice on the other end was not my dad, but my brother. I felt the sky falling even before he said, "Dad is dead." Tears rolled down my cheeks. Not sobs, but quiet tears of disbelief and pain.

That phone call changed everything. It was the second time a simple phone call had made my sky crash in. The first time was six years earlier. That time it was my dad phoning with the news that my mum had an inoperable brain tumour.

For three months, everything stopped and the only thing I did was look after my mum and my daughters. Every day, I watched as my mum slipped further away, the light in her eyes slowly going out. She was transformed from a vibrant, chatty woman of 58 into an old lady. She shuffled instead of walked, and the free flow of her speech stopped as she struggled to say even a single word.

It was a Saturday when I kissed my mum goodbye and told her I would not be seeing her the next day. As had become habit, I asked if there was anything else she needed. With all her energy, she forced the word from her lips: "YES!"

I ran through the list of things it could be: Did she need the toilet? Was she hungry? At each question, she shook her head and rolled her eyes at me. Finally, I asked, "Do you want me to come tomorrow?"

"YES," she forced out for a second time.

"Then I will be here," I replied. Right then, I knew that she would leave our world the next day.

That Sunday was to be the most traumatic yet peaceful day of my life, as this amazing woman left, held by both me and my dad. Dad was alone on the day he transitioned, which was his wish. He didn't tell anyone he was ill, but I know he wasn't truly alone. He had the invisible hand of my mum to guide him on the next step of his journey.

My parents have left me with great gifts: the strength to overcome anything, the responsibility to emulate the best of them both, and the desire to make a difference in people's lives, just as they did. My mum and dad are still part of every decision I make.

A Journey of the Heart

By Patricia Downing

My life shifted direction in a hospital examination room. The doctor had just left the room after telling us my mother had rectal cancer and needed to begin radiation and chemotherapy immediately.

We sat in stunned silence for several seconds, reaching out to each other with our eyes. Then I found myself on my knees in front of her, holding her hands, and assuring her that I would be with her every step of the way. I promised her we would make it an adventure and we would laugh every day.

It was a spontaneous act of love, the words coming from my heart without going anywhere near my rational mind. Only later did I understand the immensity of that promise – not with regret but with a dawning realization of the changes it would mean in my life.

In that moment, I had no idea that my caregiving journey with her would last for over six years, to be followed by two years of caring for my father. I soon discovered that this would be an inner journey for me, as much as an outer experience of caregiving. Only much later did I realize what a gift the journey held for me.

At that time, my husband, Larry, and I were working with at-risk teenagers and their parents. Now, my focus suddenly shifted from group sessions and family mediations to radiation, chemotherapy, and then a 13-day hospital stay.

I welcomed the opportunity to be her companion as she faced the challenges of the cancer and its aftermath. She never regained full functioning of her body, and soon we were living together so I could provide the daily care she needed.

I saw this as an opportunity to let go of old issues that had divided us in the past and just be with her now with love and acceptance, which, over time, is exactly what happened. What I learned along the way transformed my life.

Parts of our journey were rocky, but we did laugh every day. And by the time she went on her next journey, all that remained between us was love.

Transitions

By Melisa Archer

It broke my soul when my nana was moved into a nursing home, and she said, "I will never be going home again." In that moment, something within me shifted. I went into panic mode and started to *plan*. Preparing for the worst day to come, I created a list of things I wanted to say and do. I photocopied Nana's cookbook. She autographed it, *To Melisa With Love*. I got her fingerprints to make a Thumbie Necklace. I also bought her a cell phone with a plan, since she wasn't able to use the phone in the nursing home. She was so excited when she called, thanking me from the bottom of her heart.

Nana obviously thought ahead as well. She gave me her prized possession 3-D rose blanket, as well as two baby blankets she crocheted, a jar of homemade pickles, and her golf shoes.

Nana passed four months later, on Valentine's Day 2016. Later that day, my husband and I saw her spirit in our home. Days later, at her celebration of life, I took a picture as she orbed into a beautiful pink ball beside the flowers and candle I bought for her, as if to say, "I am right here."

Her cell phone was returned to me. In the drafts, I found a text that Nana had tried sending me just a few days before her passing. She wrote, *Hi Melisa. Love Nana*. What an amazing gift! I also found her voicemail, as well as videos and pictures she had taken while experimenting with the phone. In one picture, which she had accidentally taken of her leg, you could see her spirit lifting off of her body. I thought of the lines:

Do not stand at her grave and cry.
She is not there; she did not die.

How could I be sad? I had so many special memories she made with and for me. Now in spirit, Nana has traveled many places with me, free of her wheelchair. And I have peace. I know that it was her time.

Chapter 10
Living My Purpose

W*hy was I put on Earth? What am I here to do? What is my passion? What are my dreams? How can I live my purpose?* Some people spend their whole lives wrestling with these questions without ever satisfactorily answering them. Others may discover their purpose but never fully pursue it. Fortunately, however, many people make the courageous decision to follow their passions and live their dreams. You'll read many of their stories on the pages that follow.

Many of the stories in this chapter involve people leaving their comfort zones. Sometimes they were pushed out of their old lives (such as through illness or the loss of a job); at other times, they decided to take a leap of faith. Many of the authors faced a battle between security and passion – choosing to leave behind a safe but less-than-fulfilling career to start their own business, pursue a creative path, or enter a helping/healing profession. Oftentimes, they had to decide between fulfilling other people's wants and expectations and following their own dreams and desires.

Some of the authors knew their purpose from a young age; others came to it later in life – often when facing a pivotal moment such as an illness, death in the family, or the "empty nest" that came when adult children moved away. Some authors realized they were on a path that wasn't right for them; others found that they had reached the end of what had been a "right path" and were now ready to set off in a new direction that better suited the person they had now become.

No matter what life path you feel called to, we hope these stories resonate with you. And we hope the brave souls featured in this chapter inspire you to get in touch with your own passions, follow your dreams, and live your purpose!

November 16

Leaping into My Life Purpose

By Courtney Long

My heart overflowed with joy as I looked at the beautiful souls attending my retreat in Sedona, Arizona. The sun filled the room with its bright light, illuminating their smiles and curiosity as we discussed intuition and angels. This was the happiest moment of my life.

After years of confusion about my life purpose, I finally found what I was meant to do – spiritual teaching and writing. Climbing to this high peak required courage and intense leaps of faith.

College had left me feeling depressed and disillusioned, as none of the traditional career paths resonated. There wasn't a college major called "creatively pave your own path." Reluctantly, I decided on a bachelor's degree in Psychology and a master's degree in Social Work.

Working as a social worker was meaningful but draining. I wondered, *What if I never find work I truly love?*

I took a giant leap of faith by moving across the country from Michigan to Arizona and enrolling in a life-coaching program at a private college. I'll never forget what the instructor said: "Fasten your seatbelts."

Little did I know I had agreed to a roller-coaster ride of transformation. I awakened my authentic self and discovered my gifts, like coaching, writing, and angel communication. I also learned to love myself, which led to healing from an eating disorder, accepting my bisexuality, and coming out to family and friends.

As I leaped from one mountain peak to the next, intense feelings of fear continually bubbled up inside me, knowing I could fall at any moment. Yet I felt the fear and kept going. I felt alive and inspired, and the light of that passion outshined the darkness of fear.

Following my heart, I quit my job and started my own spiritual business. Seven years later, I still feel fulfilled, knowing I am making the difference I was born to make. Now, at my retreat, I felt so grateful for the opportunity to help others discover their authentic selves, purpose, and gifts. Before we know it, we'll all be shining brightly, sharing our gifts and shifting the planet.

Sail Away

By Mauri Barnes

My sister and I stood on the old wooden dock in Road Town, Tortola, staring up at a tall ship. We'd come a long way and were eager to board. "Rusty bucket," muttered someone in the crowd behind us. We nodded in agreement. This did not look like the gleaming white vessel in the brochure. Shrugging our shoulders, we clambered aboard, eager to explore the Yankee Clipper, our home for the next week.

We were so excited. This was our first vacation without our parents. We had saved vacation time, carefully planning our itinerary to fit this trip into our nursing careers. As newly certified scuba divers, we couldn't wait to dive the crystal-clear waters of the Caribbean Sea.

Later, while enjoying rum swizzles at the Welcome Aboard party, our rum-numbed brains heard the announcement, "There will be no scuba diving on this cruise."

Oh no! The wretched feelings of despair stirred us into action. We ran up to the ship's owner, a tall, tanned figure in dress whites, leaning against the ship's rail. "Captain Burke, we've come such a long way just to go scuba diving. Couldn't we borrow or rent equipment so we can dive?"

He was slow to respond, staring into the quiet island harbor, "Well, you could jump ship," he offered. "See that ship over there? Tomorrow she leaves on a delivery cruise to Belize. You could do all the diving you want."

Our minds reeled with the possibility. *What about work? How much will it cost? What would our parents say? Where is Belize?* "What do we have to do?" we asked.

"Just tell your captain you'll be leaving…"

In that moment, we chose to go for the once-in-a-lifetime opportunity. We joined the MV Yankee Trader to island-hop and dive across the Caribbean for three weeks of adventure. That impulsive, risk-taking decision shifted everything. We never returned to our jobs. Before a year had passed, we were both crewmembers living aboard the Windjammer ships, sailing the crystal-clear waters of the Caribbean!

Go West

By Ruth Donald

It's now a little more than a year since my husband's passing, and my journey through the terrain of his leaving has ultimately blessed me with the phenomenal gift of clarity of purpose and a shift into a world adorned by lights, colours, and energy forms, the likes of which I could never have imagined.

Leaving the corporate world had been presenting me with a challenge. I was resisting the change and feeling stuck when one day during my meditation, I received a crystal-clear message to "go west." It was this clear direction that I needed, and over the next few days, I began to feel a palpable yearning to be in the ancient forests and the untouched wilderness of the Southwest.

The 4,000-km journey was beset with wind and wet weather, but despite the undesirable conditions, a fascinating shift began to occur within me as I journeyed deeper into the untouched forests of the chilly, damp Southwest. The light changed – or maybe it was my perception of the light that changed, but it became other-worldly and crystal clear. The beauty of the light and the spirits of the trees pierced my heart with a poignancy that brought tears of love and gratitude. The trees and shrubs I photographed appeared to be hung with fairy lights, and exquisite sparkling discs of light danced in the air around the trees. The forest floor and the paths I walked on showed intriguing green lights shining amongst the rocks and leaves in my photographs.

My journey drew me to a small coastal hamlet on the edge of the Indian Ocean where the peace and tranquility simply took my breath away. I was guided to a beautiful house overlooking the water, and in my mind's eye I could see groups of people gathered to learn about meditation and energy healing. There was no doubt in my mind that this place held the mystical silver cord to the shift in my perception.

As I meditated the following day, I was shown the roof of the house opening to Heaven with light and angels pouring in, filling the rooms with incredible sound and a silvery-golden light. This was the clear sign I needed to leave the corporate world for good.

Leaving the Family Business

By Lauren Leduc Lemieux

Two months shy of my 40th birthday, I sat at my desk, shaking. My heart raced, my breath was heavy, and I was at a loss. The reality that I was utterly and completely miserable working with my family in the family business had slapped me right in the face. In a moment of utter desperation, I typed the words "Leaving the Family Business" into a search engine. And there it was, like a beacon of light: LeavingTheFamilyBusiness.com.

I clicked.

In awe of what I saw before me, I devoured 25 posts like a famished carnivore. The nourishment of each message nurtured my aching heart and invigorated my starving soul. Scrolling in silence, I let the validation wash over me like a gentle, warm rain shower, cleansing me of my pain. I was not alone.

I can still feel how calming that first deep breath felt. All my thoughts of leaving, feelings of contempt, beliefs of possibility, and dreams of fulfillment were real. I was not being selfish or having a mid-life crisis. I was allowing my reality to present itself. I was surrendering. The proof was right there on that screen. Others had decided to leave a family business, and not only did they survive, they thrived!

My survival instincts kicked in, and within a few weeks I had declared to my mother that I was leaving. After 18 years, the time had come for me to discover what I was put on Earth to do. After many heartfelt conversations, she uttered the words that solidified everything: she acknowledged that it was time for her to be my mom and not my boss.

That one sentence provided me with all the courage and confidence I would need to begin my new journey on my own. I had no idea what was next for me, but I was ready to start looking.

Night Closed In

By Bianca Lynn

Night closed in as I looked out over the canyon edge and asked myself: *What the hell am I doing here?*

My journey started several months earlier. While sitting at my desk at one of the world's largest banks, I thought, *Maybe I should go on a vision quest.*

If you aren't familiar with the term *vision quest*, you aren't alone. Simply put, it is a ceremony of time alone in nature for reflection, spiritual guidance, and to mark times of transition.

Months had passed since I first thought of participating in a vision quest, and there I was, alone in the desert of Death Valley National Park. As it grew darker, I realized I was terrified.

I awoke the next morning relieved to be alive. That's how it went for the three days and three nights.

I encountered scorpions, snakes, spiders, and other odd insects. Hummingbirds, butterflies, and doves visited, too. Angels and demons, both real and imagined, came out of the shadows and shared themselves with me.

I couldn't predict how profoundly that time would change me. I couldn't know how it would connect me with others, changing the focus of my work and, ultimately, my life.

I did not leave my job immediately upon returning. In fact, it was two years before my corporate job finally disappeared during a company merger. More time passed as I tried to bridge the gap between my need for security and what I was directed to do. Over time, I've transitioned into a life that is more aligned with what I learned in the desert and who I am in my heart.

Perhaps the most important lesson to share here is that sometimes a life shift is a big dramatic event that happens in a heartbeat. Other times, it may be gentler and subtler and take a bit more time to unfold. Either way, it is a journey that deeply changes you.

Letting Go of Safe Sadness

By Anita D. Marshall

My Grandpapa's love of great apes led me to adopt an orangutan for his birthday. His sudden passing before his birthday affected me deeply. In addition to grief, I felt guilty about not visiting more. These feelings began to overwhelm me as I also struggled with a job that I once loved, but something had changed and it no longer resonated with me.

As I now know, the spiritual part of our Soul Plan usually activates as you enter your 30s; at the time, however, I did not know this, so my life became a daily struggle of long, pressure-filled workdays – until the day I collapsed, unable to move or speak. I had suffered a transient ischaemic attack, putting me at risk of a stroke at just 33!

In retrospect, I see this as the universe's way of helping me, albeit through quite a painful kick in the butt! Signed off work with plenty of time at my disposal, I re-evaluated everything in my life. I created my "Want To Do" list, guided by a book that literally fell off a shelf in a bookshop. At the top of my list was *travel*…extended overseas travels plus volunteer work.

This wish was granted when I saw a newsletter that mentioned two-month placements working at a Borneo orangutan sanctuary. My heart and soul yelled *YES*! while my mind countered: *What? Give up your high-paying job, family, friends, and safety?!* But I could not ignore the calling. I chose to let go of the fear of the unknown that held me in safe sadness. When I handed in my notice at work, I waived the opportunity for sabbatical leave, knowing that the thought of returning would cast a dark cloud over my travels.

I had planned for a total of six months abroad, but it became a 16-month journey of reconnecting with myself, my capabilities, and the power of soul awareness. After two wonderful months at the orangutan sanctuary, I visited other countries where I learned meditation, energy healing, and various spiritual philosophies – all of which I now combine in my Soul Awareness Coaching, helping others align with their soul purpose and live a soul-fulfilled life.

The Next Right Step

By Susan Mullen

"'It's impossible,' said pride. 'It's risky,' said experience.
'It's pointless,' said reason. 'Give it a try,' whispered the heart."
- Unknown

I was approaching my mid-40s and was feeling burned out. I was at the top of a thriving wedding-photography career, and my two daughters were getting ready to leave the nest. I started hearing the soul whispers of "It's time" over and over while being pulled to show up more authentically as *me*.

As an intuitive, I have always had a clear connection to higher guidance. I know that souls evolve and bodies age. The truth was, I was evolving out of my work and out-aging my clients. I was being guided to pursue intuitive sessions that would help others find their next right step. But I questioned: *Who walks away from a profitable business?*

It was time to redefine success. I imagined how it would feel to be the most authentic version of myself – revealing purpose, reigniting passion, and being of service. Then I asked myself if, 10 years from now, I would regret it if I hadn't followed my heart. Yes, I would.

I said to my main spirit guide, "But I'm almost 45!"

She lovingly responded, "You're going to be 45 *anyway*."

Continuing work that I was losing passion for was a disservice to my treasured clients who deserved more than my skillset. I ultimately chose to leave money on the table in pursuit of being me – to combine my innate intuitive gifts with intuitive coach training to light the path for others as they navigate their next right steps.

I learned that discontent arises when we've fulfilled a divine contract but are still hanging on to it for non-divine reasons. If evolving to our highest selves is natural, then change is, too. It's about adjusting our sails as the winds change, not remaining in the harbor.

Looking back, taking the risk to head in the direction I was being pulled toward – even when it didn't make sense, and especially because it was scary – confirms to me that the universe does, indeed, always have my back.

Second Chances, and Then Some

By Cat Williford

I came to coaching because I believed I killed my father.

He was on dialysis and in kidney failure; my kidney was a "perfect" match. At 25, I was enthralled by the notion of *perfect*. I built an internal story that told me that I alone had been given the rare opportunity to save my father's life, and donating my kidney to him was the most worthwhile – the most *perfect* – reason to be on Earth that I could imagine.

My perfect mission didn't work out as I envisioned, though. The transplant was successful, but everything else that could possibly go wrong after a successful transplant did. Six months after the transplant, my father died in the hospital where I was born.

Unequipped to handle such loss, I spiraled into a world of devastating isolation – a world of depression, self-loathing, exhaustion, illness, and shame. I collapsed the failure of my ultimate goal – saving my father's life – into the paralyzing notion that *I* was a failure.

The question tormented me: *If I can't save my daddy's life, then what the hell am I here for?*

My body took the brunt of my inner torture: near starvation, alcohol overload, sleep deprivation.

After several years of grief and illness, I finally felt strong enough to attend an actor's workshop where a founder of The Coaches Training Institute talked about authenticity in the face of the Hollywood audition: "We all have a life purpose that enhances our lives, as well as a gremlin voice inside that makes us feel like crap about ourselves."

I felt his words echo in the core of my being. I relaxed completely into his life-purpose visualization, emerging from it with this deep knowing that was so powerful and instantaneous, I blurted it out loud: "Know the Light of Love is inside you! Share it!"

That night, I tasted a longed-for second chance to make a difference. A few months later, I entered coach training school, guided in my work by the Light of Love that lit my path forward that day and continues to do so.

Saying Yes to Writing

By Kimberly DuBoise

For me, it was a matter of listening to my inner voice. Listening to it and responding. When I did, a shift occurred that impacted my life. The voice within me had been gradually growing louder, and became louder and louder still, until I could no longer ignore it. What was the voice telling me? It was telling me that I had words within me that needed to come out. I realized that I wanted to write. What was so important about writing poetry? The fact that through it I could express my deepest feelings and give life to my dreams.

I began to write after work. I would write before work, too. Different hours with different pens would find me jotting down verses and entire poems. It was all so exciting, new, and fulfilling! I self-published some poetry books and started a poetry blog. I had to learn about a whole new world – the world of indie publishing!

In a moment, I decided to alter my career path and set my life on a different course. In doing so, I took what felt like a serious step in honoring my Self. I was standing up for a newly developed dream and daring to embrace my right to fulfillment. I know that from the outside it may have looked impulsive and reckless, but the journey up to the point where I said yes to writing was one filled with deep introspection and soul searching.

I have always been an introspective person. I am drawn to lyrics and poems that express a longing for understanding, unity, and awareness of love. Writing poetry helps me tap into that vibration and also helps me honor my feelings. It helps me feel grounded and also linked to something ethereal. Saying yes to it has been hard, wonderful, challenging, and rewarding. I am so glad I said yes!

Fulfilling My Sacred Contract

By Barbara Toller

My transition from the fast-paced hustle of the East Coast to the wide-open space and Midwestern values of Kansas City ignited the healer in me to switch careers from corporate marketing to health and wellness. But after years of fitness training, bodywork, and nutritional counseling, I yearned to explore *beyond* the physical, to the mental and spiritual connections that supported my well-being. This led to hypnosis classes, studying the power of the unconscious mind, and subsequently to Caroline Myss's book *Sacred Contracts*, which introduced me to a self-discovery method that would forever change how I viewed the world and everyone in it.

The first step of the *Sacred Contracts* process was to identify my 12 archetypes. These are energetic prototypes of thought and behavior that act as a support team guiding us toward our destiny. According to Myss, there are four core archetypes that we all share (Child, Victim, Prostitute, and Saboteur) and eight personal ones we select from reflecting upon lifelong patterns. (I selected Seeker, Healer, Artist, Athlete, Nun, Goddess, Alchemist, and Teacher.)

By studying these archetypes, I was able to dismantle myths I had been telling myself that created barriers to greater health and happiness. For instance, I saw how my Saboteur was operating in shadow with the myth of low self-worth, which undervalued my capabilities, second-guessed my decisions, and avoided the spotlight for fear I might be judged. It overwhelmed me with perfectionism and too many projects that blocked focus and clarity. As I learned to use the Saboteur as an ally, it guided me toward choices that removed obstacles in the path of great opportunities.

Now, as a Certified Archetypal Consultant, I feel free to move forward with confidence, allowing my personal archetypes to connect with others on a larger scale. I am able to consciously step into my Teacher archetype to prepare and present workshops, the Nun to enter sacred space of Divine guidance, the Athlete to navigate life's storms with strength and stamina, and the Healer to love and serve others while fulfilling my own Sacred Contract.

Do Things That Matter with Big Love

By Reina Pomeroy

She walked into my office, closed the door, and sank into the chair across from my desk with a comfortable familiarity. "It's good to see you. How are you doing?" she asked.

"I'm good," I casually answered, like I'd done a thousand times.

Then she looked at me and asked, "No, how are you *really* doing?"

She sensed my trepidation, and I told her something that I had been scared to admit to myself: I loved the job, but I didn't like the commute. Since becoming a mom eight months prior, something started to shift in me. The two-hour commute (each way) was taking a real toll on my happiness. That morning was a prime example and was fresh in my head as I had spent an hour with my baby screaming in his carseat on our way to daycare. I sat in the front seat, peeking at him in my rearview mirror, trying to remember every single soothing lullaby I knew. I arrived at work with tears of frustration streaking my face. I felt immobile, helpless, stuck.

My mentor looked back at me, nodding. A year prior, she had experienced the terrible loss of her best friend to a battle with cancer. As she grappled with grief, she searched for a more meaningful, purposeful life and resolved to create an identity that wasn't centered around how much she earned. She did some soul-searching and decided that she would pursue her dream of entrepreneurship.

During my confession, she didn't tell me what to do, she didn't tell me to quit, and she didn't tell me to just suck it up. The words she uttered were loaded – packed with meaning, heat, and purpose – and they are forever etched on my heart:

"Life is too damn short not to love every single day."

Indeed, life is too short to play small, to be meek, to not live on purpose. *Do things that matter with big love.* I took these words to heart, quit my job, and decided to do the thing I had wanted to do most: I enrolled in a coaching certification program and started my business. I now have the absolute best job, and it was a blessing that I had those shifts.

The Call to Nursing

By Julie Jones

When I entered university, I thought I wanted to be a teacher, so I took advantage of an opportunity that let students observe and help in the classroom. However, it did not take very long for me to realize that this was *not* what I wanted in a career. But what was my next step?

Fast-forward to spring 1974. My friends and I had plans to travel out of town to attend a retreat. Everyone was becoming concerned with my lack of commitment for what I was going to do. As we were returning home, we passed a hospital and I immediately knew that this was where I was supposed to go next! I had no idea the how or what, but I asked my friends to stop and allow me to go into the hospital school to ask some questions.

I was greeted by a matronly woman at the desk who informed me that she was the "house mother." I told her that I was certain that I was to come there for school and needed to pick up the paperwork as the deadline to apply was in a few days. She laughed a bit and said, "Sorry, honey, but there's a two-year wait list." That simply did not deter me.

While I had never considered a career in nursing before, I knew that this was where I needed to be – it was a deep-down knowing that I cannot explain. I picked up the paperwork and promised that I would return it in a few days. School was starting soon, and I had to be ready. The house mother reminded me that there was no chance I would be accepted into school for that year, but they would keep my application on file.

All the way home, I talked to my friends about my upcoming move to a new town and school, and they kept reminding me to make some "real" plans. I sent my paperwork in, and within a few weeks, I received my letter of acceptance.

I truly felt called in that moment to pursue nursing. My career has allowed me the sacred privilege of caring for others. I knew I was called to serve – I just had to trust and lean in to the message!

A Moment of Decision

By Robert D. White

In the summer of 2002, I was a new undergrad student unsure of the career path I wanted to pursue, let alone the degree I would need to achieve this uncertain calling. So what did I do? Predictably, what many other college students do: I pursued a degree with high financial gains. I ended up applying and being accepted into the School of Engineering.

Somehow, I had developed a vision of being this big-shot computer engineer. To my disbelief, however, I was the only person who could envision me sitting behind a desk, looking at a computer screen day after day, and partaking in what many considered to be the most dreadful job ever. Several friends and family even asked me, "How can someone with your charisma and magnetism spend his entire life sitting in a cubicle with practically no human contact?" But I was unfazed. After all, look at all the money to be made!

Oddly enough, even though I had this exceptional long-term incentive within arm's length, a plethora of influences began derailing me from fulfilling my plan. My grades mysteriously started slipping; the engineering department abruptly changed the curriculum, which extended the program length upwards of five years; and my employer was reluctant to accommodate my new class schedule. My one and only plan suddenly became a distant mirage.

I knew I had to think fast. I didn't want to quit my job, yet I couldn't bear the thought of flunking out of school. What was I to do? Suddenly, I had an epiphany. I thought to myself: *Well, I do have a natural knack for business, and most of my satisfaction has arisen from helping others. That's it! Human Resources! It would give me the ability to influence people's lives, subsequently being a key to the success of the business.* And just like that, I was venturing down a new path.

As I reflect on this pivotal moment of decision, I realize that, regardless of the financial possibilities, I was paving the way to a lifelong dedication to sharing and contributing to the lives of so many people – the ultimate reward. From this vantage point, I can clearly see that my universal plan was much bigger than I had imagined.

White Witch

By Joanne Angel Barry Colon

Everybody has a purpose for being here on Earth. Ever since I was 12 years old, I knew that my life purpose was to educate, heal, and transform lives through exercise and healthy eating, which is why I started my own business as a personal trainer and nutrition coach.

While this vision has continued, it has expanded tremendously, beginning in 2009. At that time, I had my first Reiki attunement. I studied under several masters, and by 2012, I became a Reiki Master. I started offering Reiki circles, writing workshops, and moonlight meditation rituals, which all included mini Reiki treatments.

As I administered Reiki treatments, I also worked with crystals, which helped me connect with my clients on a deeper level. It was almost as though the crystals helped me become more intuitive to my clients' pain and emotions. Sometimes, I would randomly call a client to check in on them and they would ask me how I knew they were not feeling well. I would reply by saying, "I was sitting with a crystal and suddenly had a desire to connect with you." When this happened more frequently, some of my clients started referring to me as "The White Witch."

Through these experiences, my original life-purpose vision grew into something much bigger. I realized that, yes, I am here to educate, heal, and transform lives, but on a much higher level. I am here to help people transform their mind, body, and spirit holistically with movement, nutrition, meditation, and Reiki/crystal healing. I also wanted to have unlimited access to my community and offer my healing gifts to hospitals, churches, and nursing homes. To this end, on March 17, 2016, I became an ordained minister. I do not claim to be "psychic," but I do believe that I am an intuitive healer, which is why some people still refer to me as "The White Witch."

A New Why

By Jody Wootton

Twenty years ago, I had a clear goal for where I saw myself in the future. I had planted that very seed when I walked into my guidance counselor's office in high school and stated, "I will be a pilot and live in Hawaii." Thanks to the U.S. Coast Guard and my passion, I piloted C-130 Hercules aircrafts and lived in the most beautiful place on Earth.

What I needed next was a new goal, a new purpose, a new *why*.

I decided to take a heart-centered coaching course presented by a sweet friend who I'd met while living in Hawaii. During the three-day class, I experienced significant breakthroughs. At first, I saw myself as if I were an observer. I saw that I had been reacting but not acknowledging. I was loving but not giving. I was being but not present. Surrounded by positivity and aspiring women, I let go of my fears and doubts. I embraced the wholehearted coaching. I decided that this was my time to be here, to learn, to be coached, and to coach.

I rediscovered my real self. I rediscovered my emotional purpose. And I discovered my new *why*: to live with purpose and to be real.

These experiences reminded me that we all need to adjust our why as we journey through time. And, like all of us, my why is unique to me, like a snowflake.

Moving forward, I will continue to create the life I was meant to have. I will live my dreams through my purpose. I will grow every day in relationships, beginning with cultivating love and joy with my husband and son. I will be real to myself and to others. I will be of service to others while keeping my own cup full and staying in alignment with my new why.

Being an Artful Self-Explorer

By Marihet Hammann

My story was thin before I became an Artful Self-Explorer. It felt like I'd shed a lot of my proverbial skin – too much, too often, too soon. Vulnerable, yet not visible. I can't say my life was miserable, as my soul is in essence light and playful, but her vibrant brilliance was just not embodied in living experiences.

As if on cue, this quote found its way to me: "A soul without a body is a ghost. A body without a soul is a corpse." In both cases, you'll be dead. I did not want to be either. Thank God I was neither…yet.

I soon realized that I leaned towards the *ghost* part because of abundant dreaming, planning, and innovative ideas and very little inspired action. I would go for days without remembering if I fed my body, drank water, moved, or slept enough. My soul and body were disconnected, functioning on autopilot without awareness, like being dead and alive at the same time.

I knew that a shift needed to happen for my body and soul to meet again, and so the exploring began.

I found Intentional Creativity, a 13-step painting process, and was immediately drawn to the use of story, symbol, colour, pattern, and play. There was just one problem: I had not painted a single painting until that moment. My inspired action froze and created a sense of unease with old stories. Would I be able to do this? Would my painting be good enough?

It wasn't very long before the invitation to play brought out my innate ability and soul truth. My hand danced across the canvas with ease. My body and soul were in delight. They met each other halfway, and at this midpoint, I found my Artful Self-Explorer.

I soon realized that I am enough; I am able to do this. Through Intentional Creativity, I was living experiences, insights, and breakthroughs that no theory could have taught me. I was an Artful Self-Explorer, weaving my story's threads back to me and reclaiming my brilliance.

How I Unexpectedly Became a Psychic

By Catherine M. Laub

While visiting my brother-in-law in 2011, I showed him my itinerary for a cruise that was only for people going to hear seven self-help and spiritual speakers. He shared information about a friend, Donna Cantone, who does this type of work. I immediately contacted her, and she became my life coach!

During every session, Donna did an Angel Card reading for me. I always loved the angels, so I asked her how I could learn how to read the cards. I immediately signed up for classes with Angels Teach University and, after two years, was certified as an Angel Communication Master.

Classes were all on the telephone with people throughout the world. I loved doing practice readings with my classmates. We all shared a common bond. At that time, I tried to focus on readings without my angel cards, but it didn't come easily. I believe that the timing wasn't right.

I continuously heard messages for myself that I would one day make a living doing readings. This excited me beyond belief because for years I had been searching for how I could best serve God. This was my answer because, with my readings, I guide people to plan great futures with the help of God and the angels.

I began private readings and working at psychic fairs as an Angel Card reader. What happened next really surprised me. During sessions with another spiritual teacher, I suddenly started giving her messages from her departed father. I gave her so many accurate details in that first session, and from then on, I have helped many people receive messages from loved ones.

I am now professionally doing psychic readings, with the help of the angels, using oracle cards. It gives me great gratification knowing how I have helped others hear from their angels and loved ones. This is something I never dreamed of, and I am so thrilled about this wonderful life shift.

From Failure to Success

By Tiffany Andersen

What does it take to truly succeed at something?

I remember very clearly a comment a well-meaning friend once made to me: "Tiffany, you've tried so many different things in your life and nothing ever panned out for you, so you lost credibility in my eyes. I'm glad you finally found your true mission with your skincare business."

I know she meant this as a compliment, but the truth is, the comment was cruel in my eyes and actually really hurt my feelings. You see, she was pointing out all my "failures" as if they were a bad thing. I, however, see them as important steps on the path to success.

If there is anything I can pass on to others who wish to make something of their lives, to try something beyond the ordinary, it is this: Don't ever be afraid to fail. Don't ever let anyone tell you that you're a failure or that you can't do it. The most successful people in life will fail 10,000 times before they succeed at one major thing. It takes incredible strength and perseverance to gain true accomplishments in life.

At the young age of 15, I learned how to overcome severe adversity; I had no choice after a catastrophic car accident nearly paralyzed me. But during that time, I learned one valuable lesson that many may miss: I learned how to fight...and never give up. I discovered my own courage, and I hope that others can learn from this, too.

Don't be afraid to fail, because that is how you learn who you are and what you can accomplish.

Take the Leap of Faith

By Farahana Surya Namaskar

Soon after my ex-husband and I separated and our divorce was in process, I secured employment with a local non-profit in Dallas. After working there for about five months, I began to feel frustrated with the job. I wished I could do more, but I didn't feel like I was being given the opportunity to maximize my potential in that position. I couldn't just quit, though, as I had to pay my bills and support myself and my son. I felt stuck.

Early one morning, I awoke from a dream where I heard the words, "Take the leap of faith." I knew what God was trying to tell me, but I also knew that I couldn't just quit my job. I needed the money.

I spent days meditating and praying over the message I had received. One day shortly thereafter, I somehow managed to work up the courage to submit my two weeks' notice.

The day before my last day, my co-workers treated me to a farewell lunch. When we were on our way back to the office, I noticed a homeless woman outside in the shopping plaza. I thought about giving her my food that I had packed in a to-go box. I had written a phone number on the lid of the container and realized I needed to write it down somewhere before she took the food. She insisted she would get me a piece of paper. She rummaged through her belongings and handed me a piece of stationery paper. On the bottom of the paper, in italicized writing, it said, *Rewrite your own destiny*. I smiled, and tears welled up in my eyes.

A few days later, I got a tattoo on my arm that said, *Take the Leap of Faith*. Every day, I am reminded of my unconditional faith in God, which has given me the courage to take this leap and rewrite my destiny.

The Courage to Follow My Path

By Brandon Olivares

As a visually impaired individual, I applied for vocational assistance from the New York Association for the Blind in 2014. Thanks to their help, I was offered an internship at a local non-profit agency. The problem was, I didn't know if I really wanted this position.

For the three years since I had dropped out of college, my life had been rather aimless. I was stuck between other people's expectations for me to get a "real" job and my desire to go out on my own and follow my own path.

I took the internship as a way to appease the more vocal factions in my life, whose relentless, insistent expectations made me feel like I was wasting my life. I immediately knew, however, that I would dislike the position. The job itself played to my interests, as I would be working on this agency's website, but the structure just didn't jibe with my own idea of what I wanted to be doing in life.

Initially, I felt stuck. The Association said I could not quit the internship, and I felt a responsibility to them for finding me the job. After about two weeks, however, I knew I'd had enough. I realized that I was attempting to live for others, not for myself. I realized that I would rather follow my own path, no matter what others said. Furthermore, I realized that the Association really had no control over what path I followed. My life was my own.

I told my supervisor that I was quitting. To my great surprise and relief, she was actually incredibly understanding. We parted on good terms and remain friends to this day.

Within a year of leaving that internship, I got certified in Neuro-Linguistic Programming (NLP) and became a life coach, helping others to follow their own passions in life. I'm incredibly grateful to this experience for giving me the motivation I needed to be true to myself and follow my own path.

Angelic Strings of a Life Shift

By Wendyanne Pakulsky

The universe is always talking to us in different ways, helping us discover (or *rediscover*) our passion and our gifts. We may receive messages through the encouragement of others or from a sense of angelic urging from within. It's up to us to be open to the messages and the opportunities that present themselves to us, in whatever form they may take, and to connect with our passion.

My own connection with my inner gifts and passion began at a young age, but it took many years for me to make the shifts that allowed this to become a central part of my life.

All my life, I have enjoyed writing. When I was a little girl, I would go into my bedroom and make paper books – writing the stories and drawing the illustrations. I was very happy being left in my own space to create and write in my own way.

When I wrote a story for my secondary-school English class, my teacher, Elizabeth Bolton, pulled me aside and told me that my writing was extraordinary and my imagination was a real gift. But her words never really registered until years later when I wanted to really rediscover this gift. I enrolled in a diploma program with the Australian College of Journalism in Sydney, and from that point on, Ms. Bolton's words reignited a spark within me.

After three years, I had completed my diploma and was well on my way to making my inner passion of writing a central part of my outer life. I wanted to write my own children's storybook. So the journey began, and in 2014, I stood at my own book launch.

My life shift with this journey was about finding, connecting (and reconnecting) with, and expressing my passion through my life. I'm sometimes asked, "How do we know what our passion is?" It feels like angel strings playing straight through the centre of your heart. Listening to this song – and following it – can lead you into a life-shifting journey, opening up whole new areas of self-discovery and a beautiful belief in yourself that can take you anywhere you want to go. And throughout this journey, the soul just keeps singing.

A Different Kind of More

By Freda Durden

I began a new journey in life with an old perspective. Before I let my soul lead my life, I worked as a Certified Nurse Assistant (CNA). In my family, having a job was something to celebrate. However, I had never been satisfied. Nonetheless, I learned to settle and tried to do my best in my position – to be the best adult-sitter, house cleaner, and grocery shopper who ever lived! Struggling through seven years of working overnight, all day, and sometimes even in my sleep, I built myself from employee to contractor and began to manage some home-care clients on my own and with a small team.

Then I found myself at a crossroads. I attended some spiritual seminars and received my Master certificate in Usui Reiki, but I didn't realize that I was on my way somewhere until I was given the opportunity to share what I had learned at a retreat.

As I left my clients on the Friday before the retreat, I proposed an increase in services and pay. In my limited mind, I felt I deserved more. Unbeknownst to me at the time, my soul was leading me to a different kind of "more"!

The retreat was my first time expressing my true, authentic self. I used my energy-healing training and innate ability to love and understand. I helped six women release their inner struggle and heal. And I felt a power unlike anything I'd ever known. My life shifted from that moment forward.

Still in a swirl of confusion, I returned home and to cell phone reception, only to discover that my clients had chosen to go with another service provider. Although I was heartbroken, my soul was renewed…and the rest is "her-story"!

In retrospect, my seven years as a CNA taught me divine service, a tool that I needed to become the most authentic version of myself. My life shifted when I asked for more from people and was denied. But God provided *more* in a way I had never imagined, and I have been changed ever since.

Creating a Life of Purpose and Substance

By Joy T. Barican

Emigrating to another country proved challenging – especially as I was halfway through university studies and searching for work. To gain local experience, I started full-time work in a factory and a weekend job at a supermarket. Although thankful for these opportunities, I dreamed of attaining a position that was more aligned with my skills and passion.

As I scanned through job advertisements, everything seemed to be stacked against me. Rather than be deterred by it, though, I developed a plan of action to keep me focused with my preparations, including part-time studies. The efforts paid off when I successfully passed an examination for a government post. Not long after that, I landed a corporate position.

With that accomplishment, I allowed myself to celebrate but remained fully aware that in order to create the life I wanted, I needed to raise the bar each time I succeeded. This was the driving force behind my quest to reinvent myself from a career perspective. There were times when complacency got the better of me; in time, however, the universe always sent me a wake-up call. Admittedly, these "calls" weren't always pleasant, but they certainly propelled me into action!

Through these experiences, I have learned that when I am willing to go beyond what is comfortable, safe, and familiar, I am supported, and the end result makes the calculated risk worthwhile. I've also learned not to measure my success solely on my professional accomplishments. More than a successful career and lifestyle, I want to create a life of purpose and substance. After all, we make a living by what we get, but we make a *life* by what we *give*. With this in mind, I seize every opportunity to give away smiles, spread joy, and share time and whatever spiritual or material gifts I can offer.

Pablo Picasso summed it up quite well: "The meaning of life is to find your gift. The purpose of life is to give that gift away."

Say Yes to Sacred Suggestions

By Lore Raymond

"A tiny mirror can reflect a strong beam when it faces the light."
- Angel Wisdom

Yes, our souls are love-filled mirrors, and I sought to reflect the best of myself as a writer. However, low self-esteem wouldn't allow me to see my soul's reflection in the outer world. I was blind. Helping me face the light was The Reverend Lauren, a wisdom coach.

Ten years ago, she suggested, "Why don't you start a Meetup group for writers?"

My self-sabotaging answers included: "What's Meetup?...I don't have a writing degree...I'm not published, so who would attend?"

Like an angel mirroring the Light of Truth, she replied, "You love to write, right?"

I immediately enrolled in Meetup to establish the *Creative Writing Circle*! My writing partner, Janan, agreed to be the co-host. For seven years, writers gathered monthly in my home of *Casa de la Fe* (House of Faith). As someone who always carries her passport, it was fun building the theme around a country for the prompts, food, and music.

This sacred suggestion shifted me to launch a Facebook magazine, *Women as Visionaries with Lore Raymond*. Here, many women writers and I contribute to "empower women with spiritual inspiration." I've since mentored dozens of women writers and helped start their writing circles. Over time, my daily writing practice expanded to include my spiritual evolution. I added prayer, meditation, ritual, and gratitude lists.

For the next three years, the more I lived in my truth, the more light I mirrored as a writer. The *Creative Writing Circle* transmuted to the *Divine Dialogue Writing Circle*. We just celebrated our 10-year anniversary! The new name shift also fearlessly energized me to teach the expanded writing system online.

Finally, in January 2016, four publishers made the sacred suggestion to become a co-author of their collaborative books. This time, I didn't hesitate and answered each one with, "YES!"

The Day I Chose to Stand

By Lydia Di Francesco

I sat in silence with the sun shining down on me. How could I be so unhappy on such a beautiful day? I was exhausted, frustrated, worn down, and unsure of myself. Self-doubt was in full force. I questioned my worth as a fitness professional and my value to the community I serve.

I had been working tirelessly promoting a boot camp for my fitness business. Sadly, no one was signing up. Tactics that had previously worked weren't effective this time, and a few new efforts didn't pan out either.

So I sat. I let those negative thoughts come. I acknowledged them. But then I said, "That's enough. The truth is, I have value. I have important things to share with the world. My message needs to be heard."

Suddenly, I had an idea. I stood up, invigorated and hopeful. It was a complete shift from anything I'd done before, but I chose to go for it. I posted a message recruiting volunteers for an experiment where they would exercise for 10 minutes a day for two weeks. The response shocked me. In less than one day I had over 100 volunteers! I couldn't believe it and didn't know whether to laugh or cry about the whole thing.

It was only months later that I realized that the simple act of shifting directions changed everything for me and my business. A key piece of my calling and mission – sharing short, at-home workouts – had grown out of that simple experiment. It was a turning point in my messaging and how I share a healthy lifestyle with my audience. Looking back, that shift was the catalyst for a fitness program that I know will help thousands of lives.

I'll be forever changed by what happened that sunny day. I learned that it's okay to feel down and frustrated, but it's not okay to stay there. I became braver and more open to taking risks. It confirmed that, despite ups and downs, I am on the right journey.

Slow Down to Reframe

By Tazeem Jamal

For over 20 years, I walked the same path as a spa owner and esthetician. I received great recognition from my peers and my community. I spoke on stage, was quoted in industry publications, and was featured on TV and in amazing books.

Even though I woke up with passion every day, I felt that something was shifting. I knew I needed to listen to my inner voice. I needed to slow down, to reframe what the second half of my life would look like.

As fate would have it, as soon as I realized I needed to slow down, I was *forced* to. I was unable to renegotiate my lease, and just like that, my career seemed to have come to a full stop. I was done...or was I?

It all happened so fast, it left my head spinning...and filled with questions: *What will I do? Who is Tazeem now? What will people think of me?* There I was, out on my own with no safety net, facing a stark choice: sink or swim.

At this time, I retreated from the outside world and pulled my faith and my family closer, allowing me to heal, close this chapter, and strategize what my future would look like.

I'm not the kind of person to let others determine my fate, so even though I am still unfolding, I have now regained my sparkle, my voice, and my drive! Today, I still work with clients ("changing the world, one face at a time" is my heart's true work!), but I am also now coaching others in the industry and sharing my amazing secrets of success.

I am so beyond grateful for this time of transformation. I know I am a better mother, wife, and businesswoman for it! It has also taught me some incredibly valuable lessons. I've learned that we don't have control over everything and that sometimes we need to allow the Universe to guide us. I've learned that we can never give up on our dreams. I've also learned that we are all here for a purpose, and I've learned to ask: *What is my purpose?*

Just Shy of 20 Years

By Annie Price

In November 1998, I finally received my ticket to freedom, but it came with a cost. Several months earlier, I'd returned to an office job I didn't like after a maternity leave with my first child. The job was increasingly toxic for me, and it was more difficult to show up every day. No one knew yet – I'd just found out I was pregnant with my second child. I had to stick it out a few more months! My much-needed shift would arrive even sooner.

During this time, the climate was changing in many American companies – they were downsizing and restructuring expectations of their employees. I'd worked at this large company for 19 years and wanted to complete 20 years of service, as my retirement benefits would take a nice bump up – justifying the need to hang on a little longer – but it was such a struggle.

On this November day in 1998, with no forewarning, several other employees and I were called into a meeting and terminated on the spot. Just like that – it was all over. We'd receive a package, gather up our belongings, turn in our badges, and walk out the door. As I signed the half-inch–thick pile of legalese paperwork, I tried not to think about how close I was to that bump in my benefits. The truth – it felt shady. Also, the truth – *I was free.*

I focused on *that* truth. I never had to go back again! I was free from this job obligation and many attachments of what I "should" do. We'd manage with one income, and I could stay home and really enjoy my new career – being a mom to my beautiful babies.

This life shift was a blessing in disguise. I'd never again stay in a job that wasn't good for me. My time has now become too valuable to me. I honor who I am now, filling my soaring soul with happiness and purpose. While I may have paid a price, the ticket to my freedom was priceless.

Joining the Peace Corps

By Charlotte Palmer

Three months before graduating from Ohio State University, I was in a quandary about what my next step would be. I happened to overhear a Peace Corps recruiter telling my roommate about the service programs requested by host countries. "They need all kinds of teachers and community workers to help local citizens organize to achieve their projects."

I wasn't a teacher, but I followed my curiosity to apply, stating my background in 4-H homemaking and YMCA clubs as well as a social-work aide internship, Spanish classes, and a degree in Psychology. Surprise! Peace Corps invited me to train to be a Venezuelan high school home economics teacher part time plus develop service projects.

Always adventurous, I accepted the position and completed all my trainings successfully. My placement was in El Tigre, a dusty desert oil community with citizens from many nations. Gated and open worker camps serviced the oil industry. There were Italian, Spanish, Arabian, and American social clubs. Spanish was spoken with the accents of many other languages.

I lived with two American/Venezuelan families near where I taught. My charming Venezuelan co-teacher taught me doll-making and crocheting while I showed her how to knit and make an apple pie.

Together, we got donations to furnish our classroom, decorate a childcare's nutrition center, and hold exhibitions of our students' projects. I helped scout troops earn their badges, developed and ran a summer craft program, then shared it with YMCA programs throughout Venezuela. Night school and home-based English programs were popular. The camp-dwelling Americans were pleased to see our local volunteers interacting with the area's many neighborhoods.

I discovered the fun of teaching practical skills this way! After the Peace Corps, I was confident enough as a teacher to secure a school position on a Caribbean island. Five years later, I moved to Florida where I continued to be a lifelong learner and teacher. I recently retired from a 50-year teaching career, and I continue to support others' needs as a volunteer tutor. My life is still an adventure!

Finding My Passion in Florence

By Haley Reese

I started college prep school in kindergarten, putting me squarely on a path to a four-year university to get a good degree and start a successful career. No other known paths, and no questions asked. But even in elementary school, I didn't fully buy it.

As I progressed through grade school and inevitably went to college, my internal fight with what you're supposed to do only grew stronger. This conflict manifested into chronic anxiety and depression.

Luckily, I'd made a promise to myself, one that rewarded me more than I could have ever imagined. Other than completing my degree, I promised myself I would study abroad.

After deciding on Florence, Italy, I began considering the classes I'd take. I was thrilled that all my options had to do with art, culture, and cooking – quite different from the subjects I had been focused on in school. I stumbled upon a program at a culinary school that would allow me to complete the first semester of a Culinary Arts degree program. My heart leapt for joy! I knew that this was what I'd been longing for all those years.

That fall, I spent four of the most glorious months of my life living and breathing the culinary world of Italy. I woke up every day joyful to be me and excited for the wonder that my day would bring, an entirely foreign feeling up to this point.

Between my classes of "Introduction to Culinary Arts," "Italian Bread Making," and "Wine Appreciation," I found my true passion. And my path.

Florence blew my world wide open and showed me, for the first time in my life, that I could be and do anything my heart desires, as long as I pay attention to what lights me up and follow my passion.

Where Two Paths Are One

By Ahana Lara

Many people predicted that 2012 would be quite a transformative year for our planet. Well, I don't know about you, but it completely changed the trajectory of *my* life!

As a child, I had very lofty dreams, very strong belief, and a very clear vision that I would run a company that would help thousands. As a 40-year-old, I was happy doing small workshops in my city or as an invited guest in other countries. I was helping people to the best of my ability, but the calling to expand my work often nudged me. Life had somewhat blunted my belief in my ability to build up my childhood dreams. It had taught me not to expect the big, to be satisfied with the status quo, and to ignore the restlessness I felt inside. But all of that changed when I came to Australia in 2012 and Daniel Nilon walked into my workshop – late, smug, and ready to question my beliefs.

For every metaphysical principle I presented in the workshop, Daniel offered a piece of scientific corroborating evidence, followed by a pointed question that would push me to dig deeper for answers. I believe I pushed his buttons, too. For two days, we avoided each other during lunch and tea breaks. By the end of the workshop, I could not ignore the fact that he had broken my status quo. While I was busy digging, I had found my childhood dreams surfacing and wanting to be voiced.

I've found that when purpose wants to raise its voice, it's prudent to take action, so I ended up meeting with Daniel. We compared our notes and our dreams. Daniel wanted to change the way people think through his exploration into the science of magnetic energy. I wanted to help people transform through a process of self-exploration and self-realisation. We both wanted to empower thousands through nature's path, a simple path. So we started A Simple Path coaching programs with the Sci-Meta Project as a sub-brand for our clients who wanted to build a business around innovation and creativity.

Over the last four years, we have touched hundreds of lives through our programs. As hearts open, we continue growing through purpose and moving ever closer to realising our childhood dreams.

Bigger Than Purpose

By Daniel Nilon

Life has a strange way of manifesting exactly want you need. My friend Ahana Lara and I were lucky enough to find our purpose, which brought us together to start a company and give our purpose a place to exist. However, every journey has its highs and lows, and the initial excitement of starting the company started to fizzle. As we struggled through a series of challenges. I often asked myself: *What gives? I'm following my passion and I've mapped out a plan, so what's preventing me from reaching my goals?* I questioned myself again and again over the course of several months, and when the answer came, it completely shifted my perspective, my life, and my business.

Looking back, I see my life in little cycles of transformation. Between July and October 2013, Ahana and I decided to visit Malaysia and test out some new courses. Even though we started receiving several leads, we were not able to reach a large audience or meet the cash-flow challenges of our business. It would have been easier to give up and return to our respective countries, back to what we knew before. However, we decided to give it one more month and put our heart and soul into reaching our goals.

Our renewed excitement paid off – we were invited to speak at a massive event with hundreds of people. We appeared on a TV show and did radio interviews. People started recognising us. Our business started expanding. It was a lesson in patience, persistence, and never giving up on your dreams, which we now know is a key to entrepreneurial success.

Our lessons came one after another. With each lesson, we grew stronger within ourselves, and we learned to structure our brand and business better. We started embracing a circle of gratitude and generosity, and as we felt abundant, we grew abundant. We started getting results, and so did our clients.

Beyond our business lessons, we learned to follow our true purpose and allow it to flow through us so we can help others transform their lives.

Uplifting Souls: Blessings from a Grandmother

By Pooja Shende

Ever since I started writing my newsletters and books, I have been receiving countless emails and messages from readers all over the world, sharing experiences of how their lives have changed through the wisdom they've discovered.

On the morning of May 25, 2015, I received an email from one of my subscribers who had just lost her three-year-old grandchild and felt very depressed: "I love the inspiration that I get from your emails. The inspiring words give me courage to cope with my day. May God bless you."

I read the email twice. I was amazed by her words; they touched my heart. As a mother, I could understand what she must be going through and the impact of losing her little one. From the bottom of my heart, I blessed her and her grandson. I blessed myself and expressed gratitude to myself. I expressed gratitude to her for blessing me. It meant a lot to me, especially from someone experiencing so much grief and suffering.

I realized that the motivation and inspiration I shared was helping so many people worldwide. This email provided confirmation that I was going in the right direction of my mission: to have a positive influence in the lives of others and to be the change I wish to see.

Through my talks and writings, I want to help people overcome the difficulties that are keeping them from finding direction and purpose in their lives. I want to help them increase their self-awareness, self-management, social awareness, and relationship management, identifying their strengths and weaknesses, and identifying the potential that already exists within them. I want to guide them in making positive changes and leading harmonious, abundant, and successful lives. I want to help them to be the change that *they* wish to see.

And I wish for God to bless everyone with abundance of good health, wealth, success, prosperity, support, joy, happiness, peace, harmony, and love.

Discovering Rainbows After the Storm

By Veronica Mather

A difficult experience during my career left me feeling vulnerable and with no control over my life. Although I didn't realise it at the time, the challenges I faced provided an opportunity for growth and renewal.

A work colleague was being relentlessly bullied, not by just one person but by four individuals in our workplace. He retaliated with an action that left him with his job on the line. He asked me to support him during the incident investigation, to which I agreed. While the defence of my workmate saved his job, I found myself isolated in a toxic work environment.

I realised my colleagues would be upset with me, but to be honest, the intensity of their anger and desire for payback took me by surprise. My work was sabotaged. I was socially excluded, undermined to management, and attacked online. Discussions with my colleagues and management resolved nothing. It was five people's word against mine. It was suggested that I was lying or perhaps the breakdown in relationships was my fault and I was too sensitive.

During this time, I did a lot of soul searching. I examined my life and considered the choices I make and the ripple effect of my actions. I discovered a passion for animal-welfare advocacy. I learnt about factory farming for profit, where animals have no say in the way they live or die. There is unnecessary and cruel testing of products on innocent animals and endless stories of animal cruelty and neglect worldwide. There is so much injustice in the world; I can't believe it took me so long to become aware.

My colleagues were terminated for another unrelated offence, which provided immense relief. Life gradually returned to normal but with an enlightened awareness of the imprint my lifetime will leave.

My empathy and compassion grow with each difficult life experience. Inadvertently, my colleagues helped me discover more about living a life that speaks to my soul. As is often the case, there was a beautiful rainbow waiting for me at the end of the storm.

I See You

By B. G. Friedman

I was a professional photographer for 11 years. I loved the mechanics of the camera, the chemistry of the darkroom, the physics of lighting, the creativity of setting up a shoot, and the glamour of the entertainment industry where I worked. What I loved most was capturing "The Moment" that came from establishing a special connection between clients and myself. No defenses, no posturing, just their true selves. When I gave them their photos, they often misted up, saying, "I never thought anyone would see this part of me."

It was rewarding, but I wanted my work to do more. I wanted to take pictures that changed the world the way photojournalists did, but as a single mom with two children, I didn't think this was possible. I told the Universe I didn't want to do this work anymore, but I was tied to the income and afraid to stop. My objections escalated, but my behavior stayed the same.

Well, the Universe heard me and responded with an auto accident that injured my neck and fractured my back. Bedridden, I realized I would never do professional photography again. I surrendered to the pain, the immobility, and the end of my career. After several weeks, my best friend called to say she had entered a graduate program in Psychology at a university for adults who couldn't be full-time residential students. Instantly, I felt this was *It* – the way to help people and make a difference – what I came here to do. I jumped in, heart and soul.

That was 35 years ago. Since then, I have expanded from a degree in Clinical Psychology into the field of Energy Psychology, supplemented traditional psychotherapy with psychospiritual work, and added Executive Coaching, which enables me to integrate those years of working with business people in the entertainment industry.

Although it seems like an enormous career shift, my current work still relies on establishing a deep rapport leading to those sacred moments when clients feel safe enough to be seen deeply. This leads them to change themselves and, ultimately, to change the world. Thank you, Universe.

Opening Doors to a New World

By Felicia D'Haiti

Until my junior year in high school, my dream was to become a pediatrician. I threw myself into science and math classes because I knew I needed them to achieve my dream. I didn't pay much attention to anything else. At the end of my sophomore year, I registered to take Chemistry and Human Physiology the following year. I was on track to take all available math and science classes offered in my high school before I graduated. I was excited!

Midsummer, I received a phone call from the assistant principal. She told me that I would not be able to fit both classes into my schedule because of the times they were offered. Then, she topped it off by saying she'd like to register me for a new course at the school called Humanities. My first thoughts were, *You want me to take what? What is that?* But I didn't really have a choice, so I agreed to take the class.

On my first day of Humanities, I walked into the classroom and saw a glamorously dressed teacher standing at her podium. She gave us a pre-test focusing on art, music, dance, and other items of cultural and historical significance. I don't remember knowing much of the information and still wondered why I needed to know it. Then, before she even finished teaching the first class, I was hooked.

The energy, passion, and knowledge that Madolyn Johns had about the arts was phenomenal! By the end of that first class, the door to an entire new world had opened up. Looking at the arts made me see everything in my world in a new way. I just knew that I wanted to be culturally informed and educated. By the end of the year, we had explored numerous museums and cultural centers, attended plays and ballets, and more.

This became an exciting world for me, one in which I could explore new perspectives and different aspects of creativity. At the end of the year, I signed up to take Humanities again. And when I graduated from high school, my dream had completely shifted from the medical field to the arts.

A Leap of Faith: Angel Guidance

By Cindia Carrere

As a jewelry designer who studied energy healing, I used the jewelry as a living laboratory to see if what I was learning actually worked. I experimented, creating pieces similar in color, shape, and tone, and then quietly infused intentional love into half of them – just to see what would happen. The designs I had blessed were always the first to go!

These infused pieces often included positive financial blessings, such as, "May the person who buys this piece be blessed with at least 10 times the purchase price in financial prosperity this week." It became so much fun to watch customers return with synchronicity stories – how when they wore a pair of my earrings or a necklace I'd made, they received more compliments than ever, they got the job they were looking for, or they just felt so much more confident.

But I began feeling joyfully discontent. My soul was being called to something more, though I didn't know what. One day, my inspiration angels whispered in my heart to give all of our inventory away. *What?!* It was the only job and source of income my husband and I had. Even though we'd built our business up for 22 years, we listened and gave everything away within three days.

Two months later, the answer came in the form of a divine download. Thirty minutes of facts, figures, equations, and images rapidly flowed into me. When it was over, I suddenly knew about "The Energy Grid" and how to help women remove blockages, including negative financial energy and the internal contracts holding them back.

The minute I told friends about what happened, they volunteered for practice. Word spread like wildfire, and soon I had a full-time business, making more income in the first two years than we ever had designing jewelry. I'm now on my soul path, helping authors, speakers, and heart-centered entrepreneurs experience abundance and joy.

Breaking Out of the Ordinary

By Maura Smith

After three decades of rushing around, following a routine, and working in stressful corporate jobs, doing something out of the ordinary sounded *very* appealing. So when I heard about a series of intuitive-development classes, I said YES. Little did I know that my decision to do this would lead to the transformation of my career, my health, and….well, basically my whole life.

At that point in time, I was very grateful for many things, including my family and career. However, I was tired of being unhealthy and feeling overwhelmed by a never-ending to-do list. All I really wanted to do was to retire so that I could rejuvenate myself and spend more quality time with my family. At least that's what I thought.

Underneath it all, I sensed there was more to life than what appeared, and I wanted to find out what that was.

I did retire, and I did take the intuitive classes, which became the gateway to a series of trainings in various transformational techniques, the establishment of my own coaching practice, and new connections with like-minded people all over the world. Going from analytical to intuitive energy work was quite a shift! In addition, the process of developing the structures, discipline, and know-how to create my own business was a bumpy ride, especially for someone who felt at home hiding in a corporate cubicle.

Was it worth it? Absolutely. Every day, I'm inspired by the possibilities that keep unfolding for me and everyone else I'm connected with. My mission is to help people experience a sense of fulfillment so that they can enjoy plenty of quality time *and* make a difference in the world.

I'm still feeling my way along, and although I've stumbled many times, I've found so much support along the way that it's hard to articulate how much gratitude I have.

I've found that we're often unaware of what's trying to emerge through us – that new stage of our development – which is why it's so important to embrace the invitation to do something out of the ordinary…and just say *yes!*

She Leads Fearlessly

By Nukhet Hendricks

It had been three years since I started offering intuitive angel readings as my soul business, but I was having serious challenges establishing my business solidly. Granted, I was working full time as a non-profit executive, but I was pretty sure that by the end of the third year I should have had a steady stream of clients. I had a number of awesome clients, but it was not enough. It was more like a hobby. I wanted a solid client base before moving to doing it full time.

So I decided to sign up for a coaching program to help me connect to the soul of my business and create a program that would benefit my clients. I was finally on my way to creating my business.

I was in for an awesome awakening. During the course of this program, I was led to a place where I realized that my soul was yearning to serve women leaders who were experiencing exactly what I was experiencing in my full-time position as a non-profit executive: complete dissatisfaction and disappointment in being a woman leader.

At first, I really didn't want to do this. I was looking to leave my leadership position and move on to being a full-time intuitive reader. There was so much resistance that I even surprised myself. It is funny how what we resist the most can end up being our calling.

In the end, I decided to create a program for women leaders who worked very hard to get where they are but ended up being completely miserable, just like I was. I decided to go through the program I created myself first, and by the time I was two-thirds of the way through it, I realized that it was absolutely what I needed and what women leaders like me needed. I found myself enjoying being a leader and was liking the leader I was becoming because of this program. Talk about finally awakening to the call of my soul! I realized I was born to coach women leaders to have a powerful impact and create lasting change. And "She Leads Fearlessly" was born!

What Matters Most

By Cat Smith

Over two decades ago, I pulled a muscle in my lower back and went to physical therapy for over a month with no improvement. I then took Reiki training and healed my back the following week. It was fun telling the physical therapists that I healed myself and I didn't need to return for more sessions! (Yes, they gave me strange looks!)

When I started doing energy work on others, they told me I had a gift. I had the skills and the sensitive touch, and people were seeing results. They reported that their physical pain was reduced or eliminated, and they had more energy.

Two years ago, I finally accepted that this was my life's purpose. One problem was that I also worked in the corporate world, which is the complete opposite from natural healing! How could I do both? When would I find the time?

I felt a constant tug (which felt more like guilt) indicating that I wasn't doing what I wanted to do. I wasn't making time for my natural-healing business. So, one day at work, I gave myself permission to go into a conference room for 30 minutes and call people to set up free energy sessions with me.

I felt so alive! I felt a surge rush through me like a large ocean wave. I felt it deep into my core.

In that moment, I realized that my energy work was a part of who I am. I knew I couldn't live without providing my services to others, removing blocks that keep them in physical and emotional pain. I realized that it was an important part of my life that I needed to make time for. That day, I decided to put my business first.

I now make time for what matters most. In addition to my business, I also spend quality time with my adult kids and grandson, express my creativity, and make time to take care of my health and well-being. I find that I really *do* have the time – once I determine my priorities and focus on them.

Time for Change

By Michelle Evans

There I was, sitting on the couch, when I realized that my oldest son would be entering 11ᵗʰ grade in the fall. It occurred to me how quickly he would be done with school and off on his own adventures, with my youngest son not far behind. I felt a rush of excitement for them, being young, venturing out on their own, and all the things they would learn and discover.

This was immediately followed by a feeling of terror as I realized that I, too, would be on my own. I had spent the first half of my life shutting down in order to survive my childhood. I had spent the second half of my life living for my children: playing taxi, fundraising, volunteering, and being the safe place for everyone to be.

Now I was looking at a time when I was going to be alone with *me*! It occurred to me that I didn't even know who I was outside of my work and my kids. What did this mean? What would I do? What did I even *like* to do?!

Soon, terror turned to curiosity as I sat with these questions and did something I hadn't done for a long time: I turned to spirit for guidance.

Throughout my life, I had frequently turned to spirit when I was stuck and really needed help, and spirit was always there with the answer. Due to recent life events and experiences, however, I had turned this dimmer switch way down. I had been surviving on my own, but now I wanted to do more than simply survive. So I reached out to my old friend and found that, as always, it was there for me.

Spirit reminded me that I've always wanted to help people. It reminded me that I had always known things I "couldn't know" as a child. Intrigued by these resurfacing memories, I set out to discover what this power meant. How could I strengthen it? How could it help me to heal? How could I use it to help others?

Reaching out to spirit and asking these questions were the first steps down the path to my soul reconnection – and to a new life-chapter as a claircognizant empath, intuitive, and healer.

Trusting the Magic of the Heart

By Helen Rebello

I wished I hadn't seen it, but I had. I wished I didn't have to tell the mum-to-be, but I knew that I would. The moment I saw the cleft lip on the antenatal ultrasound scan, I also knew something else: I knew I had to leave this job – this job that plunged me into depression every Sunday night as I prayed for a miracle to stop me from having to go to work on Monday.

I had known this for a long time, but now I could no longer ignore it. Halfway through my Radiography degree, I knew that this career wasn't right for me...yet I carried on. I added two years of Sonography training, thinking maybe that would be the panacea that would make each day bearable. I was wrong.

I was wrong because this career resulted from a clear decision to ignore my heart by not doing what I loved and was good at – instead, following my head into a vocation that enabled me to help people, while knowing that I was motivated more by the guaranteed income.

I left home at 18 under a cloud. After struggling to survive on my own for seven years, I wanted more ease, more money, and a reason to feel proud of myself. I also wanted external approval, to make amends, and to be a contributor. My head thought it knew the best way to achieve these things, but my heart wanted something different.

Fast-forward to the day my heart finally stamped its desires lovingly but firmly into my consciousness. The day I wanted to lie to the mum-to-be. The day I risked losing my integrity.

I wanted to help people, not spin them into moral turmoil because of something I'd seen. Having seen one (minor) abnormality too many, I wanted to pretend *not* to see, thereby taking away someone else's right to follow their heart, too.

That day, I woke up to the fact that I was in the wrong career, and I decided to leave the familiar and step cautiously onto the unknown path of my heart. I embarked on an unfolding journey of self-discovery, self-employment, serving, and stillness – learning how to help others while also honouring my heart. And my heart has never let me down since...not even on Mondays!

Playing the Game in Real Life

By Victoria L. Mai

It was always in my nature to explore the world, but my childhood didn't allow for me to venture outside much. So I immersed myself in books and video games and explored the world through my imagination. In games where you got to pick your class, I always gravitated towards the magic classes. In particular, I chose to play the healer whenever that was an option. I felt like I was a real-life mage, even though I didn't know at the time that it was real. I felt like there was more to life; I just hadn't discovered it yet.

In 2010, a series of unfortunate events made me wonder about the meaning of life. After being in two car accidents that led to my cars being totaled, I felt that I needed to get my life together. This led me to spiritual teachings and opened me up to a new world, which was not altogether unlike the one I had been fascinated with in my imagination and in the games I played! I found out that energy healing was real and that my interests growing up were not a coincidence. There had been clues all along leading me on my spiritual path – the path that led back to myself.

Back then, my spiritual gifts were not yet awakened, but I had a deep knowing of this potential. I signed up to learn Reiki and became certified in Reiki healing. I started to notice that I could feel energy, and after the Reiki attunements, I noticed I could feel even more. My friends who I practiced on also said they could feel energy when I worked on them, which was exciting and provided me with great confirmation of this gift.

Being a real-life healer, just like the characters in my games, has been a dream come true. Since beginning this journey, I have continued to uplevel as I grow and expand. In addition to my healing experiences, I've also been reminded of a subtle truth: whatever you love, you are.

A Passion for Writing

By Joanne Angel Barry Colon

I never saw myself as a writer until seven years ago. It was then that I started a monthly writing workshop, Healing Within. As time went on, I found myself writing more frequently, and writing became a passion of mine.

My writing consisted of daily journaling, guided meditations, and a chronicle of the progression and recovery of my hip surgery.

One afternoon, as I was reading my notes on my hip progress, I was inspired to share my journey. I reached out to a local paper, *The Queens Tribune*, and wrote my first article, which was featured in its May 2015 weekly edition. Since then, I have written over 50 columns for them and several articles for other local papers and online columns, such as *Mind, Body & Green*.

I was curious to know where else I could apply my writing and, as I usually do whenever I have a question, I meditated and looked to my guides. The answer I received was straightforward, "Your writing is another channel to reach people and help transform their mind, body, and spirit."

At this time, I knew what to do with most of the guided visual meditations I wrote. The universe sent me a graphic designer, an illustrator, and an editor – all at no additional expense! I gathered up 16 meditations, and we got to work. Within one year, on October 24, 2015, I self-published my first book, *Healing Within Meditation*.

My passion for writing has shifted my life. I now have the ability to educate, heal, and transform the world with my writing.

Death Unlocks a New Life

By Prameela (Pam) Sreemangalam

In 2008, life pushed me to understand my purpose at a deeper level after five people who were close to me passed away. That year, I often dreamed of them, and it felt like they were reaching out to me from some other world – trying to communicate something, although I didn't always know exactly what it was.

By day, I found myself questioning the bigger purpose of life and re-evaluating my everyday activities. As I did this, I often noticed myself feeling tired, irritable, or disinterested in things I had previously enjoyed. My decade-old corporate career felt less and less appealing, and I began to think of quitting. With support from a strong mentor, a soulful partner, friends, and family, I decided to shift to a path of healing.

I opened a private healing practice and soon realized that this was, indeed, my life's calling. The path just welcomed me, and I was blessed with a beautiful life that made me happy to the core of my soul. The Divine Creator gifted me with travel opportunities and healing experiences around the globe. Through Source, I channeled people's departed ones and helped those left behind to heal from their losses. In the process, I also created Ancestral Healers and the channeled Buddha Consciousness work, which has helped people manifest lives they truly wish to realize and live to their fullest potential.

Although the losses I experienced in 2008 were difficult, they pushed me to understand my purpose at a deeper level and to realize my higher potential, which was then lying locked within my subconscious awareness. When I look back at the hard times, I now realize what soulful experience they have been, and I feel profound gratitude that I am able to share this gift from the Divine for the healing and celebration of the spirit.

Answering the Question

By Joan B. Zietlow

Most of us have been downsized at least once; for me, it was more than once. In 2010, my downsizing experience was significantly different; at least it sure felt different from past downsizings. I allowed myself to be wooed away from a position where I had lots of perks: a window office overlooking the forest preserve, a pension, indoor parking, minimal travel (after many years of excessive travel), leading an interesting project, and working with a brilliant group of minds at a prestigious professional organization with one of the oldest political/educational histories that very few were ever invited or qualified to join.

One might wonder: *How could the grass have seemed greener to allow yourself to give up a known position for the unknown?* It was the potential of building a better and bigger mousetrap. The new team seemed genuine and the project closer to my core value: to alleviate pain and suffering. So, when the calling of my soul was enticed, I answered the invite.

Eight months into the new position, they changed their mind – no need for the original program, and I was out the door. What a gift this experience turned out to be! It led me to ask myself that all-important question: *What do I want to do with this one precious life?* My answer became crystal clear: *Alleviate the pain and suffering for as many as possible.* I chose to enroll in health coaching certification, applied for an MBA scholarship (which I won and completed), and never looked back.

I now inspire, empower, teach, and lead people to be their own "best doctor no money can buy." It feels awesome to help others in this capacity. I love coaching leaders because the ripple effect for others' health inspires me even more! I help my clients find answers to health issues they have had for years and never thought could improve. I love what I do, and I will never have to work another day in my life.

A Dream Fulfilled

By Sherri Hayter

My husband, Matt, and I had been dreaming of RV living since the very beginning of our relationship. Now, with two young sons in tow, we are harvesting the fruit of seeds sown so long ago. As I write this, we are travelling through British Columbia, Canada, to our current destination on Vancouver Island.

The process has been akin to shedding several skins. Like many couples, we owned a house with a whole heap of debt on the side, and our "stuff" was taking a financial and energetic toll on us. On the heels of a significant job loss and the pursuit of an entrepreneurial path, we made the hard decision to sell our home. We purchased a 32-foot fifth wheel and a truck to tow it, and began living the full-time RV lifestyle in earnest.

Purging 98% of our worldly possessions has taught us a great deal about attachment. It is said that attachment is the source of all human suffering, and indeed, we experienced our possessions as little anchors continuously holding us back. "How can we sell this for so little when we paid so much?" we wondered. "This was a gift – how can we donate it? What will we do without this practical little gadget?" It quickly became apparent how little we truly needed in the way of possessions to live an immensely rich life – and that richness is measured by the moments of now, not by the amassing of "stuff."

This simplified life is teaching us, moment by moment, how to live a life free from distraction and to connect to the essence of ourselves. We are learning that our incarnation is unique and our birthrights are joy, ease, and abundance. We've realized we were using the wrong gauge with which to measure these birthrights, not even recognizing them as such in favor of believing we had to *do* something to achieve them. In truth, we experience these birthrights simply by being ourselves. The magic and wonder of life unfurls daily for us through this process of simplified living and dream fulfillment.

Conclusion

Throughout this book, you've been exposed to a vast array of life shifts. As you've seen, they can be as dramatic as a near-death experience or as subtle as a change in thought. They can arise spontaneously, or they can be the result of a conscious decision. But one thing ties all these shifts together: once they occur, life can never be the same. They have a profound impact on your life, which creates positive ripples that reach out into the world and touch other hearts, minds, and lives.

We hope that you, too, have been touched by the authors' experiences described throughout this book. Perhaps the book has helped you reflect on the life shifts you've already experienced. Perhaps it's encouraged you to look for (or create) opportunities for more. Perhaps it's renewed your sense of awe and wonder at the amazing diversity of life experiences and the limitless possibilities for your own life. We certainly hope that it's done all this and more.

If you enjoyed this book, please share it with your friends and family! Inspiring someone to make a positive shift in their life is a beautiful gift! We would also be so grateful if you left a positive review for us on Amazon, which will help this book's uplifting messages reach even more people. And we would love for you to join us on our Facebook page, where you can share some of your favorite pieces, connect with the authors, and be part of our wonderfully loving and soulful community: www.facebook.com/365lifeshifts.

Thank you so much for taking the time to read our book. We hope it's been a positive experience and has inspired you to experience a soulful life shift of your own!

Hugs, love, and gratitude,

Jodi and Dan

Contributor Biographies

O ver 250 authors contributed to this book with the hopes that sharing their pivotal life shifts would provide insight, inspiration, and encouragement to those who read about them.

The co-authors come from many different walks of life from many parts of the world. The common thread that links each of us is our desire to share our words and to inspire others by doing so. That's all, and that's everything.

As you read through each author's biography on the pages that follow, you'll find some who are already bestselling authors and others who are sharing their words in print for the first time, which is such an exciting moment!

It's our hope that you'll enjoy meeting them all through their photos and biographies, and that you'll reach out to those you resonate with and let them know how much their pieces moved you. What a gift that will be for them to receive!

About the Editors

Jodi Chapman and Dan Teck are a husband-and-wife team who loves living soulfully and joyfully. Since 2005, they've been living their dream of writing books and creating products that inspire others to connect with their soul and live fully and passionately.

Jodi has a BA in English/Technical Editing and Sociology, and Dan has a BA in Religious Studies and an MFA in Creative Writing. Together, they have over 30 years of experience with editing and publishing and have sold over 35,000 books. They have written 20 books, 10 ecourses, and over 1,000 blog posts/articles.

Jodi is an award-winning blogger at www.jodichapman.com and the creator of Soul Clarity Cards. Dan is the author of the personal-growth blog *Halfway up the Mountain* (www.halfwayupthemountain.com). They are the co-creators of the *Soulful Journals Series* and the *365 Book Series*.

They live on the Oregon coast with their sweet cats. They enjoy hanging out at the beach and working, creating, and playing together.

They feel truly blessed to be able to spend each day together, doing what they love. It's their hearts' desire that their books and products bring joy to everyone they reach.

About the Contributors

Nikki Ackerman is a heart-centered, holistic business owner and a Master in Usui Reiki, Karuna® Reiki, and Holy Fire® Reiki. She recognizes that the rewards are very beneficial for mind, body, and spirit wellness. Her desire is to provide others with peace and balance through a soulful and holistic approach to self-care and well-being.

Atiya Ahmed is a passionate healer whose training includes some of the most cutting-edge healing methods available on the planet today. In her spare time, she enjoys spending time in nature and working on her personal growth in order to serve others at her best. Email: atiya_amf@icloud.com.

Aprile Alexander is a results-focused life coach and intuitive energy healer. A Certified SimplyHealed Practitioner, she specializes in distance sessions by phone for people and animals from any country. As "Jo Shepherd" she authored *Walking the Camino for Newbies*. www.TimeForFlourishing.com

Karrol Rikka S. Altarejos is the creator and author of the spiritual lifestyle blog *La Bella Energia*. She holds space for others to embrace, empower, and embody their experiences with living energy. A student of Andean Q'ero teachings and indigenous shamanic, mystical practices, she shares her explorations at www.karrolrikka.com.

Tiffany Andersen is a medical aesthetician with 20+ years' experience, stage-IV cancer survivor, and victim of a major car accident. She turned tragedy into triumph, which is described in her award-winning memoir, *Finding Faith*. On a quest for elements to repair the body, she developed the toxin-free skincare line, Gavée Gold. www.gaveegold.com

Melisa Archer, National Trainer for Tesla Wellness Energy, is certified in Pulsated Electromagnetic Frequencies, BIO Frequencies, Reiki 3, Raindrop Therapy, Vitaflex, essential oils, rejuvenation facials, Emotion Code, and Dolphin Neurostim. Her ability to see and feel energies benefits the clients' sessions. www.TeslaWellnessEnergy.com

Joy T. Barican is a life coach who is passionate in assisting you to make meaningful, exciting, and viable choices for yourself based on your individual values, personal strengths, and beliefs. When results matter, contact her via email: jbarican@hotmail.com.

Mauri Barnes, RN, is reinventing herself through writing and self-realization. Volunteering on medical missions to Kenya, Peru, Vietnam, and the Caribbean ignited her awareness of naturopathic medicine as she experienced various cultural traditions of healing and home remedies. Her passion is healing with nutrition, education, and lifestyle.

Lisa Bartello, BA (Hons), is a proud mother and international bestselling author in *Empowering Women to Succeed*. Her gifts with vibration, the brain, and spiritual alchemy form her passionate career as an intuitive, teacher, meditation guide, and writer. She is also a successful realtor and investor. www.lisabartello.ca

Katy Beaumont was born with a creative heart and a penchant for books. She loves sharing her creations of jewelry, music, and sweets. She especially loves spending time with her husband and fur babies and is currently working on her new novel. www.KatyBeaumont.com

Sarah Berkett is an animal intuitive, dream intuitive, past-life regressionist, angelic life coach, and spiritual teacher. She resides in Arizona with her husband, Jim, and German Shepard, Sasha. www.beamerslight.com

Holly Berkley, CEO of BlissSmart, is a professional-development expert and creator of the Mastering Confidence system, which helps businesswomen eliminate limiting beliefs and achieve authentic leadership and work-life-spirit balance. Co-author of *The Young Female Leader: Confidence, Communication and Charisma*. www.BlissSmart.com

Rebekah Bernard is fulfilled with her work as a spiritual counselor through hospice care. She has a master's degree in Counseling Psychology and has been a student of interdisciplinary spirituality for over 15 years. She teaches, speaks, counsels, and writes about living a love-centered, mindful existence. www.rebekah-bernard.com

Nicole Black is a certified Rolfer™, massage therapist, and writer. She lives in southern California with her daughter. When she isn't writing, she enjoys Pilates, traveling to distant lands, and chasing butterflies.

Cathie Bliss, MBA, cultivated a career in international business for two decades. When her daughter developed severe special needs in the 1990s, she reoriented to the healing arts, becoming a Certified LifeLine Practitioner and Intuitive Astrologer. Visit www.CathieBliss.com for her heart-centered offerings.

Karen Bomm is a lifestyle entrepreneur who is passionate about self-publishing strategies for business owners, entrepreneurs, artists, authors, and publishers. She is an international bestselling author and the CEO/founder of www.iWillSelfPublish.com, attracting creative professionals who value integrity, grace, growth, and community.

Natasha Botkin, Master Teacher and Intuitive Behavioral Energy Healer, is a #1 international bestselling author and creator of *Reclaiming Your Power: Empower Your Words* and *Heart Meditative Writing*. She uses healing energies by releasing blocks to help her clients empower themselves. www.magicalblessingshealingcenter.com

Mary Ann Reel Bouttu fell in love with the writing process as a pre-schooler learning to write numbers and the alphabet. She journals regularly and hopes to write a book someday. mabouttu@aol.com

Anne Bradley has always been a writer of one kind or another. Her recent transition from authoring software to memoirs is a welcome and delightful lifestyle change. She loves meeting and hanging out with her readers and author friends at www.facebook.com/annebradleyauthor.

Lisa Miles Brady believes the greatest gift we give the world is to be unapologetically *all* that we are. As a speaker, writer, and intuitive artist and coach, she mentors women in accessing their deepest truths so they can create fully expressed lives. www.LisaMilesBrady.com

Michael Brewer is a life lover. He loves his beautiful wife, Ann, and they live a spiritually enriched life on the east coast of Australia. They live each moment of each day in heartfelt gratitude. www.facebook.com/freedompathways.info

Shannon L. Brokaw is a writer, yogi, and Usui Reiki practitioner who loves the outdoors. She is a seeker of anything that makes her laugh in life and puts a smile on her face. *La Dolce Vita!* www.welliesandwhisky.com

Ted Brooks is a sage, psychologist, consultant, author, healer, and angelologist. He is blessed with the ability to communicate with the angels around us and often gives messages from Archangels Michael, Zadkiel, Hope, Mary, Amethyst, Jophiel, Gabriel, and others. www.Facebook.com/tedbrooks.980

Tonia Browne is an advocate of inviting fun back into our lives. Her writing is interwoven with spiritual insights and personal anecdotes. Check out her book *Spiritual Seas: Diving into Life* for more underwater adventures and insights. www.toniabrowne.com

Andrea Bryant spent years in the painful pursuit of her purpose. Now she helps her fellow animal lovers discover and step into their meaningful life or career! She is a certified Inspired Spirit Coach who lives in New Zealand with her two indoor rabbits. www.purposeanimal.com

Claire Bunker is a leader, aspiring writer, and seasoned educator. She believes in the profound balance of mind, body, and spirit in every life journey. After pouring her heart into public education for three decades, she welcomes the next adventure. Visit www.clairebunker.wixsite.com/mysite to see "The Interruption" drawing mentioned in her piece.

Mindi Burke spent 20 years studying human potential and now devotes her life to inspiring and empowering thousands around the globe to become a better version of themselves through her coaching, training, writing, and sharing of valuable products and services. Begin your transformational journey by visiting www.beliefactionresults.com.

Brian D. Calhoun is a heart-centred international bestselling author, psychic medium, Reiki Master, and spiritual teacher who has dedicated his life to bringing messages of love and light for healing and enlightenment to all for over 15 years. He is based in Ottawa, Ontario, Canada. www.angelswithin.ca

Sheila Callaham is an international bestselling author and motivational coach. She founded the Activate Your Braveheart platform to facilitate women through the process of identifying hidden passions and making them real. Learn more at www.SheilaCallaham.com and claim your free gift, "28 Questions to Transform Your Life."

Christine Callahan-Oke is an empowerment coach, mom, inspirational writer, and positive thinker. Through coaching and writing, she offers practical tips and straightforward wisdom to help people achieve their potential, see the beauty in everyday moments, and live authentically. Download her free *5 Keys to Loving Life* guide here: www.YourInspiredLife.ca/free-guide.

Valerie Cameron is a certified life coach and Reiki Master/Teacher. She has been an entrepreneur for over 40 years, and it is through this and her abilities as an intuitive psychic/spiritual medium that she is able to compassionately assist those who ask for guidance. www.earth-balance-healing.com

Angie Maya Campbell is an intuitive energy healer and teacher at Superhero Reiki School. She lives in Scotland and devotes her life to teaching, balancing chakras, spreading laughter, and finding superpowers! Come and hang out with her at www.angiemcampbell.com.

Maryann Candito is an author, intuitive healer, and Akashic Records consultant. By healing the past on the subconscious, energetic, and soul levels, we change current paradigms and create new realities. She would love to help you heal, connect, and transform. www.MaryannCandito.com

Donna Cantone is a Feng Shui practitioner, columnist, and author of *Live an Abundant Life with Feng Shui*. She's an Angel Healing Practitioner®, Angel Communication Master™, and Angelic Life Coach®. She empowers others to create their sacred life purpose and design a home sanctuary. www.Phoenixholisticservices.com

Debbie Carcuffe is a spiritual counselor, emotional-wellness teacher, and holistic energy practitioner who guides and empowers others toward self-awareness and self-actualization through classes, workshops, and private sessions. She owns Portal of Healing: Conscious Alignment with the Soul in New Jersey. www.portalofhealing.com

Barbara "Bobbie" Carr is a mother, grandmother, and author who enjoys gardening, choral singing, tennis, and reading. She truly believes in the power and grace of the Spirit in her life. She lives in New Jersey with her husband, Pat.

Cindia Carrere is an abundance activator and travel guide for women on their transformational paths as they evolve into their full spiritual adulthood. She helps rewire their energy grids, thus changing the story from separation, shame, and scarcity to wealth, worth, and wholeness. www.HealYourGrid.com

Angie Carter is an inspirational writer who began writing as a way to cope with the sudden loss of her 19-month-old daughter, Bella. Her blog, *A Mother's Journey Through Grief* (www.angiecarter.ca), is dedicated to Bella's memory and has deeply touched people worldwide with evidence that life is eternal.

Julie Chan, Founder of Being My Purpose, uses intuitive abilities to empower people to know and express their life purpose with courage and creativity. On a mission to bridge spirituality, business, and science, she is an entrepreneur, urban planner, singer, and graduate of Yale and MIT. www.beingmypurpose.com

Robin Chellis is the founder of Light Code Healing™ and Auroric Facets™ serving lightworkers, healers, and leaders to help with abundance, alignment, and ascension. She incorporates energetic healing work, energetically infused artwork, and other modalities to activate and amplify your true self. www.robinchellis.com

Claire Chew kicked stage IV cancer's butt at 19 and now can be found coaching, teaching, cooking, and practicing spiritual psychology. Her favorite mantra is "Let love be your bottom line." She knows her time here is short and empowers women to live fully. www.clairechew.com

Judith Clements is a perennial teacher/student who is now retired from the kindergarten classroom and continues exploring her passions for language, people, and creativity. An avid reader/writer, she enjoys collaborating in a creative writer's circle. Inspired energy comes from swing dancing, camping, and professional hockey.

Lisa Rachel Cohen, CEO of InSparkle Media, is on a sacred mission to embrace the heart and grasp the hand of every woman, child, and man. She coaches, hosts Global InSparkle Compassion Celebrations, and is the author of *Grace is Born* and *My Grace is Born Companion*. www.InSparkleMedia.com

Joanne Angel Barry Colon has been blessed with a beautiful daughter; is the business owner of Fitness "R" Us; and is a personal trainer, nutrition coach, Reiki/crystal healer, and speaker. She is the author and publisher of *Healing Within Meditation*. www.fitnessrus.org

Missy Conley has a passion for writing about all the fun you can have while creating your own reality. You can read her blog at www.missysstory.wordpress.com.

Marla David is a life coach, speaker, writer, and author of two #1 international bestsellers. She loves giving back to society. A retired stay-at-home mom of three grown daughters, she lives a life of passion, which includes spending time with family and friends, traveling, enjoying arts and culture, and advocating for animals and nature.

Donna Davis is a modern-day change agent disguised as The Menopause Fairy who celebrates the magic, mystery, and mayhem of midlife. This Fairy is taking bold action to educate, celebrate, and collaborate with women in all phases of life around the globe. www.TheMenopauseFairy.com

Netta de Beer is the creator of the successful wedding-events company Delicious and Delightful, which began in 2010. Her great passion is writing poetry for a local newspaper. She enjoys playing with unsaid words and mixed feelings.

Dr. Regina J. Dekker, MscD, PsyThD is a minister and doctor of Metaphysical Science and Theocentric Psychology. She's the founder of Authentic Living Ministries, an inspirational speaker, published writer, Certified Spiritual Life Coach/Practitioner, Certified Reiki Master, and Holistic Energy Therapist. authenticliving@roadrunner.com

Dr. Tanya Destang-Beaubrun, a family physician, certified lifestyle and empowerment expert, wife, mother, and passionate lover of life, has dedicated her career to helping people connect more deeply to themselves and their truth. She is a strong advocate for a holistic approach to health and well-being. Connect with her at www.tanyabeaubrun.com.

Andrea Detchon had a BSc. in Chemistry, a successful career in manufacturing process improvement, and looked successful. She was also stressed, depressed, and looking for alternative solutions to heal. She trained in Reiki, crystal healing, Dru Yoga, and Laughter Yoga to find her joy. She now guides people to create their own joy-filled life.

Janet Dhaenens is an author, speaker, coach, and circle facilitator. She has learned to follow emotions to uncover the thoughts that cause them, revealing true choice and personal power. She creates safe space in her circles, assisting others in finding their own power and choice. www.EmergingBalance.com

Felicia D'Haiti is a Feng Shui and Soul Coach/Teacher who guides clients in shifting their perspectives and environments to move beyond perfectionism, fear, and self-imposed limitations. She is an author and educator who lives in Maryland with her husband and four children. www.feliciadhaiti.com

Lydia Di Francesco is a Certified Personal Trainer, *Huffington Post* contributor, and frequent TV fitness expert. She founded an online fitness program, 15 Minute Workout Club, helping busy professionals get strong and stay fit through short, effective, at-home workouts. Learn more at www.15minuteWorkoutClub.com.

Ruth Donald is a strategist, coach, and educator. She works with individuals and enterprises from across the world, helping them to connect at the heart. Her number-one priority in life is seeing the love in every situation. www.ruthdonald.com.au

Jody Doty is a writer, healer, seer, internet radio host, and a bit of a mystic. She is "Jody Doty Soul Reader" to her clients. Her written words are inspired through meditation on the divine. She lives in the Pacific Northwest with her husband, Dave, and three amused cats. www.jodydoty.com

Patricia Downing is co-founder of Living with Kindness, an online community whose purpose is to recruit kindness ambassadors who inspire each other to practice kindness and help create a more compassionate world in which people join together to find creative solutions that work for everyone. www.livingwithkindness.com

Kimberly DuBoise is a poet who loves to inspire with words. When not writing, she is probably reading, cooking, or walking. She lives in the Midwest with her husband. You can find her book and blog at www.kimberlyduboise.com.

Cathy Duesterhoeft is a freelance writer from Westfield, Wisconsin. She and her husband of 36 years travel throughout the United States in their RV. When home, they enjoy spending time with their family, kayaking, and biking. She documents their many adventures on her blog at www.baldladytravels.com.

David J. Dunworth is the Chief Experiences Officer of Marketing Partners LLC, a digital marketing agency focused on helping small businesses. As a published author of several books, ghostwriter, and publisher, he stays pretty busy. He is passionate about writing and digital marketing.

Freda Durden is the owner of 813WellBeing LLC. As a master energy therapist, intuitive healer, and professionally developed counselor, her oracle-like wisdom facilitates the transformation of new beings. Her divine assignment is leading a renaissance of awakened individuals deeper into the art of living as an authentic soul.

J. L. Eck always wanted to be a writer but never dared go after her dreams until she moved to Hawaii. The islands inspired her to write her first novel, a romance based on the Hawaiian myth of the naupaka flower. Learn more about her at www.jleckthewriter.com.

Dr. Jerri Eddington is the creator of Energy Connections and the co-creator of Lighten Up and Thrive! – a sacred vision of sharing our expertise and wisdom as transformational Soul Coaches®. She facilitates powerful, transformative programs to experience joyful living for mind, body, and soul. www.LightenUpandThrive.com

Meilin Ehlke aspires to express her sacred wisdom by celebrating life's beauty in every moment. Playing with her son and two cats are a big part of it. She invites the world's wisdom seekers to walk with her to fully feel their wisdom and unfold their true beauty. www.meilinehlke.com

Tandy R. Elisala inspires women to passionately live their life purpose, learn to love themselves first, and lead a life that matters. She has 30 years of experience as an executive and coach. She is a four-time #1 international bestselling author, *Huffington Post* contributor, and Certified Success Coach. www.tandyelisala.com/freegifts

Katrina Elkins was squelched as a child in a fear-based, apocalyptic cult and now awakens us to the beauty of life in the present moment. She invites us to live fiercely with joy and to relish the power of self-love to overcome trauma. The power of play unfolds at www.katrinaelkins.com.

Kimberly A. Elliott is a believer in passionate living. She is committed to investing her time, energy, and resources in encouraging others to love lavishly, learn limitlessly, and laugh loudly…every chance you get! She enjoys reading, writing, world travel, and the amazing beauties God has given her in her children and grandchildren!

Lori Evans is an educational health expert and holds a BA in Education in the fields of English and Health. Over the course of her career, she's taught academically to children, adolescents, and young adults. Her first solo book, *The Teenage Emotional Abyss*, is in development. www.lorievans.biz

Michelle Evans is a claircognizant empath. She has experienced many trials in this human life to better understand and empathize with her clients. She connects with them in person and from a distance on a soul level to provide insight and healing, with love and the best intentions. www.rocksolidlove.ca

Shirley Ann Everingham is from HorseGirl Farm, a horse biz in the Northern Rivers of Australia. She was tired of feeling ordinary because she didn't ride horses or create anymore and hadn't found her true north. Join her as she saddles up and helps others sparkle. www.horsegirlfarm.wordpress.com

Sophia Ellen Falke has a vision for world transformation. To that end, she is a Life Mastery Consultant, speaker, and international bestselling author. Her newest book, *Never Too Late: A Guide for Living the Life You Love*, is available on Amazon. Find out more at www.EmbracingGreatness.com.

Martina E. Faulkner, LMSW, is an author, certified life coach, and Reiki Master Teacher. In addition to her book, *What if..? How to Create the Life You Want Using the Power of Possibility*, she writes *InspireBytes*™ – a weekly blog where she shares inspirational writings. www.martinafaulkner.com

Melissa Feick uses her intuition and 20 years of experience to empower spiritual aspirants to live their life purpose and assist in their ascension process. Service is her passion and purpose, so she teaches spiritual classes and offers healings and Akashic Records readings. She is available over Skype or phone. www.MelissaFeick.com

Helen Ferrara, PhD, is passionate about the world we live in, believes that we are all creative, and has experienced that the broadening of one's perspective strengthens personal transformation. She researches creativity and is a mentor who assists the nurturing of self-knowledge and authentic expression. www.creativenurture.com.au

Nancy Ferrari is passionate about the duality within her career in multi-media and intuitive life coaching. She produces and hosts *The Nancy Ferrari Show* and is a contributing writer in bestselling books and online publications where she shares her message of positivity and living an empowered life. www.nancyferrari.com

Linsey Fischer discovered her love for journalism while writing for her hometown newspaper. She went on to study Broadcast Journalism, gaining hands-on experience in editing, reporting, hosting, anchoring, producing, and script writing in both radio and TV. She is currently working on the *Empowering Women to Succeed* book *Bounce.*

Meredith Fjelsted is a Nationally Certified Health Coach and founder of Dream2bhealthy. She is a professional speaker and healthy-lifestyle expert who loves being outdoors, gardening, dogs, going on mission trips, and living healthy. She lives in Minnesota with her husband, Scott; two stepsons, Colin and Aidan; and three dogs.

Scott Fjelsted has been a Certified Personal Trainer since 1998 and is the author of *ForeverFitU: Making Fitness a Lifestyle that Lasts a Lifetime.* He is committed to the wellness of his clients, community, and home. He lives in Minnesota with his wife, Meredith, and two sons, Colin and Aidan.

Jen Flick is a *New York Times* and Amazon international bestselling author. Her writings are included in: *Eat Pray Love Made Me Do It, Cultivating Joy,* and *365 Moments of Grace,* just to name a few. Visit www.jenflick.com to learn more about her and her work.

Karen A. Foli is passionate about creating a brilliant life and desires to share her knowledge and gifts to empower others on their path. She enjoys living in harmony with nature, opens her big heart to volunteer adventures with children, and loves her furry friends. www.karenafoli.com

Diane Marie Ford, Certified Holistic Counselor and Spirit Medium, offers revolutionary counseling with you, your ancestors, and your loved ones in spirit. "The real question is not whether life exists after death. The real question is whether you are alive before death." www.ListenToThyself.com

Suzanne M. Fortino currently resides in Idaho and is a mother of five and grandmother of two. She often finds herself wandering the Northwest, visiting friends and family. She's passionate about the path she's chosen, spreading healing love and light to all she encounters on life's healing journey. www.healingjourney.com

Jane Francis credits her three children as the catalysts in awakening her heart to her soul. She facilitates past-life regressions, angel card readings and parties, and Usui Reiki sessions/classes; channels "The WE"; and is a certified Radiant Heart Healing Instructor. janesangel444@gmail.com

B. G. Friedman, MA, LMFT, helps individuals transform by reuniting them with their core selves and creating emotional safety. She facilitates business growth and success for professionals through practical solutions and strategic communication. Working by phone enables her to support clients worldwide. BF.morepositiveoptions@gmail.com

Amy Gage is an author, speaker, and poet who is passionate about beauty alchemy and transparent self-expression. She shares her voice to help others claim their own voice; overcome debilitating fears; and find more beauty, freedom, and magic in their lives through intuitive creative healing. www.moondancemuse.com

B. J. Garcia is an author and inspirational teacher. She lives in Austin, Texas, with her family and loves to share with others, in groups or individually, all the many strands of interest and wisdom she has collected and moved through in her personal journey for truth. www.bjgarcia.com

Ginger Gauldin is an intuitive creative artist, poet, and grace expander who enjoys writing, diverse reading, and holistic wellness and nutrition. As a multi-passionate entrepreneur, she operates an online business, blogs, and collaborates with heart-centered businesses as they help to raise the vibration of the planet.

Lindsay S. Godfree is the author of *Awakening Consciousness: Finding a Larger Version of Self.* She is a certified trainer of life-changing techniques. Creator of the *Consciousness Guide* website, her passion is uplifting consciousness in every part of life. www.ConsciousnessGuide.com

Bryce Goebel is an intuitive, energy healer, and empowerment coach. She's passionate about helping you find your voice and learn to completely love who you are, without guilt, shame, or apology. Get free tools to help you live a fierce, authentic life at www.BryceGoebel.com.

Randi Goodman is a mom of four beautiful boys, a 4th-Level CMA, and a 2nd Dan in Shotokan Karate. She is action oriented and enjoys supporting entrepreneurs in business. She co-founded the #1 international bestselling series, *Empowering Women to Succeed*, as well as multiple globally renowned business conferences.

Michelle Anne Gould is a soulpreneur, mother, founder of Abundant Spirit Education, and creator of SoulMagic™. She supports people who are committed to enhancing their lives through personal transformation, unlocking and activating abundance from within. She awakens people to their unique, infinite magic. www.abundantspiritedu.com

Noemi Grace has been chosen as a channel for spiritual wisdom in answer to her prayer on 9/11: "Use me for the healing of the world." She helps people find happiness through unconditional self-love and is delighted to offer you her free self-love ebook: www.noemigrace.com/self-love-ebook.

Linda Graziano is a life coach, inspired by her personal experience with bipolar disorder. She supports women with depression or bipolar disorder to overcome self-criticism, handle uncomfortable feelings, and connect to their higher selves so they can sustain their wellness and live life fully. www.embracetheinneryou.com

Judy N. Green first managed her son's ADHD through diet in 1988. She has overcome her personal battles with systemic candidiasis, chronic depression, obesity, and cancer through optimal nutrition, healthy habits, and a positive state of mind. She launched RAW 'N Green Wellness Coaching in 2015. www.rawngreen.com

Melody R. Green is an angel communicator, soul coach, award-winning author, thought leader, and qualified career adviser to women. Her blog, *Living with Angels,* is about how the angels want to help you in your everyday life. She lives in Newcastle, NSW, Australia. www.melodyrgreen.me

Norma L. Gunner is the mother of five grown children and the wife of a minister. She was born in Pennsylvania and now resides in Kansas City, Missouri. God has taught her many lessons through the years, and she understands that we are all part of a divine plan. She spends much of her time listening and following His direction.

Stacey Hall, LSH, CNTC, CAC, CRTS, is a spiritual healer, success coach, speaker, author of the bestselling *Chi-To-Be! Achieving Your Ultimate B-All*, and co-author of *Attracting Perfect Customers: The Power of Strategic Synchronicity*. Access her *Attraction Tips* to attract the aCHIevement of goals with ease for free at www.chi-to-be.com.

Marihet Hammann is an author, artist, teacher, and intentional creativity coach, guiding women to be artful self-explorers in their lives and business Queendoms by creatively disrupting their everyday living with powerful Living Life in Full Colour practices. She colours, creates, and dances her soul alive. www.marihethammann

Edna Harris, RNPA, is a Natural Health Consultant who believes that love conquers all. She is determined to make a difference in the lives of others. She is an author with the Canadian Institute of Poetry, past weekly contributor to *Women as Visionaries Magazine*, and a blogger at www.itsallgold.com.

Annalene Hart is an Enchanted Living Life Coach, poet, and visionary artist who creates soul paintings. She has inspired her clients to pursue and realize their dreams. She conducts individualized Magical Child sessions to help activate the participant's innate creativity and imagination. www.mydivineenchantedlife.wordpress.com

Mathew Hart is a sensitive, a channeler, and a Hollywood film producer. His awakening journey and channeled messages from a group soul called "The Guardians" can be found on his website: www.thelifeintended.com. He lives with his wife, Nola; their youngest daughter, Kaylin; and their Mini Golden Doodle, Maggie.

Beverly J. Harvey is a freelancer living in Virginia. A metaphysician for 20 years, she lives a spirit-filled life with her pets, books, and writing. She seeks to share positive energy and raise vibrations by writing on metaphysical topics. Other contributed works are found at www.heartandsoulezine.com.

Lisa Hawkins is a homeopath and healer who supports people who are struggling with a crisis in health or in life. She connects, communicates, supports, and holds a loving space for them to reconnect with themselves and work through their issues so they can heal and move forward in their life.

Sherri Hayter is a sacred artist intent on grounding the Divine in physical form through her art. Working with natural materials, crystals, and sound, she creates healing works of art that assist clients on their ascension journey. www.sherrihayter.com

Ellouise Heather helps women who dread going back to work after chronic illness and depression to find their calling and have the confidence to pursue it. She's an accredited Master Coach, writer, and blogger whose motto is, "Be you, be well." You can connect with her at www.ellouiseheather.com.

Cynthia Helbig is a spiritual life designer and creator of Empowered Heart. She uses powerful meditation practices plus ceremony, ritual, and other tools to invite your inner greatness to reveal itself. Download her free *The Art of Meditation* ebook and guided meditation to empower your heart at: www.empoweredheart.com.au/free-gift.

Amanda Hendricks, Ordained High Priestess Phoenix Sunshine, is an educator and certified yoga instructor who is committed to creating safe space for others to explore the depths of themselves. She offers relaxation massage and Healing Touch sessions in the Cincinnati area. She can be reached at phoenixsunshine13@gmail.com.

Nukhet Hendricks, Nonprofit Executive and Women's Leadership Coach, has over 25 years of leadership experience and holds an MS in Public and Human Service Administration. She is creating lasting change as a leader and coaches women leaders to also have a powerful impact and create lasting change. www.sheleadsfearlessly.com

Sharon Hickinbotham is an angel intuitive reader who has the ability to connect with your departed loved ones. She is an international bestselling co-author who has contributed to multiple books. She is an animal and nature lover whose passion is to inspire others to follow their heart and soul. www.facebook.com/PurpleReign444

Karen Hicks lives in Ontario, Canada, with her partner, daughters, and dog. She is passionate about people elevating their lives through discovering their brilliance. As an emotional success coach, she uses proven, powerful tools and technologies to help people along their journey. She believes in exercising the mind, body, and spirit.

Karen Hill received her bachelor's degree in Human Services from Union Institute and University in 2009. She has extensive experience working with adults in residential drug and alcohol treatment. She recently became a first-time published co-author in *365 Moments of Grace* and is very excited to be on her journey.

JoBeth Hitt holds a master's degree in Educational Psychology and works as an Instructional Coach for the Los Angeles Unified School District. She has also worked as a parent educator focusing on school and family interactions. She enjoys reading and spending time with her family.

Cindy Hively is a renowned intuitive healing coach and catalyst for women. Her life's passion and soul work is to help women experience a luscious, rhythmic life that's overflowing with love, joy, vibrant health, personal success, feminine mystery, spiritual connection, and prosperity. www.inherfullness.com

Gretchen Oehler Hogg, BSN, CCHt, is a Master Soul Coaching® and Gateway Dreaming® Practitioner and co-creator of Lighten Up and Thrive. She empowers people to transform and enrich their lives by connecting each individual to their soul's deepest truth using a variety of modalities along with aromatherapy.

Maureen Hollmeyer, LSW, is a Spiritual Love Coach who helps men and women heal their hearts to attract their soulmate. She uses her own life experiences, intuition, and guidance from her angels to help others along their love journey. www.transitional-guidance.com

Karla Joy Huber is a writer, tutor, and artist in Michigan who has both a conventional day job and is a freelance writer. She is a practicing Nichiren Buddhist who shares her Buddhist and interfaith insights about "thinking spiritually outside the box" at www.karlahuberblog.blogspot.com.

Lisa Hutchison works with empathic healers who want to recharge their depleted energies. As an intuitive licensed psychotherapist, certified angel card reader, and writing coach, she delivers therapeutic guidance with compassion. She is a published writer in two *Chicken Soup for the Soul* books. www.lisahutchison.net

Polina Ivanova holds a master's degree in International Relations and has practiced Japanese painting since 2014. Curious and open-minded, she experiences important life transitions and shares how art helps her go through them. She is of Russian descent and currently lives in Japan. She is fluent in English and French.

Lacey Dawn Jackson is an internationally known psychic who is passionate about teaching others how to listen to their inner self. She holds retreats on the coast. She also hosts *Groovy Green Goddess* – a show full of inspiration and empowerment. www.GroovyGreenGoddess.com

Tazeem Jamal, PMDT, LE, has been a highly respected clinical esthetician and spa owner for over 30 years. She is also a speaker, blogger, and business coach who inspires others to turn passions into profits with her signature Purple Carpet Client Experience, visual stories, online workshops, and coaching. www.tazeemjamal.com

Elyse Jarard helps people find wellness in themselves through her blog and essential oils. She aspires to empower others and create a ripple effect of positive change in the world. www.elysejarard.com

Sheila Jenkins is the author of *The Day Before: Eternal Bonds into the Afterlife*. She hopes to help others process their grief, and she plans to continue exploring her inner self as well as the afterlife. She loves music; dancing; laughing; reading; and spending time with her family, which includes two daughters and five grandchildren.

Julie Jones is a nurse, researcher, aromatherapist, energy practitioner, health and wellness coach, inspirational speaker, and author. Her supportive coaching with small steps inspires and empowers people to move from sick care to health care – restoring balance for wellness. www.restoretobalance.com

Andrée Joubert is a proud bilingual French Canadian, a Reiki Master, and a Certified Soul Coach®. Her purpose is to help women and men rediscover and honor their soul's independence. Connect with her to reunite with your essence and start your soul's journey: ajoubert_sc@hotmail.com.

Nancy Merrill Justice is an author, entrepreneur, and Certified Awakening Dynamics Theta Practitioner. With 25 years of succeeding in business and overcoming personal health challenges, she helps people to heal and learn techniques to maintain a "mindset of happiness" and manifest their heart's desires. www.nancyjustice.com

Kathy Kane is the owner of Kane Creative Consulting and is on a mission to liberate the world through the power of everyday creativity via creativity coaching and writing. Her heart holds a special place for those in the magical transition to the second half of life. www.kanecreativeconsulting.com

Ayeesha S. Kanji is a poet and blogger who has been writing for over 20 years. A recent MA graduate of New York University's Class of 2016, her background includes creative writing and professional training and coaching. In her spare time, she dances, practices yoga, and appreciates the value of not being busy.

Rose Kaplan was an IT professional for 22 years. A former Feng Shui practitioner, she also studied astrology and numerology. She is an author and Reiki and IET practitioner who has a special connection with the angels, especially her most cherished angel, her son, Scott.

Gina Karas is a full-time sales assistant in the construction industry. She's an avid scrapbooker, blogger, and aspiring author who loves photography, reading, and traveling. She loves living on the California coast and spending time near the ocean. www.californiascrappin.com

Donna Kater is an author and licensed acupuncturist. She holds professional degrees in Spiritual Psychology, Counseling, and Oriental Medicine. Her book, *I'm Still Alive, Now What?!? – How to Survive and Thrive After a Life-Changing Event*, is recommended by therapists and healers around the world. www.DonnaKater.com

Jenna Kelland is certified in holistic nutrition and has a PhD in Adult Education. As owner of Spark Wellness, she helps women emerging from burnout to have balanced, energized lives. A self-employed mom of three, she recognizes self-care as essential for her success and her family's well-being. www.sparkwellness.ca

Katie Kieffer blends a diversity of roles including homeschool mom, wife, and minister. As a ThetaHealing® teacher and self-awareness coach, she helps others deepen their connection with the Divine where they can experience powerful healing, restoration of self, and their own Inner Light. www.awakentheinnerlight.com

Davalynn Kim is a dedicated mother, daughter, sister, and friend. She enjoys reading, writing, painting, and bird watching. She loves dogs, cats, horses, and a beautiful brisk winter day. She believes in love at first sight. She believes in doing things that make the soul sing.

Christine King's soul journey began in 1979 after her husband died. She received a powerful message that her work was to help people on a spiritual path discover their soul's purpose. She has 35 years' experience as a metaphysical teacher and Soul Guidance Practitioner. www.soulsplanforyou.com

Elizabeth R. Kipp is a health facilitator who works in stress and chronic pain management. She helps people unleash the power of their own healing and is experienced in resolving conflict and generative communication skills. She empowers people to tap into their healing ability and build effective health-care teams. www.elizabeth-kipp.com

Margo Kirzinger is a certified Psychosomatic practitioner and Face and Body Reader who utilizes a variety of therapeutic modalities to address core-issue healing. She resides in rural Saskatchewan, Canada, and encourages all readers to visit her at her website: www.margok.ca.

Marci Kobayashi, a long-term resident of Tokyo, is a web designer and intuitive. When she is not building websites and helping people connect with and receive messages from their guides, she loves blogging about her life in Japan as a caregiver and avid Japanese learner. www.marcikobayashi.com

Ingrid Koivukangas is an award-winning environmental artist, designer, and writer. She is a word lover, dog slave, flower farmer, author of the YA fantasy trilogy *Hunters of the Dream*, and creator of the Eco Heart Oracle. www.IngridKoivukangas.com

Manpreet Komal is a writer, healer, speaker, and choreographer. She moved to the USA from India at the age of 12. She loves dancing, traveling, laughing, and deep conversations. She is the founder of Rang De Bollywood (a dance company), Magic Is Everywhere (115,000 followers), and Self Love Movement. www.manpreetkomal.org

Carrie Kondor is an author, counselor, and the owner of Caria, LLC. She utilizes sound coding, family constellation, and breathwork in her practice to support clients in unlocking their truest potential. Through her writing, workshops, and private sessions, clients can free their mind of negative distractions. www.cariatherapy.com

Malcolm James Kutner is a storyteller and adventurer who loves to travel, design, read, and write while bringing people into meaningful relationships with their surroundings. Friends, dogs, and beautiful landscapes are among his favorite things. He lives in New York and writes every day. www.malcolmjameskutner.com

Debbie Labinski is an intuitive angel communicator, speaker, and teacher. She instantly connects with her clients to create a safe place to explore feelings of hope and heartfelt answers, giving them the guidance they need to create positive adjustments in their lives. www.DebbieLabinski.com

Ahana Lara is a transformation and business coach, author, and co-creator of ASP (A Simple Path) coaching programs. She uses her experience in entrepreneurship, digital marketing, coaching, and journalism to take her clients through a journey of empowerment and launching a business with purpose. www.ahanaanddaniel.com

Jennifer Larkin is an entrepreneur offering a wide range of health and wellness initiatives, including life-altering healing remedies, delicious raw enzyme-rich food, meditation courses, personal-empowerment retreats, consciousness-raising workshops, and private coaching programs through Healing Light Center.

Catherine M. Laub is an inspirational author, speaker, psychic medium, and spiritual guide. She is a five-time bestselling author and continues her writing in upcoming anthologies. She speaks about mental illness in her campaign, "Brighten Your Day With Turquoise." www.catherinemlaub.com

Monica Laws is a proud Canadian with a degree in Business. Her career in sales and marketing has included publishing a home-décor magazine. She is a mother, coach, volunteer, friend, and lifelong learner. Her passion for travel has and will continue to take her on a journey with countless moments of grace.

Patricia LeBlanc is a dream maker. She empowers female entrepreneurs to get out of their own way and get to the next level. She is an award-winning author, speaker, manifesting strategist, and Master Energy Healer/Teacher. You can learn more about her by visiting www.LoaLifeCoaching.com.

Tara Leduc is an online entrepreneur, yoga teacher, and stepmom who lives in the suburbs and is passionate about helping you find peace in your life. Why? Because she believes that together we can change the world, peace by peace. Join in at www.TaraLeduc.com.

Rhonda Lee, MAEd, is the creator of Spirit Mist Smokeless Smudge. She is a Reiki Master, keynote speaker on stress management, and Laughter Yoga leader. She empowers others to take charge of their energy through various modalities. She chooses the path of love to guide her business and life. www.infusionoflife.com

Lauren Leduc Lemieux resides in Acushnet, Massachusetts, with her husband and daughter. After 18 years of working in a family business, she resigned in January 2013 to find her true calling and is now a Certified Life Coach from both the Coaches Training Institute and the International Coaching Federation. www.LaurenLemieux.com

Nicole Levac is working on her first solo book, a memoir of how she learned to live *her* way (not society's way) by learning from nature. You can watch her past show, "Journey to Soul-Full Connections," and read her *Nature's Wisdom* blog at www.nicolelevac.com.

Tanya Levy is a counselor in a community college and an inspirational photographer. She has worked in the human-services field for 25 years. She is a strong and passionate advocate for the healing power of each individual's own learning journey. www.facebook.com/heartladyinspiration

Janice Littler is an empowerment teacher. Her inspiring, loving, and passionate mission is helping moms create monumental shifts in their hearts, regain their sparkle, and give themselves permission to blossom. There is more to life than "just being a mom." She offers free resources here: www.JaniceLittler.com.

Elaine Lockard is The Confidence and Credibility Alchemist and Supreme Resourceress™. She helps her clients break out of their spiritual closet to gain confidence in self and their gifts and get the respect, recognition, and rewards they deserve. www.elainelockard.com

Courtney Long, MSW, LC, CHt, ATP®, is an angel communicator, life-purpose intuitive, psychic medium, author, and speaker. She inspires adults, teens, and kids to joyfully activate the angels' assistance, open their intuition, and discover their purpose and gifts. www.CourtneyLongAngels.com

Fiona Louise left marketing and management in the corporate world to heal from autoimmune disorders, learn natural therapies, and write. She re-evaluated her life in order to heal and return to a spiritual path, which she now shares with others through blogs and books, whilst also studying Educational Psychology. www.fiona-louise.com

Shelley Lundquist is an international bestselling author, motivational speaker, and Self-Mastery & Success Coach who uses her intuitive gifts and powerful transformational breakthrough processes to empower audiences all over the world in breaking through to the unlimited power of their own potential. www.shelleylundquist.com

Mary Lunnen, creator of Dare to Blossom, offers support in finding your way home to yourself through 1:1 life coaching, her own Rediscovery Cards, workshops, and online classes. Her writing, photography, and artwork are all part of her creative life, based in magical Cornwall. www.daretoblossom.co.uk

Bianca Lynn is a curious traveler who has spent years exploring different paths. Her goal is to help people embrace their wholeness and connect with their inner light. Through transformational workshops, writing, and one-on-one work, she supports people to live joyful, peaceful, and more meaningful lives. www.biancadisalvo.com

Amethyst Mahoney loves rainbows, unicorns, and riding motorcycles. She runs Spiritual Badass, a worldwide movement dedicated to helping people transcend old beliefs and awaken into their new awareness. She lives with her husband and their two cats and two dogs just outside of Chicago. www.AmethystMahoney.com

Victoria L. Mai inspires others to explore their life and connect to their soul. She is a spiritual explorer, traveler, writer, and healer. She loves playing with frequencies to create shifts in her life and for others. www.victorialmai.com

Kim Marks is a Soul Coach who helps you transform into alignment with your soul. From manifesting a new goal to understanding and moving through the depths of grief, she helps you to reconnect to your internal abundance. Learn more about her and how she can help you here: www.KimMarksCoaching.com.

Anita D. Marshall is a Soul Awareness Coach and Soul Plan Practitioner/Teacher. After discovering her life purpose during soul-guided travels, she created *A Journey Into Soul* – a sacred space for sharing insights and providing resources to empower others to deepen their own soul connection. www.ajourneyintosoul.com

Lori Kilgour Martin is an angelic counselor and musical theatre artist from Canada. This is her third contribution in the *365 Book Series*, and she is also a co-author in the book *365 Days of Angel Prayers*. She is grateful and enjoys helping others in service with the Divine. www.diamondheartangel.com

Sara Martin lives in the foothills of North Carolina and assists her clients in understanding who they are at the soul level and in making choices that are in alignment with their divine creative power. See more of her unique work at www.sarasmysticforest.com.

Veronica Mather is a writer and keen photographer. She is passionate about animal welfare and shares her life with her husband, Dale, four rescued sheep, and two high-spirited dogs, Max and Blaze.

Sophie Maya is passionate about growing peace on the planet, beginning in her own life, knowing the macrocosm and microcosm are one energetic wave of which we all belong. She offers self-love solutions, energetic healing facilitation, holistic caregiving, hospice support, and clutter-clearing services. www.prayervisionary.com

Kristy Carr McAdams shares from her "spiritual tool-belt" to show people how to discover their personal gifts. She's a mama, smile purveyor, psychic/medium, artist, Certified Angel Practitioner (ACP), Reiki/IET Practitioner, sound healing facilitator, mandala/art facilitator, author, and hugger extraordinaire. www.EnergyOfAngels.com

Tami McConnell-Finseth is a cancer survivor and single mother of two who resides in Santa Barbara where she enjoys beachside living. Her charisma is contagious, and she feels her soul's calling is to spread love and positivity to others. www.itsalwaysaboutlove.simplesite.com

Lisa McDonald is a successful author, motivational speaker, TV and radio host, and personal development coach. She believes in exercising daily gratitude, paying it forward, and being of service to others. She shares the message that the key to success and happiness comes through learning how to live life fearlessly.

Kellie McGarry is a wife, mother, and yoga lover. She is a Certified Health Coach, a Certified Nidra Instructor, and a Certified Reiki 1 and 2 Therapist who specializes in body image and mindful living. She enjoys sharing her story of eating disorder recovery. www.kelliemcgarry.com

Carolyn McGee helps empower women so they can walk with spirit, enhance their intuition, and trust their divine guidance so that they can easily manifest dreams to deepen relationships joyfully in line with their higher purpose. www.carolynmcgee.com

Victoria McGee is a writer focused on spiritual healing following trauma. Her blog, *Still Beloved*, has thousands of followers worldwide. She lives on Maui with her husband and a menagerie of dogs and cats. She practices Reiki and performs comedy improvisation – two different forms of healing! www.stillbeloved.com

Jenny McKaig is CEO, writer, and coach at JennyMcKaig.com; international bestselling author and senior editor of *Empowering Women to Succeed*; and a certified Awakening Coach. She is an award-winning writer who empowers with transformational tools. She loves surfing; yoga; her husband, Shawn; and their daughter, Liberty.

Pam McKinney loves to empower women who are challenged with "not enough." She is an author, Create Your Fabulous Life© coach, Certified Crystal Healer, dōTERRA Wellness Advocate, Soul Journeys® Heal Your Money Story coach & Akashic Records consultant, Usui Reiki practitioner, and angel card reader. www.connecttoyourlight.com

Trish Mckinnley is passionate about tuning you in to your divine energy. Utilizing her gifts and talents as a human dynamics coach, writer, and speaker, she will inspire you to find your authentic self and live life more fully. Her current project is The Sassy Goddess. www.tuneinwithtrish.com

Giuliana Melo aspires to inspire. She loves life, God, and her family. She spends her days spreading love and light and helping others heal. She is a cancer survivor who is passionate about medicine, non-traditional healing, and angel therapy. She has been married for 29 years and has one 18-year-old son. www.giulianamelo.com

Mary Meston, CHPC, is an inspiring multiple bestselling author, coach, speaker, and success strategist. As a high-performance expert and heart-centered entrepreneur, her practical, informative, and interactive processes enable her clients to elevate their level of freedom, meaning, joy, and happiness in all areas of their lives. www.MaryMeston.com

Lisa Miller left the legal field and became a stay-at-home mom after adopting her three youngest children from Russia. She is a mom and grandmother who now resides in South Carolina after relocating from New York with her husband, children, and two rescue dogs.

Vicky Mitchell uses her passion for learning and helping others to activate their healing journeys by using physical, emotional, and spiritual self-healing tools. She would be honored to guide you on your path to increased wellness. To connect with her, send an email to: vicky@vickymitchell.com.

Leslie Moe-Kaiser, PhD, is a brand and reputation management and leadership consultant. She utilizes her experiences in the corporate and academic sectors by serving on national boards, helping organizations fulfill their missions. She also coaches clients to achieve success. She is a tennis pro, certified by the US Professional Association.

Candy Motzek is a human BEING, wife, mom, engineer, dancer, dreamer, barefoot leader, sacred rebel, and joy seeker. She is a longtime senior leader in the corporate world and is a passionate life and leadership coach helping her clients gain clarity, grow in confidence, and take action on what matters most. www.candymotzek.com

Marta Mrotek has a calling to share the message of hope. She is the author of *Miracle in Progress*, an E-RYT 500 Yoga Instructor, the creator of Wellness Meetings, Lead Advocate for Heroes in Recovery, and blogger for *Something Honest* and *Jane Doe Recovery*. www.wellnessmeetings.com

Susan Mullen is a gifted intuitive and leading expert on intuitive living. She is a certified intuitive coach and founder of the Pilot Light Intuitive Sessions, where she lovingly guides clients to their next right step. She is an animal advocate and writer, currently writing her first book. www.SusanTMullen.com

Viknesvari Piche Muthu is a passionate creator of life with an open and brave heart. She empowers women to rise above the struggles in their relationships, to fulfill their heart's desires, and to live their soul purpose with more confidence! www.heartflow.in

Farahana Surya Namaskar is a published author and motivational speaker. She strives to help others find meaning and purpose in their life. Her faith in God reminds her that everything happens *for* us, not *to* us. Her purpose is to help people discover their potential and divine life purpose.

Lucy V. Nefstead lives in northern Wisconsin with her dog, Sam. She is a retired English, Speech, and Theatre teacher who is co-chair of an animal rescue, president of retired teachers, on Wisconsin's board of directors, and serves on state committees. Spirituality is an integral part of her life.

Janet G. Nestor founded the Center of Well-Being in 2003 and has not stopped since. She now works from home as a holistic mental health therapist, spiritual mentor, energy psychologist, intuitive energy healer, and professional author. She loves teaching via her workshops and classes. www.janetnestor.com

Hue Anh Nguyen is an intuitive healer and coach with 20 years of experience using her own unique, restorative process that corrects reverse polarity to create a life in balance. She has provided transformational healing for thousands of people by detecting and releasing negative energies. www.polarity4harmony.com

Daniel Nilon is the founder and director of A Simple Path Pte. Ltd. He is a blogger, success coach, and entrepreneur. He has taken hundreds of clients through personal development, life coaching, and business coaching, teaching how to follow their passion and monetize their ideas. www.ahanaanddaniel.com

Robin OK is a writer, coach, runner, poet, playwright, and rock lover. She empowers clients to see creative dreams to completion and is the founder of Laugh & Dream Creative Coaching and Visionary: Creative Collaborative ReTREAT. She is proud to be "Mama Bird" to Mallory Riley, a co-author in this book. www.creativecollaborativeretreats.com

Brandon Olivares is a Law of Attraction coach. He loves teaching people how to actually get results with the Law of Attraction and create a life they truly love. Sign up for his free 7-day LOA e-mail course by going to www.cocreationcoaching.org/join-library.

Nadean Ollech is a spiritual life coach with a degree in religion. She is the founder of Healed Daisy Intuitive Guidance, where she helps women connect with themselves, learn to recognize their guidance, and live their best life. Contact her at healeddaisy@outlook.com.

Wendyanne Pakulsky is passionate about reminding people that with every life shift comes an opportunity for growth and healing into new heights of awareness.

Charlotte Palmer, a former Peace Corps volunteer and learning disabilities and ESOL teacher, recently retired after 50 years of teaching. Now she shares her enthusiasm for creating acrostic prose poems with her Inner Guide, Abba Jesus. Join her on Facebook at SMART THINKING with Charlotte Palmer.

Lisa Anna Palmer launched her business as a career and leadership coach and Certified Passion Test® Facilitator in 2011 and has helped hundreds of people gain greater clarity about what is most important and leap out of their comfort zone.

Lynn Paterson teaches tantra and writes and explores the mysteries of life. She loves nature, travelling, visiting sacred sites, and helping people connect with their own true nature. She currently resides in Scotland. www.beinglynnpaterson.wordpress.com

Tanya Penny, Self-Love Catalyst, Vibrant Body and Abundant Life Coach, teaches and supports those ready to heal the root cause of anxiety, weight, or illness to have a healthy, balanced body and lifestyle; step into self-confidence; and fully live their passions and purpose. www.tanyapenny.com

Lupe Ramirez Peterkin remains strong in her spiritual path. She uses her experiences with God to inspire others. Time spent dancing, writing, and visiting New York keep her passion alive. She is writing her musician father's autobiography and shares her life's adventures with her husband, children, and grandsons.

Reina Pomeroy is the founder of Reina + Co, a life and business success coaching practice for creative entrepreneurs. She's a Certified Professional Co-Active Coach with over 1,000 coaching hours. She also co-hosts the Creative Empire Podcast where she interviews leaders in the creative industry.

Emma Porter is a mother, Dunisha Master, and author. Her passion is in finding practical ways to encourage people to believe that their emotional and spiritual well-being matter. She resides in Arizona and can be contacted and connected through the website: www.earthspiritcenter.org.

Annie Price is a spiritual healer who uses heartfelt, intuitive guidance to empower others in their divine purpose and in living the joyful expression of their soul. She has a BA in Psychology and loves being Mom to three teenagers. www.SoulSoaring.com

Donna S. Priesmeyer is a media professional who enjoys many creative pursuits, including: gardening; traveling; writing; creating art; and spending time with her husband, family, friends and pets. She is the publisher of a spiritually based website featuring consciousness-raising, art, music, and literature: www.LightonLife.net.

Mimi Quick is known as the "Prosperity Muse." She is a psychic business mentor and owner of the Spiritual Business Institute – a spiritual coaching and training company that empowers spirited entrepreneurs to create prosperous, aligned businesses and lives doing what they love. www.MimiQuick.com

Michelle Radomski is a book designer, graphic designer, mandala artist, and author. For 35 years she's created customized, inspiring designs for purpose-driven individuals and organizations. She creates "art with heart" designed to make words and work visible. Because, "if you want to serve, you first must be seen." www.OneVoiceCan.com

Lore Raymond is a visionary, spiritual tour guide, speaker, and world traveler who leads women through her No Regrets Living! program to "open hearts and inspire action." Other programs include VisionQuests and Divine Dialogue Writing. She's co-authored six books with three international bestsellers. www.LoreRaymond.com

Helen Rebello is a peaceful pathfinder who provides a safe sanctuary space for heart-centred women who've lost themselves a little in serving others. She helps them reconnect to their inner light to find their way back home to themselves and to a wholehearted, liberated life. www.thetranquilpath.co.uk

Haley Reese, CTNC, is a Holistic Health and Happiness Coach who empowers women entrepreneurs and coaches to free themselves from depression through the power of mindset, nutrition, and self-care. www.HaleyReese.com

L. A. Reeves was born into an Air Force family and moved often as a child. She enjoys traveling for fun as an adult. She has settled in Texas and is blessed to have a son, Ty. She is the author of the upcoming book *The Back Side of the Heart – Journeys from the Front Side to the Back Side of One's Heart*. She has her mom, a poet, to thank for her desire to write.

Brenda Reiss helps women step into their own power through forgiveness. Using her wisdom and certifications as a Radical Forgiveness® coach, Soul Journeys® Akashic Records consultant, and Heal Your Money Story coach, she helps them shift their perception and move beyond their most ardent challenges. www.brendareisscoaching.com

Mallory Riley loves pad thai; truth telling; her blond banjo-lovin' hubby; and her scruffy pup, Reggae. She is a photographer, a *Buffy* watcher, and a Guster groupie. She is blessed to be the daughter of Giggly Goddess, Robin OK, whom she calls "Mama Bird."

Sam Ritchie writes blogs and is the director of a company that helps people secure their futures and leave a legacy. She is originally from the United Kingdom but now lives in Spain with her husband and daughters. www.legacygold.eu

Rev. Aliza Bloom Robinson is a vibrational catalyst, author, speaker, and ordained Unity Minister. Founder of www.Divine-Awakening.org, she facilitates the discovery of grace, peace, passion, and fulfillment in living a dream-filled life. Her book, *Falling into Ease*, is a #1 Amazon bestseller.

Jessica Robinson believes in the strength of human connection and that happiness is rooted in authentic moments of self-discovery and awareness. www.Instagram.com/dragonfly_junction

Pauline Hosie Robinson writes about self-healing through the eyes of love. In her autobiography, *Triumph of Joy*, she utilized nature to help her cope with her husband's PTSD. After her husband's traumatic death, a shaman empowered her to heal herself. To read her healing journey through the natural world visit www.triumphofjoy.com.

Faye Rogers is an animal communicator, visionary, writer, intuitive healer, and qualified teacher of the Diana Cooper School in Angels and Ascension. She works with animals and people to bring more harmony and awareness. She is passionate about humanity and empowering others. www.animalcommunication-newzealand.com

Isabella Rose is a bestselling author, certified Angel Energy Healer, angel oracle card reader and messenger, aromatherapist, and WorldVentures representative. She is an advocate for those with no voice. Her passions include art in various media, traveling, and spending time in nature and with loved ones. www.bellarosehealinghands.com

Sharon Rothstein is an international bestselling author who contributed to *365 Ways to Connect with Your Soul* and *365 Moments of Grace*. She is a Feng Shui Practitioner who studied under Professor Thomas Lin Yun. She studies, teaches, and writes about Spirit. She may be contacted at SharonRothstein@aol.com.

Farah Joy Rupani is a Certified Reiki Practitioner and intuitive life coach who specializes in mind-body healing. Passionate about transforming lives, she powerfully guides her clients to release mental resistance and awaken the healer within. www.farahjoy.com

Cynthia L. Ryals is a bestselling author, coach, speaker, and spiritual messenger who guides you in rediscovering your highest self and life's purpose. She believes that reconnecting to our soul is key to consciously creating a life that feels good; honors our truth; and ultimately, heals the world. www.myevolvedlife.com

Tracy Ryan is a mystic and a yogi, a wife and a mom, a writer and an entrepreneur. You can find more of her work at www.intuitiveyogi.com.

Jen Salstrom is an author, blogger, Breath of Love Facilitator, life and health coach, and yoga instructor who teaches in Cincinnati and attends nationwide yoga festivals. She is a mother of two and enjoys spending time with family and friends, creating meaningful relationships and memories. www.heartistrywellness.com

Lori Santo is an artist, poet, writer, storyteller, dreamweaver, soul-recovery artist, life coach, ancient priestess, highly sensitive being, creativity maven, lover of life, and spirit. She is on a mission to bring light to the darkest caverns of our existence through writing, artistry, and creative soul recovery.

Sylvie A. Savoie has been successfully striving to make this life the best one ever! She enjoys life and retirement alongside her husband and their feline friend in Mont Tremblant, Canada. She is passionate about spreading positivity everywhere. She is the artist behind the internationally known Sylvie Angeline Collection. www.sylvieangelinecollection.com

Susan Elizabeth Schoemmell's journey as a seeker of her authentic self has led her to Hawaii, Czechoslovakia, Italy, Ireland, Scotland, and England – from the Haleakala Crater on Maui to Stonehenge in England. She is grateful for the blessings and chooses to be a light on the path for other seekers. www.sesangel.simplesite.com

Isla Selupucin is a mindful mother and intuitive empath. She is the creator of www.littlebeeandbutterfly.com, a website that journals her spiritual stories and connections. She lives in Turkey with the loves of her life: her daughter, Ceyda, and husband, Koray.

Mark Semple is an intuitive awakenings coach and healer who supports those who are ready to move forward. Utilizing a variety of coaching and energy-clearing techniques, he identifies and permanently resolves the energetic blocks that impede you from awakening to your true authentic self. www.justmarkcoaching.com

Pooja Shende is an entrepreneur, author, emotional-intelligence and NLP practitioner, and a performance coach who had over 20 successful years in a corporate career. She is the author of *365 Days of Mindfulness*. www.lotussoul9.com

Michele Silva-Neto is a middle-aged, divorced mother of three young adults. She has been unhealthy and unhappy for a long time due to living up to others' expectations. She has decided to ignore these expectations and question everything she thought she knew so that she can live authentically.

Angela B. Simmons is a personality profiler, intuitive singer, and ordained Unity Minister. She has over 30 years of experience helping women be true to themselves and is the Founder of The Mindfulness Walking Fitness Class. She can be reached through her website at www.angelabsimmons.com.

Maura Smith helps spiritually conscious people create successful coaching, healing, and creative businesses from their personal sense of fulfillment. As a result, clients invest their time in what really matters to them and express themselves through a lifestyle where they feel valued, fulfilled, and truly alive. www.maurasmith.com

Cat Smith has studied various energy-healing modalities for the last 25 years, including Reiki and energy scans. She identifies and clears deep energy blocks to transform others so they can live the life they desire, free from physical and emotional pain. www.EnergyWerks.net

Tania Smith is an Australian-born energy healer, professional musician, and jewelry designer. She is a teacher of Tibetan Soul Healing, hypnotherapist, and intuitive channel who helps people find more joy. She also co-wrote the title track to the Grammy-winning CD *Lesson of Love*. www.crystalgypsy.com

Shari Sorbo, DD, DS, MAP, RScP, is a transformational counselor and writer who blends her psychological and spiritual approach in assisting people to discover their true joy and passion for living a heartfelt life. www.sharisorbo.com

H. Michelle Spaulding is an entrepreneur and self-taught artist. She owns Crafty Diva Cottage, a business offering creativity consulting, art events, classes, and workshops in the fiber arts. She expresses her creativity through the fiber arts and storytelling.

Marie Spencer-Rowland loves working with women to help them take their personal power back to live more, love more, laugh more, and become more centred within their own lives.

Lynn Spiro is a lightworker on a mission to illuminate the path for others seeking spiritual transformation. She cultivates soulful living through meditating, working with crystals and oracle cards, and intuitive writing. Living in southeastern North Carolina, she cherishes the solitude of walks on the beach and local nature trails.

Prameela (Pam) Sreemangalam is an author, psychotherapist, and life coach who is connected to the consciousness of infinite healing through hypnotherapy, psychotherapy, and the Akashic Records. She is the founder of Mind Scan, where she conducts personalized, life-transformational workshops. www.prameelasreemangalam.com

Jeanette St. Germain is a spiritual alchemist with a passion for empowering others to embrace their own inner radiance. She offers intuitive guidance, energetic healing, and public events that include inspired angelic messages, clarity of life purpose, and deep rejuvenation through all layers of the mind, body, and spirit. www.sophiastouch.com

Rani St. Pucchi is the founder and designer of the world-renowned bridal house St. Pucchi and the author of *Your Body, Your Style*; *The SoulMate Checklist*; and her upcoming memoir, *Unveiled: A Celebrity Fashion Designer's Story*. She is a speaker and coach who is passionate about empowering women. www.ranistpucchi.com

Cynthia Starborn is an inspirational author, teacher, and soul guide. She offers transformative classes and consultations, based on the Akashic Records, for adults and children. Fluent in French, Spanish, and English, she loves helping you transcend challenges and tap into the magic of life. www.CynthiaStarborn.com

Star Staubach is a bad-ass manifestor, change agent, bestselling author, keynote speaker, BS excavator, and creator of the 21-Day Challenge to Receive. She was invited to blog for the *Huffington Post* by Arianna Huffington herself. She is a busy mother of three who knows the truth about self-love. www.igniteradiance.com

Alison M. Stokes is a native of Dublin, Ireland. She combines her qualifications in astrology, psychology, counselling, Reiki, Mystic Therapy, and animal healing to treat people (and their pets!) on a holistic level. She works online as an Akashic Records Consultant at Silver Soul Therapy. She loves laughing at comedies and reading.

Sheila Sutherland is a Certified Wholistic Life Mastery Coach, professional educator, podcaster, and founder of Reignite Your Purpose. She elevates professionals' lives and businesses through aligning their mindset, behaviours, and communication so they can live a more authentic, connected, and vibrant life. www.reigniteyourpurpose.com

Stella Tassone loves to help those in need. She lives in Geelong, Australia, and this is the third time she has been a contributing author in a book. She is a mother to two beautiful cherubs, Alessio and Claudia, and practices Reiki, massage, and angel-card readings.

Gabrielle Taylor is a psychotherapist and a transformational specialist. Her passion is to mentor visionary, sensitive women leaders to shine their light brightly and share their gifts with the world. www.gabriellebtaylor.com

Ioana Adriana Terec is a born philosopher. Moving to the United States from Romania on her own at the age of 22, she is a true testament to the power of dreaming. A Master Empowerment Coach with the S.W.A.T. Institute, she is a witty and profound writer and speaker. www.IoanaAdrianaTerec.com

Michelle R. Terry is a dietitian who keeps people healthy through prevention and chronic-disease management. When she's not working or wrangling her two children, she is writing stories and managing an unruly garden. She shares her imperfect life at www.mamamickterry.com.

Lori Thiessen lives in Alberta, Canada, where she works as an architectural tech during the day, moonlights as a writer, and is mom to five almost-grown-up kids. She is a certified NLP Practitioner, Toastmaster, and runner. www.couragefinder.com

Lori Thomas has loved bugs her entire life. As a spiritual entomologist, she combines that love with her background in interspecies communication and Reiki to receive and share their messages, helping to heal the relationship between humanity and the insect kingdom. www.spiritualecologist.com

Barbara Toller is an East Coast transplant living as a modern homesteader in Kansas. With over 20 years in the healing arts, she currently helps others discover their energetic self-portrait through Archetypal Counseling. She is certified through the Caroline Myss Sacred Contracts Program. www.sacredcontracts.net

Jody Vehr is the author of *Just Hit Send* and a graduate of the University of Santa Monica. She has her master's degree in Spiritual Psychology with an emphasis in Consciousness, Health, and Healing. She is currently the co-owner and dream manager of Timney USA, where she assists others in manifesting their heartfelt dreams.

Teresa Velardi is a leader, author, speaker, potter, and host of *Transformational Tuesdays*. She lives life authentically and gratefully while making a difference in the lives of others with passion and purpose. Her pottery illustrates life's transformation from a ball of clay to a work of art. www.teresavelardi.com

Jacynthe (Jaz) Villemaire loves to walk along the river with her dog, Maya; her husband; and her son. She is a spiritual mentor, Soul Realignment® Practitioner, and Reiki Master. She helps women entrepreneurs find their authentic voice and self-expression through a soulful design of their businesses. www.deliberatesoulcreation.com

Michelle McDonald Vlastnik, Mystic Intuitive, Healer, Certified Personal Trainer, Interdimensional Story Weaver for Soul Remembrance, Angel Abundance Ambassador, and Published Author, assists with the rediscovery of our Authentic Self and the healing of Mother Earth. www.facebook.com/HighEnergySixSensoryPersonalTraining

Linda Voogd is a holistic therapist, addictions counselor, and adjunct professor. She offers ongoing workshops and life coaching. She helps others create healthy beliefs, attitudes, and thought patterns that propel them toward personal transformation. She has over 30 years of experience and runs a private practice in northern New Jersey.

Holly Wade is a healthy lifestyle coach and mind/body expert with over two decades of experience in the fitness and wellness industry. Through her own personal struggles, she knows firsthand the toll that stress takes on the entire Being. Her passion is to help women reduce stress and increase energy.

Connie M. Warden is an entrepreneur, acupuncturist, and lifestyle coach who has a deep passion to inspire people to be their healthiest in body, mind, and spirit. She talks about the power of personal discipline to help you achieve health and success personally and at work. www.ConnieWarden.com

Rozlyn Warren, CHt, ESLC, is passionate about helping you create deeper connection with your Pure Essence through practical spirituality and creativity. She is a certified Akashic Records Practitioner and energy aligner, bestselling author, happy mystic, and spiritual cheerleader who publishes *Lean Toward Happy Magazine*. www.LeanTowardHappy.com

Dr. Robert D. White is a mental-health practitioner who is dedicated to working with children, adolescents, and adults. His passion is to guide people in recognizing and harnessing their inner truths through self-mastery. His research and areas of expertise are in human capital and self-development. www.rdwassoc.com

Simone Wiedenhöft is a sacred-sound singer, modern life magician, and a master in transforming energetic blocks into fertile soil for personal growth. She works with those who feel an urgent call to their own spiritual path and a life of expansion and fulfillment. www.simonewiedenhoeft.com

Brenda M. Wiener's mission is to inspire, educate, and equip overwhelmed women to live a life of health, harmony, faith, and prosperity. She is the owner of Pathways To Harmony and is a Christian Licensed Spiritual Healer, Certified Natural Health Professional, Zyto Elite Technician, and Certified Chi-To-Be! Coach. www.PathwaysToHarmony.com

Heather Wiest is beyond blessed to love, serve, and inspire the community as a Registered Yoga Teacher, Reiki Master, and Licensed Clinical Social Worker. Her holistic yoga sessions are engaging and rejuvenating, leaving one feeling balanced and inspired. Restore your body. Renew your mind. Refresh your spirit. www.loveserveinspire.com

Charlene Williams is a mother of five, and "Gramster/Mami" to nine! She is blessed to have these people in her life. Her thirst for knowledge of God, Angels, and Spirit have always been a huge part of who she is, and she sends light and love to all.

Cat Williford, MCC, is a 23-year pioneer of the coaching profession and founder of The Modern Goddess and The Authenticity Advantage. She has helped thousands of women overcome daunting obstacles to enjoy confidence and success on their terms. She leads retreats and ceremonies and is a speaker, writer, and frequent guest expert.

Pami Woodruff believes in empowering others to discover their inner creativity, be who they were meant to be, and fulfill their lifelong dreams. She blogs and creates videos as "Make It With Pam" and teaches long-forgotten self-reliance skills at www.TheSchoolofLostArts.com.

Jody Wootton is a heart-centered person who lives life with gratitude. She specializes in helping people find joyful vacations as a home-based travel agent with Heart Cruises LLC (CST-2119226-70) and glamorous Touchstone Crystal jewelry as an independent consultant (#2005696). www.touchstonecrystal.com/jw3

Karen L. Wythe, a lifelong Spiritualist, is dedicated to living life with passion, enthusiasm, and zest. As a Life Transformation Coach, she helps others do the same. She is an ordained minister, medium, healer, workshop presenter, writer, and fiber artist who is married to her best friend. www.enrichingliferesources.com

Laura Young is a gifted and trusted intuitive energy healer and teacher, specializing in aligning physical, emotional, mental, and spiritual bodies for optimal balanced health. She is also the founder of Spiritual YOUniversity – an online classroom developing your alignment to the YOUniverse! www.SpiritualYouniversity.com

Joan B. Zietlow, BSN, RN, CHHC, AADP, MBA, is a health coach who helps others thrive through health optimization. She inspires and educates while dispelling myths such as "it's hard to be healthy after 40." Her clients enjoy energy, joy, health, confidence, peace, and answers to longtime health concerns. www.vibranthealthandhealing.com

Suzanne Zupancic is a Registered Yoga Teacher/E-RYT200/RYT500/YACEP, aromatherapist, and creator of *Your Empowered Self* workshops and training modules. Her classes focus on alignment, intention, a little humor, and a lot of realism. She offers support in the hopes that others may come to realize their own strength. www.unwindyogallc.com

Contributor Index

For your convenience, we have listed each contributor in alphabetical order by last name and have included the page number(s) of their piece(s). We hope that this makes finding your favorite co-authors easy!

Acknowledgments

This is the third book in this special series, and we continue to be grateful to all of the contributors who bravely open their hearts and share their personal stories. It's not always an easy thing to do, and we appreciate their honesty and vulnerability.

We love that our community of authors continues to grow, and we are so happy that we get to be part of each of your journeys and connect with you in this book and beyond. We love knowing that we've all created this book together – that each of our words and stories will be read all around the world. And we hope that those who read them will be moved in some way and will be inspired to reflect on their own shifts. Thank you for being part of this.

From Jodi: As always, I give thanks to Dan for being my everything. Thank you for co-creating such a magical life with me. Thank you for all of the beach walks, the afternoon naps, the many conversations we get to share each day, and for loving me in such a full and wholehearted way that I never even knew was possible. You are my world. And I love you beyond what words could ever express.

I would also like to thank my new best friend, the ocean, for being such a loving and healing presence in my life – for calling me to it and welcoming me in such a beautiful way when I arrived. Thank you to all the forces above and here on Earth that helped to make moving close to it happen.

Also, thank you to our three cats: Biddle, Buncom, and Elsie. They bring such great comic relief for us each day, which is always appreciated. They are great nappers and snugglers, and they expand our life so much.

From Dan: Thank you, Jodi, for being the greatest shift I've ever experienced – pointing me toward love every moment of my life. Sharing our life is the most profound blessing I could ever ask for – the answer to my highest wishes and deepest prayers. I am honored to call you my wife, my best friend, my soulmate, my home; and I am so grateful we get to experience this magical life side by side. I love you with all my heart.

On a slightly more mundane (but still important) note: for their tremendous help throughout the editing process, thank you to all the writers and editors who have pored over decades' (and, in some cases, centuries') worth of dictionaries and style guides in order to distill the lessons and guidelines that have helped us create a cohesive unit out of 365 pieces from over 250 authors – with special shout-outs to Bryan A. Garner for his comprehensive and indispensable resource, *Garner's Modern English Usage*, and Mignon "Grammar Girl" Fogarty for the "Quick and Dirty Tips" from her wonderful website and surprisingly addictive books.

And thanks to all the contributing authors for reminding me that what's most important (even more than the proper use of subjunctives, semicolons, and subordinate conjunctions!) are the heartfelt pieces and, more importantly still, the people behind them. This includes not only the authors but also their friends, families, and loved ones – because behind every on-the-page story is a real-life experience with real people having real shifts. If, together, we've managed to convey even a modest reflection of these people's hearts, souls, and lives, I consider it a success.

Lastly, we would like to thank you, the reader. It's our hope that you will receive at least one shift of your own while reading this book! You may see yourself in some of the stories, or they may help you revisit some of your own shifts and see the gifts they brought. Whatever the case may be, we're so grateful that you're reading this and hope that it's a positive experience for you.

Thank you to everyone who continues to believe in our vision to create books that inspire, to give all of us a voice, and to share something loving and soulful with those who are ready to receive it. What a special gift that is.

Other Books in This Series

This is the third book in our bestselling *365 Book Series*, and we would love to invite you to learn more about the books and join us as a contributing author, a reader, or both!

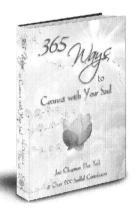

365 Ways to Connect with Your Soul

In this #1 international bestselling book, over 200 beautiful souls came together to share how they connect with their own souls with the hopes that it will help you connect with yours as well. It's a wonderful addition to your spiritual practice!

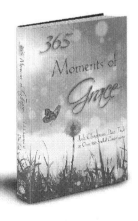

365 Moments of Grace

This #1 international bestselling book contains 365 personal stories of grace, miracles, and transformations from beautiful souls all around the world to show how magical our world is and how connected we truly are. Moments of grace are presents from the universe!

Goodness Abounds: 365 True Stories of Loving Kindness

This upcoming book will contain stories of people expressing love, goodness, and kindness. The experiences will range from huge expressions of lifelong love to small acts of kindness – each adding to an ever-growing mountain of evidence that goodness abounds! Available November 2017.

You can learn more about our current and upcoming books from this soulful series here: www.365bookseries.com.

Made in the USA
Middletown, DE
21 February 2017